New Developments and Approaches
in Consumer Behaviour Research

Ingo Balderjahn, Claudia Mennicken,
and Eric Vernette (eds.)

New Developments and Approaches in Consumer Behaviour Research

1998

Schäffer-Poeschel Verlag Stuttgart

Macmillan Press Ltd Houndmills and London

About the Editors:

Prof. Dr. Ingo Balderjahn is Professor of Marketing and Business Administration
and Chair of the Department of Marketing, School of Business Administration
and Economics, University of Postdam, Germany.

Dipl.-Ök. Claudia Mennicken is Research Assistant and Lecturer at the same department.

Prof. Dr. Eric Vernette is Professor of Marketing at the University of Savoie and Head of
the Marketing Group of the Institute of Research in Business Management
((IREGE$_{Marketing}$) at the same University in Chambéry, France.

Die Deutsche Bibliothek – CIP-Einheitsaufnahme

New Developments and Approaches in Consumer Behaviour Research :
Ingo Balderjahn, Claudia Mennicken, Eric Vernette (eds.)
- Stuttgart: Schäffer-Poeschel; Houndmills and London: Macmillan Press Ltd,1998
   ISBN 3-7910-1140-5 (Schäffer-Poeschel)
   ISBN 0-333-73907-8 (Macmillan Press Ltd)
NE: Balderjahn, Ingo; Mennicken, Claudia; Vernette, Eric (eds.)

Gedruckt auf säure- und chlorfreiem, alterungsbeständigem Papier.

ISBN 3-7910-1140-5 (Schäffer-Poeschel)
ISBN 0-333-73907-8 (Macmillan Press Ltd)

© 1998 Schäffer-Poeschel Verlag für Wirtschaft · Steuern · Recht GmbH
© 1998 Macmillan Press Ltd Houndmills and London
Einbandgestaltung: Willy Löffelhardt
Druck und Bindung: Franz Spiegel Buch GmbH, Ulm
Printed in Germany

Schäffer-Poeschel Verlag Stuttgart
Ein Tochterunternehmen der Verlagsgruppe Handelsblatt

Macmillan Press Ltd

Preface

From an international perspective, the field of consumer behaviour research is emerging and indeed dynamic. Consumer behaviour research aims to describe, explain, and predict the behavioural patterns and the underlying constructs with regard to the individuals' role as consumers. Whereas in Germany consumer behaviour is more or less a distinct area of study within the discipline of marketing, we can see that in other parts of the world the boundaries of the field have not yet been defined that clearly. But there is a consensus about the fact that it is a research field with an empirical as well as an interdisciplinary orientation.

Our goal is to produce a volume of readings which reflects some of the new developments and approaches in the European consumer behaviour research, especially those in France and Germany. Although consumer behaviour is an interdisciplinary field of research, we have noticed that it is not always an international or cross-national discipline, which means that the communication and transfer of scientific results between European researchers, and especially between French and Germans, could be improved.

This volume is one of the outcomings of a first step to improve and reinforce the exchange and discussion of research ideas between French and Germans which started with a conference held in September 1996 with the purpose to bring together researchers especially from both mentioned countries, or let's better say, from two different language domains. Nevertheless, we were open to colleagues from other countries (Austria, Denmark, and the USA) as well. Because of the backgrounds and interests of all the people who have contributed to this book, the primary perspective of the several chapters are theoretical approaches to consumer behaviour as well as empirical investigations and practical applications in marketing.

We hope that we have been able to capture some of the recent interests of consumer researchers from the different countries in the articles to be presented and to contribute to improve the dialogue and exchange of research ideas. We also wish to encourage the interested reader to discover and share with us the experience that we - however we do not share the same language - have all something in common, the excitement and the fascination for consumer behaviour research.

Potsdam and Chambéry, January 1997

Ingo Balderjahn,
Claudia Mennicken,
and Eric Vernette

Contents

Preface V

Part I: Consumer Values and Lifestyle

Food-Related Lifestyle in France and Germany
Klaus G. Grunert, Karen Brunsø and *Lone Bredahl* 1

Consumer Values in West and East Germany
Sigrid Joseph 15

Towards a Revision of Schwartz's Values Inventory:
Some Exploratory Findings
Yorick Odin, Jean-Yves Vinais and *Pierre Valette-Florence* 35

Part II: Social Beliefs and Social Meaning of Consumption

The Role of Television in the Construction of Consumer Reality
L.J. Shrum and *Thomas C. O'Guinn* 53

Sportswear as an Expression of How the Consumer Society has
Evolved: The Example of „Fun-Wear"
Patrick Hetzel 69

Part III: Communication and Information Behaviour

Market Reactions to Integrated Communication
Franz-Rudolf Esch 89

Lexical Analysis: A Method for Understanding „What is said" and
„How is it said" in Marketing Messages
Marie-Laure Gavard-Perret and *Jean Moscarola* 113

Part IV: Affect, Motivation, and Personality

Measuring Affect and Emotion toward a Brand with a
Smiling Face Scale
Eric Vernette 131

An Empirical Investigation of the Relationships between
Values, Motivations, and Personal Goals
Alain Jolibert and *Gary Baumgartner* 153

Part V: Consumer Decision Processes and Behaviour

Product Knowledge, Consumer Knowledge, and Brand Loyalty:
Some Empirical Evidence about their Relationships
Abdelmajid Amine 169

Empirical Analysis of Price Response Functions
Ingo Balderjahn 185

Optimum Stimulation Level as a Determinant of Exploratory
Behaviours: Some Empirical Evidence
Jean-Luc Giannelloni 201

Part VI: Environmental Aspects of Consumer Behaviour

The Reaction of German Consumers to French Nuclear Testing
Björn Walliser and *Thomas Froehlicher* 219

Environmental Aspects of Consumer Behaviour in Germany
Frank Wimmer 237

An Investigation of the Handling of Solid Waste in the
Consumption Cycle
Petra Buchholz 255

VIII

Part VII: Cross-Cultural Consumer Behaviour Research

Assessing Measurement Equivalence in Cross-National Consumer
Behaviour Research: Principles, Relevance and Application Issues
Rudolf Sinkovics, Thomas Salzberger and *Hartmut H. Holzmüller* 269

Measuring Cross Cultural Acceptance of an Innovation:
The Case of Low-Alcohol Wine
François d'Hauteville and *Ronald E. Goldsmith* 289

Part VIII: Qualitative Methods in Consumer Behaviour Research

Consumer Ambivalence: Perspectives Gained from Shopping
with Consumers
Tina M. Lowrey, Cele Otnes and *L.J. Shrum* 307

Hard versus Soft Laddering: Implications for Appropriate Use
Günther Botschen and *Eva Thelen* 321

About the Contributors 341

Klaus G. Grunert, Karen Brunsø and Lone Bredahl

Food-Related Lifestyle in France and Germany

1. National Food Cultures and International Food Marketing

2. The Food-Related Lifestyle Approach

3. Data Collection and Cross-Cultural Validity

4. Cross-National Differences on the 23 Dimensions of Food-Related Lifestyle

5. Comparison of National Consumer Segments

6. Discussion and Conclusions

References

Food-Related Lifestyle in France and Germany

Klaus G. Grunert, Karen Brunsø and Lone Bredahl

Abstract

Food markets are claimed to be characterised by two opposing tendencies: On the one hand, food culture seems to be a domain of increasingly transnational character. On the other hand, there is substantial evidence that food culture has considerable inertia. This papers reports a study comparing consumers' relationship to food in France and Germany. The study is based on the *food-related lifestyle instrument*, which characterises consumers by how they employ food and eating to obtain life values. The results indicate differences between French and German consumers on most of the 23 dimensions of the instrument. Nation-wise cluster analysis yielded sets of five segments per country. Grouping the segments based on the correlations of segments means using MDS results in distinct placements for the French and the German segments.

1. National Food Cultures and International Food Marketing

Two opposing tendencies seem to be at work in today's food markets. On the one hand, food culture seems to be a domain of increasingly transnational character. On the other hand, there is substantial evidence from several sources that food culture is one of the domains characterised by considerable inertia (cf. Fischler, 1990; Mennell et al., 1992). Food products are markers helping to define social situations. It is a category in which we are capable of quickly judging various products, the way they are cooked and presented as familiar or strange. It is a product category where very strong habits and preferences are often found. One can therefore speak about a relative stability that characterises eating patterns in different societies. Due to the importance of local geographical conditions for the availability of food items, regional patterns have traditionally been particularly relevant for food products. Such regional patterns persist today even if modern distribution systems have liberated local eating patterns from the constraints of climate etc. (Askegaard and Madsen, 1995; Grunert et al., 1995).

In opposition to that, food is at the same time a field of consumption where we are very often encouraged to try out new things; an invitation which bears relatively little risk since the consequences of mistakes and disappointments are normally short-term and not too serious. Recent years have seen an explosion in the supply of new food products in most markets. Improved conditions of production and transport facilities along with the international communication possibilities, immigration and tourism have caused great upheavals in the majority of European food cultures.

In this paper, we compare consumers' relationship to food in France and Germany using the *food-related lifestyle* approach.

2. The Food-Related Lifestyle Approach

In the food-related lifestyle approach (Brunsø and Grunert, 1995; Grunert, Brunsø, and Bisp, in press), lifestyle is defined as the system of cognitive categories, scripts, and their associations, which relate a set of products to a set of values. This definition

(i)   makes lifestyle distinct from values,

(ii)   makes lifestyles transcend individual brands or products, but possibly specific to a product class, so that it makes sense to talk about a food-related lifestyle, or a housing-related lifestyle,

(iii) places lifestyles clearly in a hierarchy of constructs of different levels of abstraction, where lifestyles have an intermediate place between values and product/brand perceptions or attitudes,

(iv)   covers both factual and procedural knowledge, i.e., both the subjective perceptions, based on information and experience, about which products contribute to the attainment of life values, and learned procedures concerning how to obtain, use, or dispose of products, and

(v)   refers to enduring dispositions to behave, not to single behaviour acts. Lifestyles in the way defined, change slowly and will always frame behaviour, but any single act can always be modified at will by constructing ad hoc chains linking that act to the attainment of value(s).

Figure 1 shows our model to delineate relevant parts of cognitive structure, and how they contribute to linking food products to values. The boxes indicate groups of cognitive categories, and the lines associations between them:

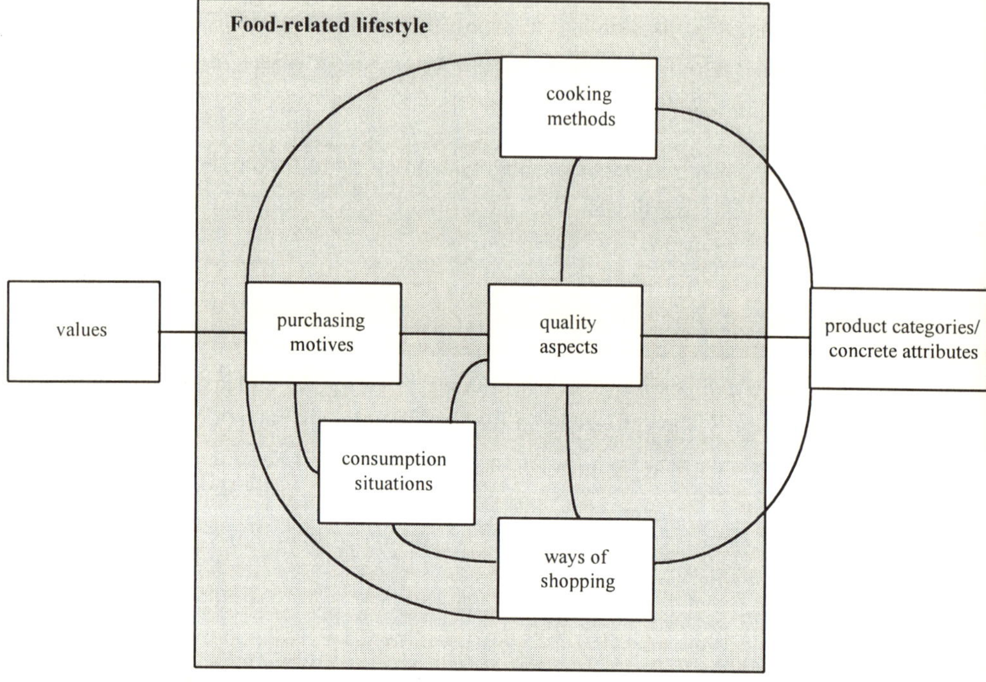

Figure 1: A cognitive structure model for food-related lifestyle

Ways of shopping. How do people shop for food products? Is their decision-making characterised by impulse buying, or by extensive deliberation? Do they read labels and other product information, or do they rely on the advice of experts, like friends or sales personnel? In which shops - one-stop shopping versus speciality food shops?

Cooking methods. How are the products purchased transformed into meals? How much time is used for preparation? Is preparation characterised by efficiency, or by indulgence? Is it a social activity, or one characterised by family division of labour? To which extent is it planned or spontaneous?

Quality aspects. This refers not to concrete attributes of individual products, but to attributes which may apply to food products in general. Examples may be healthy, natural, fresh, and tasty.

Consumption situations. How are meals spread over the day? How important is eating out?

Purchasing motives. What is expected from a meal, and what is the relative importance of these various consequences? How important are social aspects, hedonism, tradition and security?

The food-related lifestyle model is related to the means-end chain approach in consumer behaviour (Olson and Reynolds, 1983; Peter and Olson, 1993), since it also contains the basic hierarchical chain from product characteristics to values. It extends this approach, however, by incorporating procedural knowledge about shopping, preparing meals, and eating (Grunert, 1995).

We have developed a survey instrument covering 23 dimensions measured by 3 items each. Details about the development of the instrument have been described elsewhere (Brunsø and Grunert, 1995; Grunert, Brunsø, and Bisp, in press).

3. Data Collection and Cross-Cultural Validity

The FRL (Food-Related Lifestyle) instrument has been applied in representative consumer surveys in several countries, and is currently available in Danish, English, French, German, and Spanish. All items are rated on 7-point Likert-type scales. In the present paper, we compare data collected in France and Germany. Data was collected by personal interviews. In Germany, sampling was done by a random-walk procedure. In France, a quota sample based on major demographic and geographical criteria was used. Samples sizes were 1000 respondents in both France and Germany. Sampling was done on a household basis, and in each household selected the person with main responsibility for shopping for food and preparing meals was interviewed.

A cross-culturally valid measurement instrument is a precondition for cross-cultural comparisons of research results. Cross-cultural validity can be said to be present to the extent that understanding and evaluation of the research items are based on the same, or at least comparable, cognitive processes and structures in the populations investigated. Factor invariance has often been suggested as a validation instrument in cross-cultural research. A recognised way to measure this is confirmatory factor analysis, which investigates whether a set of data is compatible with a pre-specified factor structure. It can also be applied to multiple samples, and can then be used to check whether the data are compatible with the assumption that the factor structure in the samples is the same.

We have employed the approach suggested by Grunert, Grunert, and Kristensen (1994), who distinguish between different levels of cultural compatibility based on a cognitive view of cultural differences. Our results indicate that all scales can be regarded as cross-culturally valid at least at the level of weak cultural comparability. Details can be found in Brunsø, Grunert, and Bredahl (1996). The results also indicate that the cross-cultural validity when comparing France and Germany is weaker than when comparing, e.g., Germany, Denmark, and the UK.

4. Cross-National Differences on the 23 Dimensions of Food-Related Life-style

The national means for the 23 dimensions of food-related lifestyle are shown in Figures 2-6.

Concerning ways of shopping, the results show that the French enjoy shopping and advertising more than the Germans and use more speciality shops. The Germans are more interested in product information, use shopping lists more often, and look more at price. Generally one could say that the French are more interested in the hedonistic and the Germans more in the reason part of shopping.

In line with that interpretation, the French also score lower on the quality aspects health, value for money, freshness, and ecological/natural products. The also score lower on novelty, indicating a more conservative attitude to food. The only quality aspect dimension on which the French score higher is taste.

Concerning cooking methods, the French are considerably more interested in cooking, and while they are more conservative in the type of product used, they are more inclined to experiment with new recipes. In France, cooking is more a women's task and less a family matter than in Germany. There are no differences in the importance of convenience and planning.

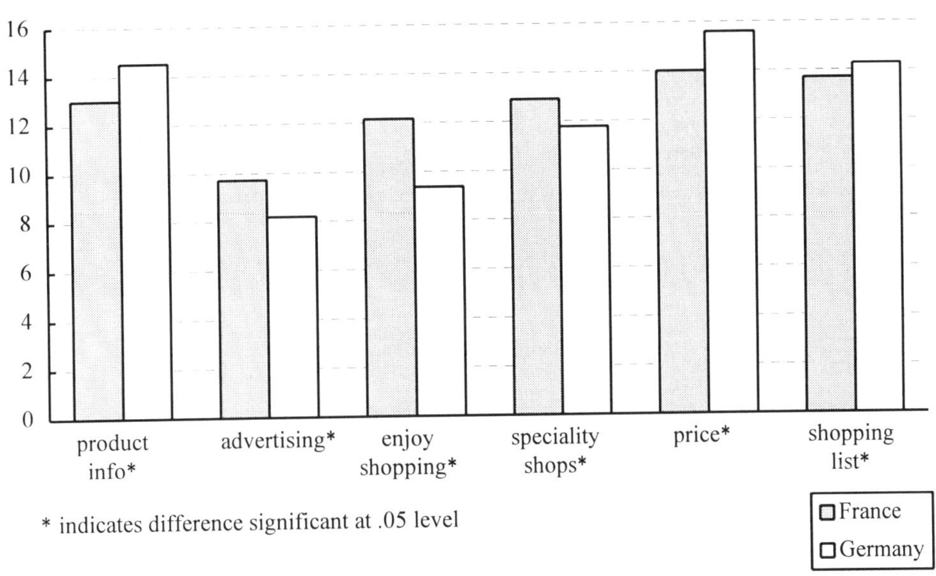

Figure 2: Mean differences on way of shopping *dimensions*

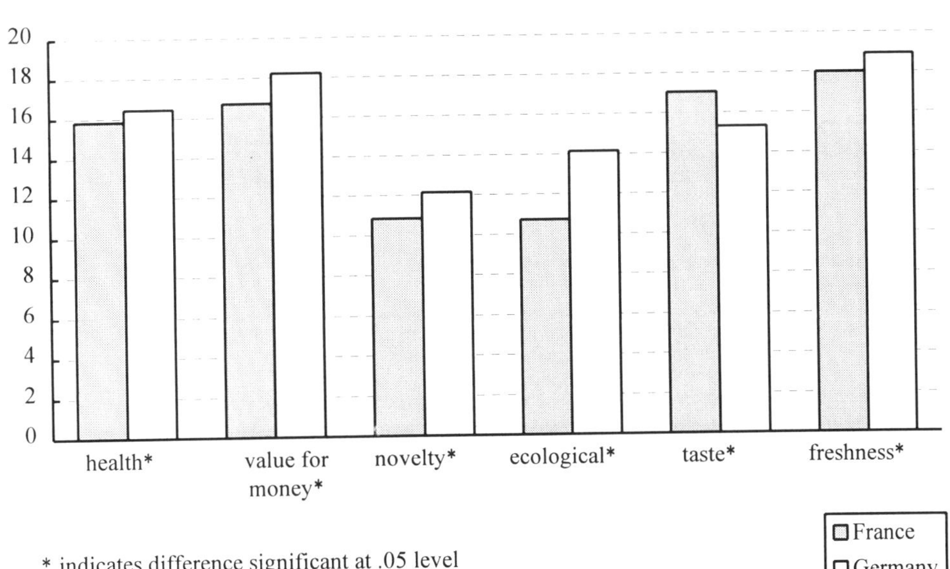

Figure 3: Mean differences on quality aspects *dimensions*

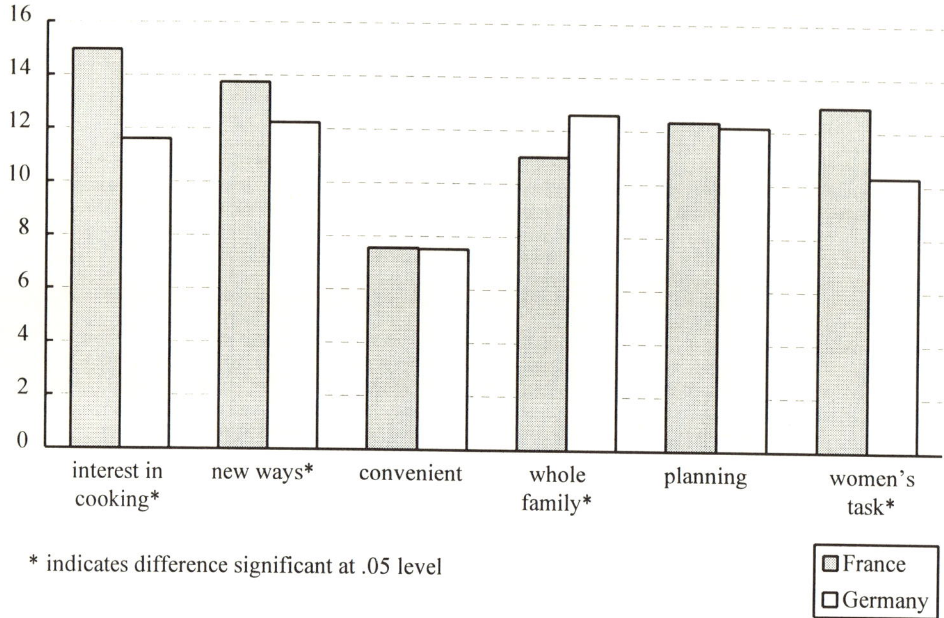

Figure 4: Mean differences on cooking methods *dimensions*

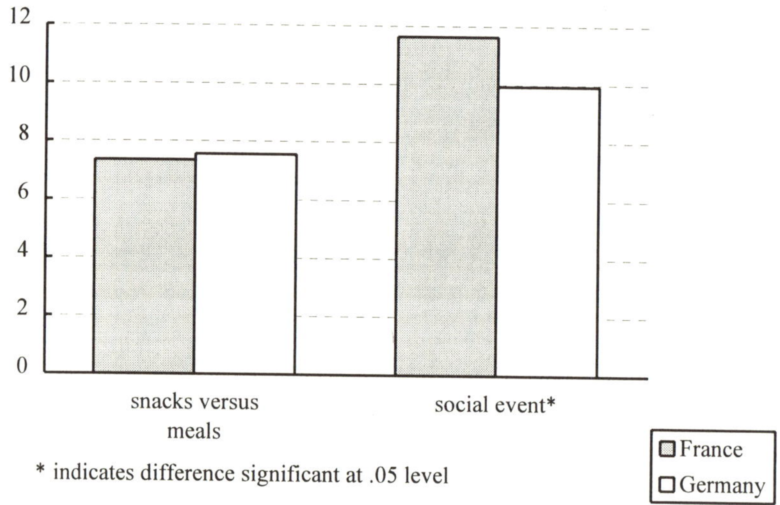

Figure 5: Mean differences on consumption situations *dimensions*

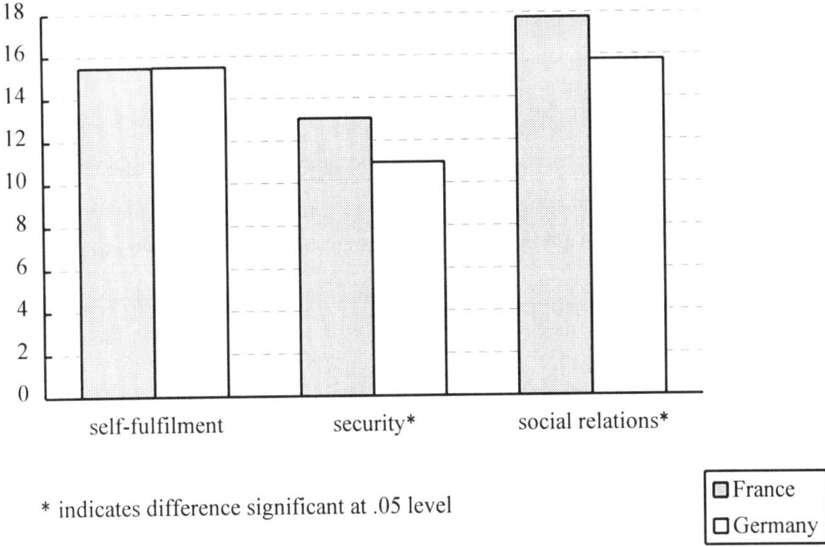

* indicates difference significant at .05 level

Figure 6: Mean differences on purchasing motives *dimensions*

As for consumption situations, the meal as a social event is more important in France than in Germany. There is no difference in the extent to which snacking has replaced regular meals.

Finally, on the three purchasing motives dimensions, the French score higher on social relations and security, underlining both the social role of the meals and the conservative attitude towards food products and eating.

5. Comparison of National Consumer Segments

For both countries, a clustering procedure based on Ward's method was performed, i.e., a minimisation of the sum of squares within as opposed to across clusters. The cluster solution finally selected was based on interpretability as well as the inspection of jumps in distance measures (scree test). Analysis of variance was used to check that significant differences exist between the clusters on all 23 scales. The interpretation of the clusters rests mainly on how the cluster means differ from the overall population means.

For both, France and Germany, five-cluster solutions were finally selected. The interpretation of the clusters, based on an inspection of how the cluster means differ from the population means, seemed quite similar for 3 out of the 5 clusters. We first describe the 3 clusters which the two countries seem to have in common.

The uninvolved food consumer. This group accounts for 21% of the cases in Germany, and 18% of the cases in France. These consumers are quite uninterested in most aspects of shopping and score below average on importance of product information, enjoyment from shopping, use of speciality shops, use of shopping lists, and use of the price criterion. Likewise, they are little interested in product characteristics. Their interest in health, price-quality relation, novelty, ecological products, taste and freshness is below average. The cooking methods dimensions also show that food is not a central element in these consumers' lives. This segment is the least interested in cooking, and aspects such as innovation and challenge are not important at all. Consumers in this group don't plan meals much, either. On the other hand, quick and easy cooking is relatively important for them. Snacks have replaced fixed meals to a greater extent among these consumers than among the population as such in two out of the four countries. Recognition in connection with cooking is less important than for the majority of consumers in all four countries, and this also applies to security through traditional eating in three out of the four countries.

As can be seen from the above, these consumers are quite uninterested in most aspects of food. Their food-related lifestyle is characterised by the fact that they hardly use food to achieve basic values at all. Whatever it is these consumers want to achieve in their lives, they achieve through other channels than food.

The conservative food consumer. This group accounts for 18% of the respondents in Germany, and 13% in France. There is no clear pattern with regard to their way of shopping, but with regard to quality aspects they clearly stand out by not wanting novelty in food products. They have a clear profile on cooking methods, which is characterised by avoiding new ways of cooking, a low emphasis on convenience, considerable planning, and a conviction that cooking is a woman's task. They also clearly stand out by high ratings on creating security by traditional meal patterns.

Food is an important part of the conservative food consumers' lives. Food and food products create stability and security in their lives. This is reflected in the careful planning of cooking, and an aversion to anything new.

The rational food consumer. This group accounts for 26% of the respondents in Germany, and 35% in France. These respondents have above-average scores on most of the ways of shopping scale, i.e., they have a stronger tendency to regard product information as important, look after prices, use shopping lists, and also enjoy shopping. They also score high on most quality aspects. As for cooking methods, they have high scores on the planning dimension, and have an above-average tendency to look for new ways in the kitchen. They also rate the purchasing motives self-fulfilment in food and security highly.

Food and food products are an important part of these consumers' lives, and are essential for achieving such basic values as self-fulfilment, recognition, and security. This gives rise to an interested-critical shopping behaviour.

We now describe those segments which seemed to be more idiosyncratic for the two countries.

The adventurous food consumer. This group accounts for 24% of the respondents in Germany. They have somewhat above average interest in most quality aspects, but their profile is most pronounced with regard to cooking methods. They are very interested in cooking, score high on looking for new ways, involve the whole family in the cooking process, are not interested in convenience and reject the notion that cooking is a woman's task. They score high on self-fulfilment in food and low on security by traditional eating patterns.

Food and food products are an important element in these consumers' lives. Cooking is a creative and social process for the whole family.

The hedonistic food consumer. 18% of the respondents in France are in this group, which can be regarded as a variant of the adventurous food consumer. Just like the adventurous food consumers in Germany, consumers in this group emphasise aspects related to creativity and social activity. What distinguishes them from the adventurous group in Germany is a lower emphasis on the 'reasonable' aspects of food purchases like health and naturalness.

The moderate food consumer. 16% of the respondents in France have been named in this way. The consumers in this segment differ in not differing. They lie close to the average for the French population as a whole in nearly all dimensions of food-related lifestyle.

The careless food consumer. This group accounts for 11% of the respondents in Germany. At first sight, this segment resembles the uninvolved food consumers: consumers also seem to be uninterested in most aspects of shopping. However, they score especially low on the use of shopping lists, i.e., buy spontaneously. This is also reflected in the quality aspects sought. Consumers in this segment are less interested in basically all quality aspects, but they are quite interested in novelty. Cooking is a spontaneous activity as well. Compared with the other segments, this segment places the most emphasis on quick and easy cooking. Meals are not planned in advance.

The overall picture is of a consumer who attaches little importance to food as a means of achieving basic values, but who are often tempted by new products - as long as they don't require a greater effort or new cooking skills.

Three of the segments looked sufficiently similar in the two countries that we have dared to give them the same name. How similar are these segments really? An answer to this is presented by the diagram in Figure 7. Correlations have been computed between the means of the 23 FRL scales for the totality of the 10 segments found in the 2 countries. The correlation matrix was then entered into a nonmetric MDS algorithm for graphic representation.

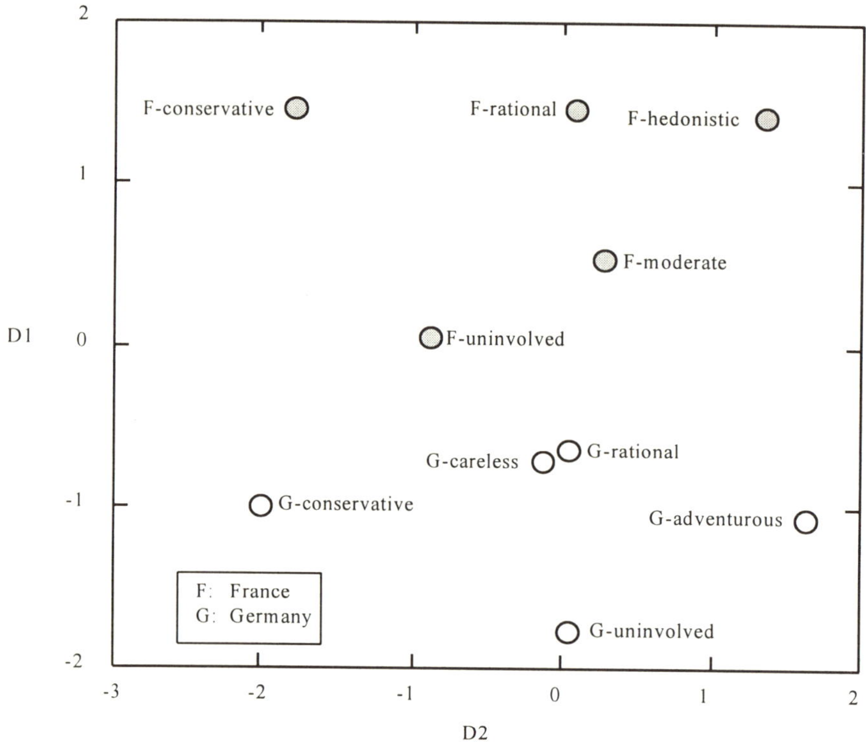

Figure 7: MDS configuration based on segment scale means

12

We see a quite clear pattern in the diagram. The French segments are on the top, and the German segments are in the lower half of the diagram, i.e., there is a clear cultural grouping of the segments. At the same time, the segments seem to be grouped according to a conservatism-modernism dimensions, with the conservative segments to the left and the adventurous/hedonistic segments to the right. The segments are thus comparable across the two countries on that dimensions, mirrored by the fact that the horizontal grouping of the segments for the two countries is quite the same. At the same time, there is a clear cultural difference, indicated by the fact that the French and the German segments are placed in disjunct parts of the space.

6. Discussion and Conclusions

In the present paper we have described research aimed at measuring consumers' food-related lifestyle France and Germany.

While we found that there is enough similarity between the countries to make it possible to develop a measurement instrument with cross-cultural validity, considerable differences between consumers in the two countries were also found. In general, the French consumers appear as more hedonistic and more conservative, while the German consumers appear as more reason-oriented and more adventurous. These cultural differences are also mirrored in the segmentation analysis, whereas the conservative-adventurous (or modern) dimension seems to have cross-cultural applicability.

Global marketing is therefore bound to be difficult in the food sector for some time to come.

References

Askegaard, S. and T.K. Madsen (1995): European Food Cultures: An Exploratory Analysis Of Food Related Preferences And Behaviour In European Regions, MAPP working paper No. 26, The Aarhus School of Business.

Brunsø, K. and K.G. Grunert (1995): Development And Testing Of A Cross-Culturally Valid Instrument: Food-Related Life Style. In: Advances in Consumer Research, Vol. 22, F. Kardes and M. Sujan (Eds.), Provo, UT: Association for Consumer Research, pp. 475-480.

Brunsø, K., Grunert, K.G., and L. Bredahl (1996): An Analysis of National and Cross-National Consumer Segments Using the Food-Related Lifestyle Instrument in Denmark, France, Germany and Great Britain, MAPP working paper No. 35, The Aarhus School of Business.

Fischler, J.-C. (1990): L'omnivore, Paris: Odile Jacob.

Grunert, K. G., Brunsø, K., and S. Bisp (in press): Food-Related Life Style: Development Of A Cross-Culturally Valid Instrument For Market Surveillance. In L. Kahle and C. Chiagouris (Eds.), Values, Lifestyles, And Psychographics, Hillsdale, NJ: Erlbaum.

Grunert, K. G., Hartvig Larsen, H., Madsen, T. K., and A. Baadsgaard (1995): Market Orientation In Food And Agriculture, Boston: Kluwer Academic.

Grunert, S. C., Grunert, K.G., and K. Kristensen (1994): Une Méthode Déstimation De La Validité Interculturelle Des Instruments De Mesure: Le Cas De La Mesure Des Valeurs Des Consommateurs Par La Liste Des Valeurs Lov. In: Recherches et Applications en Marketing, Vol. 8, No. 4, pp. 5-28.

Mennell, S., Murcott, A., and A. van Otterloo (1992): The Sociology Of Food, Eating, Diet And Culture, London: Sage.

Olson, J. C. and T. J. Reynolds (1983): Understanding Consumers Cognitive Structures: Implications For Advertising Strategy. In: L. Percy and A. G. Woodside (Eds.), Advertising and Consumer Psychology, Lexington, MA: Lexington Books, pp. 77-90.

Peter, J. P., and J.C. Olson (1993): Consumer Behavior, 3rd ed., Homewood, IL: Irwin.

Sigrid Joseph

Consumer Values in West and East Germany

1. Introduction

2. Research Issues and Research Propositions

3. Research Method

4. Results
    4.1. Comparing Importance Scores of Values
    4.2. Analysis of the Structure of Values

5. Discussion

6. Conclusion

References

Consumer Values in West and East Germany

Sigrid Joseph

Abstract

The list of values (LOV) as developed by Kahle is used in order to assess West and East German values in reunified Germany. Based on data from interviews of more than 400 respondents, priorities and structures of values are studied. „Self-respect" proved to represent the most important value for both samples. As far as structures are concerned, four groups of values could be identified.

1. Introduction

The objective of this article is to approach West and East German values based on the list of values (LOV) developed by Kahle (1983). Having introduced the subject and having outlined the method of the research, importance scores of values for a West and an East German sample are presented, and principal component analysis is conducted.

Values can be defined as characteristic conceptions of what is desirable, influencing the choice between different modes, means and objectives of behaviour for an individual person or a group (Kluckhohn, 1951). According to Grunert and Scherhorn (1990), values can be characterised by five important features. Values are 1) beliefs or concepts 2) about desirable behaviour or end states, 3) values go beyond particular situations, 4) guide the choice or evaluation of events and behaviour, and 5) are arranged in a hierarchy according to importance. Kmieciak (1976) also proposes a rather detailed definition of values, when he notes that values are culturally and socially determined and that they are dynamic, centred on the self and constituent of the self. The concept of values organises and accentuates the„input" of a person's system (i. e. perception), and it also regulates his/her output (i. e. behaviour). In this way, values allow an active and directive planning by the self, as well as an orientation of behaviour in different situations. Values themselves depend on views of the world (Stammen, 1982).

Values have been introduced into consumer research mostly as a consequence of the research undertaken by Rokeach (1973), who has developed a list of 36 values. 18 of these values are „instrumental" in nature, they rather characterise behaviour or means adopted by individuals, whereas the other 18 values represent „terminal" values, i. e. they constitute final objectives of human existence. These 36 values developed by Rokeach were reduced to 9 more general values by Kahle and his colleagues (Kahle, 1983; Kahle, Beatty, and Homer, 1986; Kahle, Poulous, and Sukhdial, 1988). In fact, the lists of values which have been developed by Rokeach and by Kahle resemble each other as far as their structures are concerned.

Furthermore, Schwartz and Bilsky (1987; 1990) have developed a theoretical framework which integrates the values developed by Rokeach into a psychological structure. This framework has been applied on an intercultural level. Actually, the authors identify different groups of values according to three criteria: according to the objective (instrumental or terminal), depending on interest (individualist, collectivist or both of them), and according to seven motivational domains (social objective, restrictive conformity, security, maturity, pleasure, accomplishment, being centred on the self). This classification allows one to compare values between different cultures and periods more easily.

Comparing the two approaches developed by Rokeach and by Kahle respectively, one finds that certain items are identical, other items in the long list have been condensed by Kahle into one term only, while certain values have simply been dropped. However, there are a few items that are only characteristic of Kahle's list. Generally speaking, the scale developed by Kahle contains more generic items and, contrary to certain terminal values, possesses a more personal orientation. Rokeach's method seems to be better adapted to research with socialimplication, whereas Kahle's approach is better suited for research on individual objectives (Valette-Florence, 1988). The list of values developed by Kahle was tested in different cultural contexts, for example in France and West Germany (Valette-Florence et al., 1991), as well as in West Germany and North America (Grunert and Scherhorn, 1990).

2. Research Issues and Research Propositions

Values in West and East Germany have been shown to differ to a certain extent. According to Millar and Restall (1991), who analysed data from the Rokeach value survey (which, as we have seen, mainly represents an extended version of the LOV developed by Kahle), priorities of values differ quite considerably between West and East Germans. According to the authors, West Germans favour more „sophisticated" values, such as tenderness, harmony and creativity, whereas East Germans search for more fundamental values, such as confidence, honesty and competence.

Bauer (1991) also states that values in East Germany are of more traditional nature, whereas West Germans rather tend to search for social and post-materialist ideals. Bauer (1991) explains this difference by differing priorities of life in West and East Germany, and compares economic conditions in East Germany immediately after reunification to those found in West Germany during the period of reconstruction after the war, in the 1950's and up to the middle of the 1960's. Actually, West Germans tend to be more idealistic, whereas East Germans seem to be more „down-to-earth". According to these findings, the first research proposition is as follows:

<u>Research Proposition 1:</u>

Priorities of values in West and East Germany differ in so far as West Germans favour values linked to self-realisation, and show a certain degree of hedonism, whereas East Germans rather search for security and are concerned with more traditional values (Bauer, 1991; Millar and Restall, 1991).

According to different authors (Klages, 1984; Huppertz, 1987; Herbert, 1988), two main groups of values can be distinguished in West Germany: values related to duty (e. g. sense of accomplishment, security) and values linked to self-realisation (e. g. a varied life, excitement). Values related to duty have been predominant until the middle of the 1960's, whereas values linked to self-realisation started to expand from this moment on (they were dominant from the middle of the 1960's up to the middle of the 1970's). In today's society both types of groups of values can be identified, and certain persons are characterised by priorities of values related to duty and of values linked to self-realisation. Klages (1988) and Herbert (1988) have named this phenomenon „synthesis of values".

Actually, values related to duty and values linked to self-realisation possess each two sub-dimensions: each sub-group can either be linked to society or to the individual person. Hence, four groups of values can be distinguished: values of duty linked to society, values of duty related to the individual person, values of self-realisation linked to society, and values of self-realisation related to the individual person. Therefore, the second research proposition is as follows:

<u>Research proposition 2:</u>

The underlying structures of values in West and East Germany are characterised by four groups of values: values related to duty towards society, values related to duty towards oneself, values linked to self-realisation towards society and values linked to self-realisation towards oneself (Klages, 1984; Huppertz, 1987; Herbert, 1988).

Security occupies different positions in West and East Germany. West Germans see security linked to society, they are used to living conditions which imply a certain risk (for example the crime in cities), whereas East Germans are confronted with a degree of insecurity today that they had not known in the past German Democratic Republic. One should not forget that crime linked to the use of drug was almost unknown in the German Democratic Republic. It was not until German monetary reunification that East Germany has become an interesting territory for drug dealers. Crime on such a scale has become a new and shocking experience for a large number of East Germans. Hence, this leads us to the third research proposition:

<u>Research proposition 3:</u>

In West Germany security is felt to be linked to society, whereas in East Germany security is felt more strongly at the individual level (Bauer, 1991).

Finally, in East Germany we can state a phenomenon which is called „apolitical interiorisation" (Merseburger, 1988). More precisely, self-realisation linked to society is linked more strongly to establishing relationships with friends and relatives. Actually, during the period of the former German Democratic Republic, many East Germans successfully tried to loose or break off their ties with an indoctrinated public life and tended to realise themselves in their private lives instead. This meant attaching special importance to relationships with friends and relatives. One has noted that many East Germans regret the lack of solidarity which they discover in Western societies (Maaz, 1991). Research proposition 4 is as follows:

<u>Research proposition 4:</u>

Values of self-realisation towards society are linked more strongly to sense of belonging in East Germany than they are in West Germany (Merseburger, 1988; Maaz, 1991).

3. Research Method

Values (as items of a questionnaire) can be evaluated by respondents in two principal ways. The first possibility is to ask respondents to rank items, but the number of items which can be ranked by a respondent is rather limited. The second possibility is to ask respondents to evaluate each item by using a scale, for example an importance scale. For the purpose of the present research (as the number of items to be evaluated was relatively high), we decided to use an importance scale developed by Mendel (1997) for German respondents. This scale contains semantic supports which are supposed to help orientation and understanding for the respondents

(Vernette, 1986). Actually, standard deviations and means of the German expressions tested allow one to place semantic supports on the following points: 0; 2,5; 5; 7,5; 10. In this way, the variables concerned possess the characteristics of interval variables, and allow one to execute various statistical tests (Evrard, Pras, and Roux, 1993).

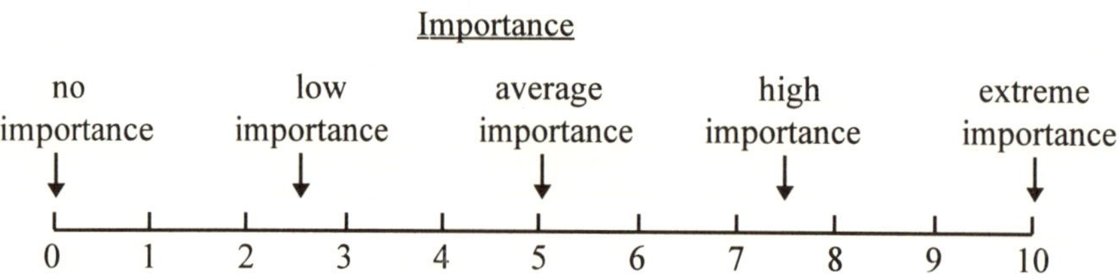

We base our research on the list of values developed by Kahle (1983), and we take Grunert's and Scherhorn's translation (1990) as a starting point. In fact, this list of values had already been used by the authors in West Germany, and we also pretested it in East Germany. As a consequence of the comments made by the interviewees, two items of the list were sub-divided into two each. In fact, several East German respondents told us that they did not per-ceive two parts of the translated phrases in the same way. These remarks concerned the Ger-man translation of „excitement" which had become „a varied life, excitement", and „sense of belonging" which had become „sense of belonging, feeling protected". In this way, the list of values now contains 11 items instead of the original 9 items.

The interviews were realised in summer 1995, and the sample of the research is com-posed of 205 West Germans and 201 East Germans. The present research only constitutes a part of a larger study. In fact, the aim was not to interview a representative sample for West or East German population, but to cover different age groups and different degrees of education. The average age of the persons interviewed is 39 years. About half of the sample serves or served an apprenticeship, and the other half studies or accomplished studies in the past (socio-demographic characteristics are the same for West and East Germany).

4. Results

4.1. Comparing Importance Scores of Values

We start our analysis by looking at the results for the first research proposition. Accord-ingly, priorities of values in West and East Germany should differ in so far as West Germans favour values linked to self-realisation, and show a certain degree of hedonism, whereas East

Germans rather search for security and are concerned with more traditional values (Bauer, 1991; Millar and Restall, 1991). First of all, let us take a look at the ranking of values in West and East Germany. Table 1 shows the ranking of values for the West and for the East German sample in descending order of importance.

Variable	West: Mean	Variable	East: Mean
1. Self-respect	9,38	1. Self-respect	9,14
2. Self-fulfilment	9,21	2. Feeling protected	9,09
3. Warm relationships with others	9,09	3. Security	9,06
4. Feeling protected	8,81	4. Self-fulfilment	8,79
5. Fun and enjoyment in life	8,60	5. Warm relationships with others	8,74
6. Security	8,48	6. Sense of accomplishment	8,67
7. A varied life	8,12	7. Being well respected	8,22
8. Sense of accomplishment	8,05	8. A varied life	8,19
9. Being well respected	7,86	9. Fun and enjoyment in life	8,14
10. Sense of belonging	6,19	10. Sense of belonging	6,59
11. Excitement	6,07	11. Excitement	6,10

Table 1: Ranking of the items of the list of values (descending importance) for the West (n=205) and for the East German sample (n=201)

„Self-respect" is the most important value for the West German as well as for the East German sample. How can we explain the importance of these values in both parts of Germany? In fact, as far as East Germans are concerned, German reunification has made them live in a daily environment which is rather new to them. Compared to what they were used during the period of the former German Democratic Republic, this new environment seems to be rather hostile: the importance of collectivity and mutual help have diminished considerably, and a „capitalist" society is more openly based on individual performance. West Germans, who are already used to this kind of environment, rather look for self-realisation (Klages, 1984;1988).

This difference in the perception of environment perceived by West and East Germans is underlined by the values with ranks 2 and 3: persons from the West German sample prefer „self-fulfilment" (rank 2) and „warm relationships with others" (rank 3), whereas those from the East German sample rather favour „feeling protected" (rank 2) and „security" (rank 3). Moreover, correlation coefficients between the values of the first three ranks are relatively high. The correlation coefficient (Pearson, two-tailed test) between „self-respect" and „self-fulfilment" attains 0,513 (p<0,000) and between „self-respect" and „warm relationships with others" amounts to 0,235 (p<0,01) for the West German sample. For the East German sample, the correlation coefficient between „self-respect" and „feeling protected" is 0,357 (p<0,000) and 0,439 between „self-respect" and „security" (p<0,000). This implies that there seems to exist a rather strong link between the first three values having just been mentioned for West Germans as well as for East Germans.

Value	West	East	p (two-tailed test)
Being well respected	7,86	8,22	0,0453
A varied life	8,12	8,19	0,7065
Excitement	6,07	6,10	0,9157
Warm relationships with others	9,09	8,74	0,0513
Sense of accomplishment	8,05	8,67	0,0020
Self-respect	9,38	9,14	0,0682
Self-fulfilment	9,21	8,79	0,0102
Security	8,48	9,06	0,0020
Fun and enjoyment in life	8,60	8,14	0,0226
Sense of belonging	6,19	6,59	0,1473
Feeling protected	8,81	9,09	0,1400

Table 2: Comparison of means between the West (n=205) and the East German sample (n=201)

Certain values are relatively more important for the West German sample than for the East German sample. This is the case for „warm relationships with others", „self-fulfilment" and „fun and enjoyment in life", for example. Actually, contrary to values related to duty, which dominated in West Germany until the middle of the 1960's, those three values aim at self-realisation, a dimension finding its roots during the period between the middle of the 1960's and the middle of the 1970's (Klages, 1984; 1988). Therefore, values of West German society have profoundly changed since this period, and this change is still visible in West German society today.

Accordingly, the values having a greater importance for the East German sample are of a more traditional nature, and therefore are closer to values related to duty („being well respected", „sense of accomplishment", „security"). Values in East Germany (and in West Germany, but probably to a lesser extent) have proved to be influenced by Prussian values (Korte, 1990), which constitute a basis of today's values oriented towards duty. This orientation towards duty was also sustained by „socialist work ethics" in the former German Democratic Republic. Examining these values one by one,„being well respected" represents a value related to Prussian society (Haffner, 1987). Hence, this value continues to be important in East German society today. Moreover, „sense of accomplishment" is related to the importance of work in East Germany. If one considers the transformation of the East German labour market today (in the German Democratic Republic, employment was guaranteed to citizens, whereas today unemployment in East Germany is by far higher than in the West), one understands the importance labour values are bound to play after reunification.

„Security" also proves to be more important for the East German sample than for the West German sample. In fact, it is noticeable that East Germans interest in security is relatively higher than for West Germans. In the former German Democratic Republic security in general was assured to people in various fields: they had the right to work (even if they often could not get the work they wanted), and young people who got married obtained a (small) flat (even if the choice had to be made from a small number proposed to them by the local administration). After reunification, these rights have disappeared, and many East Germans strongly feel the absence of security in their living conditions (Maaz, 1991). We can conclude that these findings largely confirm our first research proposition, according to which priorities of values in West and East Germany differ in so far as West Germans favour values linked to self-realisation, and show a certain degree of hedonism, whereas East Germans rather search for security and are concerned with more traditional values (Bauer, 1991; Millar and Restall, 1991).

4.2. Analysis of the Structure of Values

We conduct principal component analysis in order to determine the underlying structure of the list of values (Churchill, 1979), which will help us to evaluated our research propositions number 2, 3 and 4. Homer and Kahle (1988) distinguished three underlying dimensions in American values (by using the list of values developed by Kahle). The first dimension can be interpreted as an external factor („sense of belonging", „being well respected", „security"), the second dimension is internal in showing more individual values („self-fulfilment", „excitement", „sense of accomplishment", „self-respect"), and the third factor can be characterised as a more internal factor as well, the values being more interpersonal („fun and enjoyment in life", „warm relationships with others").

Grunert and Scherhorn (1990), in working on data drawn from a West German sample, determined three underlying dimensions which were different from those determined by Homer and Kahle (1988). Their solution was as follows: the first factor could be interpreted as being influenced simultaneously by comfort/constancy and achievement orientation („security",

„sense of accomplishment", „self-respect", „being well respected"). The second factor showed a dominance of pleasure/change („excitement", „fun and enjoyment in life", „self-fulfilment"), and the third factor could be interpreted by a combination of being loved and the orientation towards comfort/constancy („warm relationships with others", „sense of belonging"). First of all, we conduct principal component analysis on the West German sample (205 persons). Secondly, the same analysis will be made on the East German sample (201 persons).

4.2.1. Underlying Structure of West German Values

We try to determine the underlying structure of the West German list of values, and we retain the 205 persons of the sample, as all questionnaires are complete. To begin with, we want to test factorisability of the variables, which means to test if the items of the questionnaire represent a sufficiently coherent whole in order to determine common dimensions (Evrard, Pras, and Roux, 1993). The two statistical tests commonly used for this analysis are the Kaiser-Meyer-Olkin Measure of Sampling Adequacy and the Bartlett Test of Sphericity:

1. Test: Kaiser-Meyer-Olkin Measure of Sampling Adequacy = 0,73238
2. Test: Bartlett Test of Sphericity = 503,72133, Significance = 0,00000

The score of the first test is 0,73, which, according to Kim and Mueller (1990) can be considered to be „middling". The score of the second test reveals to be significant (even if this significance is almost always satisfied in big samples; Evrard, Pras, and Roux, 1993).

Factor	Eigenvalue	Percentage of Variance	Cumulated Percentages
1	3,22700	29,3	29,3
2	1,73619	15,8	45,1
3	1,14807	10,4	55,6
4	0,92567	8,4	64,0
5	0,85207	7,7	71,7
6	0,72438	6,6	78,3
7	0,64265	5,8	84,1
8	0,53243	4,8	89,0
9	0,46503	4,2	93,2
10	0,42225	3,8	97,1
11	0,32426	2,9	100,0

Table 3: Eigenvalues of factors and percentage of variance explained by the factors (West German sample, n=205)

Pursuing our analysis, we want to determine the number of factors to be retained. Mainly, there are two formal tests (Evrard, Pras and Roux, 1993): we can retain the factors with eigenvalues equal to or greater than 1 and examine the scree plot of the eigenvalues (the first eliminated factor leads to a minimum loss of information). Table 3 shows the eigenvalues and the percentage of variance explained by the factors for the West German sample.

The first three factors have eigenvalues greater than 1. We also conduct the scree test, which can be graphically examined, or can be calculated by scrutinising the sign of the differences between consecutive eigenvalues. In fact, the point of inflexion corresponds to the change of the sign. The following mathematical formulas are used (Evrard, Pras and Roux, 1993):

$$delta_k = lambda_k - lambda_{k+1} \quad \text{and} \quad difference_k = delta_k - delta_{k+1}$$

With: $lambda_k$ = eigenvalues,

$delta_k$ = differences between consecutive eigenvalues, and

$difference_k$ = difference between consecutive values of delta.

One retains k+1 factors, k being the first index for which $difference_k$ is negative (Evrard, Pras, and Roux, 1993). Table 4 indicates the calculation for analysing the scree plot of the eigenvalues of principal component analysis conducted on the list of values for the West German sample.

Factor k	Eigenvalue (lambda$_k$)	delta$_k$	difference$_k$
1	3,227	1,491	0,903
2	1,736	0,588	0,366
3	1,148	0,222	0,148
4	0,926	0,074	-0,054
5	0,852	0,128	
6	0,724		
...	...	...	...

Table 4: Calculation for analysing the scree plot of the eigenvalues (West German sample)

The index is negative with the fourth factor. Accordingly, we would retain k+1, which is to say 5 factors. Considering eigenvalues, those of the first three factors are greater than 1, which would lead to retaining 3 factors. Comparing the solutions obtained by Homer and Kahle (1988) and by Grunert and Scherhorn (1990) (see above), one can conclude that there is, on the one hand, an external as well as an internal dimension, and, on the other hand, a dimension that is influenced by comfort/constancy/achievement and one oriented towards pleasure/change.

Klages (1984; 1988), in analysing West German values, has retained a combination of these two dimensions, and the characteristics of the four dimensions that can be inferred from his research are fairly similar to the dimensions described here above. Accordingly, we expect to determine four factors among values in West Germany. As a matter of fact, according to research proposition 2, we expect to determine the following groups of values: values concerning duty oriented towards society, values concerning duty on the individual level/towards oneself, values of self-realisation oriented towards society, and values of self-realisation towards oneself (Klages, 1984; 1988).

Consequently, we opt for a four-factor-solution (which, at the same time, constitutes the most straightforward compromise between the three-factor-solution according to eigenvalues and the five-factor-solution found according to the scree plot). In fact, the values belonging to several groups are supposed to be correlated to each other. In this way, on the one hand values linked to self-realisation towards oneself and values linked to self-realisation towards society are likely to show positive correlations (as are values linked to duty towards oneself and values linked to duty towards society). On the other hand, values linked to self-realisation towards society are likely to show negative correlations with values linked to duty towards society (as are values linked to self-realisation towards oneself and values linked to duty towards oneself). We take into account these correlations by conducting an oblique rotation on the factors. For interpretation of the factors, factor loadings of the variables which are greater than 0,5 are retained (Evrard, Pras, and Roux, 1993). The results are as follows:

| | Factor 1 | Factor 2 | Factor 3 | Factor 4 |
	Duty towards society	Self-realisation towards oneself	Duty towards oneself	Self-realisation towards society
Sense of belonging	**0,722**	0,075	-0,019	-0,048
Security	**0,722**	-0,090	-0,389	-0,204
Being well respected	**0,516**	0,348	-0,446	-0,307
A varied life	0,052	**0,855**	-0,214	-0,115
Excitement	-0,021	**0,823**	-0,194	-0,055
Fun and enjoyment in life	0,145	**0,711**	-0,180	-0,273
Self-fulfilment	0,109	0,239	**-0,816**	-0,146
Self-respect	0,134	0,209	**-0,773**	-0,398
Sense of accomplishment	0,409	0,192	**-0,684**	0,115
Warm relationships with others	0,109	0,233	-0,188	**-0,859**
Feeling protected	**0,624**	0,130	-0,304	**-0,686**

Table 5: Factor loadings of the West German list of values (n=205)

26

According to our expectations, we can distinguish the four dimensions we have defined above. The first factor, which contains the values of „sense of belonging", „security", „being well respected" and „feeling protected" represents values expressing duty towards society. The second factor, by showing the values of „a varied life", „excitement", and „fun and enjoyment in life" represents values related to self-realisation towards oneself. The third factor expresses duty towards oneself (values of „self-fulfilment, „self-respect" and „sense of accomplishment"). Finally, the fourth factor corresponds to the dimension of self-realisation towards society (values of „warm relationships with others", „feeling protected"). We conduct the same type of analysis on the East German sample.

4.2.2. Underlying Structure of East German Values

The East German sample is composed of 195 persons, 6 persons having been excluded for showing missing values on the responses to the questionnaire. Factorisability of the variables is analysed by again using the Kaiser-Meyer-Olkin Measure of Sampling Adequacy and the Bartlett Test of Sphericity:

1. Test: Kaiser-Meyer-Olkin Measure of Sampling Adequacy = 0,76680
2. Test: Bartlett Test of Sphericity = 616,83496, Significance = 0,00000

The score of the first test is slightly higher than that of the West German sample, and can be considered to be „middling". The score of the second test reveals to be significant as well. We pursue our analysis. In order to determine the number of factors to be retained, we take a look at eigenvalues greater than 1 and examine the scree plot of the eigenvalues.

Factor	Eigenvalue	Percentage of Variance	Cumulated Percentages
1	3,58399	32,6	32,6
2	1,79533	16,3	48,9
3	1,19129	10,8	59,7
4	0,86319	7,8	67,6
5	0,80946	7,4	74,9
6	0,62667	5,7	80,6
7	0,59140	5,4	86,0
8	0,49702	4,5	90,5
9	0,43010	3,9	94,4
10	0,35659	3,2	97,7
11	0,25497	2,3	100,0

Table 6: Eigenvalues of factors and percentage of variance explained by the factors (East German sample, n=195)

Table 6 (above) shows us the eigenvalues and the percentage of variance explained by the factors for the East German sample. The first three factors show eigenvalues greater than 1. We also conduct the scree test (see Table 7, below):

Factor k	Eigenvalue (lambda$_k$)	delta$_k$	difference$_k$
1	3,584	1,789	1,185
2	1,795	0,604	0,276
3	1,191	0,328	0,274
4	0,863	0,054	-0,074
5	0,809	0,128	
6	0,627		
...	...	...	...

Table 7: Calculation for analysing the scree plot of the eigenvalues (East German sample)

As for the West German sample, the index is negative with the fourth factor. Accordingly, we would retain k+1, which is to say 5 factors. Considering eigenvalues, those of the first three factors are greater than 1 (as for the West German sample), which would lead to retaining 3 factors.

Values in West and East Germany resemble each other (in particular, both parts of Germany are rooted in similar cultural and social traditions over long or fairly recent periods of history, e. g. Prussia, the Reformation and the Third Reich), and values in West and East Germany show a tendency to approach each other to a certain degree (Lüthy, 1973; Brämer and Heublein, 1991). Consequently, we opt for a four-factor-solution for the East German sample. In reality, according to research proposition 2, we again expect to determine the following groups of values: values concerning duty oriented towards society, values concerning duty on the individual level/towards oneself, values of self-realisation oriented towards society, and values of self-realisation towards oneself (Klages, 1984; 1988). Consequently, we again opt for a four-factor-solution. As above, we will consider correlations between factors by conducting an oblique rotation on the factors. The results are shown in Table 8.

According to what we expected, we can distinguish the four dimensions we have defined above. The first factor, which contains the values of „excitement", „a varied life", „fun and enjoyment in life", „self-fulfilment, and „sense of belonging", represents values expressing self-realisation towards oneself. The second factor expresses duty towards oneself („self-respect", „security", „sense of accomplishment", „self-fulfilment" and „feeling protected"). The third factor shows values related to self-realisation towards society („warm relationships with others", „feeling protected", „sense of belonging"). Finally, the fourth factor can be interpreted as expressing duty towards society („being well respected").

| | Factor 1 | Factor 2 | Factor 3 | Factor 4 |
	Self-realisation towards oneself	Duty towards oneself	Self-realisation towards society	Duty towards society
Excitement	**0,865**	-0,036	0,141	0,321
A varied life	**0,817**	0,031	0,063	0,285
Fun and enjoyment in life	**0,768**	0,345	0,061	0,078
Self-fulfilment	**0,610**	**0,577**	-0,082	0,327
Sense of belonging	**0,558**	0,165	**0,468**	0,248
Self-respect	0,285	**0,776**	0,219	0,358
Security	-0,110	**0,775**	0,217	-0,023
Sense of accomplishment	0,391	**0,638**	-0,055	0,423
Warm relationships with others	0,139	0,013	**0,757**	0,183
Feeling protected	0,087	**0,459**	**0,739**	0,050
Being well respected	0,202	0,224	-0,166	**-0,940**

Table 8: Factor loadings of the East German list of values (n=195)

5. Discussion

Comparing the solutions of the two samples, one can state that the composition of the factors differs between the West and the East German sample. The values oriented to duty towards society are „sense of belonging", „security", „being well respected" and „feeling protected" in West Germany, while the comparable category of East German values is limited to „being well respected". In fact, according to research proposition 3, we can explain this difference by the different places security occupies in West and East Germany. Actually, West Germans see security linked to society, they are used to living conditions which imply a certain risk, whereas East Germans are confronted with a degree of insecurity today that they had not known in the past German Democratic Republic.

The second group of values, values related to duty towards oneself contains „self-respect", „sense of accomplishment" and „self-fulfilment" in West Germany and „self-respect", „sense of accomplishment", „self-fulfilment", „feeling protected" and „security" in East Germany. We have already noted that for East Germans, the necessity for security is felt more strongly by the individual mind. The third group of values is composed of values linked to self-realisation towards society. For both, the West and the East German sample, those comprise

„warm relationships with others" and „feeling protected", but for the East German sample we also note „sense of belonging". We can explain the presence of this latter value among the values related to self-realisation by the phenomenon of apolitical interiorisation (Merseburger, 1988), and these findings confirm research proposition 4.

Finally, values related to self-realisation towards oneself include „a varied life", „excitement", „fun and enjoyment in life" and „feeling protected" for the West German sample and „a varied life", „excitement", „fun and enjoyment in life", „self-fulfilment", and „sense of belonging" for the East German sample. In this group of values, we can note that West German values have a more hedonistic character (Klages, 1984, 1988), whereas East German values are slightly more traditional (Bauer, 1991). Indeed, these findings correspond to our first research proposition.

6. Conclusion

This research, based on the list of values developed by Kahle, was conducted in West and East Germany, in order to assess importance scores of values and underlying structures of the list of values between the former two states. Results imply similarities as well as differences: the most important value in the West and in the East German sample is „self-respect". However, the persons from the West German sample rather favour values related to self-realisation, whereas individuals from the East German sample mainly look for security.

The underlying structures of the list of values rather clearly show four main groups of values: values related to duty towards society, values related to duty towards oneself, values related to self-realisation towards society, and values related to self-realisation towards the individual. In spite of this similarity, we note a certain number of differences concerning the values composing each of the groups with regard to the West and to the East German sample. We can remark that, for example, values linked to self-realisation towards oneself are of a more hedonistic nature for the West than for the East German sample. Moreover, as far as values linked to duty are concerned, the necessity of a search for security is more strongly felt individually in the East German sample, whereas the West German sample attributes security to the level of society. Differences concerning priorities and structures of values have important implications for consumer research. According to Pras and Tarondeau (1981), identification of criteria of choice represent a necessary stage in searching for competitive advantage for a brand, for the definition of strategies of segmentation, and of strategies of positioning, and they precede studies concerning modelling of attitudes and choice. Among others, our results imply that security constitutes an important concern of East Germans, whereas West Germans rather favour self-realisation. These are premises that have to be taken into account by marketers.

References

Bauer, Petra (1991): Politische Orientierungen im Übergang. Eine Analyse politischer Einstellungen des Bürgers in West- und Ostdeutschland 1990/1991. In: Kölner Zeitschrift für Soziologie und Sozialpsychologie, Vol. 43, No. 3, pp. 433-53.

Brämer, Rainer and Heublein, Ulrich: (1990): Studenten in der Wende? Versuch einer Deutsch-Deutschen Typologie vor der Vereinigung. In: Aus Politik und Zeitgeschichte, Supplement of 'Das Parlament', No. B 44/90, 26. October, pp. 3-16.

Churchill, Gilbert A. Jr. (1979): A Paradigm for Developing Better Measures of Marketing Constructs. In: Journal of Marketing Research, Vol. 16, February, pp. 64-73.

Evrard, Yves, Pras, Bernard, and Roux, Elyette (1993): Market. Etudes et Recherches en Marketing. Fondements, Méthodes. Paris: Nathan.

Grunert, Susanne C. and Scherhorn, Gerhard (1990): Consumer Values in West Germany. Underlying Dimensions and Cross-Cultural Comparison with North America. In: Journal of Business Research, Vol. 21, No. 2, pp. 97-107.

Haffner, Sebastian (1987): Preussen ohne Legende. Hamburg: Gruner & Jahr.

Herbert, Willi (1988): Wertwandel in den 80er Jahren. Entwicklung eines neuen Wertmusters? In: Luthe, Heinz O. and Meulemann, Heiner (Eds.), Wertwandel - Faktum oder Fiktion?: Bestandsaufnahmen und Diagnosen aus kultursoziologischer Sicht, Vol. 1, Frankfurt/Main: Campus, pp. 140-60.

Huppertz, Beate M.K. (1987): Werte und Normen in ihrem konstituierenden Einfluß auf die politisch-soziale Wirklichkeit. Ein Beitrag zur Charakterisierung der politischen Kultur und deren Manifestationen in der politischen Bildung der USA und der Bundesrepublik Deutschland. Doctoral thesis, Rheinische Friedrich-Wilhelm-Universität: Bonn.

Kahle, Lynn R. (1983; Ed.): Social Values and Social Change: Adaptation to Life in America. New York: Praeger.

Kahle, Lynn R., Beatty, Sharon E., and Homer, Pamela (1986): Alternative Measurement Approaches to Consumer Values: The List of Values (LOV) and Values and Life Style (VALS). In: Journal of Consumer Research, Vol. 13, No. 3, pp. 405-409.

Kahle, Lynn R., Poulos, Basil, and Sukhdial, Ajay (1988): Changes in Social Values in the United States During the Past Decade. In: Journal of Advertising Research, Vol. 28, No. 1, pp. 35-51.

Kim, Jae-On and Mueller, Charles W. (1990): Factor Analysis. Statistical Methods and Practical Issues. London Sage Publications.

Klages, Helmut (1984): Wertorientierungen im Wandel. Rückblick, Gegenwartsanalyse, Prognosen. Frankfurt/New York: Campus.

Klages, Helmut (1988): Wertedynamik. Über die Wandelbarkeit des Selbstverständlichen. Zürich: Edition Interfrom.

Kluckhohn, Clyde (1951): Values and Value Orientations in the Theory of Action. An Exploration in Definition and Classification. In: Parsons, Talcott and Shils, Edward A. (Eds.), Toward a General Theory of Action, 3rd edition, Cambridge, pp. 388-433.

Kmieciak, Peter (1976): Wertstrukturen und Wertwandel in der Bundesrepublik Deutschland. Grundlagen einer interdisziplinären Wertforschung mit einer Sekundäranalyse von Umfragedaten. Göttingen: Otto Schwartz & Co.

Korte, Karl-Rudolf (1990): Die Folgen der Einheit. Zur politisch-kulturellen Lage der Nation. In: Aus Politik und Zeitgeschichte, Supplement of 'Das Parlament', No. B 27/90, 29. June, pp. 29-38.

Lüthy, Herbert (1973): Nochmals: Calvinismus und Kapitalismus. Über die Irrwege einer sozialhistorischen Diskussion. In: Braun, Rudolf et al. (Eds.), Gesellschaft in der industriellen Revolution, Köln, pp. 18-36.

Maaz, Hans-Joachim (1991): Der Gefühlsstau. Berlin: Argon.

Mendel, Dorothea (1997): La Perception et la Mesure de la Qualité du Service dans une Comparaison Franco-Allemande: Application au Service Après-Vente dans le Secteur Automobile. Doctoral thesis, Université Paris IX-Dauphine (forthcoming).

Merseburger, Peter (1988): Grenzgänger. Innenansichten der anderen Deutschen Republik. München: Bertelsmann.

Millar, Carla and Restall, Christine (1991): The Embryonic Consumer. Markets and Values in Transition in Eastern Europe. In: Proceedings of the 44th E.S.O.M.A.R. Marketing Research Congress, General Sessions, Vol. 1, pp. 593-611.

Pras, Bernard and Tarondeau, Jean-Claude (1981): Comportement de l'acheteur. Paris: Sirey.

Rokeach, Milton (1973): The Nature of Human Values. New York: The Free Press.

Schwartz, Shalom H. and Bilsky, Wolfgang (1987): Toward an Universal Psychological Structure of Human Values. In: Journal of Personality and Social Psychology, Vol. 53, No. 3, pp. 550-562.

Schwartz, Shalom H. and Bilsky, Wolfgang (1990): Toward a Theory of the Universal Content and Structure of Values: Extensions and Cross-Cultural Replications. In: Journal of Personality and Social Psychology, Vol. 58, No. 5, pp. 878-891.

Valette-Florence, Pierre (1988): Analyse Structurelle Comparative des Composantes de Systèmes de Valeurs selon Kahle et Rokeach. In: Recherche et Applications en Marketing, Vol. 3, No. 1, pp. 15-34.

Valette-Florence, Pierre, Grunert, Susanne C., Grunert, Klaus G., and Beatty, Sharon (1991): Une Comparaison Franco-Allemande de l'Adhésion aux Valeurs Personnelles. In: Recherche et Applications en Marketing, Vol. 6, No. 3 (Special Issue: France-Germany), pp. 5-20.

Vernette, Eric (1986): Comparaison des Méthodes d'Identification de Critères de Choix d'un Produit. Doctoral thesis, Université Paris X-Nanterre.

Yorick Odin, Jean-Yves Vinais and Pierre Valette-Florence

Towards a Revision of Schwartz's Values Inventory: Some Exploratory Findings

1. Introduction

2. Schwartz's Values Inventory
    2.1. Definition
    2.2. Motivational Areas

3. New Developments in Schwartz's Values Inventory
    3.1. A Revised Model Based on Schwartz's Structure
    3.2. The Agorametrie Referential

4. Methodological Aspects
    4.1. Sample
    4.2. Statistical Method: Canonical Analysis

5. Results
    5.1. Canonical Roots Tests
    5.2. Interpretation of Canonical Roots
    5.3. Synthesis of the Results

6. Conclusion

References

Towards a Revision of Schwartz's Values Inventory: Some Exploratory Findings

Yorick Odin, Jean-Yves Vinais and Pierre Valette-Florence[1]

Abstract

Recently, the research undertaken by Schwartz and his colleagues (Schwartz and Bilsky, 1987, 1990; Schwartz, 1992; 1994; Schwartz and Sagiv, 1995) have revived the interest on the study of values. Schwartz proposes an universal structure, organised in ten motivational areas that are supposed to represent the totality of human aspirations. Despite the interest and the extent of the research led by Schwartz, Odin et al. (1996) have recently tried to refine Schwartz's inventory of values: refinements on structural aspects, but also in terms of nomological validity. This article tries to confirm the superiority of the revised inventory proposed by Odin et al. (1996) on Schwartz's structure, through the comparison of the impact of both models on the Agorametrie Conflicts. Therefore, this paper has three complementary parts. Firstly, Schwartz's values inventory is briefly described. Secondly, the revised structure used in the framework of this research will be presented, as well as peculiarities of the inventory Agorametrie Conflicts. Finally, the third part presents the statistical method, canonical analysis, and discusses the results obtained.

1. Introduction

Recently, research undertaken by Schwartz and his colleagues (Schwartz and Bilsky, 1987, 1990; Schwartz, 1992; 1994; Schwartz and Sagiv, 1995) have revived the interest on the study of values. Based on results obtained on more than 80 samples in 40 different countries, Schwartz proposes an universal structure, organised in ten motivational areas that are supposed to represent the totality of human aspirations. The methodological process is always based on multidimensional analyses: such an approach implies that the researcher verifies *a posteriori* that the obtained configuration fits well the supposed theoretical structure.

---

[1] The authors would like to thank the GRETS department of the E.D.F Company for the data, and STATSOFT Inc. for the use of the canonical analysis module.

Despite the interest and the extent of research led by Schwartz, Odin et al. (1996) have recently tried to refine Schwartz's inventory of values: refinements on structural aspects, but also in terms of nomological validity. Their methodological process is based on the use of confirmatory analyses. Moreover, their research is carried out on a representative sample of the French population (2522 respondents). The results guided the authors to propose, based on Schwartz's inventory, a revised structure including only 42 values that are grouped in 13 motivational types. A comparison of the nomological validity of the revised model and Schwartz's inventory was made on selected media habits. The results led to the conclusion that the revised model was superior in terms of predictive validity.

This article tries to confirm the superiority of the revised inventory proposed by Odin et al. (1996) on Schwartz's structure, through the comparison of the impact of both models on the Agorametrie Conflicts. Therefore, this paper articulates around three complementary parts. Firstly, Schwartz's values inventory is briefly described. Secondly, the revised structure used in the framework of this research will be presented, as well as specificities of the inventory Agorametrie Conflicts. Finally, the third part presents the statistical method, canonical analysis, and discusses the results obtained.

2. Schwartz's Values Inventory

2.1. Definition[2]

In the area of psychology (Rokeach, 1968), anthropology (Kluckhohn, 1951) or sociology (Williams, 1968), scientists regard values as criteria that the individual uses to select and justify actions, and to evaluate others (and themselves) as well as events (Schwartz, 1992, p. 1). It is this point of view that Schwartz and Bilsky (1987, p. 551) elaborate in their definition of values. From their perspective, „values are concepts or beliefs, about desirable end states or behaviours, that transcend specific situations, guide selection or evaluation of behaviour and events, and are ordered by relative importance." (Schwartz and Bilsky, 1987, p. 551).

In fact, values are cognitive representations of three types of universal human requirements:

---

2 For a review of literature on the subject of values, the interested reader is refered to the work of Valette-Florence (1994).

1) **Biologically based needs of organism**: sexual need of the individual can for example be transformed into values such as intimacy or love.

2) **Social interactional requirements for interpersonal coordination**: this type of need can for example be transformed into values such as honesty or equality.

3) **Social institutional demands for group welfare and survival**: this need can for example be transformed into values such as national security or world in peace.

Their definition of values enunciate three distinct facets. According to them, values can be considered as the adhesion of individuals to **objectives** (terminal or instrumental), conducting to satisfy **interest** (individual, collective or both). These values belong to eleven **motivational areas** (ten today, since the universalism dimension seems questionable) and they are more or less important in the individuals' every day life (Valette-Florence, 1994, p. 47). Our research concentrates more particularly on Schwartz's values structure, that is to say on motivational types.

2.2. Motivational Areas

Areas are presented here in a succinct manner. They are synthesised in the form of a radex in Figure 1. The interest of such a representation resides on the one hand in the compatibility of two adjacent areas and on the other hand in the contradictory position of two opposite areas, as compared to the origin (Valette-Florence, 1994). The three types of interest are also presented in Figure 1.

The eleven motivational types can be described as follows:

- *Self-direction:* search for independence in thoughts and actions of the individual.
- *Stimulation:* values connected to needs of excitement, novelty, and challenge.
- *Hedonism:* close to the stimulation area; search for pleasure and personal gratification.
- *Achievement:* search for personal success, by demonstrating one's competencies in the milieu of a social group.
- *Power:* the goal associated to this area is obtaining a social status, the achievement of prestige, control, or domination of others.
- *Security:* search for security, harmony, and stability in the society.
- *Conformity:* objectives are here to restrain actions, inclinations, and impulses that could hurt others or transgress social norms.

- *Tradition:* corresponds to the motivation to conform to beliefs, types of behaviour, or customs that culture or religion impose on the individual.
- *Spirituality:* meets the need of the individual to find the ultimate sense of the reality of things. The objective is personal harmony through the transcendence of daily realities.
- *Benevolence:* the main objective of this area is the preservation and/or the improvement of the well-being of people with whom the individual is frequently in contact.
- *Universalism:* the main motivational objective linked to this area is understanding, appreciation, tolerance, and protection of the well-being of all men and nature. In his recent works (Schwartz, 1994; Schwartz and Sagiv, 1995), the author did not succeed in validating the structure of this area, and then chose to remove it from the inventory.

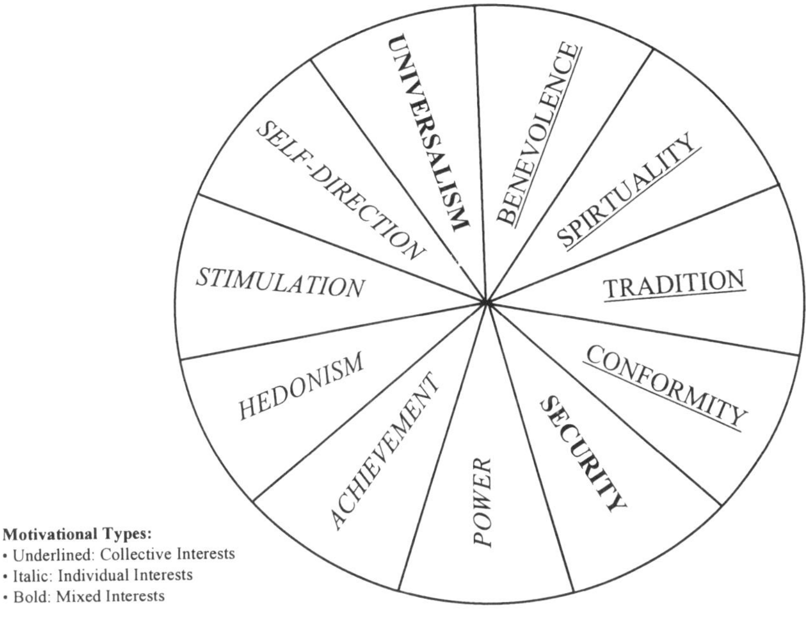

Figure 1: Schwartz's motivational types

3. New Developments in Schwartz's Values Inventory

3.1. A Revised Model Based on Schwartz's Structure

Odin et al. (1996) highlighted a certain number of problems in Schwartz's value structure. These problems can be summarised in four main aspects:

- With one or two exceptions, the sample sizes, that vary from 200 to 400 respondents, remains relatively modest with regard to the number of values incorporated in the inventory (56 to the total). Moreover, all samples are convenience samples, based exclusively on students and their professors.

- The statistical method used, the multidimensional analysis, is an exploratory method, the researcher is checking *a posteriori* whether the obtained configuration fits well to the areas presupposed.

- Apart particular cases, the grouping of values in motivational areas is undertaken through the projection of these values on a plan, while the dimensionality is at least of order 3, perhaps more.

- The proposed statistical analysis follows a deterministic orientation, considering that each value is perfectly measured, and this, without any residuals or measurement error. Besides, it is surprising to observe that Schwartz himself has never used other multidimensional analyses following a probabilistic orientation, even if they are more effective (Example: MULTISCALE, see Ramsay, 1982).

To circumvent these criticisms, Odin et al. (1996) have tested Schwartz's structure on a representative and large sample of the French population (2522 respondents), using a structural equation model restricted to a confirmatory factor analysis. This methodology leads the authors to develop a more parsimonious and more shaded measurement instrument (42 values against 56, no cross-affectations[3]), that has proven superior to Schwartz's model. The differences between the revised inventory and Schwartz's structure is described in Table 1. The final revised structure composed of 13 motivational types is presented in Exhibit 1 (see Appendix).

The authors have compared the nomological validity of Schwartz's inventory to the validity of the revised model on media habits. Results have shown that, though the nomological validity of values on media practices remained weak, the two models were comparable in terms of explained variance (approximately 8%). However, the revised model seems superior through its more parsimonious and more tinged aspects.

In the present case, the same type of procedure is adopted, but this time on general opinions, measured by the Agorametrie Referential. From a theoretical point of view, it seems

---

[3] One value is affected to only one motivational type, which is not the case in Schwartz's structure.

appropriate to think that the values system of an individual explains his opinions on subjects as wide as those approached by Agorametrie.

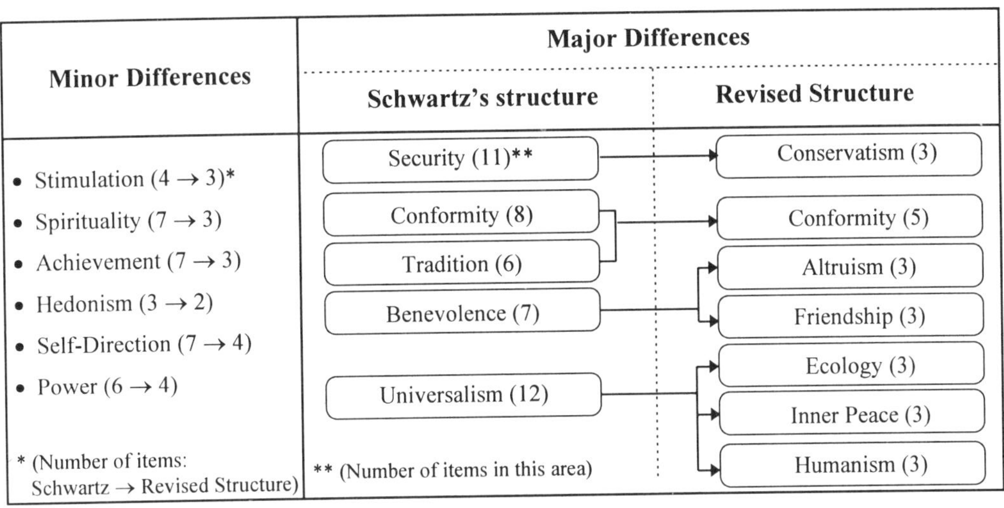

Minor Differences	Major Differences	
	Schwartz's structure	Revised Structure
• Stimulation (4 → 3)*	Security (11)**	Conservatism (3)
• Spirituality (7 → 3)	Conformity (8)	Conformity (5)
• Achievement (7 → 3)	Tradition (6)	Altruism (3)
• Hedonism (3 → 2)	Benevolence (7)	Friendship (3)
• Self-Direction (7 → 4)		Ecology (3)
• Power (6 → 4)	Universalism (12)	Inner Peace (3)
* (Number of items: Schwartz → Revised Structure)	** (Number of items in this area)	Humanism (3)

Table 1: Differences between Schwartz's structure and the revised structure

3.2. The Agorametrie Referential[4]

The Agorametrie[5] association strives to study the evolution of public opinion structures through the identification, each year, of current themes largely discussed in the French population. These themes are extracted from a thorough analysis of the national press and focus on subjects as varied as politics or environment. The procedure followed here is totally original, since it uses current conflicts to express individuals' opinions. The subjects tackled in Agorametrie then become themes of expression, measured by means of 5-points Likert scales.

In this paper, the authors use the sixteen items selected in 1995 by Agorametrie, because they approach current controversial themes which were frequently debated in France in the course of last year. This referential, not based on a theoretical framework, remains mostly empirical. The Agorametrie items were included in our survey are presented in Exhibit 2 (see Appendix).

---

4 For more information, the interested reader may consult Valette-Florence (1994) and Arnoux and Du Malet (1984).

5 Also known as AESOP (Association pour l'Etude des Structures de l'Opinion Publique).

4. Methodological Aspects

4.1. Sample

Electricité de France (EDF), the state-owned company providing electricity in France, through their research department (G.R.E.T.S.), regularly undertake opinion surveys. Some of them are specifically related to their commercial activity, but others, more general, focus on the sociological study of the French population and its attitude concerning current social problems such as environment protection. In this framework, approximately every two years, the SOFRES (a French leading company of marketing research) carries out a survey on behalf of the GRETS. This survey, based on a sample of 2522 respondents, mainly explores the attitude towards environment, using several referentials, including Schwartz's values system, and the Agorametrie inventory.

4.2. Statistical Method: Canonical Analysis

According to the nature of our variables (continuous variables) and the structure of our data (two distinct sets of variables), canonical analysis seems to be the best statistical method to investigate the relationship between motivational types and Agorametrie opinions. Indeed the empirical nature of the referential implies that there is no underlying structure in the 16 items (The authors have confirmed this assumption using a maximum likelihood factor analysis). Therefore, canonical analysis was chosen instead of structural modeling.

In the first set, motivational types are measured by their factor scores. The second set includes the 16 Agorametrie items. In canonical analysis, the number of roots is equal to the minimum number of variables in each set. Each successive root explains an unique additional proportion of variability in the two sets of variables. Therefore, consecutive extracted roots are uncorrelated with each other and account for less and less variability.

In our case, the number of canonical roots is equal to the number of motivational types in Schwartz's structure (11), as described in Table 2.

Only those roots that are statistically significant will then be retained for interpretation. Instead of testing each root one by one, the significance of all roots combined was evaluated in a first time, then the significance of the roots remaining after removing the first root, the second root, etc. Mendoza et al. (1978), in a Monte Carlo study, showed that this testing procedure allows to detect canonical correlations of small magnitude.

	First Canonical Model Revised Motivational Types		Second Canonical Model Schwartz Motivational Types	
	Left set - Modified motivational types	Right set Agorametrie items	Left set - Schwartz motivational types	Right set Agorametrie items
Extracted Variance	100 %	87,13 %	100 %	76,3 %
Total Redundancy	9,95 %	11,63 %	10,81 %	10,05 %
Number of variables	13 types	16 items	11 types	16 items

Table 2: Canonical analysis summary

5. Results

5.1. Canonical Roots Tests

In the two canonical analyses, using the revised model and Schwartz's structure, six roots were significant (see Table 3). However, only the first three roots in the two models were interpreted, because of the very low redundancy indices given for the last three canonical roots. The redundancy indices given in Table 2 shows that $R^2_{right/left} > R^2_{left/right}$.

	Modified Motivational Structure				Schwartz Motivational Structure			
Canonical roots	Canonical correlations	Eigen-values	Chi-sqre values[6]	d.f.	Canonical correlations	Eigen-values	Chi-sqre values	d.f.
1	0,67	0,45	2077,01*	208	0,63	0,40	1746,60*	176
2	0,45	0,20	1033,29*	180	0,43	0,19	850,76*	150
3	0,41	0,17	645,45*	154	0,36	0,13	486,59*	126
4	0,27	0,073	322,78*	130	0,21	0,04	237,17*	104
5	0,19	0,036	189,38*	108	0,18	0,03	159,87*	84
6	0,14	0,019	124,60*	88	0,14	0,02	100,52*	66

* p<0,01

Table 3: Results of the Chi-square tests of significant canonical roots

---

[6] The χ^2 test on canonical roots is computed to validate the hypothesis that eigenvalues are different from 0. Values of χ^2 are calculated with the following formula: $\chi^2 = -[N-1-\frac{(p+q+1)}{2}] \times \lambda'$, with N the number of respondents, p and q respectively the number of variables of the first and the second set. The Lambda prime is the Napiarien Logarithm of the product of $(1-\lambda)$ for the remaining λ. The degree of freedom is given by (p-k)(q-k) for k = 0 to (i-1) with i the number of canonical roots.

Practically, we can conclude that the revised model variables compose the predictive set, whereas the Agorametrie items compose the explained set. In our case, values explain around 11% of the variance of the Agorametrie opinions items. This conclusion, based on the results of statistical analyses, is consistent with the underlying theory of values: the values of an individual influence his opinions.

However, the results obtained with Schwartz's structure did not converge to this conclusion. Indeed, Table 2 reports that $R^2_{right/left} < R^2_{left/right}$, which would mean that opinions of an individual explain his values orientation. This conclusion appears to be inconsistent with the theory of values, and then raises the problem of Schwartz structure's validity.

Yet, the difference between these results and the results obtained with the revised model could be explained by the higher difference in the number of variables in each set. While the revised model includes 13 variables (against 16 in the Agorametrie set), Schwartz structure is composed of 11 variables. If the number of variables was more homogeneous, the results might be slightly different (i.e. the direction of the relation could be reversed, with $R^2_{right/left} > R^2_{left/right}$), but still inferior to the results obtained with the revised model.

5.2. Interpretation of Canonical Roots

In this part, detailed interpretation is only made on the results obtained with the revised model. Indeed, it was previously emphasised that Schwartz's structure didn't succeed in giving interpretable results. Nevertheless, Figure 2 and Tables 4 and 5 report the canonical roots obtained from both models, to show that there is a convergence in meaning in the two canonical analyses.

		Root 1		Root 2		Root 3	
Modified Values System	**Values**	Conformity*	**-0,72**	Achievement	-0,30	Altruism	0,38
		Conservatism	**-0,70**	Altruism	0,40	Conformity	0,41
		Hedonism	0,35	Hedonism	-0,47	Ecology	0,44
				Power	-0,32	Humanism	**0,74**
				Spirituality	**0,66**		
	Label	**Anticonformism**		**Asceticism**		**Normative Humanism**	
	Agora-metrie Items	Immigration	**-0,58**	Immigration	**-0,56**	Retirement	0,42
		Family	-0,44	Retirement	-0,37	Robots	**0,60**
		Sacrifice	**-0,63**	Pornography	0,46	Military	0,38
		Safe	**-0,51**	Russia	**0,51**	Energy	0,37
		Proprieties	**-0,59**			Income	**0,80**
		Hashish	0,34			Birth	0,36
		Military	0,49				
		Pornography	**-0,55**				
	Label	**Hippie opinions**		**Rigid open-minded opinions**		**Progressive opinions**	

* Only variables with canonical loadings higher than 0,30 are reported in the Table. Highlighted loadings for values are higher than 0,5.

Table 4: Interpretation of canonical roots / Revised Model

		Root 1		Root 2		Root 3	
Schwartz Values System	**Values**	Achievement	0,25	Achievement	-0,29	Benevolence	-0,36
		Conformity	**0,69**	Benevolence	0,29	Conformity	-0,32
		Hedonism	-0,33	Hedonism	**-0,53**	Power	0,36
		Power	0,32	Power	-0,37	Tradition	-0,38
		Security	**0,61**	Spirituality	**0,69**	Universalism	**-0,56**
		Spirituality	0,31				
		Tradition	**0,68**				
	Label	**Conformism**		**Asceticism**		**Individualism**	
	Agora-metrie Items	Immigration	**0,60**	Immigration	**-0,50**	Retirement	-0,36
		Family	0,45	Retirement	-0,46	Robots	**-0,55**
		Sacrifice	**0,57**	Pornography	0,49	Military	-0,48
		Robots	0,40	Russia	0,49	Energy	-0,34
		Safe	**0,55**			Income	**-0,73**
		Proprieties	**0,60**				
		Hashish	-0,36				
		Military	-0,41				
		Pornography	**0,57**				
		Russia	-0,30				
	Label	**Traditional conserva-tive opinions**		**Rigid open-minded opinions**		**Reactionary opinions**	

* Only variables with canonical loadings higher than 0,30 are reported in the Table. Highlighted loadings for values are higher than 0,5.

Table 5: Interpretation of canonical roots / Schwartz Model

5.2.1. First Canonical Root

In the value set, it appears that conformity, conservatism, and hedonism values prevail, the first two values being opposed to the third one. This opposition seems to evoke a notion of anticonformism. In the Agorametrie set, eight items have canonical weights higher than 0,3. Immigration, family, sacrifice, safe, proprieties, and pornography have negative loadings. Therefore, they are opposed to opinions on hashish and military (positive loadings). This dimension seems to group „hippie opinions".

The interpretation of this canonical root is very important, because „anticonformism" values explain the inclination of an individual to hold to hippie ideas. According to the canonical correlation coefficient, the „anticonformism" dimension explains approximately 44% of „hippie opinions". However, the validity of this result is questionable because of low extracted variances (Left set: 10,8%; Right set: 15,9%) and a weak redundancy index (7,1%).

5.2.2. Second Canonical Root

In the value set, five variables compose the left dimension. Two of them have positive loadings (spirituality and altruism), and are then opposed to values such as hedonism, power, and achievement. According to the dimension structure and the loadings distribution, this dimension is named „Asceticism".

Considering the Agorametrie set, an interpretation of the underlying dimension is difficult. Indeed, the dimension structure evokes on the one hand open-minded opinions (Immigration with a negative loading, help Russia with a positive loading), and on the other hand traditional or conservative opinions through the variables Pornography (positive loading) and Retirement (negative loading). For these reasons, this dimension was named „rigid open-minded opinions".

The analysis of the global redundancy index allows us to conclude that individuals who share asceticism values hold to rigid open-minded opinions. However, the direction of this root remains vague with a weak redundancy index (1,6%), even if the basic meaning appears to be relatively relevant. According to the canonical correlation coefficient, the „asceticism" dimension explains approximately 20% of „rigid open-minded opinions". However, the validity of this result is questionable because of low extracted variances (Left set: 9,9%; Right set: 7,9%).

5.2.3. Third Canonical Root

In the value set, four variables are extracted with positive loadings higher than 0,35 (humanism, ecology, conformity, altruism). The meaning of this dimension seems clear: three variables are consistent with the notion of humanism, and the last one includes the idea of conformity. Therefore, this dimension was named „Normative Humanism", to express a humanism complying with social or moral norms. In the Agorametrie set, the dimension is composed of seven variables with positive loadings. Most of them concern social or political improvement: retirement, robots, military, energy, income, and birth. This subset evokes the idea of social progress.

Therefore, this dimension was labelled „Progressive opinions". This canonical axis seems easily interpretable: it is possible to say that individuals with humanist values will defend opinions of social progress. According to the canonical correlation coefficient, the „normative humanism" dimension explains approximately 17% of „progressive opinions". However, the validity of this result is questionable because of low extracted variances (Left set: 9,3%; Right set: 11,2%) and a weak redundancy index (1,9%).

5.2.4. Overview of the Results on Schwartz's Structure

Only a brief analysis is proposed here, because, as aforementioned, the nomological validity of Schwartz's structure is questionable as opinions explain values. The first canonical root links a set of „traditional conservative opinions" to „conformism" values. It is worth noting that the „anticonformism" dimension obtained with the revised model has changed into conformism values, while hippie opinions have become „traditional conservative opinions". Therefore, the meaning of each dimension remain unchanged, but in an opposite direction. The interpretation of the second canonical axis leads to the same results, whatever model is used. Indeed, the Agorametrie subset, namely „rigid open-minded opinions" explains „asceticism" values. For the third canonical root, we can make the same remarks as for the first axis. „Normative humanism" becomes „individualism", whereas „progressive opinions" become „reactionary opinions". An analysis of correlations between the canonical scores computed for both canonical models (revised and Schwartz models) confirms the accuracy of our interpretations (see Table 3).

5.3. Synthesis of the Results

Figure 2 summarises the different results obtained through the two canonical analyses. Extracted variance for each root on each set is reported, as well as canonical correlations and redundancy indices per axis. Arrow directions indicate which set explains the other.

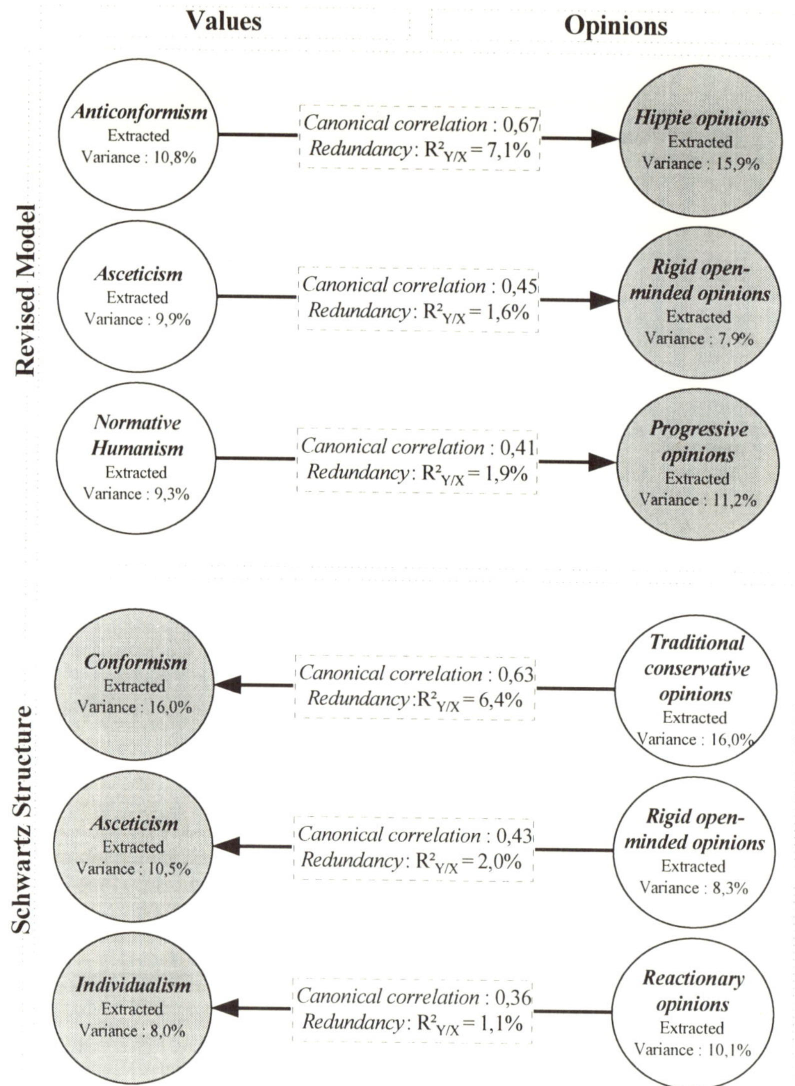

*Figure 2: Results synthesis**
* For further explanation of the global redundancy index and the redundancy index see Exhibit 3 (Appendix).

6. Conclusion

The results obtained in this research confirm the relevance of the structure recently proposed by Odin et al. (1996). More particularly, the revised structure turned out to have a better nomological validity on the Agorametrie Conflicts than the original inventory of Schwartz. Actually, only the modified inventory is consistent with the theory of values which postulates individual values influence opinions, whereas Schwartz's structure failed in validating such a hypothesis.

Despite the interesting results highlighted in this paper, several directions for future research deserve to be mentioned:

- The first research direction focus on two conceptual questions:
  - Is the theory underlying Schwartz's structure consistent with the actual organization of the individuals' values system?
  - As Schwartz's structure was accepted in the current research, a second question arises: is the underlying structure of Schwartz's inventory universal or not?

  We should remind that in their work, Odin, Vinais, and Valette-Florence (1996) have simply tried to refine and improve Schwartz's motivational structure, and not to challenge it. A relevant investigation direction would consist in defining a structure based on the values of Schwartz's inventory, but without any preconceived opinions concerning its nature or its number of dimensions.

- The explanatory power of the revised inventory is not insignificant, but it remains weak (approximately 11%). It might be more relevant to undertake analyses using the different values system held by groups in a given population. Cluster analysis could turn out to be a useful statistical method to identify these groups. A segmentation of the population on such a basis could be interesting to explain the differences observed in the Agorametrie Conflicts.

- Finally, a future research direction could be to estimate the impact of the revised motivational structure on other consumption practices, and to evaluate its stability in other cultural environments.

The analyses that have been already carried out confirm the relevance of the structure Odin et al. (1996) recently proposed. We hope that this research will encourage other researchers to replicate and deepen their works.

References

Arnoux, P. and Malet, E. du (1984): La Fin du Prêt à Penser. In: L'Express, October 5/11 1984.

Kluckhohn, C. (1951): Values and Value Orientation in the Theory of Action: An Exploration in Definition and Classification. In: T. Parsons and E. Shils (Eds.), Towards a General Theory of Action, Harper and Row: New York, pp. 388-433.

Mendoza, J.L., Markos, V.H., and Gonter, R. (1978): A New Perspective on Sequential Testing Procedures in Canonical Analysis: A Monte Carlo Evaluation. In: Multivariate Behavioral Research, Vol. 13, pp. 371-382.

Odin, Y., Vinais, J.-Y., and Valette-Florence, P. (1996): Analyse Confirmatoire des Domaines Motivationnels de Schwartz: Une Application au Domaine des Media. In: Proceedings of the XIIth International Congress of the French Marketing Association: Poitiers, pp. 125-139.

Ramsay, J.O. (1982): Some Statistical Approaches to Multidimensional Scaling Data. In:Journal of the Royal Statistical Society, Vol. 145 (A), pp. 488-494.

Rokeach, M. (1968): Beliefs, attitudes and values. Jossey-Bass.

Schwartz, S. (1992): Universals in the Content and Structure of Values: Theoretical Advance and Empirical Tests in 20 Countries. In: M. Zanna (Ed.): Advances in Experimental Psychology, Academic Press, Vol. 25, pp. 1-65.

Schwartz, S. (1994): Are there Universal Aspects in the Structure and Content of Human Values. In: Journal of Social Issues, Vol. 50, No. 4, pp. 19-45.

Schwartz, S. and Bilsky, W. (1987): Toward an Universal Psychological Structure of Human Values. In: Journal of Personality and Social Psychology, Vol. 53, No. 3, pp. 550-562.

Schwartz, S. and Bilsky, W. (1990): Toward a Theory of the Universal Content and Structure of Values: Extensions and Cross-Cultural Replications. In: Journal of Personality and Social Psychology, Vol. 58, No. 5, pp. 878-891.

Schwartz, S. and Sagiv, L. (1995): Identifying Culture-Specifics in the Content and Structure of Values. In: Journal of Cross-Cultural Psychology, Vol. 26, No. 1, pp. 92-116.

Valette-Florence, P. (1994): Les styles de vie: bilan, critiques et perspectives. Nathan: Paris.

Williams, R.M. Jr. (1968): Values. In: E. Sills (Ed.), International Encyclopedia of the Social Sciences. MacMillan: New York.

Appendix

Exhibit 1: Values Inventory of the Revised Model

Motivational types	*Values*	*Motivational types*	*Values*
Self-Direction *4 Values*	Self-respect Creativity Choosing own goals Intelligent	**Conformity** *(From Conformity and Tradition)* *5 Values*	Politeness Respect of traditions Honouring parents and elders Obedient Clean
Stimulation *3 Values*	An exciting life A varied life Daring	**Power** *4 Values*	Social power Authority Influential Preserving my public image
Hedonism *2 Values*	Pleasure Enjoying life		
Achievement *3 Values*	Ambitious Capable Successful	**Spirituality** *3 Values*	A spiritual life Detachment Devout
Altruism *(From Benevolence)* *3 Values*	Helpful Forgiving Responsible	**Ecology** *(From Universalism)* *3 Values*	Unity with nature A world of beauty Protecting the environment
Friendship *(From Benevolence)* *3 Values*	True friendship Loyal Honest	**Inner peace** *(From Universalism)* *3 Values*	Inner harmony A meaning in life Mature love
Conservatism *(From Security)* *3 Values*	Social order National security Social recognition	**Humanism** *(From Universalism)* *3 Values*	Equality A world at peace Social justice

Exhibit 2: The Agorametrie Referential - Selected Items

„Here is a list of frequently mentioned opinions in France. You will indicate if you agree or disagree with each of these opinions" (Likert Scale ranging from 1 „strongly disagree" to 5 „strongly agree"):

Variable label	*Items wording*
FOREIGN	There are too many foreign workers
RETIREMENT	The age of retirement must be lowered
FAMILY	The family must remain the foundation of society
SACRIFICE	One must sacrifice oneself for one's country
ROBOTS	The use of robots in industry must be limited
SAFE	One can not feel safe anymore
POLITIC	In general, politicians are good fellows
PROPRIETIES	One must respect the proprieties
HASHISH	Hashish should be legally sold
MILITARY	Military expanses must be reduced
PORNOGRAPHY	We must fight forcefully against pornography
MARRIED	One shouldn't get married anymore
ENERGY	The energy crisis is extremely worrying
INCOME	Income differentials should be reduced
RUSSIA	France must help Russia
BIRTH	The Government must pay everybody a minimum income from birth on

Exhibit 3: Global Redundancy Index and Redundancy Index

The global redundancy index is given by the formula:
$$R^2_{N/P} = \sum_{i=1}^{N} \lambda_i \left(\frac{\sum_{j=1}^{P} L^2_{ij}}{P} \right) \quad \text{with:}$$

L_{ij} = Canonical loadings of variable j on root i P = Number of variables of the set being analysed

λ_i = Eigenvalue of root i N = Number of significant canonical roots

From the former formula, it is then possible to calculate a redundancy index for each set on each root, that will represent the variance of one set explained by the other on a given canonical root:
$$R^2_{Root/P} = \lambda \frac{\sum_{j=1}^{P} L^2_j}{P}$$
with:

i = Canonical root being analysed λ_i = Eigenvalue of the root being analysed

P = Number of variables of the set being analysed L_j = Canonical loadings of the set being analysed

L.J. Shrum and Thomas C. O'Guinn

The Role of Television in the Construction of Consumer Reality

1. Introduction
2. Television, Social Reality and Consumption
   2.1. Cultivation Theory and Research
3. Proposed Model
   3.1. Hypotheses
   3.2. Psychological Process
4. Study 1
   4.1. Method
   4.2. Results and Discussion
5. Study 2
   5.1. Method
   5.2. Results and Discussion
6. General Discussion
References

The Role of Television in the Construction of Consumer Reality

L.J. Shrum and Thomas C. O'Guinn [1]

Abstract

Two studies investigated a particular type of consumer socialization: the construction of consumer social reality via exposure to television. In Study 1, estimates of the prevalence of products and behaviours associated with an affluent lifestyle were positively related to the total amount of television respondents watched. Television viewing mediated the relation between income and education and the affluence estimates. In Study 2, participants not only provided higher prevalence estimates, but they also constructed their estimates significantly faster, suggesting that relevant information is more accessible in memory for heavy viewers than light viewers. The results are consistent with heuristic processing strategies, where individuals infer prevalence from the ease of exemplar retrieval (Tversky and Kahneman, 1973).

1. Introduction

For many scholars (e.g., Fiske, 1987; McLuhan, 1964), one of the more socially significant events of the 20th century was the introduction and rapid diffusion of television. They hold that television has forever changed our families, the way we elect our leaders, set social policy, judge the accused, and view ourselves in relation to others. Some believe this is because television has supplanted reading and interpersonal narrative as our primary means of story telling and myth delivery (Silverstone, 1991), and has thus fundamentally changed our culture (McLuhan, 1964). Across diverse theoretical formulations, television is widely acknowledged as a powerful agent of socialization.

Our intent in this paper is to explore television's role as a possible agent of consumer socialization and further, to better understand the mental mechanisms by which this process may occur. Two studies investigate television programming's role in providing consumers with information used in constructing their mental representations of the material world (i.e., that

[1] This research was supported by grants from the Harry Frank Guggenheim Foundation, New York City, and the Research Council of Rutgers University to the first author, and from the James Webb Young Fund, Department of Advertising, University of Illinois, to the second author.

portion of the environment pertaining to the ownership or consumption of goods and services). In the first study, we report survey data that test the relationship between television exposure and the perceived prevalence of specific consumption-related indicators of affluence. In the second study, we more directly examine psychological process through a quasi-experiment, in order to suggest how, from a memory retrieval perspective, television information contributes to these consumption-related beliefs.

2. Television, Social Reality and Consumption

Television has a number of essential qualities that may contribute to its impact as an agent of consumer socialization. For one, television is ubiquitous. Today more American families have television sets than have telephones (US Bureau of the Census, 1995). The average American family watches more than seven hours of television per day; the average individual more than four hours (Nielsen, 1995). In terms of mere amount of exposure, television rivals many traditional socialization agents such as school, church, and even parental contact. Second, television's effects are often „invisible“. Because so many Americans watch television, its effects can become obscured. Watching television is so common that we may simply be too immersed to easily observe its influence. Third, television supplies its viewers with images, accounts and stories of life that are often far removed from the viewer's daily experience and social milieu (O'Guinn and Faber, 1991; Richins, 1995). It offers a view of what Goffman (1966) referred to as „backstage behaviours“, or those private moments of others to which we are typically not afforded access other than through reading or dramatisation.

It is also important to understand that television's representations of social reality are often discrepant from so-called „objective“ reality (i.e., census data, surveys, etc.). Content analyses of television programs have consistently identified important differences between the „television world“ and the „real world“. Examples of such differences include findings that violence is ten times more prevalent on television than in the real world (Gerbner et al., 1980a), male television characters outnumber female characters 3 to 1 (Gerbner et al., 1980a), and characters in the 25 to 45 year old age range are overrepresented, but young and old people are underrepresented relative to their real world frequencies (Gerbner et al., 1980b). Particularly relevant to the present study, professionals - especially doctors, lawyers and wealthy businessmen - predominate on television, as does the upper middle class. On the other hand, blue collar and „low status" occupations (with the exception of police officers) are significantly underrepresented compared to the real world (Lichter et al., 1994).

Television is also full of representations of consumption (DeFleur, 1964), many involving members of social classes and spheres very different from those of most Americans. Television commonly uses consumption symbols as a means of visual shorthand; what consumers have, and the activities in which they participate, mark their social status with an economy of explanatory dialogue. Viewers see and hear what members of other social classes have, and how they consume, even behind their closed doors.

2.1. Cultivation Theory and Research

Cultivation theory (Gerbner et al., 1977) holds that television viewing significantly assists in creating or „cultivating" a view of reality that is biased toward the highly formulaic and stylized narrative content of television. Given that television is a medium in which viewers regularly „suspend their disbelief", often in what some believe to be a passive cognitive state, for an average of over four hours per day, cultivation theory posits that heavier viewers of television will have beliefs about the social world that are more consistent with televised social representations than will light viewers. To the heavy television viewer, the real world becomes more like the „TV world".

Cultivation research has shown consistent correlational support for the assertion that television programming, with its constant and relatively narrow messages, produces a conformity of social perceptions, norms and even values. For example, studies have found that heavy television viewing correlates with higher estimates of the prevalence of prostitution, alcoholism, and drug use (Shrum and O'Guinn, 1993), greater faith in doctors (Volgy and Schwarz, 1980), and higher estimates of crime and violence (Gerbner et al., 1977; Shrum, 1996; Shrum and O'Guinn, 1993). Moreover, these findings persist in the presence of a number of control variables (e.g., demographics, various individual differences variables).

3. Proposed Model

Because of the aforementioned qualities of television, and the predictions of cultivation theory, we believe that exposure to the world as it is portrayed on television has the potential to influence consumers' perceptions of the very existence or incidence of things, including consumption objects and activities often associated with a more affluent lifestyle. If unchallenged, these perceptions can become part of enduring mental and social representations. Consumers may begin to believe the material and consuming world, or at least part of it, exists as it is constituted on television. This effect may be subtle, and go largely unnoticed, because so few are left untouched by the consensus of television reality. It is important to note, however, that we are not claiming that television viewing is the only consumer socialization agent that may influence perceptions of the material world. Clearly, one's daily life experiences, outside of the context of television viewing, will also influence social perceptions. In fact, it is the concurrent effect of such daily experience variables on both social perceptions and amount of television viewing that has necessitated the use of demographic variables as statistical controls in previous cultivation research. The model we propose incorporates these demographic variables, in particular education and income, along with actual direct experience measures, and our socialization variable of primary interest, television viewing.

3.1. Hypotheses

In Study 1, we hypothesize and test the following relationships (see Figure 1). First, we expect amount of television viewing to positively correlate with estimates of the prevalence of particular products and behaviours associated with affluence (affluence estimates), indicating a cultivation effect (H_1). Second, we expect that the extent of direct experience with these products and activities will be positively associated with the affluence estimates (H_2). However, we do not expect that these effects occur in isolation. We also expect that income and education will correlate negatively with amount of television viewing (H_3 and H_4, respectively), and we expect that income will positively correlate with direct experience with affluent products and behaviours (H_5). Additionally, we predict that education will function as an accuracy or knowledge variable, and will therefore be negatively related to estimates of affluence (H_6). Thus, we expect that television viewing will mediate the relation between demographic variables (income and education) and the affluence estimates. Similarly, we expect that direct experience will mediate the relation between income and the affluence estimates.

3.2. Psychological Process

Along with documenting the effects of television viewing and how it is situated within a broader social context, we are also interested in how the effect occurs at the individual level.

One of the major criticisms of cultivation theory is that a mental mechanism that can account for cultivation effects has not been explicated (Shrum, 1995). In other words, why is it that television information apparently influences these perceptions, even though most people do not think television portrayals are necessarily veridical?

One psychological process explanation for television's effect on social judgements relates to the research on information accessibility. This research suggests that when individuals are asked to make a social judgement, they typically do not perform an exhaustive search of memory for information pertaining to that judgement. Rather, they tend to rely on a subset of information that is most accessible from memory (for reviews see Sherman and Corty, 1984; Wyer and Srull, 1989). Research has shown that a number of factors influence either the momentary or enduring accessibility of particular information. Such factors include recency and frequency of activation of a construct (for reviews see Wyer and Srull, 1989), vivid or easily imagined objects or events (Sherman et al., 1985), distinctiveness, prominence, self relevance, and similarity to other constructs (Higgins and King, 1981).

Recency, frequency, vividness, distinctiveness, and prominence have particular relevance to cultivation research. Heavy viewers by definition watch television more frequently than light viewers, and have a higher probability of having watched television more recently. Also, television portrayals are often very vivid and distinctive. Thus, it is reasonable to think that information obtained from television would be more accessible for heavy viewers than light viewers. Moreover, given the topics frequently portrayed on television that were discussed earlier (e.g., crime, affluence, white-collar occupations), it is likely that images pertaining to these specific topics are highly accessible for heavier viewers.

Finally, research on judgement and decision making provides insight as to how the accessibility of information, in this case television information, may influence estimates of the prevalence of particular products and activities. The availability heuristic suggests that individuals may estimate frequency or probability of occurrence based on the ease of retrieval, or accessibility, of the information from memory (Tversky and Kahneman, 1973). Specifically, the easier instances of a particular construct come to mind, the higher are the frequency and probability estimates that people make. Thus, if television viewing does indeed make relevant information more accessible for those who view more often, heavy viewers should give higher estimates than light viewers.

Study 2 directly tests these propositions. Specifically, heavy viewers should give higher estimates of the prevalence of particular products and behaviours associated with affluence (H_7), consistent with a cultivation effect, and replicating the findings of Study 1. Additionally, information used in constructing the judgements should be more accessible for heavy viewers than light viewers (H_8), indicating an accessibility effect.

4. Study 1

4.1. Method

A stratified random sample of the general population of Illinois (Midwestern state in the US) was used for this study. Nth name sampling was used to pick the sample from each strata. A total of 2,929 units were selected using telephone directories as the sampling frame, and a mail survey was administered. Of the 2,929 surveys mailed, 169 were returned as undeliverable, leaving 2,760 presumably delivered. Of these 2,760 surveys, 801 were returned by the respondents, yielding a response rate of 29%. Of the 801 returned, 16 were discarded for various reasons (unreadable, partially completed, etc.), yielding 785 valid surveys. Demographic characteristics of the sample were very similar to those of the state and country.

Five items were used to measure perceptions of affluence. The items were developed based on a content analysis of prime time and day time television programs. These five items asked respondents to provide percentage estimates of the prevalence of US households owning a car telephone, a convertible automobile, a hot tub or jacuzzi, having maids or servants, and having wine with dinner. These possessions and behaviours are similar to those noted by Hirschman (1988) in her analysis of the television programs „Dallas“ and „Dynasty“.

Television viewing was assessed by having respondents indicate the number of hours per week they view particular program categories, then summing across categories. These categories were soap operas, news, sports, movies, comedy, action/adventure, and drama. Demographics (age, income, education) were measured, as was materialism (Belk, 1985).

4.2. Results and Discussion

Viewers' estimates of the prevalence of the five products and activities associated with affluence were combined to form one latent structure (affluence estimates, α = .79). The two exogenous variables are years of formal education of the respondent and household income.

Age and materialism were uncorrelated with the intervening and dependent variables, and are not included in the model. The model is specified such that the exogenous demographic variables both directly and indirectly (through their effect on television viewing and direct experience) affect the affluence estimates.

The covariance matrix of the observed variables was used as input, and the model parameters were estimated using Generalized Least Squares (GLS). GLS was used because it does not assume multinormality among the observed variables. The model was fit using LISREL VIII (Jöreskog and Sörbom, 1993).

Three alternative models were tested against the proposed model using a nesting approach (Anderson and Gerbing, 1988). The best-fitting and most parsimonious model was the model we proposed, and various fit statistics indicate that the model fit the data very well. The ratio of χ^2 to degrees of freedom was low (58.90/ 24 = 2.45), as was the root mean square residual (RMR = 0.04). GFI (.98) and AGFI (.96), both of which are robust against nonnormality, also indicated a good fit, as did the CFI (.98) and IFI (.98).

The standardized path coefficients are shown in Figure 1. All coefficients were significant ($p < .05$). These results are consistent with our predictions. Most critically, the path between television viewing and the affluence estimates was positive and significant, consistent with a cultivation effect, thus confirming H_1. Direct experience was also a significant positive predictor of affluence estimates, consistent with H_2. Additionally, income and education were both associated with less total television viewing, and income was positively related to direct experience, confirming H_3 - H_5. Also, education had a negative direct effect on the affluence estimates over and above the mediated effect, consistent with H_6.

Overall, the results support a model in which television viewing significantly affects the perceptions of affluence. Those who watch comparatively more television tend to believe more people have possessions and engage in behaviours associated with a more affluent lifestyle. However, although Study 1 provided evidence that the cultivation effect exists in the consumption domain, and situated this finding within important demographic and experiential measures, the study offers limited insights into the psychological mechanisms through which the effect works. Study 2 was designed to not only replicate the findings of Study 1, but to also explain the effects in terms of mental processes. The study empirically tests the notion that relevant information is more accessible for heavy viewers than for light viewers, thus offering evidence of at least one possible psychological mechanism involved in this phenomenon.

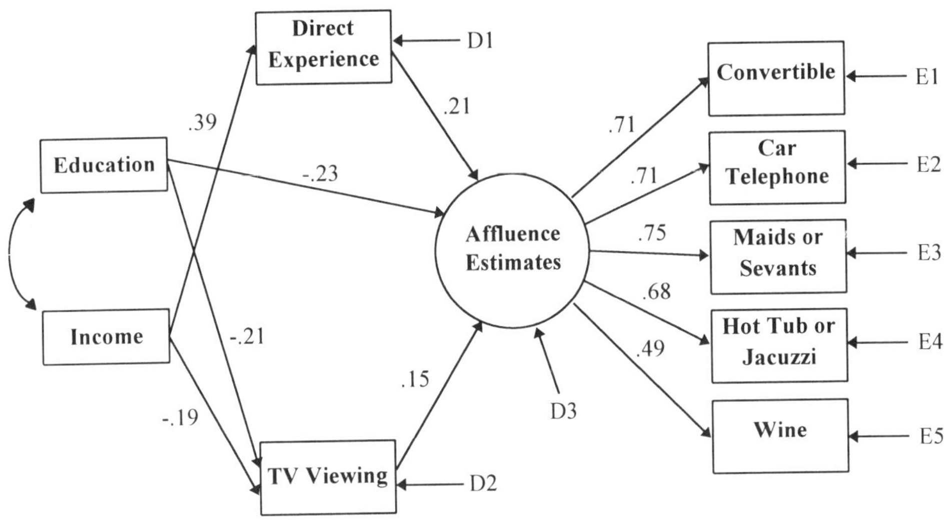

Figure 1: Model Results from Study 1

5. Study 2

5.1. Method

The sample consisted of students from an introductory class at the University of Illinois, in the US. The viewing habits of the entire subject pool were measured at the beginning of the term. Participants were selected to participate in the study if they were very heavy viewers of soap operas (indicated they watched at least 5 hours of soap opera programming in an average week or indicated they watched four L. A. Law episodes in an average month) or if they were very light soap opera viewers (indicated they watched 0 hours of soap operas in an average week and 0 hours of L. A. Law in an average month). In total, 51 participants took part in the study.

As with Study 1, a content analysis was conducted of day time soap operas and L. A. Law, and this content analysis allowed for the development of the dependent measures. Eight items were developed that asked for percentage estimates of the ownership of such things as a diamond necklace, swimming pools and luxury cars, and estimates of participation in activities such as having wine with dinner, attending charity balls, belonging to a country club, getting a manicure and travelling outside the US on business. These estimates served as dependent measures in testing for a cultivation effect (H_7).

We were also interested in determining whether, during the construction of the judgements (affluence estimates), relevant information was more accessible for heavy viewers than light viewers. A frequently accepted method of testing for accessibility is to measure reaction time (response latency), which is the time needed to generate a response (for a review see Fazio, 1990). The logic is that the faster one is able to generate a response, the more accessible is the information retrieved. Thus, the response latencies to the above eight items served as dependent measures for testing for an accessibility effect (H_8).

Potential confounding variables were measured in order to minimize the possibility of alternative explanations for the observed effects. These included gender, grade point average (GPA), income of the student's family, materialism (Belk, 1985), need for cognition (Cacioppo and Petty, 1982), impulsivity (Eysenck and Eysenck, 1968), baseline response latencies (Fazio, 1990), and total television viewing.

Participants in the study performed the exercise on a microcomputer, which recorded both their response to the dependent measures and the time needed to respond (reaction time).

5.2. Results and Discussion

Our first step, prior to testing for effects, was to factor analyze the eight dependent variables. The results initially indicated a two-factor solution. However, two of the items (owning a diamond necklace and travelling outside the US on business) loaded on both factors. Removal of these two items resulted in a one-factor solution that was internally consistent ($\alpha = .84$). Thus, a composite variable (affluence estimates) was computed by averaging the responses to the six remaining items.

To test the hypotheses that heavy viewers will give higher affluence estimates and respond faster to the dependent measures than light viewers, hierarchical multiple regression analyses were performed (analysis indicated no violation of the assumption of equal slopes). In the first entry step, the control variables were entered as a block. In the next step, soap opera viewing (dummy coded as 0 for the light viewer group and 1 for the heavy viewer group) was entered. The R^2 represents the amount of variance accounted for by the soap opera viewing variable, after controlling for the potential confounding variables entered in the first step.

We expected that heavy viewers would give higher affluence estimates than light viewers, consistent with a cultivation effect (H_7). This hypothesis was supported. The results indicate that after accounting for the effects of the control variables, amount of soap opera viewing still accounted for a significant portion of the variance in the affluence estimates (β = .32, ΔR^2 = .10, F = 5.76, p < .05). The positive β indicates that higher estimates were associated with heavier viewing, and examination of the means for each viewing level indicates that heavy viewers gave estimates that averaged about six percentage points higher than light viewers (16.7% vs. 10.9%). We also expected that heavy viewers would respond faster than light viewers when constructing their estimates, consistent with an accessibility effect (H_8). This hypothesis was also supported. The results indicate that level of soap opera viewing was a significant predictor of speed of response (β = -.37, ΔR^2 = .14, F = 8.05, p < .05). The negative β indicates that heavier soap opera viewing was associated with faster (smaller) latencies, and examination of the means indicates that heavy viewers responded about a second and a half faster than light viewers (3.2 sec. vs. 4.9 sec.).

An alternative explanation for the cultivation effect noted in this study is that heavy soap opera viewers simply gave higher estimates than light viewers to all types of questions. However, two pieces of evidence suggest otherwise. Baseline latencies (e.g., % of birds that are blue, cars that are brown, etc.) were included to control for individual differences in response time. If in fact heavy viewers overestimate all questions, we should see this effect in their responses to the baseline measures. However, soap opera viewing was not significantly related to these responses (p > .50). We also included two questions that pertained to things underrepresented on soap operas (% of households that have pets; % of population that is African-American). Neither of the estimates were related to level of soap opera viewing (pets: p > .54; African-Americans: p > .70). A similar argument may be made that heavy soap opera viewers respond faster than light viewers to all types of questions. However, as with the estimates, level of soap opera viewing was not related to speed of response to the baseline estimates (p > .50), to the percentage of households owning pets (p > .40), or to the percentage of the population that is African-American (p > .40).

These results provide information on two levels. First, what people watch on television appears to influence their perceptions of what the material world is like. Our content analysis pinpointed particular possessions and behaviours associated with affluence that were prominent in soap operas, and we found that those who watch these programs tend to give higher estimates of how frequently these possessions and behaviours occur in real life than those who do not watch soap operas. These results replicate the findings from Study 1, and also conceptually replicate previous cultivation research by showing that the effects of television viewing include consumption-related social perceptions. Second, we also provided evidence of how this socialization effect may work at the psychological level. Specifically, we found that the information that people use in the construction of their affluence estimates appears to be more accessible for heavy viewers than light viewers. Given the research on the availability heuristic (people base frequency and probability estimates on degree of accessibility), these results provide a plausible explanation for why heavy viewers give higher estimates than light viewers.

A comparison of the results of the effect of soap opera viewing on the estimates and latencies of those things overportrayed on television to the viewing effect on things underportrayed on television may be instructive in understanding how „learning from television" takes place. Our assumption has been that when people construct their estimates of the prevalence of the particular possessions and behaviours, they do so in real time through the recall of relevant information (exemplars), rather than retrieving any type of prior judgement. An alternative possibility is that viewers update their general beliefs as they receive new information (i.e., during viewing), and then recall and use this general belief in constructing their estimates. However, if this process is in fact what is occurring, we should have noted no differences in response times between heavy and light viewers, only differences in the estimates. Similarly, for those things underportrayed on television, if beliefs are updated during viewing, we would expect that heavy viewers would give lower estimates than light viewers.

The data indicate this is not the case. Rather, the data support a process whereby viewers „catalogue" information in memory, and retrieve this information when they construct their judgements. Following the availability heuristic predictions, they estimate frequency by the ease with which this information is retrieved. This notion is also supported by the null findings for things underportrayed on television. In this instance, both heavy and light viewers should have relatively few television-supplied exemplars stored in memory (all else being equal), and thus should show no differences in either accessibility or magnitude of the estimates. This was in fact what we found. Although there may be many reasons for null findings, it is the case that the overall pattern of the data is consistent with the proposed model.

These results suggest that „learning" from television may be conceived of as a process that begins with an often passive acquisition of social information, with few goal-directed processing objectives other than to comprehend the information in an effort to be entertained. At a later time, when some judgement is required, this information is likely to be retrieved due to qualities such as the frequency, recency, and prominence of the memory stores. In a sense, then, „learning" occurs at the time of judgement, rather than at the time of encoding, and this learning is a function of the accessibility of relevant information. Given this premise, and the notion that information is stored or catalogued in memory for use at the time of judgement (see Wyer and Srull 1989 for a review of such evidence), then it seems reasonable to view such accumulation of information, and the resultant accessibility of this information, as a socialization effect.

6. General Discussion

This paper investigated the effect of exposure to television programming on normative social beliefs about the prevalence of products and activities associated with a more affluent consumer lifestyle. We examined this effect with two different methods, and obtained consistent results. Both studies produced findings supported by theory, and point to a common conclusion: Heavy exposure to the consumption-rich portrayals of television programming is significantly associated with beliefs about what other consumers have and do. The results not only provide evidence that this effect occurs in the consumption domain, but also an idea of how it occurs.

This work departs from mainstream consumer socialization research in several ways. For one, it investigated a different type of socialization than is typical in consumer behaviour; we dealt with perceptions or beliefs about the social world, as opposed to attitudes or beliefs about the veracity of advertised claims, and the associated processing limitations of „special audiences" (i.e., children, the elderly). In doing so, we believe we are investigating the type of „indirect" and „subtle" consumer socialization that early socialization researchers (i.e., Parsons et al. 1953; Ward 1974) suggested. The results of this study imply that the subtle and covert influence of television affects normative consumption-related beliefs, and just as importantly, the accessibility of those beliefs, both of which we see as socialization outcomes. Secondly, we studied adults rather than children, something that has long been called for in consumer socialization research. The majority of research has addressed the effect of socializing agents on the attitudes and behaviours of younger people. Our results imply that these socializing effects are discernible over the adult life span. Third, we studied television programming, as opposed to the field's typical operational definition of „mass communication" as only advertising. Our results imply that when it comes to the formation and maintenance of social beliefs, television programming should not be overlooked in an attempt to better understand consumer socialization. Fourth, we incorporated measures of direct experience. Fifth, we added a psychological component to what had been largely a „black box" formulation. Our results indicate that accessibility is an important factor in explaining how consumers form impressions from television about how other consumers live.

In conclusion, the finding that television viewing does seem to affect normative perceptions of consumer behaviour suggests that the mass media in general, and television in particular, deserve a prominent place in models of consumer socialization.

References

Anderson, J.C. and Gerbing, D.W. (1988): Structural Equation Modeling in Practice: A Review and Recommended Two Step Approach. In: Psychological Bulletin, Vol. 103, pp. 411-423.

Belk, R.W. (1985): Materialism: Trait Aspects of Living in the Material World. In: Journal of Consumer Research, Vol. 12, pp. 265-280.

Cacioppo, J.T. and Petty, R.E. (1982): The Need for Cognition. In: Journal of Personality and Social Psychology, Vol. 42, pp.116-131.

DeFleur, M.L. (1964): Occupational Roles as Portrayed on Television. In: Public Opinion Quarterly, Vol. 28, pp. 57-74.

Eysenck, H.J. and Eysenck, S.B.G. (1968): Eysenck Personality Inventory. Educational and Industrial Testing Service: San Diego, CA.

Fazio, R.H. (1990): A Practical Guide to the Use of Response Latency in Social Psychological Research. In: Wheeler, L. (Ed.), Review of Personality and Social Psychology, Vol. 11, Sage: Beverly Hills, pp. 74-97.

Fiske, J. (1987): Television Culture. Methuen: London.

Gerbner, G., Gross, L., Elley, M., Jackson-Beeck, M., Jeffries-Fox, S., and Signorielli, M. (1977): TV Violence Profile No. 8. In: Journal of Communication, Vol. 27, pp. 171-180.

Gerbner, G., Gross, L., Morgan, M., and Signorielli, N. (1980a): The 'Mainstreaming' of America: Violence Profile No. 11. In: Journal of Communication, Vol. 30, pp. 10-29.

Gerbner, G., Gross, L., Morgan, M., and Signorielli, N. (1980b): Aging with Television: Images on Television Drama and Conceptions of Social Reality. In: Journal of Communication, Vol. 30, pp. 37-47.

Goffman, E. (1966): Behavior in Public Places: Notes on the Social Organization of Gatherings. Free Press: Glencoe, IL.

Higgins, E.T. and King, G. (1981): Accessibility of Social Constructs: Information Processing Consequences of Individual and Contextual Variability. In: Cantor, N. and Kihlstrom, B. F. (Eds.), Personality, Cognition and Social Interaction, Erlbaum: Hillsdale, NJ, pp. 69-121.

Hirschman, E.C. (1988): The Ideology of Consumption: A Structural-Syntactical Analysis of 'Dallas' and 'Dynasty'. In: Journal of Consumer Research, Vol. 15, pp. 344-359.

Jöreskog, K.G. and Sörbom, D. (1993): LISREL VIII: Users Reference Guide. Scientific Software International Inc.: Chicago.

Lichter, S.R., Lichter, L.S., and Rothman, S. (1994): Prime Time: How TV Portrays American Culture. Regnery: Washington, DC.

McLuhan, M. (1964): Understanding Media: The Extensions of Man, McGraw-Hill: New York.

Nielsen, A. C. (1995): Nielsen Report on Television, Author: Northbrook, IL.

O'Guinn, T.C. and Faber, R.J. (1991): Mass Communication and Consumer Behavior. In: Robertson, T.S. and Kassarjian, H.H. (Eds.), Handbook of Consumer Behavior, Prentice Hall: Englewood Cliffs, NJ, pp. 349-400.

Parsons, T., Bales, B.F., and Shils, E.A. (1953): Working Papers in the Theory of Action. The Free Press: Glencoe, IL.

Richins, M.L. (1995): Social Comparison, Advertising, and Consumer Discontent. In: American Behavioral Scientist, Vol. 38, pp. 593-607.

Sherman, S.J., Cialdini, R.B., Schwartzman, D.F., and Reynolds, K.D. (1985): Imagining Can Heighten or Lower the Perceived Likelihood of Contracting a Social Disease: The Mediating Effect of Ease of Imagery. In: Personality and Social Psychology Bulletin, Vol. 11, pp. 118-127.

Sherman, S.J. and Corty, E.A. (1984): Cognitive Heuristics. In: Wyer, R.S. and Srull, T.K. (Eds.), Handbook of Social Cognition, Vol. 1, Lawrence Erlbaum: Hillsdale, NJ, pp. 189-286.

Shrum, L.J. (1995): Assessing the Social Influence of Television: A Social Cognition Perspective on Cultivation Effects. In: Communication Research, Vol. 22, pp. 402-429.

Shrum, L.J. (1996): Psychological Processes Underlying Cultivation Effects: Further Tests of Construct Accessibility. In: Human Communication Research, Vol. 22, pp. 482-509.

Shrum, L.J. and O'Guinn, T.C. (1993): Processes and Effects in the Construction of Social Reality: Accessibility as an Explanatory Variable. In: Communication Research, Vol. 20, pp. 436-471.

Silverstone, R. (1991): Television, Rhetoric, and the Return of the Unconscious in Secondary Oral Culture. In: Gronbeck, B.E., Farrell, T.J., and Soukup, P. (Eds.), Media, Consciousness, and Culture, Sage: Newbury Park, CA, pp. 147-159.

Tversky, A. and Kahneman, D. (1973): Availability: A Heuristic for Judging Frequency and Probability. In: Cognitive Psychology, Vol. 5, pp. 207-232.

US Bureau of the Census (1995): Statistical Abstracts of the United States. Government Printing Office: Washington, DC.

Volgy, T. and Schwarz, J. (1980): Television Entertainment Programming and Sociopolitical Attitudes. In: Journalism Quarterly, Vol. 57, pp. 150-155.

Ward, S. (1974): Consumer Socialization. In: Journal of Consumer Research, Vol. 1, pp. 1-14.

Wyer, R.S. and Srull, T.K. (1989): Memory and Cognition in Its Social Context. Lawrence Erlbaum: Hillsdale, NJ.

Patrick Hetzel

Sportswear as an Expression of How the Consumer Society has Evolved: The Example of „Fun-Wear"

1. Introduction
2. Methodological Aspects
    2.1. The Aim of the Investigation
    2.2. The Data Collecting Method
    2.3. The Method for Processing the Collated Data
    2.4. Short Review of the Existing Literature
3. A Short Anthology of Sportswear
    3.1. Sportswear as an Object of Distinction and Elegance
    3.2. Sportswear as a Rallying Sign for a Modern Culture: The American Myth
    3.3. The Example of „Jogging"
4. The Emergence of „Fun-Wear"
    4.1. What is „Fun-Wear"?
    4.2. How do We Interpret the „Fun" Movement?
    4.3. Looking Back: The „Beat" Origins of the „Fun" Movement
5. From the „American Way of Life" to the „Fun Way of Life": From Polo Ralph Lauren to Gotcha
6. The Revival of the Phenomenon by the Big Brands
7. The Implications of this Trend on Research in Consumer Behaviour and Consumer Sociology
    7.1. The „Fun" Movement as „Hedonist" Movement: An Appeal to Emotional Awareness
    7.2. Not Forgetting the Importance of Semiotics in Consumer Sociology
8. Conclusion
References

Sportswear as an Expression of How the Consumer Society has Evolved: The Example of „Fun-Wear"

Patrick Hetzel

Abstract

We have been witnessing the massive transition of sportswear into our everyday lives. This phenomenon becomes even clearer when we look at the dress codes of certain youths in urban or border-line urban environments. We notice that there are virtually no longer any barriers between the clothes worn by streetball players and their every day clothes. This phenomenon is extremely interesting since it is indicative of a deep change within our consumer society. That is why, this paper is looking successively at the following points: a short anthology of sportswear, the emergence of „fun-wear", an illustration of the phenomenon through a compared semiotic approach between Ralph Lauren and Gotcha, the reflection of the phenomenon by the world's great sports labels, and finally, the implications of theses changes on the research in consumer behaviour.

1. Introduction

For many years, sportswear had largely remained confined to the world of sports. In other words, it was used in a sociological context that was highly specific and, more importantly, perfectly demarcated within a spatial and temporal framework from which it did not spill out. However, for some years now, we have been witnessing the massive transition of sportswear into our everyday lives, as mentioned already for example by de Certeau (1984) and Yonnet (1985) on the subject of „jogging". This phenomenon becomes even clearer when we look at the dress codes of certain youths in urban or border-line urban environments. We notice that there are virtually no longer any barriers between the clothes worn by streetball players and their everyday clothes. They are all very ample straight clothes characterised by XXL sizes. This parallel is even more interesting since, as far as these youths are concerned, the street itself has become a sports ground. There is a fusion, not to say confusion, between the street and the sports ground, daily life and sport, everyday clothes and sports clothes: in fact, a form of sport has become their daily lives. This phenomenon is extremely interesting since it is indicative of a deep change within our consumer society. However, to fully understand our present approach, we need to re-situate it using two theses put forward by sociologists. The first, which is also the oldest, is by Caillois (1967), who asks whether a society's cultural identity is directly related to the nature of the games or sports it enjoys or, on the contrary, rejects. This question posed by Caillois can be applied perfectly to what is referred to as „fun" sports in the sense that it is one of the clues towards understanding the future of our consumer society, which already tolerates them to a very large extent and is even in the process of completely integrating them. The second thesis we will be using here is the one put forward by McCracken (1988), who insists on the symbolic dimension of consumer goods, as an expression of culture, a view he re-affirms in particular with regard to clothes in an article co-written by Roth (McCracken and Roth, 1989). This proposition emphasises the fact that clothes are both a consumer object and a communication object for a culture and a system of values. Consideration of both theses lead us to believe that sportswear is likely to provide us with information on the way the consumer society has changed. That is why, in the following, we shall be successively looking at the following points: the methodological aspects of this investigation, a short anthology of sportswear, the emergence of „fun-wear", an illustration of the phenomenon through a compared semiotic approach between Ralph Lauren and Gotcha, the reflection of the phenomenon by the world's great sports labels, and, finally, the implications of these changes on the research in consumer behaviour.

2. Methodological Aspects

In this section we shall be examining the aim of our investigation, the data collection method, the data processing method as well as a brief review of the existing literature.

2.1. The Aim of the Investigation

The aim of this investigation is first and foremost to show that the trend discernible through sportswear and in the world of „fun-wear" in particular is not simply a superficial trend but rather profoundly affects the trend in the consumer society as a whole. We shall also be investigating „upstream", somewhat in the manner of consumer anthropologists, to locate the origins of the movement and „downstream" to specify its implications for research in consumer behaviour and consumer sociology.

2.2. The Data Collecting Method

To grasp a phenomenon such as „fun-wear" several approaches are possible; for our part, we have opted for a method which consists of gathering, in France, catalogues of brand label clothes such as Billabong (Australia), Freestyle/Gotcha (USA), Oxbow (France), O'Neill (Netherlands), Rusty (USA) for the „fun" trend, and Ralph Lauren and Façonnable for the „traditional" sports trend; press articles from Le Journal du Textile, Sport-Première, etc.; and finally, excerpts from „fun" trend magazines such as Surface Mag, Body Rider, Wind Magazine, AlpiRando, Surf Session, Jogging International, Nouvelles Sensations, VTT Magazine, B. Side, Planche-Mag, Snow Surf, Fall-Line, Surf'n Fun, Freestyle, Vertical, Vol Libre, Les Nouveaux Aventuriers, etc. The sheer number of these magazines already proves just how sizeable the „fun" phenomenon has become over the past few years; indeed, if the market for these magazines were not viable, there would undoubtedly not be that many. Moreover, it also illustrates the heterogeneity of a movement that is nonetheless perceived as homogeneous when its main characteristics are examined.

2.3. The Method for Processing the Collated Data

Evidently, given such an abundance of qualitative data, it is no longer a matter of measurement but of interpretation as defined by Spiggle (1994), who states: „(...); interpretation makes sense of data through more abstract conceptualisations. (...) The intuitive, subjective, particularistic nature of interpretation renders it difficult to model or present in a linear way. (...) The interpreter translates some distant - less familiar, abstract, indirectly apprehended - object, experience, or domain (encoded in signs) into one that is near." Any such interpretation will therefore evidently be subjective, debatable and even refutable; however, it should enable the portrayal of stakes which, otherwise, could not be so. It is a matter, for us, of obtaining meaning with regard to a phenomenon of our consumer society.

2.4. Short Review of the Existing Literature

While there is no shortage of either sports sociologists or anthropologists clothing habits in the international literature, it is also interesting to note that it is very often in France that we find sociological and anthropological studies on the „fun" trend. Evidently, the very strong attraction of „fun" sports on the French must play a part in this. The most recent and most complete of these works is undoubtedly by Loret (1995), who runs the Sports Innovation Research and Management Centre at Caen University; he shows that political, institutional and economic players will have to provide solutions to these sports people of a new kind emerging from the „fun" trend. To the extent that they prefer to share their emotions and excitement by participating in a festive event rather than by testing one another within the regulated framework of an ordinary competition, it will be necessary to respond to their new needs by offering services which, for the most part, do not exist at present. We can also mention older works by Vigarello (1981), which show the influence of the „Californian school" of surfing on contemporary sporting habits, and those of Midol (1987), Pociello (1987), Lacroix (1991), Augustin (1994), and Defrance (1995), all of them looking at „alternative" behaviours to understand the profound transformations operating in the world of contemporary sports.

3. A Short Anthology of Sportswear

In this section, we have no pretension to being exhaustive. However, this brief historical overview should enable us to grasp more clearly the changes that have occurred in the sports domain in the course of time. We shall deal successively with sportswear as an „elegant" object, then as a sign of alliance to a culture and, finally, we shall look at the rather exemplary case of jogging, which has largely invaded our daily lives and is a case in point of sportswear that has outgrown its original functional use.

3.1. Sportswear as an Object of Distinction and Elegance

At the end of the 19th century and the beginning of the 20th century, sport was considered as the privilege of the wealthy classes which saw it as a means of standing out from ordinary people and of recognising one another as members belonging to the same category. Quite naturally, then, sportswear's prime purpose was to be elegant rather than practical. To illustrate this, we merely need to take emblematic sports of the time such a tennis or even polo.

The first tennis championships were held at Wimbledon in 1877. At this time, the classic outfit worn by the tennis player consisted of long trousers and a light coloured flannel jacket, a situation which remained unchanged until the eve of the First World War. In 1885, the white outfit was adopted at the initiative of the Watson sisters and long remained the only colour accepted on court. Wimbledon is undoubtedly the venue which has maintained this traditional constraint the longest. Even in 1983, a player such as Martina Navratilova was refused access to the courts before the umpires felt that her T-shirt was too brightly coloured for such hallowed ground ...

As for polo, British officers had taken up the sport in India and a number of them brought it back to Britain in 1869. Here again, the notion elegance was to prevail over the functional aspect of the clothes: initially, players wore jockey silk. Later, the two-colour jacket was replaced by a short-sleeved jersey, with a button-up opening at the front, which made its entrance in the fashion world under the name of „polo shirt", as pointed out for example by Toussaint-Samat (1985). In 1901, the Maharajah of Jodhpur played wearing a knitted vest that covered his hips, with a crew neck and horizontal stripes, as well as riding breeches that tapered down the leg, the use of which then became widespread under the name of „jodhpurs". As for the colonial hat, a symbol of conservatism if ever there was one, it remained the headgear for polo players up until 1936.

In summary, then, the cases mentioned above show that sportswear was firmly established in the domain of sports and conveyed, first and foremost, membership of the ruling social class since it was so much a source of distinction as defined by Pierre Bourdieu (1984).

3.2. Sportswear as a Rallying Sign for a Modern Culture: The American Myth

On the eve of the First World War, sportswear was essentially shaped by the ideology of the aristocracy and the middle classes, particularly through the importance of their „elegant" dimension, which often takes its origins in Britain; however, the end of World War I would gradually bring out a rather radical change within that universe. Indeed, the United States of America, a young, rich and dynamic country, would come to represent innovation and progress and act as a reference after the manner of Britain, ruined by war. And so, during the twenties, as Bailleux and Remaury (1995) point most accurately out, „(...) an industry of entertainment was born in the United States which would very quickly conquer the world and export the products of its cultural roots". Those products include the T-shirt and many models of blousons, clothes generally designed for sports by the stylists of the American army. Like Levi Strauss jeans, they would become the symbols of the American dream and enjoy a runaway success, even more so as they are made famous by the stars of Hollywood with which the young people of these days identified. To wear such attributes of „Americanness" and of the North-American sports culture was therefore clearly an alternative dress style for populations who were not necessary middle class but resolutely modern. Thus, sportswear was starting to be diverted from its original function and, more importantly, it communicated modernity as opposed to the traditional mentioned above.

3.3. The Example of „Jogging"

While, historically, T-shirts and blousons were the first specifically sporty clothes to have an impact on everyday dress codes, jogging, which appeared at the beginning of the seventies, was to constitute another important milestone in the sports/society relationship. Indeed, very quickly, it represented a lifestyle in its own right, with repercussions on ready-to-wear clothes in general. Yonnet (1986) even maintains that a veritable „jogging fashion" was born, radically upsetting - as one would expect - the shape of shoes (especially town shoes), introducing new designs and colours, providing a new concept in footwear comfort and instituting new demands based on the new practices of leisure time. Sports clothes, which had long been limited to its specific domain, the boundaries of its stadia and its courts, ceased to be unacceptable. To wear shorts in the street was no longer an attack on morality, a form of indecent, ridiculous or suspect behaviour. Here again, a major step forward had been taken and there was no going back: the attributes of the sports world are conveyed in our daily lives because the connotation of that world is very largely positive. Even those who are not involved in sporting activities want to benefit from it.

4. The Emergence of „Fun-Wear"

Now that we have briefly shown that sportswear gradually left the confines of the stadia and training grounds to enter our towns and our daily lives, we shall closely look at describing the emergence of a specific phenomenon now referred to as „fun-wear", which, more than a mere dress habit, reveals the emergence of new „visions of the world" on the part of those who wear sportswear of the „fun" trend. In the following, we shall therefore attempt, on the one hand, to describe what characterises this trend and, on the other hand, to determine its philosophical and ideological origins.

4.1. What is „Fun-Wear"?

The eighties confirmed a new interest on the part of certain consumers for an „alternative" type of sports, which took on the name „fun" in most Anglo-Saxon countries and which in France is also referred to the term „glisse". This trend is essentially characterised by the quest for extremist excitement and translates into new sports such as wind surfing, snowboarding, climbing, mountain biking, etc. The development of this trend has been accompanied by the market launch of consumer goods with new labels, such as Rusty, Oxbow, O'Neill, Billabong, Rip Curl, Sun Valley, Quicksilver, most of which market the equipment needed for „fun" sports as well as the specific and characteristic clothes of that sporting world. For instance, the original activity of the Californian make Rusty was to manufacture surfboards. Its founder, Rusty Preisendorfer, who used his first name for the brand, is a surfer who became a „shaper" (board manufacturer). He then led his company to diversity into clothes for surfing, snowboarding, windsurfing, ..., basically any sport that involves a board and the spirit of „fun". Rusty Preisendorfer chose the first letter of his name as his logo, a capital R followed by a full stop, which he first put onto a board in 1983, as if to sign it, while still employed by the board manufacturing company Canyon Surfboard, which he had joined in 1976. Likewise, Gordon Merchant, who founded the Australian make Billabong, was also a surfer. For his brand he chose a name of aboriginal origin in order to position himself clearly within an alternative creative strategy: clothes inspired by the Australian lands where nature has retained its rights. In the aboriginal language the word „billabong" means: „watering hole in a desert landscape". Naturally, the origin of these brands, their identity, i.e. their name, their logo, their founder, the place in which they were created, are the first blocks they use to erect their culture and their image among „fun" consumers. However, beyond their specificity, a common characteristic shared by all these „fun-wear" brands is the use of highly specific fabrics, colours and emblems that make them easily identifiable.

The aspect of the fabrics used by „funs" makes can be divided into two categories. Firstly, we have fabrics that seem technical such as outfits made of „Neoprene" (a trademark registered by DuPont, which has become a generic term for designating a synthetic rubber), surfing gear made partly of „Lycra", surfing shorts made of quick-drying fabrics, snowboarding trousers and jackets that are waterproof, wind-cheating and non-slip. Secondly, they use fabrics with a worn look: „stone-washed" denims, brushed cotton, etc ...

With „fun-wear", the colours, like the shapes and the fabrics of the clothes, are representative of the anti-conventionalism of „fun" sports practice. Loret (1995) for example emphasises the fact that these brands have abandoned the use of traditional colours: „The black, red and royal blue, with white stripes, were replaced in the eighties by pastel colours commonly referred to as „signal colours“. Loret (1995) maintains that there are five of these colours, which are always identical: purple, apple green, pink, yellow and bright red. These are not just any colours: they were made fashionable in California in the early sixties by Timothy Leary, one of the principal leaders of the „psychedelic“ movement, and that is no coincidence for a trend that seeks to „escape” and discover new sensations.

What's more, „fun-wear“ brands use a large number of motifs with ethnological references and aboriginal or African origins whose naïf style blends in perfectly with the general mood conveyed by the „fun“ trend, with its ethnic and exotic images and symbols. They convey the image of a cosmopolitan and primitive world, close to nature. For example they use fabrics printed using the batik technique that originated in India or that of the „tye and dye“, originally from Black Africa. Moreover, many „fun“ graphics take their references from pictorial movements as diverse as they are unexpected; nonetheless, they all have a common characteristic: they are inspired by movements which have been qualified as „extremist“ such as abstract art, Pop Art, free figuration, etc.

In 1987, the Gotcha brand made the following statement in an editorial ad placed in the magazine „Surface Mag“: „The traditional rules of good taste, elegance and clothing have been hit over the head. Out the window with perfectly matched fabrics and colours! Into the bin with three-piece suits; an anti-conventional theme dominates the look: cool(...). The keys are there, the blend of flashy and trashy: mixing textures, daring to superpose, forget the standard spirit, let your body and your imagination express themselves freely in the clothes you wear“. That same idea is also to be found in an article published in the magazine „Nouvelles Sensations“ in 1987, which explains why there is a fundamental difference between the F.F.S. (the French Ski Federation) and the F.U.G. (the Unified „Glisse” Federation): „For all information on the flying start competitions, two choices: if you like three-piece tailored suits, houndstooth, polished shoes, contact the F.F.S. (...) If you're a bit of a rebel, dyed hair, Rip Curl sweatshirt, Gotcha shorts and Vuarnet accessories, there's only one address: F.U.G.“. The tone is set; the „fun“ trend is a definite breakaway from the „traditional“ vision of sport. In short, it's a genuine „Copernican“ revolution taking place in the sports domain in particular, not to mention society in general.

4.2. How do We Interpret the „Fun" Movement?

To try and understand the changes that are occurring through this „fun" trend, we shall be referring to the work of Caillois (1958). Caillois (1958) defines four main families of games or sports. To designate them he uses the terms „Agon, Alea, Mimicry, and Ilinx", to which he associates the concepts of competition, chance, simulation, and vertigo, respectively. Here we shall merely be looking at the concepts of „Agon" (competition) and „Ilinx" (vertigo). He associates competition with an active sportsman who is keen to be recognised as excellent in his field, who claims a personal responsibility in the sport and who is seeking a level playing field. To vertigo he associates a sportsman who wants to generate a state of confusion, who seeks to destroy, for a specific amount of time, an instant, the stability of perception. According to Caillois, such a sportsman will have a penchant, usually repressed by society, for disorder and destruction; his aim is to play with the system's limitations. The games that correspond to „Agon" are racing, combat sports, athletics, boxing and fencing. By contrast, in „Ilinx"-type sports he lists skiing, mountaineering and bunjee jumping.

Evidently, Caillois's classification is useful to us for understanding what is happening today in our consumer society; indeed, everything is happening as if the „Ilinx" trend (not to say „fun") is gaining the upper hand on the „Agon" trend, which corresponds in a more conventional way to the world of „traditional" sports. Another way of expressing this would be to say that, on the one hand, the history of sport is one of measure, performance and rules that establish the game and, on the other hand, by opposition or even reaction, the „fun" trend is one of the sports experience, the rejection of the rules and free will of the sportsman who then becomes much more than a player. The lucid, sensorial, emotive aspect would be gaining the upper hand over the rational, symbolic and social dimension of sport. In fact, is „fun" not also the assertion of the famous phrase: „no coach, no rules"? In this way, „fun" becomes a form of free expression through sport. Indeed, it is important to understand that while traditional sports seek to measure, time, compare, classify, in other words, encourage rivalry and competition, „fun" sports have no purpose other than to promote perceptions, excitement, emotions beyond the scope of any rules and regulations, of any reference point. The most blatant illustration of this attitude is the refusal by certain sometimes highly acknowledged sportsmen and women to take part in competitions. If we refer once again to Caillois's work, especially where he states that „Agon" and „Ilinx" are incompatible and irreconcilable, we understand more easily why the „fun" movement is in the process of generating a deep revolution within mentalities and that it is more than merely a fashion phenomenon.

To illustrate this, we can quote the text published in the magazine „Wind" in spring 1993, under the heading „Neither god nor master: neither bible, nor code, nor morals", which describes „fun" behaviours:

> *„- You will never have a second chance.*
> *- Love your neighbour. Be nice.*
> *- Never let anyone dictate your style.*
> *- Confront fear.*
> *- Refuse authority. Betray authority.*
> *- Don't talk too much. Learn to be silent. It broadens the mind.*
> *- The worst is always yet to come.*
> *- Seek to elevate yourself. Not to show off in a crowd.*
> *- Surf is an art and the mountain is a never-ending canvas.*
> *- Refuse all schools. Follow your inspiration.*
> *- No pain. No gain. No guts. No glory. No work. No pride.*
> *- The day is dawning (...) it belongs to you and no-one else.*
> *- Go in peace. "*

This text perfectly illustrates the type of radical thinking that hides behind the „fun" trend and leads us to believe that it is a form of „counter-culture" that appeared in the West in the eighties but undoubtedly draws its roots in a most older movement that emerged as early as the forties: the „beat" movement. But let's see precisely what lead us to make that statement.

4.3. Looking Back: The „Beat" Origins of the „Fun" Movement

In spring 1996, the „Walker Art Museum" in Minneapolis, Minnesota, organised a retrospective on the „beat generation". It enabled us to fully realise how much the philosophical thinking of the years between 1944 and 1960, of people like William Everson, Kenneth Rexroth, Lawrence Ferlinghetti, Jack Kerouac, or even Allen Ginsberg, was implicitly present in the „fun" trend which began to develop in the Western world in the eighties. In this respect, the work by Watson (1995) is very interesting since it perfectly shows to what extent the „beat" movement was, in its day, an unprecedented form of „counter-culture". Accordingly, for the „beat" movement, society is likely to be divided into two opposed groups: the „squares", who obey the rules of American society, and the „beats", who reject those community rules to promote other ones, far different from those of the dominant American society of these days, since they are linked to the privileged expression of the private individual, with the emphasis on personal emotions and feelings. The „square" is the conformist individual ridiculed by the beatniks, with whom they do not want to have anything in common. In actual fact, the „alternative" behaviour of the „beatniks" is nothing but the visible part of a far greater iceberg that was to give rise to what American sociologists during the sixties called the „counter-culture". To fully understand what is involved, we simply need to look at the definition given by O'Neill (1971): „Counter-culture as a term appeared rather late in the decade. It largely replaced the term youth culture, which finally proved too limited. Counter-culture meant all things to all men and embraced everything new from clothing to politics". We can then easily draw up a parallel between the text published in the „Wind" magazine in spring 1993, as mentioned above, and the writings of the „beat" movement such as „On the Road" by Jack Kerouac (1957). Indeed, Kerouac's heroes have only one purpose: to transcend their life by escaping the constraints of rules and regulations; for that reason, they have hit the road ... To a certain extent, today's „traditional" sports federations are the „squares" of that time and the players of the current „fun" trend might the direct heirs to the „beatniks" of the fifties (we might also add that the „non-conventional" surfers on the Californian beaches of the fifties were very close to the „beat" movement and let's not forget that the „fun" movement also seeks to rediscover the spirit of those out-of-the-ordinary surfers, without limits or constraints ...).

5. From the „American Way of Life" to the „Fun Way of Life": From Polo Ralph Lauren to Gotcha

In California, at the late fifties and early sixties, surfing was more than just a sport. It was a truly out-of-sync way of life. It goes back to alternative lifestyles resulting from deep rejection of the American consumer society. The „surf way of life" was therefore in opposition to the „American way of life". In fact, Edgar Morin, who fully realised this situation, wrote in his Californian diary (Morin, 1970): „They go surfing in their hundreds of thousands, they go and play with the ocean, and it becomes the most important thing in life". Likewise, we can say that, today, the „fun way of life", the heir to the „surf way of life", is essentially out-of-sync with the „American way of life", not to say the „Western way of life". To show just how opposed these two trends are and how they refer to different value systems, we carried out a semiological analysis of the Polo Ralph Lauren and Gotcha catalogues. The results of the study are shown in Table 1 below. Indeed, what better brands than Polo Ralph Lauren and Gotcha to illustrate such differences? The former refers to the archly conservative Boston style of America's East Coast, to the point of inscribing the word „polo", which refers to the British most traditional neo-colonial sport while the latter refers to one of the most extravagant „fun" brands ever to have come out of the States in eighties.

The American Way of Life: Polo Ralph Lauren	The „Fun" Way of Life: Gotcha
- <u>Performance</u> - <u>Competition</u> - *The catalogues show the products*	- <u>Excitement</u>- *The catalogues emphasise the atmosphere with the products taking second place*
- <u>Regulations</u> - <u>Discipline</u> - *Impeccably styled clothes* *Regulation colours*	- <u>Freedom</u> - <u>Excess</u> - *„Oversized" look: XXL sizes* *Signal colours, very bright and sensational*
- <u>Conformism</u> - <u>Elitism</u>- *Club stripes*	- <u>Marginalism</u> - <u>Provocation</u> - *Aggressive graphics - Totemic symbols*
- <u>Tradition</u> - *Basic, timeless products*	- <u>Innovation</u> - *Very „hip" products, with built-in obsolescence*

Table 1: Differences between Polo Ralph Lauren and Gotcha

6. The Revival of the Phenomenon by the Big Brands

So far, we have stressed the fact that the „fun" phenomenon developed thanks to highly specialised brands such as Billabong, Freestyle/Gotcha, Oxbow, O'Neill, Rusty and Quicksilver. However, it is also worth noting that, as of the early nineties, the phenomenon become institutionalised and affected an important section of the market for buyers of sports clothes and articles. In other words, during the eighties, the phenomenon shifted from the periphery to the centre of the sports market. So much, that brands such as Nike and Reebok began to take an interest and claim it for themselves. Thus, in „On the road" (Kerouac, 1957), Kerouac attempts to explain through Dean, the novel's hero and principal character, the meaning of what he calls „it", i.e. an emotion, a free interpretation, a free figure, ... It is even more surprising, then, to see an internationally recognised sports firm such as Nike using a phrase such as: „Just do it" in 1993 as its advertising slogan and to use the Beatles's song „Revolution". In the „fun" world the message is well received. It is even more explicit that the entire theme is re-used and explained by the Ukrainian pole vaulter Sergueo Bubka, who says in an ad: „Too often we're scared. Scared of not being capable. Scared of the judgement of others. We let our fears obstruct our hopes and we say No when we want to say Yes. We stay silent when we want to cry out and howl with the rest when we want to keep quiet. Why? After all, you only go round once and there's no time for fear. So stop. Do as I do. Try something you've never dared before. Run down the paths of freedom. Be cross-training body and soul. Take part in a triathlon. Climb the peaks on a mountain bike. Stand up against injustices. Ask for a rise. Throw out your TV. Apply for a patent. Call her. You have nothing to loose and everything, everything, everything to win". No doubt such a statement would not be rejected by any member of the „beat" generation, as they are so many similarities of thought.

Nike did not stop there. In 1994, the brand even called upon Eric Cantona to develop an extremely provocative communication campaign. And so, in an ad, we see and hear Eric Cantona saying the following sentence, even before the Nike logo appears by way of conclusion: „I was sanctioned for hitting a goalkeeper, for spitting at a supporter, for throwing my jersey at a referee, for calling my coach a sh.. bag, then I called the jury who sanctioned me a bunch of idiots. I thought I would find it difficult to find a sponsor." At first sight, such an advertising campaign would seem to indicate that Nike's communication strategy consists of using the register of social protest to develop its communication campaign. In fact, the strategy is even more subtle: it is simply a matter of positioning oneself on a clearly different register (for purposes of differentiation) compared with the other great rival, namely Adidas, which, at that time, was still very clearly marked by the culture of sporting performance which, in the past, had enabled the brand soaring development for which measurement was all (the brand's three parallel stripes clearly refer to a geometric symbol, synonymous with measurement and performance, more than excitement).

Evidently, Nike's objective was to stand out clearly from its direct and main rivals, i.e. Adidas and Reebok. With Adidas, the move was even more successful as Adidas continued, in the early nineties, i.e. at the height of the „fun" trend, to plug the merits of sport's „traditional" values. The brand has since changed its strategy and made great efforts in particular to try and recover „street-ball", another specific manifestation of the „fun" trend. With Reebok, however, the move failed. Indeed, the company engaged into a very direct battle with Nike and even launched an ad campaign with the slogan: „Break the rules", another leitmotiv in common with the „beat generation" and the „fun" movement. In summary, the race was on between Nike and Reebok to determine which of them would use the most „counter-cultural" references of the „fun" movement.

7. The Implications of this Trend on Research in Consumer Behaviour and Consumer Sociology

7.1. The „Fun" Movement as „Hedonist" Movement: An Appeal to Emotional Awareness

For a little more than a decade now, the experiential approach has occupied an increasingly important place in research in consumer behaviour and more specifically following the work by Holbrook and Hirschman (1982). Likewise, greater importance is now also attached to the „hedonist" variable in explaining consumer behaviour following the work of the same authors (Hirschman and Holbrook, 1982). Indeed, consumption is not merely an act of destruction carried out by a consumer; rather, it is a social act through which symbolic meanings, identities, etc., are produced and reproduced. What characterises the stage referred to as consumption is that images will be generated that are linked to the object/consumer interaction. Consumption then becomes a means for the consumer to express and identify himself. By consuming, the individual exists, establishes himself and draws up his social image; that is how consumption contains a process of production and it is interesting a very recent academic paper (1996) such as the „Journal of Material Culture" should have set itself the task of gaining a better understanding of these processes of construction carried out by consumers themselves through the goods with which they surround themselves.

The approach retained by researchers situated in the paradigm of „hedonist consumption" or „phenomenological" approaches (Thomson et al., 1989) is to go beyond the models hitherto recommended by new economic theory. Indeed, preference analysis models insist too much on the cognitive component while excluding the affective component of the behaviour. In a certain sectors of activity, it is necessary to take account of the emotions and feelings of individuals to explain their behaviour: the „fun" movement is a very good example of it. The experiential model calls into question the classic hierarchy of the behavioural components used for explaining the decisions of the consumer. Experiential choice is mainly based on symbolic and non-verbal evocations which replace cognitive attitude components retained by traditional models. Therefore, this model aims to give account of the aesthetic pleasure and emotion which a consumer may feel before a product or service. And, evidently, as shown by our interpretations above, as far as the „fun" movement is concerned, the „emotional" dimension is by far the most important over all the others for enthusiasts of „fun" sports. In this context, it is also interesting to note that it was not only the works of Hirschman and Holbrook that were precursors in this specific area of research in consumer behaviour. Indeed, and that is probably what is most surprising, they emphasised a dimension which today is more and more significant in the consumer society although at the time they published their work it was only starting to gain momentum. We feel it is essential to emphasise the consumption of the product and not merely its purchase. Indeed, it is the use of the product that allows the consumer to extract from it not only the functional use provided by its attributes, but also all the affective gratification provided by the symbolic and social functions of this object. How can we hope to understand the „fun" trend if we forget to consider that the specific system of the movement's objects refer to a „counter-culture" and that the aspirations of the players who acquire them are mainly to experience new sensations? If, in the past, the emphasis has been on the „reason" dimension of the consumer when studying his behaviour, we have to admit that it is more and more imperative, especially in a number of sectors such as leisure, the arts, tourism and culture, to place the emphasis also on the „passion" dimension and to substitute the (Cognition/Affect/Behaviour) sequence with another structured around affective processes (Imaginary/Emotions/Pleasure), as explained for example by Filser (1996).

7.2. Not Forgetting the Importance of Semiotics in Consumer Sociology

Semiotics, especially structural semiotics, is part of a paradigm that advocates a „constructed" vision of the world. Hence, the consumer does not exist merely on the consumption side of things but also virtually upstream from it, i.e. right from the phase at which the products and messages are constituted (as in the case of the brands Gotcha, Quicksilver, etc., above). To take on board this vision of the world and thereby contribute to the renewal of research in consumer behaviour, semiotic theory proposes two particularly useful notions: the notion of „interpretative co-operation" (also called „co-interpretation") and the notion of enunciation (Hetzel and Marion, 1995). Moreover, semiotic formalisation also has the merit of enabling an awareness on the part of the players of the importance of the symbolic dimension of the offer, something for which researchers such as Levy have been pleading for several decades (Levy, 1959). At the theoretical level, semiotics advocate a vision where work is carried out on „constructions"; rather than claiming to have an ontological vision of the research object, there is a constructed vision of reality. This has considerable repercussions with regard to the definition of scientific criteria and research methodologies. That is why it is believed that semiotics will contribute towards significant advances in consumer sociology.

8. Conclusion

For more than a century, the world of sport had not been called into question so radically and so profoundly. The „fun trend" is a total departure from the principles set forth by the spiritual father of the modern Olympic movement, Pierre de Coubertin, for whom athletes should always go „faster, higher, stronger" („citius, altius, fortius" to quote the Latin). Indeed, the new slogan that emerges from it, which is in fact the motto of „streetball", another alternative sporting practice, is: „no coach, no ref, no rules". It is interesting to note, then, that such a situation leads to similar conclusions in other areas of consumption, where more and more the consumer seems to be seeking the „Ilinx", as defined by Caillois. In other words, the vertigo that allows him to escape the dullness and monotony of everyday life. We have, for example, reached conclusions of the same type in previous works when explaining the key factors of success in the development of a French gaming company: „La Française des Jeux", whose turnover has risen significantly since the eighties (Hetzel, 1996); and also in the sector of distribution and in the retail trade, where consumers are more and more receptive to the stimulation of their five senses and even an organoleptic saturation synonymous with vertigo (Hetzel, 1995). It is also conceivable that the astonishing success of these new venues where it is now possible for consumers to experience „virtual reality" is part of the same process of attraction of the „Ilinx", the vertigo and rejection of reality, which all too often refers back to harsh rivalry and the laws of competition. Evidently, we can no longer ignore this strong trend of the eighties and nineties if we are to understand the present, not to mention the future, of our consumer society.

References

Augustin, Jean-Pierre (1994): Surf Atlantique: les territoires de l'éphémère. Maison des sciences de l'homme: Bordeaux.

Bailleux, Nathalie and Bruno Remaury (1995): Mode et vêtement. Gallimard: Paris.

Bourdieu, Pierre (1984): Distinction: A Social Critique of the Judgement of Taste (Translated by R. Nice). Routledge: London.

Caillois, Roger (1958): Les Jeux et les Hommes. Gallimard: Paris.

Caillois, Roger (1967): Jeux et Sports. Gallimard: Paris.

De Certeau, Michel (1984): The practice of everyday life. University of California Press: Berkeley, CA.

Defrance, Jacques (1995): Sociologie du sport. La Découverte: Paris.

Filser, Marc (1996): Comportement de consommation et recherche d'expériences: vers une consommation plus affective? In: Revue Française de Gestion, Septembre-Octobre.

Gotcha (1987): Les rebelles du surf (advertising). In: Surface Mag, No. 11, p. 53.

Hetzel, Patrick (1995): Systemising the Awareness of the Consumer's Five Senses at the Point of Sale: An essential Challenge for Marketing Theory and Practice. In: Proceedings of the 24th Annual EMAC Conference, Cergy-Pontoise, France, pp. 471-482.

Hetzel, Patrick (1996): Formalizing the gambling market: what are the interaction strategies between the gambling copanies and their clients? Presentation at the French-German Workshop on Services Marketing Research, February 28 to March 1, Innsbruck, Austria

Hetzel, Patrick and Gilles Marion (1995): Contributions of French Semiotics to marketing research knowledge. In: Marketing & Research Today, February and May Issues, pp. 35-40 and 75-85.

Hirshman, Elizabeth and Morris Holbrook (1982): Hedonic consumption: emerging concepts, methods and propositions. In: Journal of Marketing, Vol. 46, Summer, pp. 92-101.

Holbrook, Morris and Elizabeth Hirschman (1982): The experiential aspects of consumption: consumer Fantasies, Feelings and Fun. In: Journal of Consumer Research, Vol. 9, pp. 132-140.

Kerouac, Jack (1957): On the road. Penguin Books: Harmondsworth.

Lacroix, Gisèle (1991): Le look fun et ses enjeux. In: Proceedings of the Symposium „Géopolitique du sport", University of Besançon.

Levy, Sidney (1959): Interpreting Consumer Mythology: a structural approach to consumer behavior. In: Journal of Marketing, Vol. 45, Summer, pp. 49-61.

Loret, Alain (1995): Génération Glisse. Revue Autrement, Série Mutations, No. 155-156, Paris.

McCracken, Grant (1988): Culture and consumption: New Approaches to the Symbolic Character of Consumer Goods and Activities. Indiana University Press: Bloomington.

McCracken, Grant and Victor Roth (1989): Does clothing have a code? Empirical findings and theoretical implications in the study of clothing as a means of communication. In: International Journal of Research in Marketing, No. 6, pp. 13-33.

Midol, Nancy (1987): Motricité et culture fun. In: Proceedings of the Conference „Sport et changement social", University of Bordeaux.

Morin, Edgar (1970): Journal de Californie. Seuil: Paris.

O'Neill, William, L. (1971): Coming Apart. Times Publisher: New-York.

Pedron, Blandine (1995): Influence du sport sur la mode, Mémoire de maitrise, Université Lumière Lyon 2, Unpublished paper.

Pociello, Christian (1987): Le nouvel âge du sport. Esprit, Avril 1987.

Spiggle, Susan (1994): Analysis and Interpretation of Qualitative Data in Consumer Research. In: Journal of Consumer Research, Vol. 21, December, pp. 491 - 503.

Thomson, Craig et al. (1989): Putting Consumer Experience Back into Consumer Research: the Philosophy and Method of Existential-Phenomenology. In: Journal of Consumer Research, Vol. 16, September, pp. 133-146.

Toussaint-Sama, Maguelonne (1985): Histoire technique et morale du vêtement. Bordas: Paris.

Vigarello, Georges (1981): Le Corps redressé. Editions Delarge: Paris.

Yonnet, Paul (1985): Jeux, Modes et Masses. Gallimard: Paris.

Franz-Rudolf Esch

Market Reactions to Integrated Communication

1. Introduction: Framework Conditions for Integrated Communication

2. Theoretical Approach to Integrated Communication

3. Means and Dimensions of Integration

4. Investigations on Integrated Communication
    4.1. The Situation of Integrated Communication in Business Practice: Mixed Semiotic Content Analyses
    4.2. Experiments for the Integration of Communication over a Certain Period of Time

5. Outlook: Challenges for the Science and Practice of Marketing

References

Market Reactions to Integrated Communication

Prof. Dr. Franz-Rudolf Esch

Abstract

Communication conditions have drastically changed during the last few years. Companies have growing difficulties to convey their advertising messages. By using integrated communication one can harmonise and reinforce all brand impressions over time. Integrated communication means to co-ordinate all communication instruments through content and/or formal elements. The result is an increasing advertising efficiency. This article discusses a range of investigations which analyse effects of integrated communication on consumer's memory. Three different levels of integration were tested: integration by slogan, semantic picture integration and integration by key visuals. The present situation of integrated communication in business practice was examined in an other investigation.

1. Introduction: Framework Conditions for Integrated Communication

Both, companies and individuals profit from the age of information: An incredible amount of information is at their disposal, data highways allow to gather the most sophisticated information in a few seconds, virtual libraries can be visited and physically non-existing books can be scanned. From a purely technical point of view even one-to-one communication can be established with ultimate customers and it is only due to exorbitant prices that this possibility is still out of question. Yet all these qualities are not sufficient for transforming our society into Eldorado. Advertising companies have growing difficulties to convey their messages to the consumers and to influence their preference for specific brands. This study will be focused on the problem of how to forge a link with the consumer with emphasis given to the role of integrated communication.

These questions cannot be answered without considering the relevant market and communication conditions. We must distinguish supply from demand. Since 1975 the number of advertised brands on the supply side has more than doubled in Germany. The number of different media as well as advertisements within a particular media channel are permanently increasing. Advertising spots in Germany have risen from 444 daily spots in 1986 to 3049 spots in 1994 (GfK Advertising Research, 1995).

90

On the other hand, consumers' interest in information is rapidly decreasing. Information is only perceived in fragments. Consumers prefer pictorial to verbal information. Consequently, the growing information offer and the decreasing information demand must result in an information overload in our society. Information overload does not refer to information stress (Jacoby, 1977), but it is used in the sense of information overflow. Information overflow is defined as an information excess ranging between information offered and information perceived (Kroeber-Riel, 1987). In Germany on average more than 98 percent of advertising information end up in the waste-paper basket (Kroeber-Riel and Weinberg, 1996). Communication effects must be fragmented under such conditions. The effects of individual communication contacts are constantly decreasing. Figures published by all great German market-research groups acknowledge these results, i.e. the efficiency of advertising expenses for communication decreases rapidly. From 1985 to 1993 there was a decrease from 18 to 12 percent.

This tendency will expand in the future. Our society will be dominated by pictures (Kroeber-Riel, 1993; Schultz et al., 1994). Today's consumers prefer information divided in small understandable portions. Companies cannot alter these changing conditions. Communication, especially integrated communication, must be adapted to these new habits, otherwise marketers risk to loose contact with consumers. Looking at today's communication scene one can hardly speak of the integration of communication. The opposite is true: Impressions for a brand given by print ads differ from impressions given by radio or TV ads. Additionally, many companies change their communication campaigns too often. Let's consider the TV ads for the **Citroen Xantia** as a negative example. **Seven different** TV spots were broadcasted from November 1993 until now (Esch and Andresen, 1996). Consumers must digest constantly changing impressions and messages for Xantia. Pieces of information eclipse each other, no link is forged with the customer. For building brand preferences, one needs time. This is not the case when campaigns are permanently changed. These changes are leading to further fragmentation caused by the company itself. **Fragmented communication** means conveying different impressions and messages for the same brand. For that reason advertising expenses are not efficiently invested in the creation of a strong brand image. For example: The Citroen Xantia has an advertising recall below 10 percent. This result is the worst in the car sector, if one compares advertising expenses and advertising recall (see Figure 1 and 3).

Coordination and integration are indispensable. But there is still a huge lack of integration, caused by organizational and personal problems within companies, such as turf battles between different communication departments (Duncan and Everett, 1993). Additionally, there exist three further essential **barriers to integrated communication**: One psychological problem and two widespread errors (Esch, 1995).

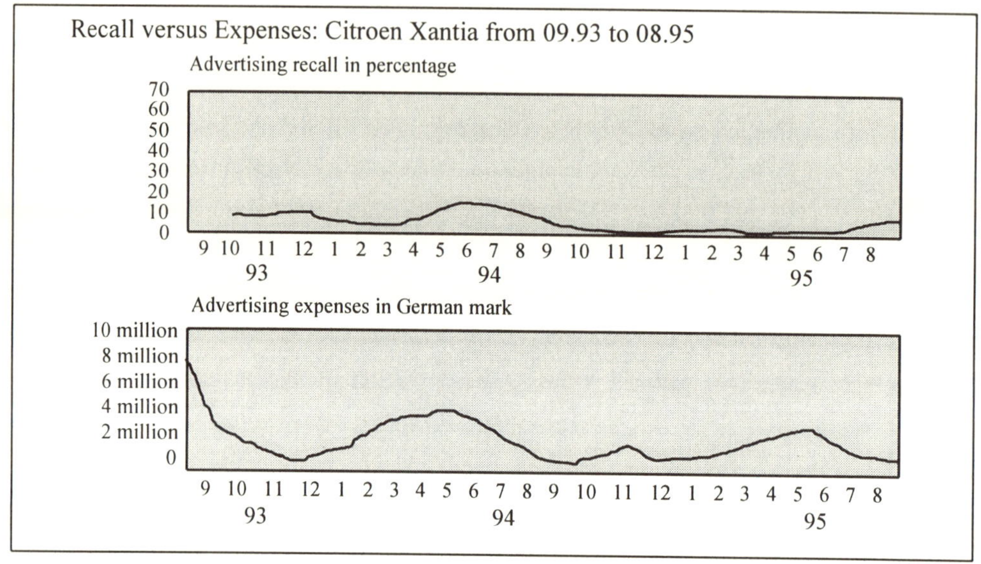

Figure 1: Relation between advertising recall and advertising expenses for Citroen Xantia, source: icon, „Forschung und Consulting", Germany

The **psychological problem**: Having seen their advertising campaigns more often and more consciously than the actual target group managers and advertisers have strong **internal wear-outs**. Supposing similar effects on the target group they tend to frequent campaign changes, although there is no measurable external wear-out.

The **misconceptions**: Companies feel forced to adapt communication to different target groups who may be interested in different information. Salesmen, for example, are interested in other information than customers or shareholders. This does not mean, however, that communication cannot be harmonised. Shareholders and salesmen as well as customers read popular magazines and watch television. They cannot be exclusively reached by a one-to-one communication. Furthermore a brand and its key positioning is constant independent of the relevant target group. Communication must be integrated in such an intelligent manner that its integration elements remain perceivable without excluding target-group-specific contacts!

A further misconconception, that media-adapted communication within different media can hardly be integrated (i.e. print, radio, TV) is not true. What matters above all is to examine, whether integration elements can be transferred and transformed to diverse types of media

(Kroeber-Riel, 1993). These are today's challenges to integrated communication. In the following context **integrated communication** will be defined as the coordination of all communication instruments through content and/or formal elements. The aim is to harmonise and to reinforce all brand impressions over time (Kroeber-Riel, 1993). Integrated communication is not limited to individual or mass communication. From our point of view all marketing-mix-instruments help to communicate with the consumer, i.e. packaging, store design etc. (Shimp and DeLozier, 1986). Though other definitions also refer to internal and external communication including planning and organization aspects (Wells et al., 1989; Duncan and Everett, 1993), we consciously restrict our investigation to the application of external communication. Here the business sector sees the main need for action. According to research results from Bruhn and Zimmermann (1993) managers who are concerned with integrated communication are primarily interested in goals referring to external communication.

A positive example of integrated communication are the advertisements for the Renault Clio. Three spots have been broadcasted since 1991. The slogan „made in paradise"and the pictures of Adam and Eve in paradise are exactly translating the emotional positioning of Clio without neglecting technical information as face-lifting or equipment variations.

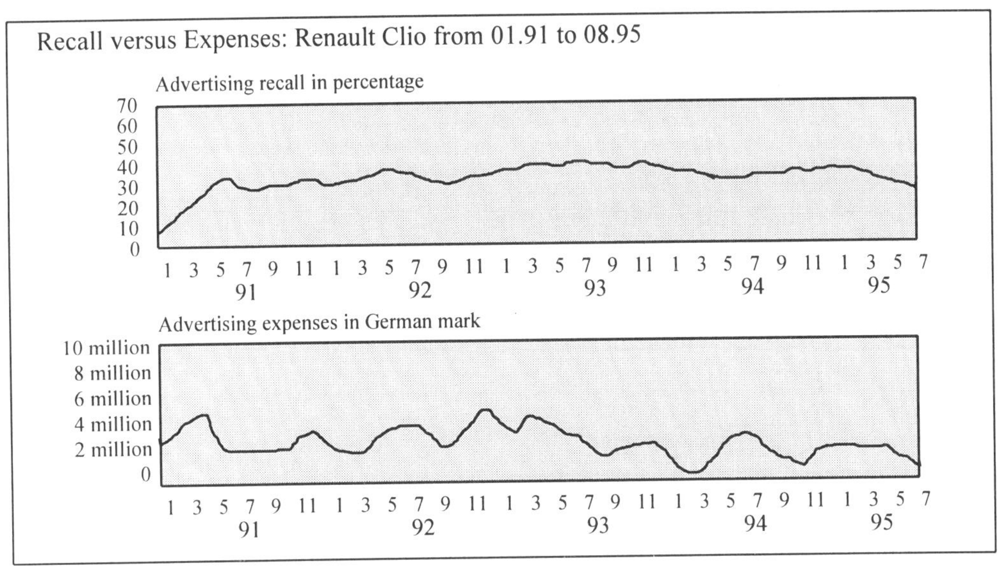

Figure 2: Relation between advertising recall and advertising expenses for Renault Clio, source: icon, „Forschung und Consulting", Germany

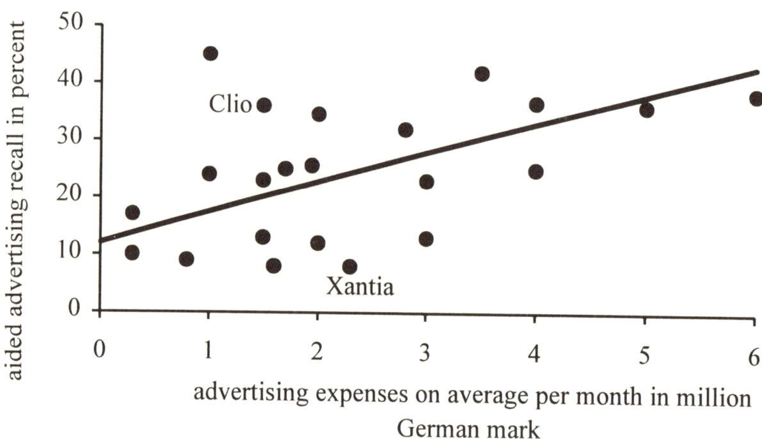

Figure 3: Ranks of Renault Clio and Citroen Xantia in an advertising efficiency test of car advertisements, source: icon, „Forschung und Consulting"

The advertising campaign for Clio is one of the best of car industry regarding the relation between advertising recall and advertising expenses (see Figure 2 and 3).

2. Theoretical Approach to Integrated Communication

From the point of view of consumer behavior research integrated communication can be seen as a concept of learning. Memory structures are to be created for brands and companies. Clearly defined emotional or informational brand attributes shall be cemented into the consumer's mind. For the reinforcement of these contents repetition is necessary (see Esch, 1997). For integrated communication two aspects of learning must be differentiated:

- initial learning of brand associations, and
- refreshing of contents of former learned associations.

According to cognitive psychology once acquired brand information and brand impressions cannot be forgotten anymore. Without appropriate stimuli, however, the consumer finds it difficult to make the necessary associations. Memory contents fade away due to passage of time or to interference with other information (Anderson, 1989; Underwood, 1957). The construction of clear memory structures for a brand by communication demands concrete information about knowledge structures and the representation of knowledge in the consumer's mind. Previously

94

acquired knowledge considerably determines the way new information is perceived, processed and stored.

The representation of knowledge in the consumer's mind can be described by schemata (Bartlett, 1932). *A schema is a large, complex unit of knowledge containing typical characteristics and fixed standardised ideas about objects, persons and events* (Esch, 1997; Rumelhart, 1980, p. 34; Alba and Hasher, 1983). Schemata can be visualised by semantic networks (Fiske and Pavelchak, 1986). Such schemata exist for products, brands and companies as well. With the chocolate brand „Milka", for example, we spontaneously associate the colour purple, the Milka cow, the Alps, a delicate chocolate produced with milk from the Alps and so on.

Precondition for building strong schemata, however, is the consistency of the presented information over a period of time! (Smith and Houston, 1985, p. 215; Taylor and Crocker, 1981). Schemata exert an essential influence on the perception of information. During the advertising contact schemata serve as framework for the selection of relevant information (Neisser, 1976). Three conditions must be fulfiled, if schemata shall influence the perception and processing of information (Abelson, 1981, p. 719):

1) The consumer must have a stable cognitive representation of a brand schema, i.e. the clear schema of „Milka".
2) There must be a relevant context which activates the brand schema. In Milka ads, for example, this might be the Alps and the purple cow.
3) The consumer must use the learned schema.

If communication activates an already existing brand schema, such a schema determines the selection of information as well as rapidity and manner of information processing (Fiske and Taylor, 1991). Information which is in accordance with a brand schema, facilitates and automates information processing. In this context it is important that central or salient attributes of a schema are recognised considerably faster as a part of the learned schema than peripheral attributes (Abelson, 1981, p. 718; Taylor et al., 1979; Arbib et al., 1987, p. 12; Friedman, 1979). The Milka schema is faster activated by the purple cow than by the Alps.

If the information structure perceived does not match the formerly acquired knowledge, the recall effects for this information will be poor. Such **„mismatches"** can occur, because

- the information perceived is too different from the stored brand schema, or
- the person does not have a brand schema (Esch, 1997; Alba and Hasher, 1983).

The activation of a schema through communication strongly depends on the consumer's involvement, that means how attentively the consumer concentrates on communication (Zaichkowsky, 1985; Krugman, 1965; Laurent and Kapferer, 1985). *The more casual the perception of an ad is, the more consistent with a formerly acquired schema the presented advertisements must be to activate the stored brand schema.* If the consumer, however, gives his full attention to the ad, the information may differ more from a previously acquired schema. But the target group's attention at the moment of communication should not be overestimated. In general consumer's involvement with advertising is low (Kroeber-Riel, 1994).

When communicating with low involved consumers the use of pictures is very important. The results of imagery research show that pictures are better perceived and remembered than words. Imagery results dealing with the perception, processing and storage of pictures (Paivio, 1971, 1986; Ruge, 1988; Esch, 1997) are therefore very important for the shaping of integrated communication under low involvement conditions. The superiority of pictures over words is known for a long time. Contrary to words pictures are processed automatically, with low cognitive control, and holistically. The findings of imagery research are of crucial importance for the communication with low involved consumers (Kroeber-Riel, 1993; Esch, 1993). The consistent use of pictures which communicate similar contents, helps to create fixed and clear brand schemata at low involved customers. The integration of communication just by verbal elements would not have such an effect.

3. Means and Dimensions of Integration

More detailed investigations on integrated communication should differentiate between dimensions (integration over a period of time and integration between different media channels) and means of integration (Esch, 1997; Kroeber-Riel, 1993). Means of integration can be subdivided according to form and content (see Table 1).

Pictorial retrieval signs and corporate design are examples for means of formal integration (Lutz and Lutz, 1977). Nivea, for example, uses the colours blue and white together with the character of Nivea in order to create a formal integration. The Michelin man, on the other side, is an example of a pictorial retrieval signal for Michelin tyres.

Formal integration is useful, if the advertisement is for special offers, the main aim is the actualisation of a brand in order to become top of the mind or the creation of formal links between different departments and brands with different positioning is aimed at. Formal integration helps to fix the brand in the consumer's mind and simplifies the access to a brand, but it does not create a bond between the positioning contents and the brand. For the positioning of brands and companies, therefore, integration should be obtained by pictures and words. Recent investigations on integrated communication are considered in the following chapter.

means of integration / dimensions of integration	integration by formal elements i.e. corporate design, pictorial retrieval signs	integration as regards content		
		verbal slogan	**non-verbal** semantic picture integration	key visuals
over time				
between different media				

Table 1: Integration matrix, source: Esch (1997)

4. Investigations on Integrated Communication

It was the aim of these investigations to register the present situation of integrated communication in business practice by mixed semiotic content analyses, and to examine the effects of integrated communication.

4.1. The Situation of Integrated Communication in Business Practice: Mixed Semiotic Content Analyses

Mixed semiotic content analyses of advertisements in the journals „Stern" and „Spiegel" were made in order to find out the actual situation of integration (Semiotics as science of signs see Eco, 1991; Peirce, 1931-35; Morris, 1946; de Saussure, 1916; for content analysis see Berelson, 1952; Kassarjian, 1977). The following results are focused on the journal „Stern". The survey indicates to which extent advertising has been integrated between 1990 and 1992. A system of three categories was applied: the pragmatic, the semantic and the syntactic level. On the pragmatic level - relations between signs and persons - it is examined, if or if not and for which reason an advertising campaign for a brand can be regarded as integrated. The semantic level contains the degree of consistency of contents communicated by pictures, headlines and advertising copy. On the syntactic level the congruity of formal elements (i.e. textual structure, typography, pictorial design and total advertising structure) is analysed. By means of 250 categories 1418 ads for brands and companies were analysed (as to the classification of signs on pragmatic, semantic and syntactic levels see Morris, 1946, p. 219).

The representation below is limited to some results about the perception of integration. The following can be noticed: As to formal integration only 31 percent of the ads are non or low integrated, whereas 16 percent of the ads are strongly integrated. There is a clear difference between consumer goods on the one hand and user goods and services on the other hand (see Table 2). Contrary to formal integration 71 percent of the ads are perceived as weak and non-integrated regarding their content. Here as well the results of the ads for consumer goods are better than those of the user goods and services.

	formal integration				content integration			
	strong	middle	weak	n	strong	middle	weak	n
service goods	7%	37%	56%	332	16%	2%	82%	332
user goods	15%	64%	21%	672	14%	0%	86%	672
consumer goods	26%	49%	25%	361	30%	37%	33%	361

Table 2: Results concerning formal integration and content integration of communication, source: Esch, 1997

4.2. Experiments for the Integration of Communication over a Certain Period of Time

4.2.1. Experimental Design

In experimental studies relations were examined among differently integrated communication under low involvement conditions. We investigated the effects of integration of communication between different media (i.e. TV, print advertising), and print ads over a certain period of time.

A large number of US studies were carried out under high involvement conditions. The subjects had often twenty seconds and more to regard an advertising spot (Keller 1987, 1991; Schumann et al., 1990; Burke and Srull, 1988). Recent research results show, however, that a one page advertisement is generally regarded for two seconds only (Kroeber-Riel and Weinberg, 1996). For that reason we simulated low involvement conditions in our experiment.

Our examination of integrated communication over a certain period of time shall now be discussed in more detail.[1] As for their effects on communication we examined **four different ways of integration regarding the content** of communication of **four different brands** and **variable numbers of repetitions**. For the investigation we produced **128 new test ads**. As a typical example of the four levels of integration several ads are selected for one brand („Württembergische Versicherung"; for examples see figures 4a to 4d). For another brand („Singapore Airlines") some different ads are described below. The formal design for all ads remained constant. First some examples of **fragmented communication**: In each of these ads one can find a different text, picture and slogan for a brand. The „Württembergische Versicherung" once pictures an old couple for underlining the issue of „retirement insurance", another time a consultant appears in order to emphasise the idea of personal contact and so on. The ads for Singapore Airlines once showed a passenger sitting in the first class, another time one can see a plane above the clouds.

Figure 4 a: Example of fragmented communication

[1] This study was sponsored by icon 'Forschung und Consulting', Germany.

Figure 4 b: Example of integration by slogan

Figure 4 c: Example of semantic integration

Fig. 4 d: Example of integration by key visuals

As for **integration by slogan** the advertising copy differs except for the slogan in every ad. The message for the „Württembergische Versicherung" shows the company always as a solid insurance company. The slogan of the „Singapore Airlines" shows the company always as an exotic airline.

For **semantic integration** different pictures are used which always show the „Württembergische Versicherung" as solid (e.g. the German oak tree, the Alps etc.) and the „Singapore Airlines" as exotic (e.g. exotic fruits, a Toucan etc.). The comprehension of the motives based on their messages was proved by a pilot study. On the highest level of integration **key visuals** were used. Salient pictorial elements are considered as key visuals. They embody the visual heart of an ad's message. The advertisements show the „Württembergische Versicherung" as solid and the „Singapore Airlines" as exotic. The **key visual** of the ads for the „Württembergische Versicherung" was the „rock in the surf", in the ads for the „Singapore Airlines" it was the „Singapore Girl".

In the experimental design four different integration levels were tested from the highest level of key visual integration until complete absence of any integration (see Table 3). The subjects had four or eight contacts with the different ads. This number of repetitions was chosen, because other experiments had shown that wear-out effects - in case there are some - occur after five or six repetitions (Pechman and Stewart, 1989). Every different level of integration was investigated for four brands. Two brands existed in real life and two were fictitious. Therefore treatment group 1 saw four times an integration of the key visuals for brand „A“, for brand „B“ a semantic integration by using different pictures with similar contents. For brand „C“ the subjects saw an integration by slogan and for brand „D“ there was no integration at all.

integration by number of repetitions	I key visuals	II semantic picture inte- gration	III slogan	IV no integration	treatment group
4	A	B	C	D	1
	B	C	D	A	2
	C	D	A	B	3
	D	A	B	C	4
8	A	B	C	D	5
	B	C	D	A	6
	C	D	A	B	7
	D	A	B	C	8

Table 3: Test design of the investigation on integrated communication within a certain period of time, source: Esch, 1997

The laboratory investigation simulated a low involvement situation. The subjects had to read two different magazines. Each magazine had 40 pages, 50 percent of them were ads. Apart from the stimuli there were ads from the competitors of the examined brands. The reason for this is the fact that ads of competitive companies reinforce interference in the consumer's mind (Burke and Srull, 1988). To cause a necessary distraction the subjects had to assess the formal design of the magazine. After 20 minutes the subjects had to leave the room. The retrieval of learned information becomes more difficult in a foreign environment (Baddeley, 1986). This corresponds to reality. Most of the time products are not bought in the same place where communication contacts are established. Questions about integration were only asked in the second room. Up to this moment 95 percent of the subjects were convinced that the test was performed for a publishing company. The real investigation purpose was therefore effectively disguised.

The **main hypothesis** of this experiment is that under low involvement conditions the integration of key visuals has the best advertising effect. The semantic integration has a better advertising efficiency than the other levels of integration. Furthermore, it was assumed that there is no difference at all between the advertising effect of integration by slogan and the ads without any integration. It was expected that four to eight repetitions do not create a wear-out effect. In contrast the results for key visual integration and for semantic integration should improve. Integration by slogan and fragmented integration under low involvement conditions do not improve any results after four to eight repetitions. These hypotheses were tested with the following dependent variables (see Table 4).

measured variables / measurement	verbal based measurement	non-verbal based measurement
memory recall	• brand recall • associations (thinking aloud)	• picture recall
memory recognition	• brand recognition • headline recognition • slogan recognition	• picture recognition

attitude (and buying intention)	• attitude towards the ad (scales)
	• overall attitude towards the ad
	• attitude towards the brand (scales)
	• overall attitude towards the brand
	• scale of buying intention
		awareness of memory pictures:
		• ease of evocation
		• vividness:
		    - Marks-Scale
		    - pictorial scales
		    - clearness scale

Table 4: Measured dependent variables, source: Esch, 1997

Attention will now be focused on the recall and recognition results, because they are important for the building of a clear brand schema. The „Württembergische Versicherung" will be used as an example, since the results of all brands were approximately the same.

4.2.2. Results

The retrieval of brand image related associations: The subjects were asked to say everything they associated with a brand. The integration of the key visuals produced the largest number of positive associations (Esch, 1997; see Table 5). The integration of the key visuals produced the most relevant associations for the brand image (see Figure 5).

Additionally that kind of integration produced the best memory for pictures. Furthermore the subjects had least confusion in assigning pictures to a brand.

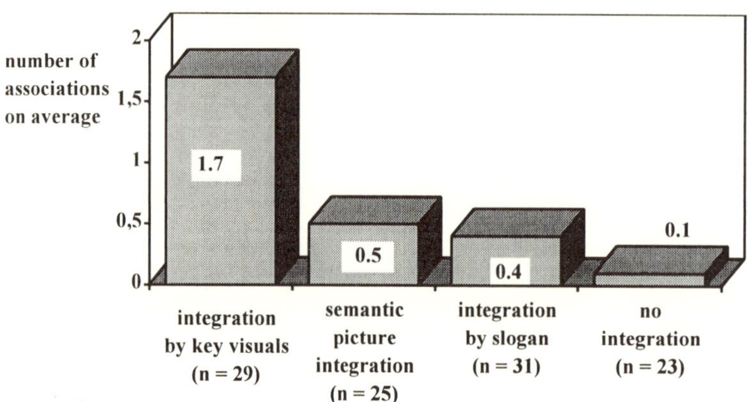

Figure 5: Brand image related associations for „Württembergische Versicherung", source: Esch, 1997

form of integration associations	integration by key visuals			integration by key visuals			integration by slogan			no integration		
	total	4 rep.	8 rep.	total	4 rep.	8 rep.	total	4 rep.	8 rep.	total	4 rep.	8 rep.
Number of associations	7.3 (4.0)	8.0 (4.8)	6.6 (3.1)	5.3 (3.8)	5.6 (3.6)	5.0 (4.2)	5.2 (4.6)	4.2 (3.2)	5.8 (5.3)	6.0 (4.3)	4.7 (3.7)	6.5 (4.6)
positive associations	3.3 (3.4)	4.1 (3.7)	2.6 (3.1)	1.8 (1.8)	1.8 (1.9)	1.8 (1.7)	1.6 (1.8)	1.2 (1.4)	1.9 (2.1)	2.8 (3.1)	1.3 (1.9)	3.5 (3.3)
negative associations	0.6 (0.9)	0.6 (1.0)	0.5 (0.8)	1.0 (1.3)	1.5 (1.6)	0.5 (0.7)	0.9 (1.4)	1.0 (1.5)	0.9 (1.4)	1.0 (1.5)	1.0 (1.4)	1.0 (1.5)
neutral associations	3.3 (2.7)	3.2 (2.7)	3.5 (2.8)	2.1 (2.1)	2.4 (1.9)	1.8 (2.3)	2.6 (3.4)	2.1 (1.8)	3.0 (4.2)	2.5 (2.6)	2.4 (2.1)	2.5 (2.8)
brand image related associations	1.7 (1.7)	1.4 (1.5)	1.9 (1.8)	0.5 (0.8)	0.6 (1.0)	0.4 (0.5)	0.4 (0.6)	0.3 (0.5)	0.4 (0.6)	0.1 (0.5)	0.0 (0.0)	0.2 (0.5)
n	29	14	15	25	13	12	30	12	18	23	7	16

Note: Mean and standard deviation (in brackets).

Tab. 5: Associations with „Württembergische Versicherung", source: Esch, 1997.

Key visual integration showed by far the best picture recall (see Figure 6). There was no confusion with pictorial motives from competitors whereas interference effects with competitors happened on other integration levels (semantic integration: 28 percent; verbal integration: 37.8 percent; fragmented communication: 21 percent).

There are similar results for the recognition of pictures, headlines and slogans (see figures 6 - 9). In all cases, even if the slogan was re-cognised, integration of key visuals was superior to other kinds of integration.

Associations with „Württembergische Versicherung"	form of integration (I)			source of variation number of repetitions (R)			interaction (I × R)			mistake (within and residual)	DF
	MS	F	Sign.	MS	F	Sign.	MS	F	Sign.	MS	
number of associations	31.8	1.8	0.16	3.2	0.2	0.68	16.4	0.9	0.44	18.1	104
positive associations	18.5	2.8	0.05	3.6	0.5	0.46	14.2	2.1	0.10	6.7	104
negative associations	1.2	0.7	0.53	2.4	1.5	0.23	1.1	0.7	0.57	1.6	104
neutral associations	7.3	0.9	0.44	0.6	0.1	0.79	2.5	0.3	0.82	8.0	104
brand image related associations	13.2	12.7	0.00	0.5	0.5	0.48	0.6	0.6	0.65	1.0	107

Note: Number of degree of freedom: form of integration (DF = 3); number of repetitions (DF = 1).

Table 6: Bi-factorial variance analysis of relations between associations, form of integration, and number of repetitions, source: Esch, 1997

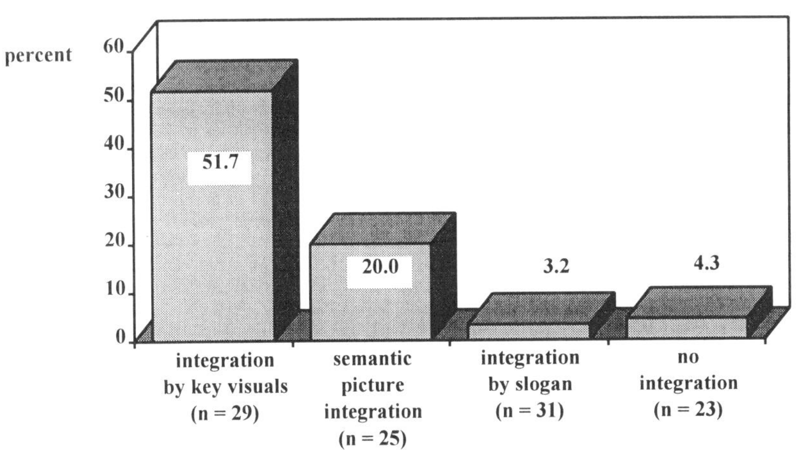

Note: Chi-square value according to Pearson: 28,8 (DF = 3; Sign. = 0,00); Cramer's V = 0,50.

Figure 6: Picture recall of „Württembergische Versicherung", source: Esch, 1997

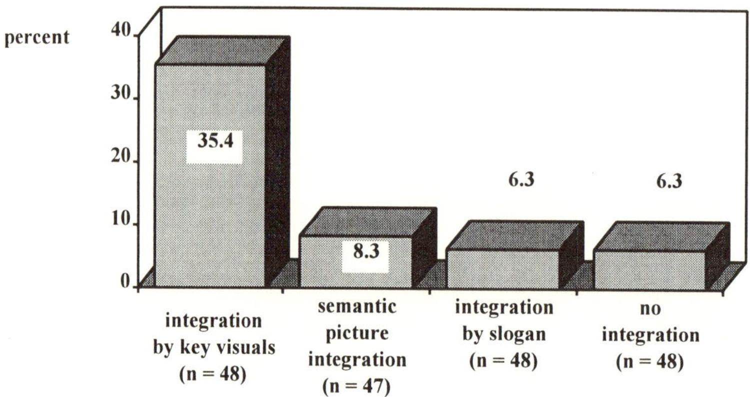

Note: Chi-square value according to Pearson: 24,3 (DF = 3; Sign. = 0,00); Cramer's V = 0,36

Figure 7: Picture recognition of „Württembergische Versicherung", source: Esch, 1997

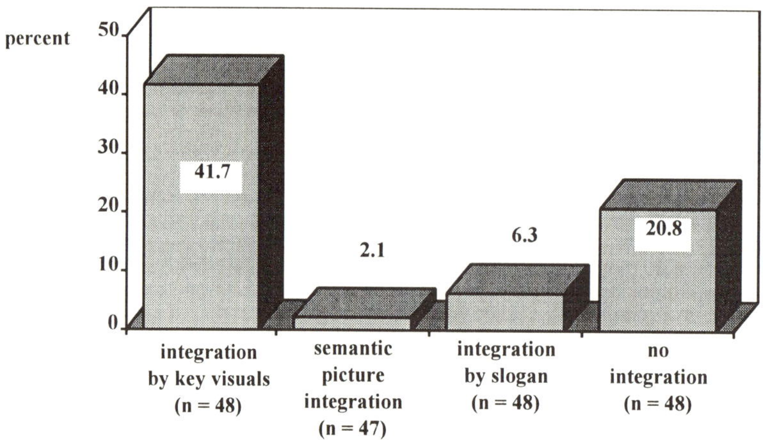

Note: Chi-square value according to Pearson: 31,6 (DF = 3; Sign. = 0,00); Cramer's V = 0,41

Figure 8: Headline recognition of „Württembergische Versicherung", source: Esch, 1997

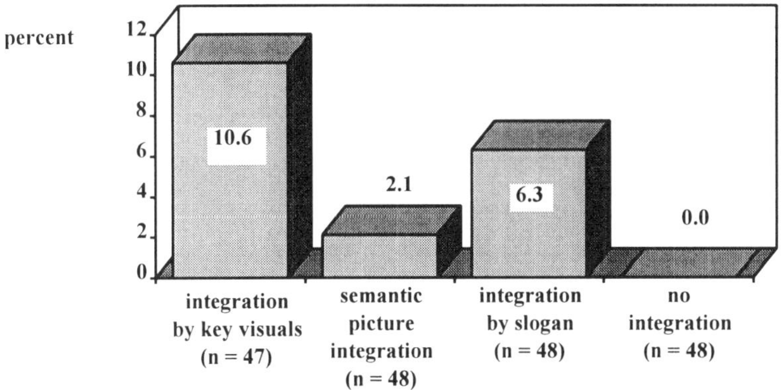

Note: In some categories there were not enough observations to implement a chi-square test.

Figure 9: Slogan recognition of „Württembergische Versicherung", source: Esch, 1997

In **conclusion** the results of the investigations show the superiority of integration by key visuals. The poor results of semantic integration are disappointing. However, the poor results of the integration by slogan in the case of low involvement are not surprising. Therefore, the integration by slogan in a low involvement situation seems to be no effective instrument of integration.

5. Outlook: Challenges for the Science and Practice of Marketing

The effects of communication integrated on different levels have been investigated and first results turned out. Further investigation has to be done in this field. Such research could refer to specific transfers of individually integrated instruments, examine the integration of short-termed tactical communication in an integrated concept, investigate the supporting effect of jingles in the field of verbal integration, analyse aspects on the point of sale or a harmonisation of communication with packaging as already partly checked by Keller (1987, 1991) in his experimental investigations. It will also be important to investigate the possibilities of integrated communication with regard to heterogeneous target groups with different information interests, since in this case target group specific and core brand information must be furnished. Interested researchers will find a large play ground of fascinating questions. Marketing in practice, however, must say farewell to a one-sided application of integration by slogan. This widespread normative preference for using verbal means of integration - based on the idea of rational consumers - cannot be seen as an effective way of integration any longer. In order to create clear brand schemata stronger means of integration - especially non verbal means - are necessary under the present low involvement communication conditions.

References

Abelson, R. P. (1981): Psychological Status of the Script Concept. In: American Psychologist, Vol. 36, pp. 715-729.

Alba, J. W. and Hasher, L. (1983): Is Memory Schematic? In: Psychological Bulletin, Vol. 93, pp. 201-231.

Anderson, J. R. (1989): Kognitive Psychologie. Eine Einführung, 2. ed. Spektrum der Wissenschaft Verlagsgesellschaft: Heidelberg.

Arbib, M. A., Conklin, E. J., and Hill, J. C. (1987): From Schema Theory to Language. Oxford University Press: New York, Oxford.

Baddeley, A. (1986): So denkt der Mensch. Unser Gedächtnis und wie es funktioniert. Droemer Knaur: München.

Bartlett, F. C. (1932): Remembering. Cambridge University Press: Cambridge.

Berelson, B. (1952): Content Analysis in Communication Research. Free Press: Glencoe.

Bruhn, M. and Zimmermann, A. (1993): Integrierte Kommunikationsarbeit in deutschen Unternehmen - Ergebnisse einer Unternehmensbefragung, Working paper No. 12. European Business School e. V., Schloß Reichartshausen: Rheingau.

Burke, R. R. and Srull, T. K. (1988): Competitive Interference and Consumer Memory for Advertising. In: Journal of Consumer Research, Vol. 15, pp. 55 68.

Duncan, T. R. and Everett, S. E. (1993): Client Perceptions of Integrated Marketing Communications. In: Journal of Advertising Research, Vol. 33, pp. 30-39.

Eco, U. (1991): Einführung in die Semiotik, 7. ed. UTB, Wilhelm Fink Verlag: München.

Esch, F.-R. (1993): Verhaltenswissenschaftliche Aspekte der integrierten Marketingkommunikation. In: Werbeforschung & Praxis, Vol. 38, pp. 20-28.

Esch, F.-R. (1995): Die Spur zum Konsumenten. Neue Erkenntnisse zur Durchgängigkeit der Werbung über Zeit und Medien. In: Bericht zum icon-Kongreß 1995, pp. 1-21.

Esch, F.-R. (1997): Marktreaktionen auf integrierte Kommunikation. Reihe Konsum und Verhalten, Physica-Verlag: Heidelberg (in print).

Esch, F.-R. and Andresen, Th. (1996): 10 Barrieren für eine erfolgreiche Markenpositionierung und Ansätze zu deren Überwindung. In: Tomczak, Th., Rudolph, Th., and Roosdorp, A. (Eds.), Positionierung - Kernentscheidung des Marketing. Thexis: St. Gallen.

Fiske, S. T. and Taylor, S. E. (1991): Social Cognition, 2 ed. (1 ed. 1984). McGraw-Hill: New York, St. Louis et al.

Fiske, S. T. and Pavelchak, E. (1986): Category-Based versus Piecemeal-Based Affective Responses. Developments in Schema-Triggered Affect. In: Sorrentino, R. M. and Higgins, T. E. (Eds.), The Handbook of Motivation and Cognition: Foundations of Social Behavior. Guilford Press: New York.

Friedman, L. (1979): Framing Pictures: The Role of Knowledge in Automized Encoding and Memory for Gist. In: Journal of Experimental Psychology: General, Vol. 108, pp. 316-355.

Jacoby, J. (1977): Information Load and Decision Quality: Some Contest Issues. In: Journal of Marketing Research, Vol. 14, pp. 569-573.

Kassarjian, H. H. (1977): Content Analysis in Consumer Research. In: Journal of Consumer Research, Vol. 4, pp. 8-18.

Keller, K. L. (1987): Memory Factors in Advertising: The Effect of Advertising Retrieval Cues on Brand Evaluations. In: Journal of Consumer Research, Vol. 14, pp. 316-333.

Keller, K. L. (1991): Cue Compatibility and Framing in Advertising. In: Journal of Marketing Research, Vol. 28, pp. 42-57.

Kroeber-Riel, W. (1987): Informationsüberlastung durch Massenmedien und Werbung in Deutschland. In: Die Betriebswirtschaft, Vol. 47, pp. 257-264.

Kroeber-Riel, W. (1993): Bildkommunikation. Vahlen: München.

Kroeber-Riel, W. (1994): Strategie und Technik der Werbung. Verhaltenswissenschaftliche Ansätze, 4. ed. Kohlhammer Verlag: Stuttgart, Berlin, Köln, Mainz.

Kroeber-Riel, W. and Weinberg, P. (1996): Konsumentenverhalten, 6. ed. Vahlen: München.

Krugman, H. E. (1965): The Impact of Television Advertising: Learning Without Involvement. In: Public Opinion Quarterly, Vol. 29, pp. 349-356.

Laurent, G. and Kapferer, J.-N. (1985): Measuring Consumer Involvement Profiles. In: Journal of Marketing Research, Vol. 22, pp. 41-53.

Lutz, K. A. and Lutz, R. J.(1977): Effects of Interactive Imagery on Learning: Application to Advertising. In: Journal of Applied Psychology, Vol. 62, pp. 493-498.

Morris, C. S. (1946): Signs, Language and Behavior. George Braziller Inc.: New York.

Neisser, U. (1976): Cognition and Reality: Principles and Implications of Cognitive Psychology. Freeman Press: San Francisco.

Paivio, A. (1971): Imagery and Verbal Processes. Holt, Rinehart & Winston: New York et al.

Paivio, A. (1986): Mental Representations, Oxford Psychology Series No. 9, Oxford University Press. New York, Clarendon Press: Oxford.

Pechmann, C. and Stewart D. W. (1989): Advertising Repetition: A Critical Review of Wearin and Wearout. In: Leigh, J. H. and Martin Jr., C. R. (Eds.), Current Issues & Research in Advertising. Reviews of Selected Areas, Vol. 11, No. 1 & 2, Division of Research, Graduate School of Business Administration, The University of Michigan: Ann Arbor, pp. 285-329.

Peirce, C. S. (1931-35): Collected Papers. Harvard University Press: Cambridge.

Ruge, H.-D. (1988): Die Messung bildhafter Konsumerlebnisse. Entwicklung und Test einer neuen Meßmethode. Reihe Konsum und Verhalten, Bd. 16, Physica-Verlag: Heidelberg.

Rumelhart, D. E. (1980): Schemata: The Building Blocks of Cognition. In: Spiro, R. J., Bruce, B. C., and Brewer, W. F. (Eds.), Theoretical Issues in Reading Comprehension: Perspectives from Cognitive Psychology, Linguistics, Artificial Intelligence, and Education. Lawrence Erlbaum Ass.: Hillsdale, NJ., pp. 33-58.

Saussure, F. de (1916): Cours de linguistique générale. Payot: Paris.

Shimp, T. A., DeLozier, M. W. (1986): Promotion Management and Marketing Communications. Dryden Press: Chicago.

Schultz, D. E., Tannenbaum, S. I., and Lauterborn R. F. (1994): Integrated Marketing Communications. NTC Business Books, Lincolnwood: Chicago, Ill.

Schumann, D. W., Petty, R. E., and Clemons, D. S. (1990): Predicting the Effectiveness of Different Strategies of Advertising Variation: A Test of the Repetition-Variation Hypotheses. In: Journal of Consumer Research, Vol. 17, pp. 192-202.

Smith, R. A. and Houston, M. J. (1985): A Psychometric Assessment of Measures of Scripts in Consumer Memory. In: Journal of Consumer Research, Vol. 12, pp. 214-224.

Taylor, S. E., Crocker, J., Fiske, S. T., Sprinzen, M., and Winkler, J. D. (1979): The Generalizability of Salience Effects. In: Journal of Personality and Social Psychology, Vol. 37, pp. 357-368.

Taylor, S. E. and Crocker, J. (1981): Schematic Bases of Social Information Processing. In: Higgins, E. T., Herman, C. P., nd Zanna, M. P. (Eds.), pp. 89-135.

Underwood, B. J. (1957): Interference and Forgetting. In: Psychological Review, Vol. 64, pp. 40-60.

Wells, W., Burnett, J., and Moriarty, S. (1989): Advertising, Principles and Practice. Prentice-Hall: Englewood Cliffs, NJ.

Zaichkowsky, J. L. (1985): Measuring the Involvement Construct. In: Journal of Consumer Research, Vol. 12, pp. 341-352.

Marie-Laure Gavard-Perret and Jean Moscarola

Lexical Analysis: A Method for Understanding „What is said" and „How it is said" in Marketing Messages

1. Introduction

2. Descriptive Lexical Analysis: Recognition of the Utterances
    2.1. Statistical Characterisation of a Corpus and Lexis
    2.2. Lexical Approximation
    2.3. Lexical Navigation

3. Interpretive Lexical Analysis: Discovering the Models of Enunciation
    3.1. Speech Acts and the Characteristics of the Enunciation
    3.2. Speech Acts: Specificities and Lexical Intensities
    3.3. Speech Acts: Models of Enunciation
    3.4. Speech Acts and Associations

4. Conclusion

References

Lexical Analysis: A Method for Understanding „What is said" and „How it is said" in Marketing Messages

Marie-Laure Gavard-Perret and Jean Moscarola

Abstract

The authors consider that there are two possiblities to use textual statistics. They develop a differentiation between the content of the message or „what the message says", in other words the utterance, and the enunciation of the message or „how it is formulated". The lexical analysis is useful firstly to discover quickly the contents and secondly to recognize the models of enunciation and to understand the utterer of the message (the one who expresses the message). They use examples[1] in order to illustrate this new reading of lexical analysis.

1. Introduction

Marketing has helped to make information an essential resource for understanding the consumer, for comparing oneself with the competition, establishing clear marketing orientation (product conception, positioning etc.), for choosing and publishing adequate messages for the various publics of an organisation, for checking the efficiency and relevance of the means used. This information unfortunately forms a very disparate, heterogenous mass of data: answers to open-ended questions, contents of interviews, company documents, advertising messages, journalistic glosses etc. However, one common factor unites this colossal mass of information and turns it into a gold-mine: the will to organize, classify and categorize, to bring out the similarities and differences, to compare them to the intentions of the communication and the expectations of the target audience, in order to identify the sense and estimate its relevance.

Statistical tools can, in this case, reveal their great utility in forming an efficient aid in the discovery of textual corpuses, in the categorisation and the relating of the lexical elements with each other or with external contextual data. However, it is necessary to make good use of the method and for that, to distinguish between two levels of possible use, still too often con-

---

[1] All the data in the examples quoted in this document have been processed with the SPHINX Plus software.

fused. Lexical analysis founded on an ensemble of more or less elaborated textual statistics, can in fact serve two different objectives:

- the discovery of utterances and

- the recognition of models of enunciation.

Indeed all communication can be approached from the point of view of its contents and its constituent characteritics (the utterance) or, more complicated and further along the road to interpretation, from the point of view of the personal adaptation that every individual, consciously or unconsciously, brings to the linguistic tool (the enunciation).

Therefore, the developments below will be centered firstly on lexical statistics as tools for the description of utterances (which Hetzel and Marion, 1992 call the content) and secondly will show the usefulness of lexical analysis to discover models of enunciations(which the same authors call „ways of delivering the content"). The interest of both is obviously to lead to a more rigourous interpretative reading and a more argued commentary.

2. Descriptive Lexical Analysis: Recognition of the Utterances

Descriptive lexical analysis can, in fact, be seen as a macro-analysis of the corpus. The researcher focusses his attention on the sense of the surface as it emerges from a reading of the elementary corpus in its integrality. Lexical analysis thus leads us firstly to a„destructuration" of a corpus in order to „break the apparent structure of language and number the elements" (Chaniac, 1980). The first linguistic units considered are the graphic forms (contiguous alphanumeric characters[2]).

2.1. Statistical Characterisation of a Corpus and Lexis

The first calculable element of the corpus is its **size**, i.e. the total number of its graphic forms, which gives a first indication of the volume of the text to be studied (see Table 1).Another interesting element characterizes the studied corpus: the **richness** of its lexis which is expressed by the ratio between the number of different graphic forms and the total number of graphic forms (see Table 1). The more a corpus contains distinct linguistic forms, the more it

---

[2] A graphic form, in computer language, corresponds to a sub-group of the text which does not contain a separator, for example, gaps, hyphens, brackets, or punctuation marks.

can be considered as „rich". This operation of computerized counting of different graphic forms can be applied to a reduced lexis (full words only) or to the total lexis (including grammatical words). It is linked to a third notion, the average **repetition** of graphic forms in the corpus. Richness and repetition can considerably vary between differentiated corpuses (see Table 1):

1) corpus „discourses" with scientific summaries of the meeting of the *Association Française du Marketing* (Bourgel, Moscarola, and Thieblemont, 1992), propositions of *Bush* and *Clinton* during the American Presidential Elections in 1993 and non-directive interviews realised on the theme of waiting for public transport (Durrande-Moreau,1994);

2) corpus „sentences" with ads for cars in English (Gavard-Perret, Domenjoz, and Moscarola, 1995); and

3) corpus „words" with words association on the salesperson in general and the ideal salesperson (Ganassali and Moscarola, 1994) or on athletes and brand-names linked to sport (Ganassali, 1993).

Example	Nb.Obs	Total Size	Richness	Repetit°	Reduced corpus	Reduced lexis	Repetit°
Corpus discours							
Scientific summaries	90	10352	2378	4,35	5208	2220	2,35
Positions Bush Clinton	18	27704	3853	7,19	17508	3714	4,71
Non directives interviews	10	59282	3626	16,35	22893	3417	6,70
Corpus phrases							
Car advertisements	52	10158	2472	4,11	5872	2331	2,52
Corpus words							
Salesperson in a few word	370	1454	460	3,16	1171	401	2,92
Ideal salesperson	370	2121	485	4,37	1487	420	3,54
Adjectives: athletes	43	195	98	1,99	191	95	2,01
Adjectives: brand names	43	158	114	1,39	150	107	1,4

Table 1: Statistical characterisation of a textual corpus

These first statistical elements concerning a corpus and its lexis allow to characterise and quantify them but do not really give access to the sense of the corpus. To access the contents of the corpus (to its utterance), the researcher can use different techniques each having the function of approaching a text by its lexis. Hence the choice of the term „lexical approximation".

2.2. Lexical Approximation

2.2.1. Graphic Forms: Frequency and Lexicality

Computing allow us to construct, quickly and automatically, from a given text a list of all the elementary graphic forms. This process gives an accelerated reading of the corpus, an examination of the lexis as a tool of knowledge of the text as a whole thus similar to a knowledge of the text through its key-words, summary, or index.

Full lexis		Reduced lexis after suppression of tool-words	
The	571 (occurences)	car	71 (occurences)
a	282	new	58
of	249	but	48
to	220	more	40
and	214	engine	34
you	156	free	32
in	132	safety	30
is	120	only	25
it	108	drive	22
for	107	road	21
with	102	system	21
as	76	than	21
that	74	power	19
we	73	year	19
all	72	doors	18
car	71	range	18
on	67	years	17
at	62	air	16
be	59	cars	14
new	58	door	14

Table 2: Lexis of advertising copies

For example 55 ads for cars in English were reduced by Gavard-Perret, Domenjoz and Moscarola (1995) to the 20 most frequently encountered graphic forms. They brought an instructive approach to the original corpus (Table 2). We can see a discourse largely articulated around „you" and „we", on „cars" which offer „ all" and especially „novelty".

It is possible to accelerate the reading of the lexis and the identification of the most characteristic graphic forms by eliminating „tool-words". These grammatical words (articles, conjunctions etc.) can usually be removed without changing the general sense of the message, a sense given more especially by the „full-words". Thus the height of the lexis reduced to its full-words highlights the leitmotivs of car ads: „new", „free", „more", „safety", „power", among others.

It can also be interesting to estimate the weight of the full-words in the interior of the corpus by using an index of **lexicality**: the number of appearances of full-words/total number of words. In the case of the advertisements for cars the lexicality is of more than one full-word, on average for two words of the corpus considered (58%), whereas in the corpus of non-directive interviews on waiting for public transport, it falls to 38% only.

2.2.2. Homonymie / Polysemie: Lemmatisation, Correspondances, and Environment

By their very nature, languages contain great ambiguities and an approximation of the content of a text simply by its elementary graphic forms, by neglecting the rules of syntax and an examination of the lexical context, risks leading us into contradictions or an absence of clarity in the exact meaning carried by the words. Hence the necessity of approaching more normal reading conditions through a study of wider and more complete **units of meaning:** a sentence, an advertising claim, the complete answer to an open-ended question etc.

In fact, a uniquely defined word can bring divergent appreciations, and hence meanings, according to the context used and its immediate **lexical environment**. For example the examination of an open-ended question concerning the butchery department of a hypermarket revealed a frequent usage of the word „big", an adjective, a priori, without any semantic ambiguity. However, the association of the word „big" with other words caused the meaning and subsequent analysis to considerably vary. Linked to the word „slice", in only 5 cases was this adjective associated with „not enough" and in all other cases with „too much".

For in the present state of the language industries, syntactical analysers allow us to solve correctly ambiguities linked to syntax. By applying the rules of grammar to a sentence and its propositions, we can, in most cases, distinguish between verbs, nouns and adjectives and substitute their canonic form (singular of a noun, infinitive of a verb etc.). We can also identify compound words and locutions. This examination of a text is called **lemmatisation** (see Table 3).

In the example below, there is no longer any ambiguity possible between „ plant", a verb and „plant", a noun which after lemmatisation are clearly identified as „verb" (v) and „noun" (n).

Corpus and lexis	Corpus and lexis after lemmatisation
The gardener planted the green plant with his garden tools on the green outside the plant where he always plants plants	gardener_n, to_plant _v, green_a, plant_n, garden_tool _n, green _n, outside_g, plant _n, always_g, to_plant _v, plant_n.
Plant (2), plants (2), planted, green (2), garden, tool, the (4), gardener, where, he, always, outside, with, his.	plant_n (3), to_plant_v (2), gardener, garden_tool, green_n, green_a, always, outside

Table 3: Lemmatisation

As lexical analysis is also enriched by techniques of factorial analysis of correspondances, it is extremely simple nowadays to visualise the table of lexical contingency and to show the **correspondances** or proximity between the units of meaning by means of mappings (Figure 1).

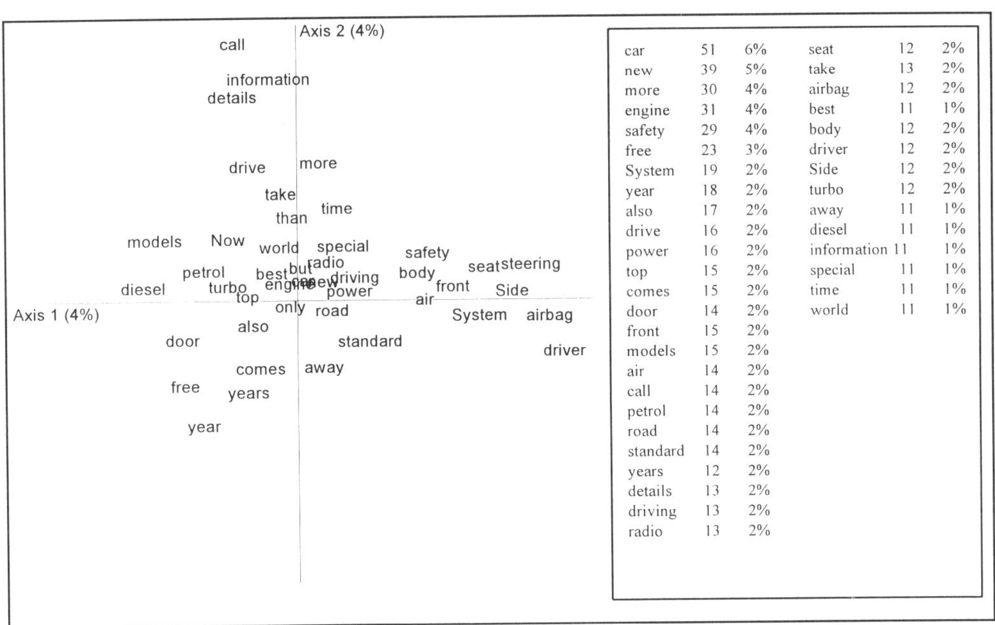

car	51	6%	seat	12	2%
new	39	5%	take	13	2%
more	30	4%	airbag	12	2%
engine	31	4%	best	11	1%
safety	29	4%	body	12	2%
free	23	3%	driver	12	2%
System	19	2%	Side	12	2%
year	18	2%	turbo	12	2%
also	17	2%	away	11	1%
drive	16	2%	diesel	11	1%
power	16	2%	information	11	1%
top	15	2%	special	11	1%
comes	15	2%	time	11	1%
door	14	2%	world	11	1%
front	15	2%			
models	15	2%			
air	14	2%			
call	14	2%			
petrol	14	2%			
road	14	2%			
standard	14	2%			
years	12	2%			
details	13	2%			
driving	13	2%			
radio	13	2%			

Figure 1: Factorial chart - Word associations

The lexical map above (Figure 1) is obtained from a multiple factorial chart based on the corpus of the car advertisements. This analysis brings to light the structure of associations existing between the 46 full-words most frequently repeated (more than 11 times).

119

2.2.3. Lexes: Contextualisation and Categorisation

This contextual data is even more important as the textual material studied comes from many sources. This is the case for example in the collection of car advertisements. Each ad, in order to have a sense and a representative value, must be characterised by the name of the advertiser, for example. In the case of interviews or questionnaire enquiries, the socio-demographic identity of the respondent, his behaviour or opinion, observed with traditional variables, help to grasp the sense of his answers to open-ended questions and to categorise them. Figure 2, a factorial chart of the contingency of the most frequent terms with the brands, brings out from the car advertisements the advertising characteristics of each make. For example for „Mercedes", we find „new" and „world" - in other words the slogan of the make.

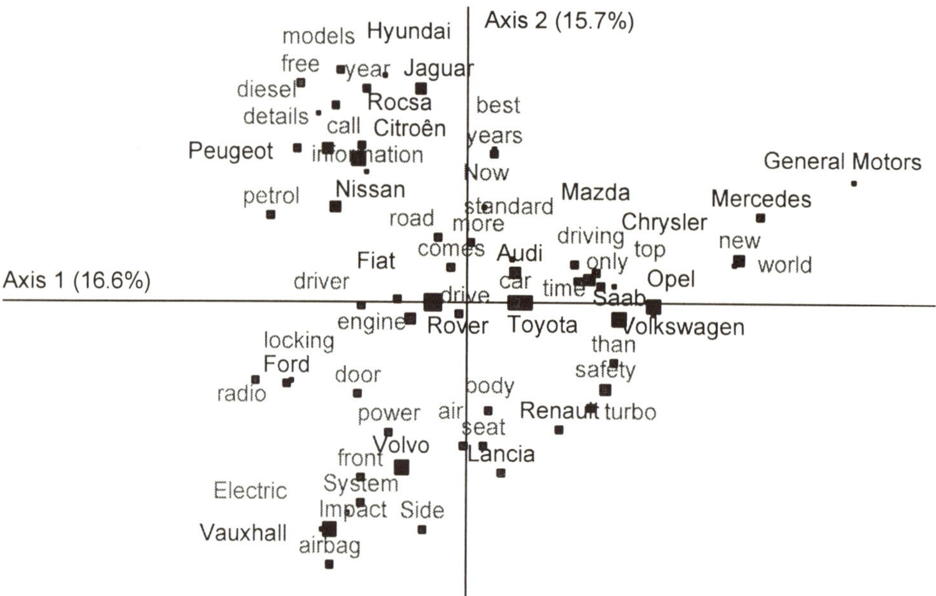

Figure 2: Factorial chart of the most frequent words

However, lexical statistics can never lead to more than an approximation of the text through its lexis. For this reason it is sometimes necessary to return to the text.

2.3. Lexical Navigation

In fact, whatever the efficiency of lexical reductions, of revealing the evidence of structures of proximity between graphic forms, or the taking into account of relative environments, the return to the text is indispensible in lexical analysis to raise certain possible equivocations or to illustrate the analysis of the original material. Lexical navigation allows us quickly and easily to look for a text corresponding to a chosen lexical input, to read it for rediscovering the real sense and the context of the exact use of a word and to annotate it if necessary.

As we have presented it so far, lexical analysis serves on the one hand to list and quantify a corpus and its lexical elements and on the other hand to contribute to an approximation of the sense of the texts through their lexes. It has the advantage of helping both the work of revealing the corpus through an automation of a part of its reading, thus similar to a kind of rapid reading articulated around the key or principal word (Richaudeau, 1984) and the work of quantifying the textual data. In this way, descriptive lexical analysis or the lexical analysis of utterances provides an opportunity for an accelerated research and description of the content and more especially one that is more systematic and hence more objective.

However, a simple description or quantification of lexical elements quickly becomes sterile if it is not completed by a willingness to understand the meaning and origins of the frequencies, the textual structures, associations, or lexical categories. Analysis must become the privileged support of interpretation. As Foucault (1966) says „to comment is to admit, by definition, an excess of the signified over the signifying". It should also allow us to find, in the signifying, the traces of the utterer or the circumstances of the utterance. From a „macro-analysis" of a communication, the researcher is going to move to a kind of„micro-analysis" of lexical decisions or speech acts. Why this word rather than another? His studies will be directed onto a fact clearly underlined by Morin (1991), „Man speaks a language that speaks him".

One preoccupation of lexical analysis is to reveal what is hidden behind the word. No longer considered for its semantic content but for its capacity to translate the interior mechanisms specific to the utterer or the intentions dependent on the conditions of the enunciation, the word has more than a superficial value. We move from an analysis of the content in „Berelsonian" style to an analysis which gives more value to inference (Bardin, 1993).

3. Interpretive Lexical Analysis: Discovering the Models of Enunciation

Statistical reasoning applied to texts led Muller (1979; 1993), the founder of lexical statistics, to consider the choice of words as the result of a decision. This decision can be characterized by the frequency with which each word appears in the corpus. In fact, if there were no choice, the appearance of each of the words of the vocabulary used would be of equal probability. We can thus reveal the words which significantly appear more or less frequently than the average repetition. This leads to a revelation of certain characteristics of the enunciation.

3.1. Speech Acts and the Characteristics of the Enunciation

The main lexical measures represent the first indicators of speech acts. From an analysis of the corpus made up of *Bush - Clinton* propositions during the American Presidential election campaign (Table 4), it is striking to see that these messages, each having the same objective and forming together a corpus of equivalent length, do not carry identical features of enunciation. The length of the text devoted to each position varies sensibly between the two candidates. *Bush* develops a much longer argument on agriculture whereas *Clinton* enlarges upon crime. They both come together again to give their largest arguments to small companies.

Position on:	Bush	Clinton
Agriculture	2407	673
Aids	478	1227
Abortion	903	460
Crime	888	2288
Education	867	353
Environment	1676	3867
Health	2948	739
Immigration	686	915
Small business	3171	3229
Total	14024	13751

Table 4: Corpus length of Bush's and Clinton's positions

These global indicators give signs of the relative interest of each theme for the candidates. These differences are sufficiently important to be able to speak already of a certain positioning, desired or not (?), in the discourse. Other measurements could also be made of modes of enunciations: the number and average length of sentences, the longest and shortest sentence, etc.

This highlighting can be refined by considering the richness of the vocabulary (number of graphic forms used) and the degree of repetition (Size/Richness). Table 5 below allows a comparison of the enunciation of the two candidates. Neither the richness of their vocabulary, nor its degree of repetition allows really to distinguish between *Bush* and *Clinton*. Their discourses are fairly repetitive, much more, by the way, than the discourse of car ads!

	Corpus size	Lexis richness	Repetition	Repetition without tool words
Car advertising	10158	2472	4,11	2,7
Bush	14024	2669	5,25	3,54
Clinton	13751	2696	5,10	3,07

Table 5: Lexical rates relative to characteristics of the enunciation

3.2. Speech Acts: Specificities and Lexical Intensities

Specificities and lexical intensities contribute also to a better understanding of the enunciation.

3.2.1. Lexical Specificity

Specificity characterises the decision, voluntary or involuntary, to choose one word rather another. Muller (1979) proposes to establish it from a comparison between the theoretical frequency, based on the equiprobability of the appearance of the word and its actual frequency. Let us illustrate this with the positions of *Bush* and *Clinton* in the Presidential Elections.

The height of the lexis proper to each candidate (Table 6) supplies an overview of the speech acts of the two political leaders. In order to concentrate on the informative content, the examination has been limited to the graphic forms (without tool-words) present more than 15 times.

At first glance, Table 6 shows that „President" comes at the top of the list. This is obviously the result of the common communication context imposed on both candidates: the nature of the elections. In other places, considerable differences are revealed. „People" frequently quoted by *Clinton* (55 times) is not used as frequently by *Bush* (6 times). Conversely *Bush* overemploys „plan" (63 times) while *Clinton* underemploys it (9 times).

It is necessary however to go beyond this first evidence, for it could be misleading, as the size of the corpuses has been ignored. The lexical specificity makes clear the fact of accentuating (+) or neglecting (-) the use of a particular form (a chi-square test estimates the gap).

Bush		Clinton		Bush		Clinton	
President	229+	I	104+++	reform	31	education	27
Bush	114+	President	89--	reduce	28	government	24
care	72	American	57+	farmers	27	billion	23-
plan	63+	people	55++	American	24--	state	21
billion	60+	business	46	help	22	insurance	19+
insurance	58+	Bush	45-	environmental	20	help	19
tax	51	care	42	State	20	Increase	18
million	50++	want	41+++	education	19	plan	16--
costs	48++	Clinton	37	aids	16-	pay	15
year	44	environmental	36+	America	13--	million	14-
percent	42++	tax	35	years	10	costs	14-
business	41	growth	35	I	9-	reduce	13
Administrat°	41++	aids	35++	people	6---	percent	10 --
Americans	33	years	30++	want	1---	reform	10--
programs	32	America	28+	*Total Bush*	*9266*	*Total Clinton*	*8253*

Table 6: Frequencies and lexical specificities according to the candidates

For example, Bush uses the word „President" much more than a proportionality calculation would have predicted. „President" clearly belongs to a specific lexicality of *Bush*, as do „administration", „billion", „costs". Conversely, *Clinton* underuses these terms and has a positive specificity for the terms „I", „want", „American" and „people".

These lexical specificities usefully complete the notion of lexes by categories discussed in the section „Approximation" and enable us to compose veritable specific lexes, to compare them and to identify at the same time both the common features and the divergences.

This is very useful for marketing, which supposes either adjustments or adaptations, some of them verbal, to the multiple segments of its clientele or, on the contrary, the willingness to find the common denominator between several clienteles or markets, notably within a policy of standardisation or globalisation. Advertising campaigns, sales arguments, direct marketing operations, products or brand-names represent direct and obvious areas for such analysis.

3.2.2. Lexical Intensities

The notion of lexical intensity can be applied to a particular lexical category (personal pronouns, possessive adjectives) or to a thematic lexical field. In the following example (Table

7), we calculate the ratio between the number of graphic forms relative to a given lexical field and the total number of forms. Table 7 recapitulates the lexical intensity of some personal pronouns:

The Interlocutors	Bush	Clinton	Together
I, my	0.08	**0.83**	0,46
We, our	0.23	**1.86**	0,47
You, your	0,01	0,47	0,24

Table 7: Lexical intensity of „interlocutors"

The personal pronouns underline significant differences in the mode of dialogue established between the candidate and his potential electors. *Clinton* personalizes his discourse and implicates his listeners by using „we" and „our" much more than *Bush*. *Bush* stays more impersonal and clearly shows his status of „President" through the vocabulary employed.

These steps again have numerous possible applications in marketing both to find the preferences or dislikes of a group of consumers, the positionings and images of products and brands and to analyse letters of complaint, for example. It is therefore essential to easily visualise the positions of the different segments according to their respective discourses.

3.3. Speech Acts: Models of Enunciation

The enunciation is characterised mainly by the choice of personal pronouns which show the position of the utterer in relation to his utterance or to the receiver. Table 8 below operates an examination of the lexis of personal pronouns, which reveals 4 styles of discourse:

- ads choose an interactive interpellation of the receiver and the „*You / We*" is clearly stated.
- French scientific communications accentuate their objectivity by an absence of „*I*" and the choice of a normative agreed and largely impersonal discourse.
- the non-directive interviews on waiting for public transport confirm the clear engagement of the subject in his answers and lead us to think that these interviews were successful, if we accept the strong implication of the individuals questioned through their use of „I".
- the positions of *Bush* and *Clinton* show the same interpellations as the advertisements (we/you). However the terms of this interpellation are reversed. While the ads implicate directly and personally the receiver through „you", the political communication privileges the

entire collectivity in advancing the utterer „we". The associative „ we" of the politician is contrasted to the involving „you" of the adman (Cotteret, 1986).

Car Ads (10 079 words)		Scientific summaries (27704 words)		Clinton and Bush (27704 words)		Non-directive interviews (59 282 words)	
you	156	il	40	we	182	Je	1636
it	108	nous	28	our	136	il	873
We	73	elle	21	their	125	j	817
our	37	on	16	I	113	vous	748
Your	35	celui	10	it	98	on	709
They	18	Elles	8	you	68	tu	260
their	5	ceux	7	They	42	ils	235
I	3	ils	5	He	39	elle	143
		celle	4	your	12	nous	57
		celles	2	she	1	Elles	39

Table 8: Pronouns and enunciation patterns

3.4. Speech Acts and Associations

The enunciation can also be seen as guided by mental models revealed by association of terms. A survey carried out on 46 students in 1992 about the efficiency of sponsoring in sport illustrates well this lexical exploitation. The 5 questions - organized on the basis of a word association test - leads the interviewee to connect two strata of his immediate memory, that of sport and that of brand names (inclusive of all sectors) and the lexical fields linked to them:

1) *If you hear the word „athlete", which names of great athletes spontaneously spring to mind.*
2) *Quote 5 adjectives which spring to mind to qualify high level athletes.*
3) *Quote 5 verbs which spring to mind to qualify high level athletes.*
4) *Quote 5 brand names which are linked to sport in your mind.*
5) *Quote 5 adjectives which best characterise the brand names you have just quoted.*

The map below (Figure 3) clearly shows the existence of associations (questions 1 and 4) reflected by the enunciations which can be taken as revealing connections operated by the interviewees.

So we can see the associations connecting brand names to athletes with a logic of sport (skiers / „ski-brands") or of sponsorings. This does not mean that these associations are correct but they reveal mental connections. Killy, Picard with Salomon? Papin, Jordan with Nike, Adidas or Puma? Some sponsors would ask themselves a few questions.

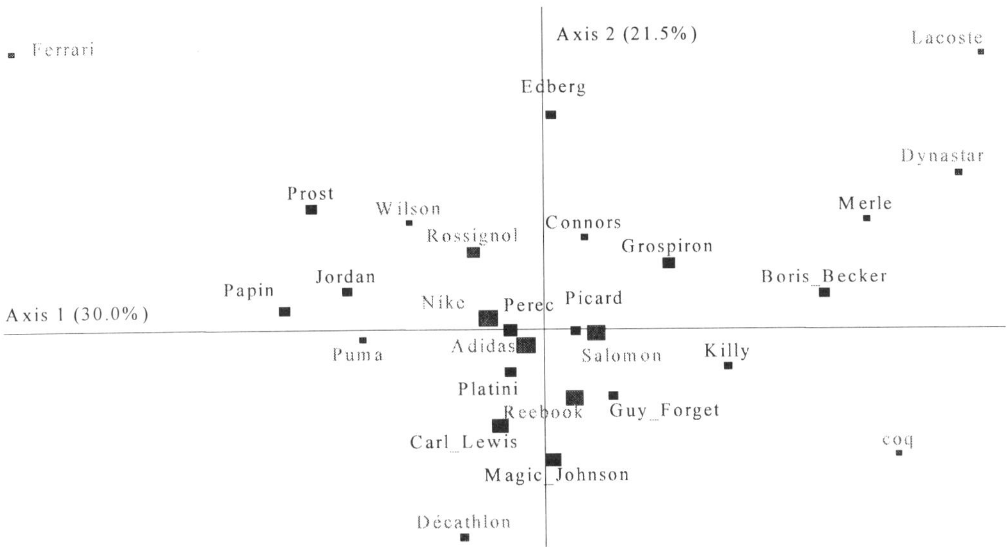

Figure 3: Factorial chart athlets / brand names

Lexical intensities also allow us to characterise the messages that the image of an athlete helps to communicate. To do this we define 4 lexical fields built from the answers to question 3 (see Table 9).

Each field - with the words all refering to a same idea - evokes a different message carried by the athlete and which a brand would like to communicate. Is it possible to reveal the specialisation of the image of an athlete in relation to each of these fields? We then calculated the average value of the intensity of each field in each sub-group of the interviewees who quoted one or another athlete (se Table 9).This data was then analysed through a factorial chart (see Figure 4).

	to train	to fight	to win	to gain
Carl_Lewis	12.39	5.00	9.00	3.27
Magic_Johnson	12.43	8.11	3.94	2.50
Boris_Becker	29.90	10.00	2.86	4.00
Grospiron	19.33	11.83	8.10	8.10
Papin	14.64	15.07	11.43	4.23
Platini	13.89	13.49	0.00	9.52
Prost	14.76	4.23	1.67	6.30
Edberg	22.14	2.86	6.67	0.00
Picard	13.89	0.00	2.22	0.00
#Guy_Forget	11.11	6.94	2.78	0.00
Jordan	8.33	0.00	0.00	10.42
#Perec	15.85	12.38	5.51	3.47
Connors	16.67	4.76	0.00	14.29
Killy	8.33	13.89	2.78	8.33
Merle	39.29	0.00	4.76	0.00
TOTAL	17.42	7.52	5.16	4.62

Table 9: Lexical intensity of lexical fields / athlets

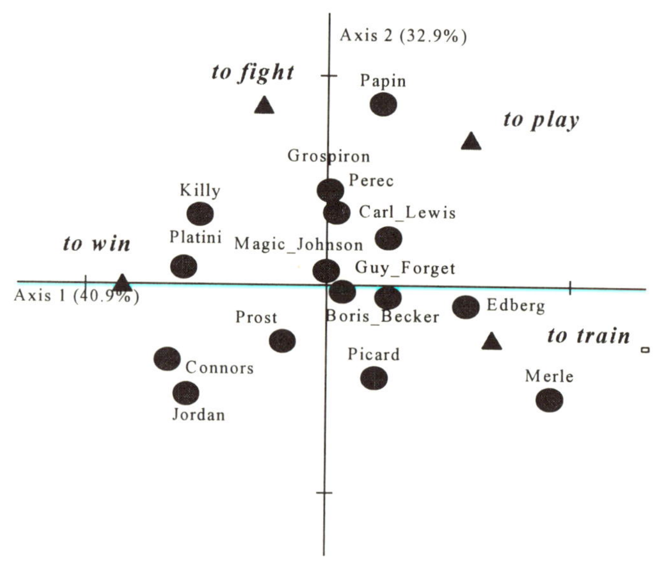

Figure 4: Factorial chart (component analysis) lexical fields / athlets

It does not seem unreasonable to deduce, for example, that a brand name needing to communicate around a positioning and image of combativity would do better to choose Grospiron, Papin or Killy to express this quality than Merle. The image of a company as a winner would also be carried better by an athlete like Platini or Killy than Merle. The practical implications in marketing of similar methods are immense: advertising communications, sponsoring, research for positioning, creation and control of the image and the positioning, etc.

4. Conclusion

The re-reading of lexical statistics which we have just carried out shows clearly the usefulness of such analysis in marketing. Indeed, from the moment when, on the one hand, „language, the tool of communication (a trivial idea) is operated as a strategic instrument (a recent idea)" (Peninou, 1986) and when it must not be, on the other hand, considered as a „simple means of communication, but the expression of a mind and a conception of a world of the speaking subjects" (Humboldt, 1969), it becomes indispensible to analyse language minutely, as much in its simplest utterance as in its most complex enunciation. Only in doing so, it will give to decision makers and marketing experts the means of both improving the efficiency of their communication and being better at listening to the organisation's publics.

These perspectives demonstrate the interest in the methods and tools of lexical analysis. Consequently, more and more efficient techniques of lexical approximation and of capturing and reading the utterances will have to respond to the abundance of lexical material. They will also have to give access to a systematic management of the available information: to calculate, observe, summarise, and synthesise. This is the first level of the contribution of lexical statistics.

But beyond that, they can lead to a deeper understanding of the behavioural mechanisms by looking at the remarkable structures revealed by the enunciation. As Foucault (1966) so aptly said: „We must question the words we speak, denounce the grammatical track of our ideas, dissipate the myths that animate our words and render once again noisy and audible that part of silence that each discourse brings with it when it is uttered (...) to turn words upside down and see everything that is said through and in spite of them".

References

Bardin, L. (1993): L'Analyse de Contenu. PUF: Paris.

Bourgel, G., Moscarola, J., and Thieblemont, R. (1992): 7 Ans de Communications aux Congrès de l'AFM. In: Actes du Congrès de l'Association Française du Marketing, Vol. 8, Lyon.

Chaniac, A. (1980): L'Analyse Lexicologique: Principes et Applications à la Communication Publicitaire. In: Cahier de l'IREP, June, pp. 257-268.

Cotteret, J.M. (1986): Comment Parler le Language de vos Clients? In: Revue Française du Marketing, Vol. 109, No. 4, pp. 47-54.

Durrande-Moreau, A. (1994): Qualité de Service et Perception du Temps: L'Attente propositions Théoriques et Étude Emipirique. Doctoral Thesis, University de Grenoble II.

Foucault, M. (1966): Les Mots et les Choses. Gallimard.

Ganassali, S. (1993): Le Transfert comme Principe Central du. Unpublished working paper of the IUP, Annecy.

Ganassali, S. and Moscarola, J. (1994): La Vente et les Vendeurs. Unpublished working paper of the IUP, Annecy.

Gavard-Perret, M.-L., Domenjoz, P., and Moscarola, J. (1995): Le Texte et L'Image dans la Publicité Automobile. In: 11th Congress of the Association Française du Marketing.

Hetzel, P. and Marion, G. (1992): Les Contributions Françaises de la Sémiotique au Marketing et à la Publicité Automobile. In: 11th Congress of the Association Française du Marketing.

Humboldt, G. de (1969): De l'Origine des Formes Grammaticales. Bordeaux.

Morin, E. (1991): La Méthode. Vol. 4: Les Idées. Seuil: Paris.

Muller, C. (1979): Langue Française et Linguistique Quantitative. Edition Slatkine.

Muller, C. (1993): Principes et Méthodes de Statistique Lexicale. Champion: Genève.

Peninou, G. (1986): Langage et Marketing. In: Revue Française du Marketing, Vol. 109, No. 4, pp. 5-10.

Richaudeau, F. (1984): Méthode de Lecture Rapide. Retz: Paris.

Eric Vernette

Measuring Affect or Emotion toward a Brand with a Smiling Faces Scale

1. Introduction
2. A Smiling Face Scale for Affect Measurement
   2.1. Affect, Emotion and Mood
   2.2. Measuring Affect and Emotions with Faces
   2.3. Smiling Face Potential
3. Methodology
   3.1. Scale Calibration and Face Selection
   3.2. Sampling
4. Results and Discussion
   4.1. Mean Scores for Occupational Status
   4.2. Faces Rating according to Sex and Age
5. Implications and Suggestions
   5.1. Choice of Style
   5.2. Selecting Scale Anchor Points
6. Limitations and Conclusions
References

Measuring Affect or Emotion toward a Brand with a Smiling Face Scale[1]

Eric Vernette

Abstract

The rise of affect and emotion research has been significantly perceivable in consumer research literature during the last years. But, despite this increasing interest, there are very few publications in the area of measurement development for these concepts. This paper aims to verify the methodological qualities of two different smiling face scales, especially interval properties and robustness. The results show that it is possible to construct a quasi-interval scale, with 5 faces used as anchor points; moreover, these faces have no statistically significant differences of perception according to sex, age or social class.

1. Introduction

The role and the influence of affect in consumer behaviour are now clearly established and emphasised in the literature, especially in North-American handbooks (Mowen 1993, p. 181; Engel et al. 1995, p. 406). Each step of the consumer decision-making process can be re-investigated and better understood from this perspective.

For example, it has been recognised that positive affect could speed up information processing and reduce decision time (Gardner, 1987), or that emotion-seeking could lead to a drive state (Mowen 1993, p. 181). Brand choice may also be holistically processed with regard to the consumer systematically selecting the brand most closely corresponding to a specific feeling, according to an „Affect Referral Heuristic": the more exciting or surprising brand will be chosen first. For example, over 90% of consumers had something positive to say about the brand purchased (Hoyer, 1984). Finally, the affective dimension is crucial in post-purchase evaluations, especially for satisfaction, brand loyalty and complaints. If product performance is below (or above) expectations, emotional dissatisfaction (or satisfaction) occurs (Woodruff et al., 1983); very close correlations have been established between post-purchasing satisfaction

---

[1] We are grateful for the help and assistance in data collection provided by the students of Consumer Behaviour Course: „Maitrise LEA, 1992, Université de Savoie".

(or dissatisfaction) level and positive (or negative) emotions experienced by consumers (Dube-Rioux, 1990; Westbrook and Oliver, 1991; Oliver, 1994).

Emotion is a key element in advertising, especially in the „star-strategy" approach (Filser 1994, p. 392). It has been proved that an emotional appeal in an advertisement increases message attention and its memorisation (Ray and Batra, 1983), raises consumer message involvement (Deighton, 1985), and at the same time, is a very efficient means of persuasion („peripheral road") in case of low product involvement (Petty and Cacioppo, 1983).

Faced with so many affective elements, the marketing researcher may have trouble measuring them. Existing scales have in fact been developed to capture the cognitive side of judgements and, consequently, demand a verbalisation from the respondent; transposing these scales to the affective field is questionable, because eliciting an affective reaction is very difficult (Derbaix and Pham, 1989). On the other hand, a large inventory of physiological measures is available, like heart rate, galvanic skin response, electroencephalogram, pupil dilatation, eye movement, but none of these have been widely accepted as useful in consumer research, because they are inadequate (if not too complex) to capture a full range of emotions (Morris and Mc Mullen, 1994).

One specific scale does exist - „the smiling faces"- with a lot of potential strength capable of circumventing previous difficulties. With this instrument, the respondent has only to show which face (among a series of smiling faces) best approaches the emotion experienced during an evaluation process, a choice, or brand consumption. But using smiling faces has its problems. First, as shown in Figure 1 the researcher is confronted with a large variety of forms in the literature. Is one form superior to another? Do two different consumers understand the emotion expressed by a specific face in the same way? What are the properties (nominal, ordinal, interval) that the smiling face scale offers?

More precisely, this article will try to:

1) Expose the potential strength of the smiling face scale as an instrument for measuring affect or emotion experienced by consumers toward a brand;

2) Verify the stability of judgements evoked by different faces, by testing them with demographically different respondents (occupational status, sex, age); and

3) Examine the possibility of calibrating the smiling face scale so that the intervals
between icons remain constant and similar, regardless of the respondent's demographic profile[2].

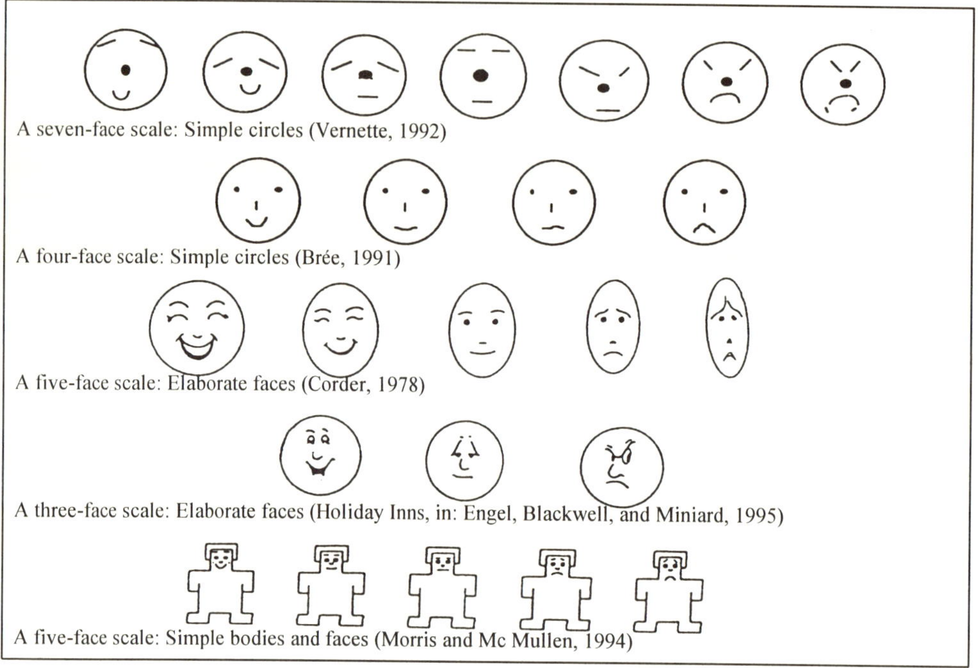

Figure 1: Some examples of smiling face scales

2. A Smiling Face Scale for Affect Measurement

2.1. Affect, Emotion and Mood

For many concepts frequently used in different research areas, it is difficult to find convergent definitions in existing literature. The concepts of emotion, mood or affect are no exception. The most frequent definition of affect seems to be Gardner's (1987), who defines it as
a „class of mental phenomena uniquely characterised by a consciously experienced, subjective
feeling state, commonly accompanying emotions and moods". Engel et al. (1995, p. 406) reduce it to „a positive or negative feeling state".

---

[2] A first attempt in this direction has produced very encouraging results (Vernette, 1992), but only three
faces were validated in a student convenience sample as being at equivalent perceptual intervals from
each other.

134

The concept of emotion is not precisely circumscribed, even if we admit that it is a particular form of affective reaction (Derbaix and Pham, 1989, p. 77). Establishing an inventory of emotions is a very difficult problem: the most frequent typology is probably Izard's (1977), which proposes 10 categories (interest, joy, surprise, anger, distress, disgust, satisfaction, fear, shame, culpability). Others exist which, contrary to the former approach based on discrete categories, propose a dimensional view limited to 2 or 3 principal components: for example, emotional responses to advertisements could be structured in three dimensions named pleasure, arousal, and dominance. If it is noticeable that the relevant literature is now in favour of a dimensional perspective, results also clearly show the „pleasure-unpleasure" dimension explains by far the greatest percentage of variance of the concept[3]. According to Mc Innis and Jaworski (1989) mood differs from emotion in its lower intensity and lesser psychological urgency.

In a worthy effort at synthesis, Derbaix and Pham (1989) propose a typology of the affective reactions founded on a seven-category fractionable continuum: emotion is considered the most affective reaction, followed by feeling, mood, character, preference, attitude, and appreciation, judged as the most cognitive reaction. They also note that a consensus characterises emotion as having intensity, strength, polarity (positive or negative appreciation), and content (expression, substance).

2.2. Measuring Affect and Emotions with Faces

The reversal of the cognitive primauty in favour of affect opens new perspectives for the comprehension of brand choice processing. But we are obliged to note that most verbal attitude rating scales which exist in marketing research (Likert scale, the semantic differential, semantic properties) are not really suitable to capture affect, due to the fact that they are above all developed from a cognitivistic point of view. Moreover, verbalisation could increase rational judgements leading consumers to think out loud might artificially raise the information processing load and the number of rating judgements, and finally, might determine tautological decision rules, resulting, for example, in a halo effect.

Compared to these difficulties, facial expression study offers an interesting alternative for the affective measurement of attitude or other related concepts (emotion, preference, satisfaction). A brief review of psychology literature clearly shows the numerous advantages offered by studies using faces:

---

3 For a good overview on this topic, see Feyereisen et de Lannoy (1985), pp. 165-173.

1) A facial expression doesn't lie. According to Ekman (1993), it is possible, through attentive face observation, to detect contradictions between the emotion announced by a person and what he or she really feels. For instance, a smile can be qualified as „true" or „false"; the latter, the sign of a lie, is produced by mouth muscle contraction alone; the true smile also involves the action of the muscles surrounding the eye (Ekman, 1985).

2) The same range of emotion can be expressed by different facial expressions, but these expressions share enough common points, so that it is possible to determine, with reasonable risk, their original family. This observation made by Ekman and his colleagues has given rise to a very precise facial reference system, the „Facial Action Coding System" (Ekman and Friesen, 1978).

3) A number of facial expressions are universal (Ekman, 1989). This point, particularly important from an ethnological or sociological perspective, is also very interesting for cross-cultural market studies which would use faces as an affective measurement tool.

4) The risk of bias due to perceived social desirability or the presence of the interviewer is reduced, especially in the area of child research (Derbaix et al., 1994).

Despite these favourable arguments, some unanswered questions and problems remain. Among them, the influence of context and situation in face interpretation is frequently evoked: the information produced by a face would depend, for a great part, on circumstances and conditions producing the expression (Feyereisen and de Lannoy, 1985, p. 175). It is accepted that in non-verbal communication some messages are, by nature, ambiguous and can only be processed in context. For example, in social interaction, a person will seem more attractive, if he or she was initially reserved, and then friendly, than if it was the contrary (first friendly, then reserved, or reserved throughout the entire meeting) (Clore et al., 1975). Another problem could be the possible discrepancy between males and females, the faces of the latter producing clearer messages than males (Buck et al., 1972).

2.3. Smiling Face Potential

Once we have admitted that a smile indicates emotion or a specific affect, the construction of an affective measurement tool, based on a variety of expressions, becomes legitimate. According to Ekman (1985; 1993), attentive observation of a smile enables the observer to determine the nature and strength of the emotion experienced. Most emotions can be analysed, independently of the inventory selected, in terms of negative polarity (disgust, distress, fear, suffering) or positive (joy, pleasure, satisfaction): the analysis of a smile - or its absence- is potentially rich in revelations for product marketing or brand image research. The smiling face scale has only been investigated by a few researchers. Results indicate reasonably good performance in terms of theory and practice (Vernette, 1991).

Its reliability is excellent, around .99, with an adult population using half-split procedure (Vernette, 1992); with a child population aged from 7 to 10 years, results remain acceptable: a Cronbach's α varies in a .69 - .72 range (Brée, 1991). Its convergence with other verbal scales is more difficult to establish. For adults, it strongly converges with the semantic properties scale, but not significantly with rank order (Brignier, 1991); for children, convergence with the Likert scale is rather weak (Brée, 1991). In fact, theses divergences are not surprising, if we keep in mind the fact that smiling faces enhance the affective component of attitude, whereas the other forms are focused on cognitive elements.

The practical superiority of the smiling face scales, compared to the alternatives is widely recognised: it is easily understood by respondents, even if their educational level is low (Parasuraman, 1986), well-accepted by young children (Macklin and Machleit, 1989; Brée, 1991). Its communicative qualities are undeniable: a drawing is more eloquent than a long speech. In a very natural manner, and without tedious explanations, the respondent links a facial expression to an emotion, to an attitude or to a satisfied or unsatisfied judgement[4]. The playful aspect of the drawings leads to a significantly higher response rate and to fewer unanswered questions in a mail study (Jolibert and Baumgartner, 1981).

Finally, the smiling face scale is very useful in the case of cross-cultural market research, since it avoids the problems of establishing and calibrating semantic terms questions, which are unavoidable with other attitude scales[5]. This solution obviously supposes that respondents from different cultures perceive different facial expressions in the same manner. This is coherent with Ekman's (1985) research, and confirmed by Vernette's results (1993). In underdeveloped countries, attitude scales appear to be unpracticable, because they are too complex: respondents have a lot of trouble understanding the meaning of the different scale

---

[4] A very interesting analogy exists between smiling faces, used in data collection, and Chernoff faces (1973), which represent MDS analysis results with different kinds of faces.

[5] Angelmar and Pras (1978) have shown that a simple literal word translation is not adequate: it is necessary to verify systematically the intensity of adjectives (excellent, good, bad, ...) which differs from one language to the other. For example „OK" equals 12/20 in France, but only 10/20 in the USA; the counterpart of „Excellent" is 18/20 in France and 19/20 in the US.

items (Douglas and Craig, 1983). Smiling faces are a good alternative, if not the only solution, in countries where illiteracy is high, because the interviewer doesn't have to keep reiterating the different possible responses: he or she simply shows the drawing as necessary.

3. Methodology

3.1. Scale Calibration and Face Selection

The method used for testing the interval properties of smiling faces is adapted from Myers and Warner's (1968) procedure, originally developed for calibrating semantic term scales. This application has been previously presented in detail (Vernette, 1992), therefore we will only summarise key issues.

The first step consists in drawing the greatest number of faces covering the largest span of emotional expressions or affects. Here we have adopted an illustration for the „Emotion" and „Appreciation" categories in the Derbaix and Pham (1989) affect inventory[6]. For semantic term scales, Myers and Warner (1968) recommend collecting a minimum of twenty terms, for each kind of scale (conventional or colloquial terms). Since lot of facial expressions exist, it wouldn't be too difficult to collect a large number of graphic illustrations. For example, Ekman and Freisen (1978) have shown that, at minimum, 50 different kinds of smiles exist; combinations of mouth and eye muscles allow a large variety of emotional expressions. Unfortunately, a preliminary investigation reveals that it is almost impossible to draw, in a single style, more than fifteen or so faces perceived as a representation of different emotions[7]. So we decided to enhance our range by drawing four series of faces with different styles. Students with some graphic expertise produced first a series of simple circle faces, followed by three other more creative and humorous series. Figure 2 presents some of the drawings composing each series. Instructions was given for illustrating „all possible expressions from a consumer rating brand

---

[6] More precisely, we wished to illustrate the „Satisfaction-Unsatisfaction" marketing concept linked to brand use. In our opinion, it is possible, with sustainable risk, to consider that we had also represented a variety of emotions („Pleasant, Surprise vs. Disappointment"). Besides this conceptual categorisation, one should not forget that, anyway, along a dimensional approach, a strong „Pleasure-Displeasure" component exists in every affective state. This dimension was often evoked by respondents during pretests.

[7] Ekman himself (1985) recognizes that a lot of training hours are necessary to become competent in identifying the meanings of similar facial expressions. In our case, a measurement scale aimed to be the most speedily administered possible to „ordinary" consumers, needs to select a sufficiently contrasted face series.

qualities or defaults". Each drawing series should be homogeneous in style and standardised enough for easy replication by another illustrator. For example „Series A" is supposed to cover the most expressive and creative feelings of the pleasure dimension, „Series B" is rather creative, „Series C" has an intermediate position, and finally, „Series D" represents a classical and simple form. Moreover, the drawers should include about the same number of favourable and unfavourable expressions in each collection. In the same series, the number of drawings varies between 13 and 15 pictures. Surprisingly, drawers spontaneously modified the forehead, eyebrows, eyes, and mouth to translate different emotions, just as Ekman and Freisen (1975) observed.

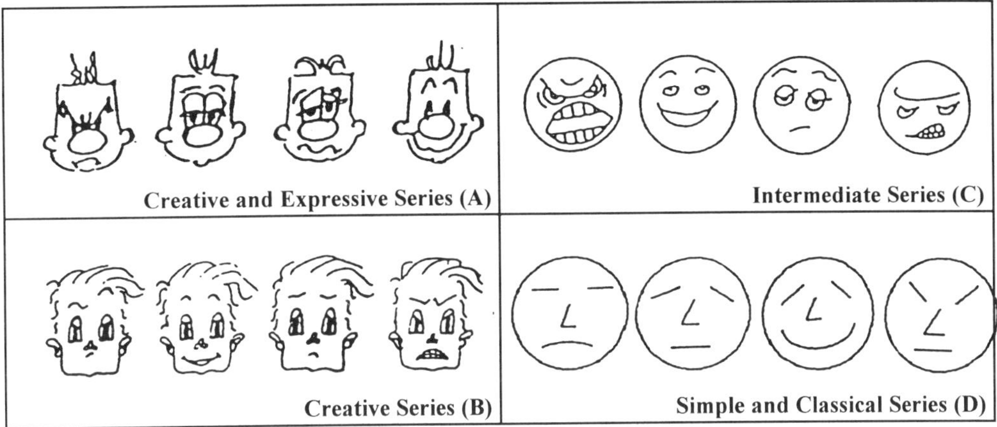

Figure 2: Samples of drawings used for pre-test

A pre-test conducted on a convenience sample (20 undergraduate French students) enabled us to select the best two series representing the greatest homogeneity of respondents' judgements (i.e. the lowest distribution of standard deviations). The „D" (simple) and „B" (elaborate) series had the two lowest scores, respectively 1.20 and 1.13. Finally each selected palette contains 14 different figures to be calibrated.

As a second step - in fact the main experimentation described below - another sample of judges must rank faces („From the picture corresponding to the worst brand rating to the best"), then assess each face (on a graduated scale of 0 to 10 points), according to the perceived intervals in intensity (greater or lesser) between each face. The mean and standard deviation was calculated for each face. The final choice of calibrated-scale pictures was dictated by an even perceptual distance between each face, without overlapping between their respective standard deviations.

3.2. Sampling

Two convenience samples were constructed composed of males and females living in the Rhône-Alpes area[8]. Occupational status was chosen as stratification criteria. For reasons of simplification, only four levels were kept: executives, manual and clerical workers, under-graduate students and secondary students. This *a priori* segmentation enables us, in accordance with our major goal, to test the effect of occupational status and/or education level upon face ratings. Respondents' age and sex were also recorded.

A first sample of 116 respondents received a questionnaire composed of simple smiling faces; a second sample, composed of 150 persons, has filled in the elaborate smiling face questionnaire. Table 1 gives cross-tabulations between type of questionnaire and occupational status. In order to avoid an eventual bias due to the order of presentation of the smiling faces, we have developed, for each face form, two different series, obtained by randomising all 14 faces. Respondents rate one series or the other.

Type of Questionnaire	Executives	Undergraduate Students	Manual & Clerical Workers	Secondary students
Simple Smiling Faces	29	29	28	30
Elaborate Smiling Faces	38	52	30	30

Table 1: Type of questionnaire and sample sizes

4. Results and Discussion

4.1. Mean Scores for Occupational Status

Means scores obtained are exposed in Figures 3 and 4. The proposed smiling faces appear to cover the emotional range well, because the total magnitude (the highest mean score minus the lowest mean score) varies between 9.4 and 7.9 points, depending on occupational status and face series.

---

[8] No doubt, this is a clear limitation in terms of external validity for our results, but we are following Derbaix et Pham's (1989) recommendation, who advocate (in the development phase of affective measurement tool) working with convenience samples, in order to facilitate manipulations of affective reactions.

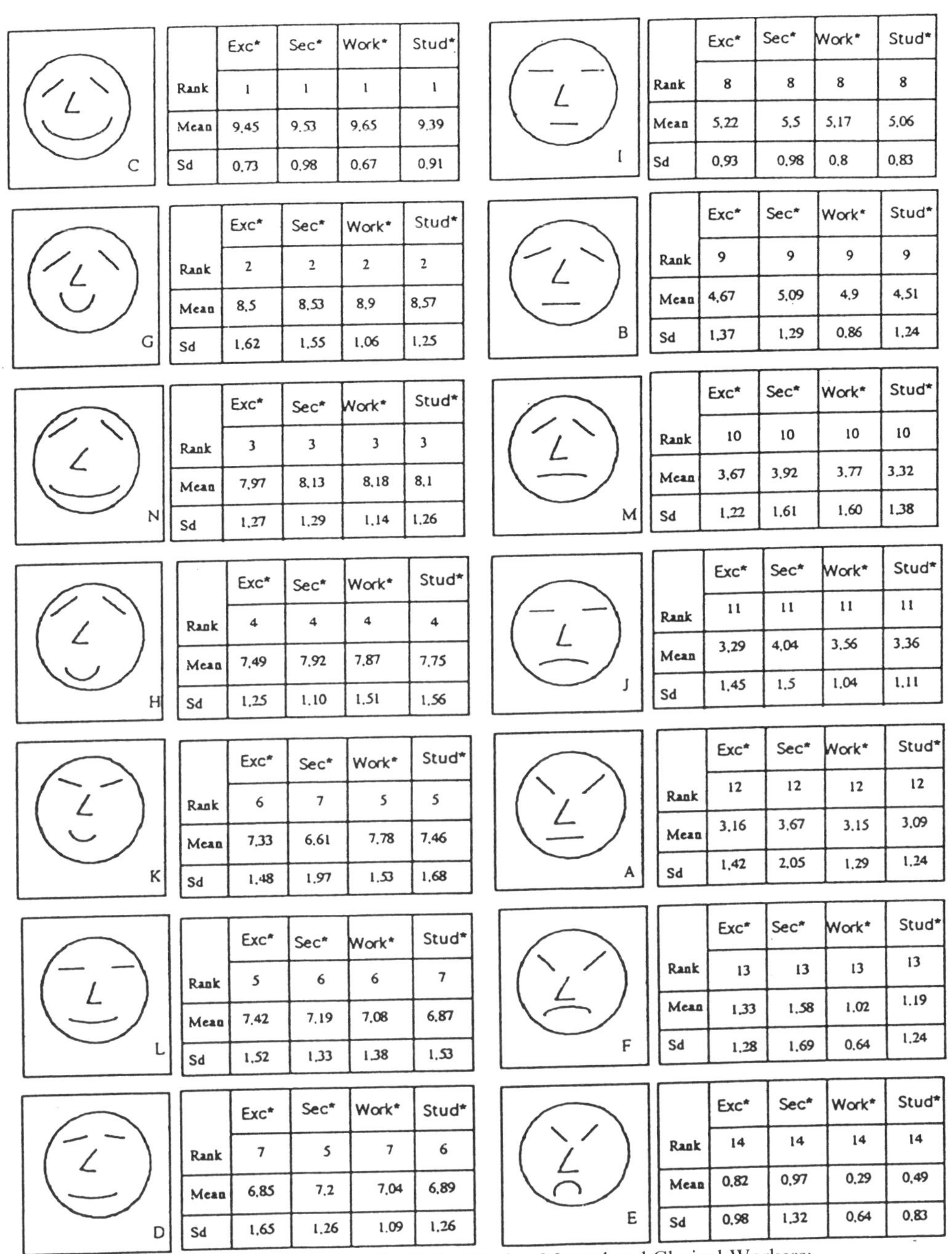

C

	Exc*	Sec*	Work*	Stud*
Rank	1	1	1	1
Mean	9.45	9.53	9.65	9.39
Sd	0.73	0.98	0.67	0.91

I

	Exc*	Sec*	Work*	Stud*
Rank	8	8	8	8
Mean	5.22	5.5	5.17	5.06
Sd	0.93	0.98	0.8	0.83

G

	Exc*	Sec*	Work*	Stud*
Rank	2	2	2	2
Mean	8.5	8.53	8.9	8.57
Sd	1.62	1.55	1.06	1.25

B

	Exc*	Sec*	Work*	Stud*
Rank	9	9	9	9
Mean	4.67	5.09	4.9	4.51
Sd	1.37	1.29	0.86	1.24

N

	Exc*	Sec*	Work*	Stud*
Rank	3	3	3	3
Mean	7.97	8.13	8.18	8.1
Sd	1.27	1.29	1.14	1.26

M

	Exc*	Sec*	Work*	Stud*
Rank	10	10	10	10
Mean	3.67	3.92	3.77	3.32
Sd	1.22	1.61	1.60	1.38

H

	Exc*	Sec*	Work*	Stud*
Rank	4	4	4	4
Mean	7.49	7.92	7.87	7.75
Sd	1.25	1.10	1.51	1.56

J

	Exc*	Sec*	Work*	Stud*
Rank	11	11	11	11
Mean	3.29	4.04	3.56	3.36
Sd	1.45	1.5	1.04	1.11

K

	Exc*	Sec*	Work*	Stud*
Rank	6	7	5	5
Mean	7.33	6.61	7.78	7.46
Sd	1.48	1.97	1.53	1.68

A

	Exc*	Sec*	Work*	Stud*
Rank	12	12	12	12
Mean	3.16	3.67	3.15	3.09
Sd	1.42	2.05	1.29	1.24

L

	Exc*	Sec*	Work*	Stud*
Rank	5	6	6	7
Mean	7.42	7.19	7.08	6.87
Sd	1.52	1.33	1.38	1.53

F

	Exc*	Sec*	Work*	Stud*
Rank	13	13	13	13
Mean	1.33	1.58	1.02	1.19
Sd	1.28	1.69	0.64	1.24

D

	Exc*	Sec*	Work*	Stud*
Rank	7	5	7	6
Mean	6.85	7.2	7.04	6.89
Sd	1.65	1.26	1.09	1.26

E

	Exc*	Sec*	Work*	Stud*
Rank	14	14	14	14
Mean	0.82	0.97	0.29	0.49
Sd	0.98	1.32	0.64	0.83

(*) Exc = Executives; Sec = Secondary Students; Work = Manual and Clerical Workers; Stud = Undergraduate Students

Figure 3: Simple smiling face calibration according to occupational status

G

	Exc*	Sec*	Work*	Stud*
Rank	1	1	2	1
Mean	9.36	9.20	8.79	9.25
Sd	2.28	2.50	2.63	2.20

I

	Exc*	Sec*	Work*	Stud*
Rank	7	8	9	8
Mean	5.6	4.8	4.8	4.8
Sd	1.13	1.14	1.81	1.71

L

	Exc*	Sec*	Work*	Stud*
Rank	2	2	1	2
Mean	9.00	9.11	8.81	8.82
Sd	1.35	1.67	1.61	1.35

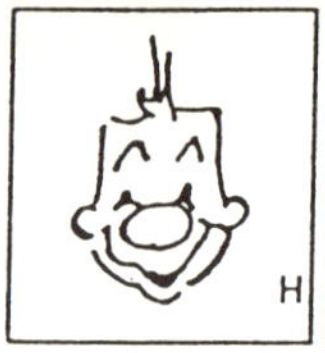

D

	Exc*	Sec*	Work*	Stud*
Rank	9	9	8	9
Mean	4.46	4.55	4.88	4.18
Sd	1.37	1.31	1.84	1.49

H

	Exc*	Sec*	Work*	Stud*
Rank	3	3	3	3
Mean	8.58	8.49	8.10	8.33
Sd	0.63	1.35	1.98	0.75

B

	Exc*	Sec*	Work*	Stud*
Rank	10	12	10	10
Mean	3.65	3.47	4.7	2.93
Sd	1.62	1.18	1.86	1.43

N

	Exc*	Sec*	Work*	Stud*
Rank	4	4	4	4
Mean	7.85	8.02	7.77	7.93
Sd	0.93	1.02	1.65	0.85

J

	Exc*	Sec*	Work*	Stud*
Rank	11	10	11	12
Mean	3.31	3.64	3.75	2.87
Sd	1.73	1.48	1.55	1.41

C

	Exc*	Sec*	Work*	Stud*
Rank	5	5	5	5
Mean	6.63	6.78	6.6	6.48
Sd	1.25	1.25	1.42	0.87

M

	Exc*	Sec*	Work*	Stud*
Rank	12	11	12	11
Mean	2.86	3.57	3.04	2.91
Sd	1.42	1.44	1.49	1.65

K

	Exc*	Sec*	Work*	Stud*
Rank	6	6	6	6
Mean	5.8	5.64	5.52	5.28
Sd	1.61	1.52	1.83	1.12

A

	Exc*	Sec*	Work*	Stud*
Rank	13	13	13	13
Mean	2.14	1.72	2.54	1.57
Sd	1.62	1.18	2.07	1.44

E

	Exc*	Sec*	Work*	Stud*
Rank	8	7	7	7
Mean	5.42	5.09	5.46	5.08
Sd	1.07	1.22	1.77	1.55

F

	Exc*	Sec*	Work*	Stud*
Rank	14	14	14	14
Mean	0.41	0.7	0.85	0.53
Sd	0.8	0.92	1.26	1.25

(*) Exc = Executives; Sec = Secondary Students; Work = Manual and Clerical Workers;
Stud = Undergraduate Students

Figure 4: Elaborate smiling face calibration according to occupational status

Figures 3 and 4 reveal an almost identical ranking order for the 14 simple or elaborate smiling faces, whatever the respondent's occupational status is. This convergence - almost perfect - gives rank correlation coefficients (Spearman's Rho) that are clearly significant, and all above .97 ($p < .001$) (see Table 2).

Comparisons Between Type of Occupational Status	Simple Smiling Faces	Elaborate Smiling Faces
Executives vs. Secondary Students	.984	.979
Executives vs. Manual and Clerical Workers	.995	.979
Executives vs. Undergraduate Students	.979	.989
Secondary Students vs. Manual & Clerical Workers	.979	.974
Secondary Students vs. Undergraduate Students	.979	.979
Manual and Clerical Workers vs. Undergraduate Students	.989	.984

Table 2: Spearman rank correlations between smiling face ratings according to the occupational status of respondents

Since a strong correlation doesn't automatically mean that smiling faces produce equivalent mean scores in each of the 4 levels of occupational status, we have conducted, for all 14 simple smiling faces, a one-way variance analysis (with occupational status as factor) and 4 levels (executives, manual and clerical workers, undergraduate students, and secondary students). We repeated this analysis for the 14 elaborate faces. Results are very close, whatever the type of faces is: if we consider the set of 14 simple smiling faces, only two present a significant difference (at $p < .05$ level) depending upon occupational status: faces E and K. Likewise, only three elaborate faces (figures A, B, and J) out of 14 reveal a statistical difference ($p < .05$).

An attentive examination of the „overall mean" (average of the mean scores for all 14 faces) doesn't reveal leniency bias with any occupational status (see Table 3). Variation of these scores is slight, since the maximum magnitude between means of the same series equals .27 for the simple faces, and .33 for elaborate faces.

Type of Smiling Faces	Executives	Undergraduate Students	Manual and Clerical Workers	Secondary Students
Simple	5.51	5.43	5.60	5.70
Elaborate	5.38	5.07	5.40	5.34

Table 3: Occupational status and overall mean variation of smiling faces

We wanted to refine these preceding statements, by taking into consideration the global effect of occupational status on smiling face interpretation. First we conducted a two-way variance analysis, with only the simple faces[9]. As expected, smiling face ratings do not statistically differ between different occupational status categories: $F_{(3, 112)}$ = .12. On the other hand, a slight interaction appears between occupational status and the faces (F = 2.06): for certain figures only, ratings differ slightly from one occupational status to another. We next replicated this analysis with the elaborate faces. Results are quite similar to simple face analysis: the effect of occupational status is not significant (F = 1.64), and we note again a slight interaction between occupational status and faces. These different analyses clearly show that the respondent's occupational status doesn't have a significant influence on face ratings, whatever the drawing style is.

Type of Smiling Faces	Executives	Undergraduate Students	Manual and Clerical Workers	Secondary Students
Simple	1,30	1,23	1,01	1,42
Elaborate	1,34	1,30	1,76	1,39

Table 4: Means of standard deviations for smiling face evaluations

Afterwards we compared the distributions of the different standard deviations ratings, as reported in Figures 3 and 4 above. A first reading reveals these scores to be very similar to those obtained in another study aiming to calibrate semantic terms (Pras, 1976). We verified the possible existence of significant differences for each set of standard deviations (two-sided t test, independent samples): the only significant difference concerns the Manual and Clerical Workers category, where the standard deviation distribution is statistically higher than for other

---

[9] A two-way variance analysis model has been used (with countries and faces as factors), with repeated measure on the second factor and unequal cells (see Winer, 1971, pp. 599-603).

categories. Surprisingly, the direction of differences depends on the forms of the faces: with simple faces, score dispersion for Manual and Clerical Workers is statistically lower than for other occupational status categories ($p < .05$ level); on the contrary, with elaborate faces, this same dispersion is significantly higher ($p < .05$).

4.2. Faces Rating according to Sex and Age

The same analyses have been repeated in order to verify face rating convergence according to respondent's sex. Table 5 summarises means and standard deviations (for letters corresponding to drawings, see Figures 3 and 4). Smiling face ratings convergence is very strong, whether for the simple face series (Spearman Rho = .98) or for the elaborate faces (Spearman Rho = .99). If we consider the mean scores of all 14 faces, only the „F" face presents a significant difference ($p < .05$) for the simple faces, and „H" ($p < .10$) and „J" ($p < .05$) for the elaborate faces.

Smiling Faces Identification Letters	Simple Smiling Faces				Elaborate Smiling Faces			
	Males		Females		Males		Females	
	Mean	Sd	Mean	Sd	Mean	Sd	Mean	Sd
A	3.28	1.48	3.36	1.61	2.06	1.68	1.62	1.12
B	4.61	1.12	4.95	1.29	3.28	1.70	3.2	1.41
C	9.48	0.69	9.56	0.92	6.49	1.39	6.58	1.14
D	7.08	1.24	6.99	1.41	4.45	1.67	4.40	1.08
E	0.64	0.95	0.62	1.06	5.28	1.11	5.18	1.21
F	1.27	1.18	1.32	1.37	0.49	0.81	0.47	0.92
G	8.40	1.39	8.83	1.37	8.93	2.86	9.58	1.95
H	7.52	1.66	8.00	1.33	8.68	0.77	8.24	1.25
I	7.24	1.44	5.25	0.97	5.20	1.47	5.10	0.99
J	3.64	1.38	3.58	1.39	2.60	1.23	3.40	1.76
K	7.57	1.66	7.20	1.74	5.44	1.73	5.55	1.46
L	7.24	1.44	7.17	1.44	8.82	1.82	8.95	1.30
M	3.64	1.38	3.82	1.53	2.76	1.35	2.99	1.48
N	8.07	1.23	8.17	1.23	7.96	1.07	7.85	0.91

Table 5: Means and standard deviations for males and females

The different sets of dispersion scores, illustrated by the distributions of standard deviation of face ratings, don't significantly differ between males and females, whatever the considered set (elaborate faces: t = -1.21; simple faces: t = .72). Similarly, no effect of the respondent's age on face assessment has been detected by correlation, for both sets of 14 faces, between rating scores and the respondent's age. For simple faces, none of Pearson's 14 r coefficients are significant at p < .05 level; the highest of them equals .13. On the contrary, with the elaborate faces, the results are more balanced, since that four coefficients are significant at p < .05 (faces A, B, I, J) and two others at p < .10 (faces D, L); but these coefficients, although significant, remain moderate: variation is in a range of .37 to .19; all other coefficients are below .15.

5. Implications and Suggestions

The major aim of this research was to create a scale, formed by different faces representing quasi-equivalent gradations in feeling. Based on the results observed in this article, which faces and forms should be chosen?

5.1. Choice of Style

From a theoretical point of view, our results don't suggest a clear preference for one type of smiling face, since we haven't detected, in either of these two sets, significant effects between occupational status or age with face ratings. If we consider the possibility of correlation between ratings and age for 6 elaborate figures out of 14, as a precaution, we shall prefer the simple smiling faces.

From a practical perspective, as we shall see in the following section, the advantage is clearly in favour of the simple smiling faces, because it appears to be very difficult to fit anchor point with equivalent intervals with the elaborate scale, and relatively easy with the simple faces.

5.2. Selecting Scale Anchor Points

A major precaution must be taken in order to determine the number of scale anchor points. As Pras (1976) recalls, it's not the number of scale-points which is important, but rather the fact that selected terms (here: drawings) should be at equivalent perceptual intervals. Moreover a balance must be respected between the number of favourable and unfavourable terms.

Finally, an ideal smiling face must respect three constraints: having the most unvarying mean score possible (independent of the respondent's occupational status, age, and sex), representing an interval equivalent to that of either of the surrounding faces, and having a low standard deviation.

We have applied these three rules in creating the simple smiling face scale. Mean scores and standard deviation have been calculated, for each of the two series of 14 figures, with all the respondents from each sample.

We propose a five-face scale (see Figure 5), with an average interval between two faces which is equal to approximately 2 points. Scores indicated between brackets correspond to the average score for each face across the sample. So it will be noted that none of these 5 faces present significant differences for occupational status, age and sex. Because the average standard deviation varies from 1.5 to .8 depending on the faces, it is not possible to construct a more discriminating scale, since standard deviations plus anchor-point means would overlap.

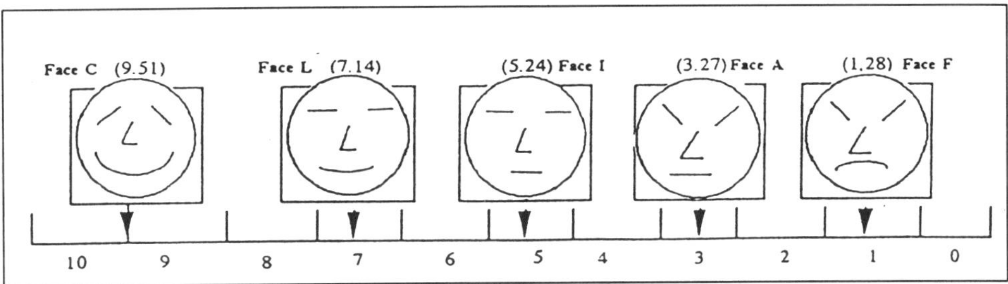

Figure 5: Simple smiling face scale (with 5 anchor points)

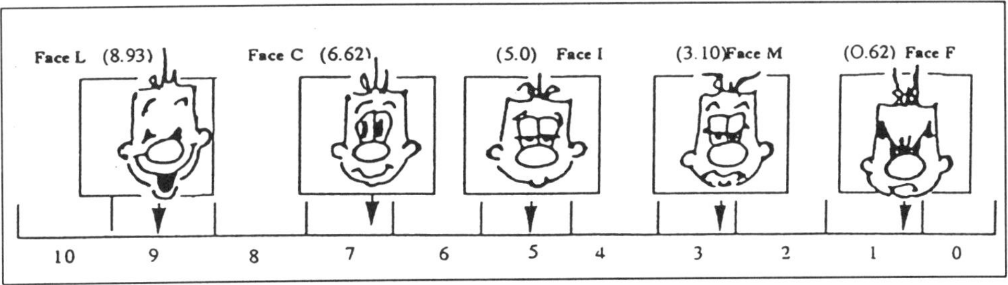

Figure 6: Elaborate smiling face scale (with 5 anchor points)

Creating an elaborate smiling face scale is more questionable. Considering the mean score for each face, it is not possible to keep a strictly equivalent interval from one figure to another. We could offer a five-point scale, but with a slight distortion in graduation, since the interval fluctuates between 2.5 and 1.6 points depending on the face; the average interval however remains roughly equal to 2 points (see Figure 6).

6. Limitations and Conclusions

Our research is not without some serious limitations that we must keep in mind before hasty generalisations. Firstly, our sample doesn't represent the French population. Our results are only a first attempt to validate some initial hypotheses. In this perspective, we consider our conclusions very encouraging: we have demonstrated good stability for simple or elaborate smiling faces, and the possibility selecting 5 faces with an approximately equivalent interval between them. This seems quite an interesting result, because other research in related fields (verbal semantic ratings), and with comparable limitations, had reported some divergence between occupational status or countries (Pras, 1976; Angelmar and Pras, 1978). Secondly, our research is limited only to the pleasure-unpleasure dimension of the concept of emotion, with no attention paid to arousal; this latter represents an important part of the concept, however, and could be successfully combined with the former (Spreng, 1995).

In conclusion, we encourage the use of the smiling face scale, especially the simple face forms, and we believe faces have valid interval properties for measurement of emotions or affect towards brands or products. Future studies must - in addition to improving external validity - compare the predictive capacity of these smiling faces (for preference, brand choice, satisfaction) to other verbal instruments.

References

Angelmar, R. and Pras, B. (1978): Verbal ratings scales for multinational research. In: European Research, Vol. 6, No. 2, pp. 62-67.

Brée, J. (1991): Quelques problèmes de choix d'échelles pour mesurer l'attitude chez les enfants. In: Recherche et Applications en Marketing, Vol. 6, No. 4, pp. 27-58.

Brignier, J.M. (1991): L'influence des échelles de mesure sur les réponses collectées dans les enquêtes. In: Recherche et Applications en Marketing, Vol. 6, No. 1, pp.1-26.

Buck, R., Savin, V., and Caul, W. (1972): Communication of affect trough facial expressions in humans. In: Journal of Personality and Social Psychology, Vol. 23, pp. 362-371.

Chernoff, H. (1973): Using faces to represent points in K-dimensional space graphically. In: Journal of the American Statistical Association, Vol. 68, June, pp. 361-368.

Clore et al. (1975): Quoted in: Feyereisen, P. and de Lannoy, J.D., Psychologie du geste, p. 176, Ed. P. Mardaga: Bruxelles.

Corder, C. (1978): Problems and pitfalls in conducting marketing research in Africa. Marketing Expansion in a shrinking world. In: Proceedings of the American Marketing Association, pp. 86-90.

Deighton, J. (1985): Rhetorical strategies in advertising. In: Advances in Consumer Research, Vol. 12, pp. 432-436.

Derbaix, C., Brée, J., and Masson, S. (1994): La mesure des réactions affectives dans la réception des films publicitaires chez les enfants: une approche expérimentale. In: Actes de l'Association Française du Marketing, Vol. 10, pp. 471-499.

Derbaix, C. and Pham, M. (1989): Pour un développement des mesures de l'affectif en marketing: synthèse et prérequis. In: Recherche et Applications en Marketing, Vol. 4, No. 4, pp. 71-87.

Douglas, S. P. and Craig, C.S. (1983): International Marketing Research. Prentice Hall: Englewood Cliffs, NJ.

Dube-Rioux, L. (1990): The power of affective reports in predicting satisfaction judgments. In: Advances in Consumer Research, Vol. 17, pp. 571-576.

Ekman, P. (1985): Telling Lies: Clues to Deceit in the Marketplace, Mariage and Politics. Norton: NY. (French Translation: (1986): Menteurs et mensonges. Belfond: Paris)

Ekman, P. (1989): The arguments of evidences about universals in facial expressions of emotions. In: Wagner and Manstead (Eds.), Handbook of Social Psychophysiology, Chister: England, pp. 143-164.

Ekman, P. (1993): Facial Expression and Emotion, In: American Psychologist, Vol. 48, No. 4, pp. 384-392.

Ekman, P. and Freisen, W. (1978): Facial Action Coding System: a technique for the measurement of facial movement. Consulting Psychologists Press: Palo Alto, CA.

Engel, J. F., Blackwell, R. D., and Miniard, P. W. (1995): Consumer Behavior, 8th ed. Dryden Press.

Feyereisen, P. and de Lannoy, J. D. (1985): Psychologie du geste. Ed. P. Mardaga: Bruxelles.

Filser, M. (1994): Le comportement du consommateur. Précis-Dalloz: Paris.

Gardner, M. (1987): Effect of Mood States on Consumer Information Processing. In: Research in Consumer Behavior, Vol. 2, pp. 113-135.

Hoyer, W. (1984): An examination of consumer decision making for a common repeat-purchase product. In: Journal of Consumer Research, Vol. 11, December, pp. 822-829.

Izard, C. (1977): Human Emotion. Peplum Press: NY.

Jolibert, A. and Baumgartner, G. (1981): L'influence des échelles de mesure sur les résultats d'une enquête postale. In: Proceedings of the 3rd Seminar on Research Methodology, Lille, pp. 108-129.

Macklin, M. C. and Machleit, K. A. (1989): The development of an attitude scale appropriate for use with preschoolers. In: Advances in Consumer Research, Vol. 16, pp. 792.

Mc Innis, D. and Jaworski, B. (1989): Information processing from advertisements,: toward an integrative framework. In: Journal of Marketing, Vol. 53, October, pp. 1-23.

Morris, J. D. and Mc Mullen, J. S. (1994): Measuring multiple emotional responses to a single television commercial. In: Advances in Consumer Research, Vol. 21, pp. 175-180.

Mowen, J. C. (1993): Consumer Behavior, 3rd ed. Mc Millan: NY.

Myers, J. H. and Warner, G. (1968): Semantic properties of selected evaluation adjectives. In: Journal of Marketing Research, November, pp. 409-412.

Oliver, R. L. (1994): Conceptual Issues in the structural analysis of consumption of emotion, satisfaction, and quality: evidence in a service testing. In: Advances in Consumer Research, Vol. 21, pp. 16-22.

Parasuraman, A. (1986): Marketing Research. Addison-Wesley: Reading, Mass.

Petty, R., Cacioppo, J., and Schuman, D. (1983): Central route and peripheral routes to advertising effect: the moderating role of involvement. In: Journal of Consumer Research, Vol. 10, September, pp. 135-146.

Pras, B. (1976): Echelles d'intervalle à supports sémantiques. In: Revue Française du Marketing, Vol. 61, pp. 87-95.

Ray, M. and Batra, R. (1983): Emotion and persuasion in advertising: what we know and don't know about affect. In: Advances in Consumer Research, Vol. 10, pp. 543-548.

Spreng, R. (1995): New directions in affect and consumer satisfaction. In: Advances in Consumer Research, Vol. 22, pp. 453.

Vernette, E. (1991): L'efficacité des instruments d'étude: évaluation des échelles de mesure. In: Recherche et Applications en Marketing, Vol. 6, No. 2, pp. 43-66.

Vernette, E. (1992): Evaluation des propriétés d'intervalle des échelles à icones. In: Actes de l'Association Française du Marketing, Vol. 8, pp. 447-461.

Vernette, E. (1993): Les qualités de l'échelle de mesure à icones pour une étude internationale. In: Proceeding of the 20th International Research Seminar in Marketing, IAE: Aix-en-Provence, pp. 444-468.

Westbrook, R. and Oliver, R. (1991): Dimensionality of consumption emotion patterns and consumer satisfaction. In: Journal of Consumer Research, Vol. 18, pp. 84-91.

Winer, B. J. (1971): Statistical principles in experimental designs. Mc Graw Hill: New York.

Woodruff, R., Cadotte, E., and Jenkins, R. (1983): Modeling consumer satisfaction process using experience-based norms. In: Journal of Marketing Research, Vol. 20, pp. 296-304.

Alain Jolibert and Gary Baumgartner

An Empirical Investigation of the Relationships between Values, Motivations, and Personal Goals

1. Introduction
   1.1. Values, Motivations, Personal Goals: The Conceptual Standpoint
   1.2. Values, Motivations, Personal Goals: The Operational Standpoint

2. Research Plan

3. Methodology

4. Design of a Scale to Measure Personal Goals

5. Data Collection

6. Analysis

7. Results

8. Discussion and Conclusion

References

An Empirical Investigation of the Relationships between Values, Motivations, and Personal Goals

Alain Jolibert and Gary Baumgartner

Abstract

This paper deals with the concepts of values, motivations and personal goals. These concepts are first analysed from a conceptual standpoint. In spite of numerous attempts to define them, clear-cut definitions have yet to be found.

An empirical survey confirms this theoretical analysis. It shows that individuals structure these three concepts into four meaningful dimensions characterised by social, personal, achievement, and humanistic orientations. Strong associations between the three concepts of values, motivations, and personal goals have been detected. This suggests that the differentiation between these three concepts is not conceptual but may be due to some artifacts inherent in the measurement process.

1. Introduction

Personal goals, motivations, and values have been of great interest to marketing and consumer behaviour researchers. They are used as determinants of choice criteria in evaluating brands, a basis for segmentation, vectors of communications, antecedents of involvement, etc. However, the degree of their importance is not reflected in the clarity of their definitions, and this can be said both from a theoretical and practical standpoint. Before applying these concepts in marketing research, a certain effort will be necessary in order to clarify their significance.

Personal goals have been defined by certain researchers (Markus, 1983; Bandura, 1986) as being an individual's cognitive representation of his personal motivations; others (Solomon, 1992) consider them to be an end state.

Values have been referred to as a mode of conduct or an end state of existence (Rokeach, 1985). Maslow (1970), however, has defined them as being needs.

"

Finally, motivations have been defined as tendencies to strive for a personal class of incentive (McClelland, 1985). They have also been considered as something created by needs (Brehm and Self, 1989).

Recent developments in the conceptualization of values by Schwartz and Bilsky (1987; 1990) indicate the existence of nine motivational categories based on three fundamental needs of all human beings: biological, social, and societal needs. According to them, the nine motivational domains are represented by facets which are built upon cognitive representations of needs. Their research findings, if indeed very interesting, seem to only reinforce the vagueness of the frontiers between values, motivations and personal goals.

Figure 1 represents a summary of how key researchers have defined the conceptual relationships between values and personal goals, motivations, and needs. Values and motivations are defined to be strictly equivalent. On the other hand, personal goals, well known in psychology (Emmons, 1989) as being one of the principal components of personality, are used as synonyms for values. Finally, the same equivalency is observed for the relationship between values and needs.

Relations Authors	Values and personal goals	Values and motivations	Values and needs
Schwartz and Bilsky (1987)	„Values represent either terminal or instrumental goals.“	„Values express motivational concern.“	„Values are cognitive representations of three needs (biological interactional, societal needs).“
Rokeach (1973)	„Values are preferred end states, either terminal or instrumental.“	„Values have strong motivational components. Terminal and instrumental values are motivations.“	„Values are cognitive representations and transformations of needs, give expressions to human needs.“
Murray (1951)	„Values are an interest of bringing about some end state.“		„Needs operate in the service of values.“
Maslow (1970)		„Values are motivations.“	„The gratification of any need is a value.“

Figure 1: Interrelationships between values, goals, and motivations

A brief examination of these definitions indicates a type of circular causality among these three constructs. In defining each of the three concepts, usage is made of the definitions of one or both of the other two concepts.

What then are values? Are they motivations, or are they in fact personal goals close to the personality of the individual? In light of the ambiguities in the definitions found in the research literature, this article discusses the relationships between the three concepts from a conceptual as well as an operational standpoint. An applied investigation is then presented in a modest attempt to clarify certain links between these three concepts.

1.1. Values, Motivations, Personal Goals: The Conceptual Standpoint

In order to satisfy one's needs, it is evident that they must first be concretised. This is the role played by motivations. In fact, motivations correspond to one's capacity to obtain satisfaction from a class of stimuli which can be numerous: money, prestige, power, curiosity, achievement, co-operation with authorities, ... etc. Murray (1938) and McClelland (1961) have identified and suggested several inventories of motivations.

In turn, motivations are translated consciously in terms of personal goals and values. The confusion between personal goals and values is therefore scarcely surprising. Murray (1951) already indicated that motivations are represented by values centred on the body (comfort, well-being), property (objects of value, financial ease), authority (the power of decision-making), sociability (affection, friendship, charity), knowledge (facts, theories, history, science), aesthetic shapes (beauty, art), and ideology (religion, philosophy).

Murray's definition of motivations is very close to that of Rokeach (1974) who defines values as having a strong motivational component. In other words, when one furnishes information concerning personal values, at the same time information is given on one's needs. In justifying his theory, Rokeach also suggested the existence of a hierarchy of values derived directly from the hierarchy of motivations proposed by Maslow (1970).

More than forty years after Murray, and after having seen values transformed into a specific concept, one is forced to admit that the present state of knowledge has confirmed Murray's and Rokeach's original conception whereby values can be considered to be surrogates for motivations.

In fact, motivations have two origins. The first proceeds from instinct, the second from cognition. Personal goals belong to the cognitive factor. From the standpoint of the individual, they are indeed a source of motivation (Bandura, 1989). Personal goals are a part of a hierarchy, the ultimate point of which is a motivation which can only be satisfied when the associated personal goals have been attained (Emmons, 1988). For this reason, it appears difficult to theoretically differentiate the two concepts of motivations and personal goals. However, it appears that personal goals are subordinate to motivations.

The theoretical difference between personal goals and values also appears to be quite slight. The relative similarity between the two concepts is derived from the fact that a value is a desirable objective, an ideal (Maslow, 1970), or what one *must do*, whereas a personal goal concerns what one *wishes to do* (Emmons, 1989). Personal goals seem to be closer to behaviour than values which are in turn related to objectives, normally considered as desirable by one's social system. To summarise, personal goals correspond to the objectives of the individual himself, whereas values are very much influenced by the social norms which guide people in their behaviour.

1.2. Values, Motivations, Personal Goals: The Operational Standpoint

From a theoretical standpoint, there is a lack of clear-cut definitions for the three concepts, and this has led to a certain confusion in the literature. On the other hand, it is relatively surprising to note that a very clear differentiation exists in the ways in which they are measured. Excluding the measurement of personal goals, generally neglected by consumer behaviour researchers, values and motivations are operationalized in very different ways.

Values are generally measured by means of questionnaires which focus either on general or specific values. The most common general values inventory has been provided by Rokeach (1973). Other general inventories have been derived from the Rokeach survey for practical or cross-cultural purposes; the most well known are the List of Values (LOV) (Kahle, 1983) and the Schwartz-Bilsky inventory (1987; 1995). Other scales have also been developed to measure very specific values such as materialism etc. ... (Bearden et al., 1993).

On the other hand, the measurement of motivations offers a greater variety of techniques which are not at all related to values. Projective measures of human motivation are used as well as questionnaires. Questionnaires have been largely preferred to the projective measurement technique because of their ease of administration and their reliability (Brody, 1980). The technique of the questionnaire has given birth to a multiplicity of scales focusing on specific motivations (i.e. need for power, need for achievement ...) as well as more general inventories. This diversity is probably due to the absence of a comprehensive framework for motivations (Brody, 1980).

2. Research Plan

The objective of this research is to study the relationships between the three concepts previously cited. We have chosen to measure and to analyse them by means of non-linear canonical correlation analysis. The choice of this technique was justified on two grounds. Firstly, by taking into account the non-linear relationships in the data, the obtained results will be more robust and therefore more reliable. Secondly, there is no theoretical basis to limiting the study to linear relationships.

Based on previous research findings (Jolibert and Baumgartner, 1995), we limited the investigation to four factorial dimensions.

3. Methodology

Three different scales were used. The first was destined to measure values. Rokeach's scale (1973) was chosen despite its weaknesses brought to light by Braithwaite and Law (1985), Schwartz and Bilsky (1987) and Bond (1988). Two reasons justify this choice. Firstly, Rokeach's scale has been incorporated in several more recent scales as the LOV (Kahle, 1983). Secondly, it has served as a benchmark for the construction of larger and more recent scales such as Schwartz's (1992) scale.

The second scale was used to identify the robust components of individual motivations. Murray (1951) has already pointed out the existing similarities between values and motivations, and his theory represents the theoretical backbone for the EPPS test. Designed to identify fifteen separate motivations, this test was used in the French-speaking version designed by Gauthier (1964). The EPPS offers the additional advantage of being able to verify the consistency of the answers provided by the subjects. This permitted the detection and elimination from the sample those respondents who filled out the questionnaire in an erratic fashion.

As for the scale whose purpose was to measure the personal goals of the respondents, it was necessary to design one specifically for the study. The only existing scale in research literature has been provided by Emmons (1986), whose research was oriented more to the identification of the personal goals than to their measurement. Not having *a priori* a list of personal goals, it was necessary to first establish one before attempting to measure the relative importance of the personal goals for each respondent.

4. Design of a Scale to Measure Personal Goals

In order to identify the personal goals associated with our sample, sixty students of the same age as that of the sample but from another French university were questioned. Each student was asked anonymously to provide a list of goals „that he has attained or attempts to attain."

The individual lists thus obtained were then merged and analysed by two judges in order to retain only the non redundant objectives. After discussion and agreement on the formulation, nine personal goals were retained. This list became thus part of the final questionnaire in which the respondents were asked to indicate the relative importance of each personal goal on a scale of 0 to 100.

5. Data Collection

One hundred and sixty three students in their junior year in a major French university constituted the sampling frame. All incomplete questionnaires were eliminated. The final sample on which the results are based includes one hundred and fifty-six persons. It should be noted that the student participants did not receive credit for their participation in the study as this is not permitted by the French educational system. On the other hand, to motivate the students, it was explained that the questionnaire, in addition to being a part of a research effort, would provide certain benefits such as a better understanding of oneself as well as a preparation for employment tests. The questionnaires were completely anonymous. A code chosen by the respondent, usually containing a part of either the social security number or the student enrolment code was used for identification. The students completed the personal value scale, then those regarding personal goals, and finally the EPPS.

6. Analysis

The responses obtained from the one hundred and fifty-six respondents (i.e. the scores on the fifteen motivational scales of the EPPS, the nine personal goals evaluations, and the eighteen terminal values obtained from the Rokeach test) constitute the data bank to be analysed. The instrumental values of the Rokeach test were not used in the analysis. Since the measurement scales of the results were not identical (for example, the motivational scales vary from 0 to 28, the personal goal scale from 0 to 100, and the value scales from 1 to 6), the motivational and personal goal scales were transformed to be in conformity with the values scale. The data were submitted to the OVERALS procedure (Van Der Burg and De Leeuws, 1988). OVERALS performs non-linear canonical correlation analysis. It summarises the relationships between the three sets of variables (Values, Motivations, and Personal Objectives) in the form of four dimensions and permits the identification of their characteristics.

7. Results

Table 1 presents the results obtained in four dimensions. The fit and the loss values indicate how well the solution fits the data based on the associations between the sets. The maximum value of the fit equals the number of dimensions (four). The loss value indicates the difference between the maximum and the actual fit. A Determination Coefficient (R^2) may be computed for the relationship between each set and each dimension (R^2 equals 1 - the loss value per set). The eigenvalue indicates how much of the relationship is captured by the dimension.

		Dimension			
	Sum	**1**	**2**	**3**	**4**
Values	.644	.136	.163	.176	.168
Motivations	.814	.151	.166	.232	.265
Objectives	.894	.125	.264	.241	.264
Mean	.784	.137	.198	.216	.232
Fit	3.216				
Eigenvalue		.863	.802	.784	.768

Table 1: Loss per set

The global fit is very good. 80.4% of the global variance is explained by the four dimensions. The Determination Coefficients for each set-dimension show that Values, Motivations, and Personal Objectives explain equally well each dimension, i.e. for the first dimension Personal Objectives explain 87.5%, Motivations 84.9%, and Values 86.4%. The eigenvalues show that the three sets taken as a whole explain more than 75% of each dimension. Therefore, these results imply the existence of a strong association between the three constructs.

The weights presented in Table 2 represent the relative importance of each variable to each dimension.

The first dimension is characterised by the value „equality", the personal objective „helping others" as well as the motivation „to be helped by others" (succorance). This dimension seems to represent the social dimension of the three sets.

The second dimension can be interpreted as a positive tendency toward the value „freedom" and the motivation „heterosexuality" and a negative tendency toward the values „comfortable life" and „self respect", motivation „aggression", and personal objectives „succeed one's sentimental and domestic life", „living in accordance with one's principles". This dimension seems to be related to a personal orientation.

The third dimension is principally defined by the values „happiness", „pleasure", by the motivations „achievement", „aggression", „dominance", „intraception", and personal objectives „professional success", „succeeding one's social life". This dimension emphasises an achievement orientation within the society.

The last dimension can be characterised by a negative tendency toward the values „freedom" and „salvation", the motivations „to help friends (nurturance)", „change", „achievement" and the personal objective „succeed one's sentimental and domestic life" and a positive tendency toward the personal objective „financial ease". This dimension can be characterised by a humanistic tendency.

Dimension	1	2	3	4
Values				
A Comfortable Life	-.195	-.305	-.210	-.048
An Exciting Life	.017	-.018	-.171	.211
A Sense of Accomplishment	-.229	-.054	-.063	-.273
A World at Peace	-.114	.213	-.093	-.124
A World of Beauty	-.053	-.210	-.265	.145
Equality	.456	.091	-.124	-.058
Family Security	.207	-.249	.210	.105
Freedom	-.386	.378	.189	-.410
Happiness	-.219	.164	.390	.026
Inner Harmony	.178	-.176	.135	-.262
Mature Love	-.096	-.155	-.206	-.206
National Security	.000	.031	.094	-.200
Pleasure	-.045	.218	.547	.213
Salvation	-.102	.231	.147	-.343
Self Respect	.279	-.353	-.092	.168
Social Recognition	-.123	-.003	-.206	.235
True Friendship	.230	.304	-.203	.269
Wisdom	.070	.031	.061	.330
Motivations				
Abasement	-.288	-.124	.207	-.360
Achievement	-.069	-.338	.772	-.455
Affiliation	.177	-.473	.235	-.324
Aggression	.033	-.827	.594	.002
Individualism	-.444	.049	.084	-.210
Change	-.003	.600	.376	-.519
Deference	-.240	-.095	-.022	.376
Dominance	.093	.336	.693	.076
Perseverance	-.111	.058	-.223	-.274
Exhibitionism	-.266	.169	-.014	-.196
Heterosexuality	.165	.672	.305	-.102
Intraception	.445	-.177	.646	-.319
Nurturance	.068	-.176	-.098	-.695
Order	.140	-.321	.082	-.119
Succordance	.590	-.384	.168	-.316
Objectives				
Professional Success	-.277	.092	.354	-.124
Succeed One's Sentimental and Domestic Life	.134	-.430	-.171	-.379
Being in Good Health	-.045	-.065	-.081	.113
Living in Accordance with One's Principles	.274	-.409	.372	-.226
Succeeding One's Social Life	-.003	.036	.396	.305
Intellectual and Stimulating Life	.054	-.085	-.251	.271
Financial Ease	-.401	-.185	.043	.317
Being in Contact with Other Cultures	-.241	.171	-.306	.069
Helping Others	.573	.396	-.095	.241

Table 2: Canonical Weights

8. Discussion and Conclusion

Our results indicate the existence of four major dimensions structuring the values, motivations, and personal objectives. These dimensions relate to social, personal, achievement, and humanistic orientations.

These results confirm and at the same time complement a certain number of published results. The EPPS test results are recapitulated by the three major factors of altruism, egocentrism, and activity. Altruism is found in the humanistic dimension, egocentrism in the personal life dimension and activity in the achievement dimension.

Published observations based on the Rokeach and Kahle scales also seem to be at least in partial conformity with the results. Indeed, the reported existence of personal or social orientations (Kahle, 1986; Valette Florence, 1988) have also been identified.

Of the four major observed dimensions in this study, the social, personal, and achievement factors can be found in the publications of Schwartz and Bilsky (1987), Hofstede (1980) as well as in those of Vinson et al. (1977). They are also confirmed by Prenshaw's (1993) comparative analysis in which she claims the existence of these dimensions in all analyses performed thus far. The specific content of these three dimensions correspond partially to those reported in the literature. Prenshaw's classification claims that the social dimension is composed of three values (equality, a world of beauty, and true friendship), which is partially confirmed by the weights of „equality" within the social dimension. The same phenomenon could be observed for Prenshaw's individualistic dimension which associates certain personal values (wisdom, feeling of accomplishment, self respect) whereas our results show that „self respect" is the only concept with a strong weight on that dimension. On the other hand, our achievement dimension is not based upon the values attributed to that dimension by Prenshaw.

Two other dimensions found by Prenshaw (1993): security and pleasure orientations don't appear in this study's classifications. On the other hand, one new factor, a humanistic dimension, is found.

The comparison of the results of this study with those already published suggests that eventual differences could be the result of how values and motivations are measured. The terms which are applied to measure values as well as motivations could be polysemous for the average individual if they are not associated with more precise terms. In this respect, the categories obtained in this survey provide a more complete and detailed vision than that which is usually obtained by analysing separately values, motivations, and personal goals. It is perhaps for this reason that a humanistic dimension, unknown in previous published studies on values, can be found in this study. It is interesting to note that humanism has been in previous studies integrated in the individualistic or social orientations.

The strong association between the three concepts (values, motivations, and personal goals) poses the question concerning the reality of their very existence. Should one speak of values if they are confused with motivations? Can one substitute the notion of personal goals for values which are very abstract and highly influenced by societal norms? The answers to these questions will only be answered by a thorough theoretical analysis coupled to a more universal population sampling than that provided here.

A possible explanation for the association between the three concepts could be the existence of an inherent hierarchical relationship among them. If such a hierarchy exists, it would explain why variables from different origins are found as a part of the same motivational category. If values, motivations, and personal goals form a hierarchy, it remains to be shown how these three concepts are ordered.

It is also interesting to note that, whereas the usage of values has been suggested as a tool for market segmentation and the prediction of consumption modes, their predictive power has always been rather disappointing (Henry, 1976; Beatty et al., 1991). Could it be that the operationalization of values be the reason for their poor practical significance? If so, a more comprehensive inventory of the theoretical dimensionality of values, which should include both personal objectives and motivations, could well improve their predictive power. Here again, it is necessary to pursue additional research in order to discover and perhaps understand the explanatory power of the three concepts, take both separately and jointly.

Finally, the concept of personal goals seems to be very similar to the more familiar concepts of motivations and values. However, its very nature makes it much closer to individual behaviour and thus personal goals could prove to be an interesting surrogate for motivations and values. It could in effect be more pertinent in individualistic societies such as western society. However, the experimental character of its operationalization would necessitate a serious verification based on other samples of persons in order to conclude on the relevance of the dimensions retained in this research.

References

Bandura, A. (1986): Social foundations of thought and action: a social cognitive theory. Prentice Hall: Englewood Cliffs, New Jersey.

Bandura, A. (1989): Self regulation of motivation and action through internal standards and goal systems. In: Pervin, L.A. (Ed.), Goal concepts in personality and social psychology, Lawrence Erlbaum: Hillsdale, New Jersey, pp. 19-56.

Bearden, W.O., Netemeyer, R.G., and Mobley, M.F. (1993): Handbook of marketing scales. Sage: Newbury Park, California.

Beatty, S.E., Kahle, L.R., and Homer, P. (1991): Personal values and gift-giving behaviors: a study across cultures. In: Journal of Business Research, Vol. 22, pp. 149-157.

Braithwaite, V.A. and Law, H.G. (1985): Structure of human values: testing the adequacy of the Rokeach value survey. In: Journal of Personality and Social Psychology, Vol. 49, pp. 250-263.

Brehm, J.W. and Self, E.A. (1989): The intensity of motivations. In: Annual Review of Psychology, Vol. 40, pp.109-132.

Bond, M.H. (1988): Finding universal dimensions of individual variation in multicultural studies of values: the Rokeach and Chinese value surveys. In: Journal of Personality and Social Psychology, Vol. 55, pp. 1009-1015.

Brody, N. (1980): Social motivation. In: Annual Review of Psychology, Vol. 31, pp. 143-168.

Emmons, R.A. (1986): Personal strivings: an approach to personality and subjective well-being. In: Journal of Personality and Social Psychology, Vol. 51, pp. 1058-1068.

Emmons, R.A. (1989): The personal striving approach to personality. In: Pervin, L.A. (Ed.), Goal Concept in Personality and Social Psychology, Lawrence Erlbaum: Hillsdale, New Jersey, pp. 87-125.

Henry, W.A. (1976): Cultural values do correlate with consumer behavior. In: Journal of Marketing Research, Vol. 13, pp. 121-127.

Hofstede, G. (1980): Culture's consequences: international differences in work-related values. Sage: Newbury Park.

Gauthier, G. (1964): Test de Tendances Personnelles. Institut de Recherches Psychologiques: Montréal.

Jolibert, A. and Baumgartner, G. (1995): Values, Motivations, Personal Goals: A Conceptual and Empirical Analysis. In: Jolibert, A., Peterson, R., and Strazzieri, A. (Eds), Marketing Communications and Consumer Behavior, IAE: Aix en Provence, pp. 312-323.

Kahle, L (1983): Social values and social change: adaptation to life in America. Praeger: New York.

Markus, H.(1983): Self knowledge: an Expanded View. In: Journal of Personality, Vol. 51, pp. 543-565.

Maslow, A.H. (1970): Motivation and Personality, 2nd edition. Harper and Row: New York.

McClelland, D.C. (1985): Human Motivation. Scott Fresman and Company: Glenview, Illinois.

Murray, H.A. et al. (1938): Explorations in Personality. Oxford Press: New York.

Murray, H.A. (1951): Some Basic Psychological Assumptions and Conceptions. In: Dialectica, Vol. 5, pp. 266-292.

Prenshaw, P. (1993): The Dimensions of Values: a Measurement Approach for International Marketing Research. In: Proceedings of the A.M.A., Winter, American Marketing Association: Chicago, pp. 62-70.

Rokeach, M. (1973): The Nature of Human Values. Free Press: New York.

Schwartz, S.H. and Bilsky, W. (1987): Toward a Theory of the Universal Psychological Structure of Human Values. In: Journal of Personality and Social Psychology, Vol. 53, pp. 550-562.

Schwartz, S.H. and Bilsky, W. (1990): Toward a Theory of the Universal Content and Structure of Values: Extensions and Cross Cultural Replications. In: Journal of Personality and Social Psychology, Vol. 58, pp. 878-891.

Schwartz, S.H. (1992): Universals in the Content and Structure of Values: Theoretical Advances and Empirical Tests in 20 Countries. In: Advances in Experimental Social Psychology, Vol. 25, pp. 1-62.

Solomon, M.R. (1992): Consumer Behavior. Allyn and Bacon: Needham Heights, Massachusetts.

Valette-Florence, P.(1988): Analyse Structurelle Comparative des Composantes des Systèmes de Valeurs selon Kahle et Rokeach. In: Recherche et Applications en Marketing, Vol. 3, pp. 15-35.

Van Der Burg, E. and De Leeuws, J. (1988): Homogeneity Analysis With k Sets of Variables: An Alternating Least Squares Method with Optimal Scaling Features. In: Psychometrika, Vol. 53, pp. 177-197.

Vinson, D. E., Munson, J. M., and Nakanishi, M.(1977): An Investigation of the Rokeach Value Survey for Consumer Research Application. In: Perreault, D. (Ed.), Advances in Consumer Behavior, Vol. 4, Atlanta: Association for Consumer Research, pp. 247-252.

Abdelmajid Amine

Product Knowledge, Consumer Knowledge, and Brand Loyalty: Some Empirical Evidence about their Relationships

1. Introduction

2. Defining the Constructs under Study
    2.1. Brand Loyalty versus Inertia Repurchase
    2.2. Product Importance or Enduring Involvement
    2.3. Consumer Prior Knowledge

3. Research Hypotheses and Methodology
    3.1. Hypotheses
    3.2. Sample
    3.3. Constructs Measurement

4. Results and Discussion

5. Implications and Further Research

References

Product Importance, Consumer Knowledge, and Brand Loyalty: Some Empirical Evidence about their Relationships

Abdelmajid Amine

Abstract

In marketing literature, much theoretical work has been devoted to each of the concepts of brand loyalty, consumer knowledge and product importance. However little attention has been given to their empirical relationships. In this paper, these constructs are first conceptualised and their measurement tools proposed. Then an empirical study was designed to test mainly the assumption that product importance is a predictor of brand loyalty. Our findings show that, if product importance significantly affects consumer loyalty to a brand, this relation is not as strong as desired and could not be generalised to various product classes. Moreover, it seems that consumer knowledge intervenes as a moderator variable in this relationship.

1. Introduction

Several studies have shown that the perceived importance of a product class enhances the consumer brand loyalty in the same category (Robertson, 1976; Traylor, 1981; Assael, 1992). Nevertheless this conclusion is only based on some theoretical assumptions and has a weak empirical evidence.

Kapferer and Laurent's study (1983) shows that the relationship between the consumer's involvement and his brand loyalty must be analysed at the desaggregate level of the involvement components (enduring and situational). However, these authors defined the consumer brand loyalty concept restrictively as a repetitive purchase of a brand in a period of time. This behavioural approach doesn't take into account the consumer's affective relation to the brand which can alone distinguish the actual situations of brand loyalty from those of spurious loyalty when the same brand is purchased only to reduce the external search effort.

Consumer knowledge construct received an accurate attention from researchers in the last decades and especially through the analysis of the relationship between this construct and some of its antecedents such as enduring involvement or product importance (Bloch and Richins, 1983; Brucks, 1985). These studies conclude a positive link between the perceived product class importance and the amount of information stored in memory (prior knowledge). In addition, other previous research show that brand loyal consumers become progressively more confident in their ability to make a good choice on the basis of their internal information search.

This paper presents first the conceptualisation and measurement of the three concepts under study. It analyses next the strongness of their relationships. Mainly, two research statements will be answered: Does product importance enhance true brand loyalty? and Does consumer knowledge moderate product importance effects on brand loyalty? A survey was designed to answer these questions. Data were collected via face to face interviews from a convenience sample of French females.

2. Defining the Constructs under Study

2.1. Brand Loyalty versus Inertia Repurchase

The concept of brand loyalty has been understood during a long time as the act of buying repeatedly the same brand by consumers. However, brand repurchase behaviour can have numerous and different sources such as brand commitment, limited number of brands proposed by the customary retail store, lowest (or highest) price brand, store loyalty, absence of promotions on competitive brands, etc. But can we talk about brand loyalty in all of these situations?

Some previous studies (Cunningham, 1967; Day, 1969; Jacoby and Kyner, 1973; Jacoby, 1975; Schiffman and Kanuk, 1987) provide a preliminary response to this question. They suggest that the brand loyalty cannot be reduced to its behavioural dimension (repurchasing the same brand). It is progressively admitted that this concept cannot be measured only by observing the consumer behaviour or tracking the purchase frequency of a brand via store scanning or panel data. It seems then necessary to be sure that this repurchase is intentional and can be continued in the future before concluding an effective brand loyalty.

Two approaches have been used in the literature to define the brand loyalty construct: The behavioural one suggests that the action of repurchase the same brand by a consumer expresses his loyalty while the attitudinal view assumes that brand repurchasing behaviour is a necessary but not sufficient condition to brand loyalty so it must be completed with a positive attitude towards the brand.

In the behavioural approach, brand loyalty measures are based on panel and/or scanning data and present the advantage of their simplicity and the inconvenient of hiding different phenomena like inertia repurchase, brands substitution, multi-brand loyalty. Attitudinal approach introduces in the definition and measurement of brand loyalty the notion of brand commitment which expresses the consumer's tendency to resist to brand substitution when some situational changes occur in the store assortment or selling conditions (promotion on a competitive brand, brand out of stock, ...).

Jacoby (1975) notes that in order to consider a repetitive buyer of a brand as a loyal consumer it is necessary to check that this consistent behaviour is intentional. Three major conditions seem then to be required to true brand loyalty:

- an effective buying behaviour (and not only an intention to buy),

- its repetition over time, and

- reinforcement with a commitment to the purchased brand.

The latter characteristic can be conceived as the non-substitution between the competitive brands which can result in the case of the absence of the habitual brand in the retail store frequented in delaying the purchase or looking for the same brand in another store.

Recently, Bloemer and Kasper (1993) highlighted the theoretical and managerial implications of this distinction between the two kinds of loyalty: the spurious loyalty based on the minimisation of effort (inertia repurchase) and the effective loyalty based on the brand commitment. It is essential for the retailer or the producer to know if consistent purchase of a brand can be pursued further (true loyalty) or can be stopped when there is a change in the store assortment or in the selling conditions. Then the role of brand commitment seems to be crucial in distinguishing true loyalty from inertia repurchase.

2.2. Product Importance or Enduring Involvement

The concept of product importance is closely related to enduring involvement which indicates the centrality of a product class to the consumer and the amount of interest associated with this product category.

Several researchers have stressed that personal interest and perceived importance of a product class are good indicators of consumer involvement (Howard and Sheth, 1969; Hupfer and Gardner, 1971; Lastovicka, 1979; Antil, 1984). Zaichkowsky (1985) as well as Celsi and Olson (1988) considered that consumer's involvement with a product is function of the personal relevance or centrality of that product to him.

Nevertheless, consumer's involvement cannot be reduced to product importance because the first construct can be due to other factors (than interest or importance) such as product badge value or perceived risk. Houston and Rothschild (1978) identified two types of involvement: situational and enduring. The former occurs only in specific situations and is temporary. The latter is more permanent and takes place continuously. Situational involvement happens when particular purchase decisions are required and it seems to predict episodic behaviours (gift buying). Enduring involvement requires an ongoing interest and perceived importance of the product class whether a purchase is intended or not. So it is assumed to predict regular consumer behaviours (brand loyalty).

Kapferer and Laurent (1985) operationalise these two types of the involvement construct by distinguishing five major sources: interest/importance, hedonic value, badge value, risk importance and error probability. Interest/importance and hedonic value represent the enduring type of involvement where the remaining facets cover the situational involvement. In the following developments of this research, product importance deals only with enduring component of involvement.

Concerning the theoretical relationship between product importance and brand loyalty, there is only a weak empirical support. Robertson (1976) suggests that true brand loyalty can be met only under high-involvement conditions. He notes that a low-involved consumer cannot be considered as loyal to a brand even if he buys it several times, because he/she will be tempted to purchase another competitive brand in the same product category if there is a change in the habitual offer (sales promotion, brand stock break).

A study by Thompson (1980) found that brand loyalty is highest when consumers are personally involved in the product. The brand is then a source of self-identification (e.g., cars, cigarettes, cosmetics). In the opposite, when consumers are low-involved in a product class, they have no strong beliefs or feelings about the brand and consequently they are not committed to a brand.

2.3. Consumer Prior Knowledge

An overview of the literature on the consumer information theory reveals that the construct of consumer prior knowledge has been mainly studied as an indicator of the internal information (quantitatively and qualitatively) accumulated by the consumer and used either to solve his/her own choice tasks or to provide advice to others in order to improve their choice.

This construct covers the amount of information stored in memory, the ability to transmit it to others and consequently to influence them in their choices. Prior knowledge develops over time an increasing familiarity and expertise in the domain and could lead knowledgeable consumers to be recognised by other people as information holders or „gate-keepers".

Consumer knowledge is an important construct in understanding consumer behaviours such as information searching and information processing (Alba and Hutchinson, 1987). Kass (1982) showed that as consumers became more experienced and knowledgeable the number of information sources used in evaluating products and the amount of information sought decreases.

Two knowledge constructs have been distinguished in earlier studies: objective knowledge (accurate information about the product class stored in memory) and subjective knowledge (one's perception of the quantity and quality of what he knows about a product category). Nevertheless, some researches found that these two constructs are quite related and because of the difficulty to capture the accurate knowledge, they used the self-assessed knowledge as a proxy measure for consumer knowledge. This construct is determined by product related experiences defined as memory about relationships between the self and the product in terms of information search, product usage and purchase experience (Park et al., 1994).

For some product categories a great knowledge of the product could result into brand loyalty especially if there are some substantial perceived differences between the brands on the main selection criteria. Moreover, the brand loyal consumer tends to be more self-confident in his choice (Day, 1969). So, as the probability of purchasing the same brand grows, the amount of external information search and prepurchase deliberation decreases, and consequently the use of internal information (or prior knowledge) increases.

3. Research Hypotheses and Methodology

3.1. Hypotheses

We noted earlier that basically the concept of product importance is a recognition that certain product classes may be more or less central to an individual. Strictly speaking, no prouct is inherently important or unimportant. So, only consumers can perceive the importance of any product category. According to this, and in accordance with Robertson's theoretical assumption (1976) that brand loyalty is only met when the product class is perceived as important, the following propositions can be formulated:

> H1a: Consumers who perceive tights as a highly important product are strongly loyal to a specific brand.

> H1b: Individuals who perceive tights as a less important product are not brand loyal.

Concerning the moderating role of consumer prior knowledge, past research have shown that for some product categories a high level of prior knowledge can produce true brand loyalty especially when there are significant perceived differences between the brands offered in the marketplace. However, extensive knowledge in a product class could result into a low brand commitment if there are no substantial differences among the competitive brands. Therefore we hypothesise that:

> H2: Consumer prior knowledge on tights moderates product importance effects on brand loyalty.

3.2. Sample

Questionnaires were completed in face to face interviews by a convenience sample of one hundred and fifteen French females aged from 18 to 50 years and varied in terms of occupation. Only 103 questionnaires were finally retained for analysis. The product class of interest was women pairs of *tights* because of its high purchase frequency that suggests a sufficient variation in the perceived product importance, prior knowledge and loyalty to warrant reliability of data analyses. Moreover, Raj (1985) shows that brand loyalty level in a product class varies with the number of brands in it. When only few brands are offered within a product class the loyalty level to a brand increases autometically. In the chosen product category in our study (tights), numerous national and retail brands are available in the French Marketplace which allow brand substitution phenomena (Dim, Well, Chersterfield, Golden Lady, Le Bourget, Bomo, Wolford, Miss Helen, etc.).

Respondents were asked to indicate the brand names and the average number of pairs of tights they buy per month. They were asked next to answer a battery of five-point Likert scales measuring brand loyalty (three items), product importance (six items) and prior knowledge (four items). These measures were used in past research and revealed good psychometric properties.

3.3. Constructs Measurement

Product importance measure corresponds to the facets of interest/importance and hedonic value in the Laurent and Kapferer's involvement scale. These facets include three items each and were tested and validated successfully in previous studies (Laurent and Kapferer, 1985; Valette-Florence, 1989). Depending on the product studied, the amount of interest/importance and the hedonic value of the product can either load each on a separate factor or load simultaneously on the same factor. The first factor solution means that consumers perceive a product class as important but it doesn't procure them any pleasure (i.e. vacuum cleaner). The second factor solution suggests that consumers can be interested in a product category and at the same time associate some pleasure to its use or consumption (i.e. cigars, perfume).

True brand loyalty measure requires an attitudinal measure combined with a behavioural measure (Assael, 1992). Three items asking respondents to imagine how would they behave if a sudden change in the habitual assortment (habitual brand out of stock, promotion on a competitive brand) was proposed. Consumers who answer that they don't mind to visit another store looking for their brand or to delay their purchase are considered as truly loyal, when those who answer that they will purchase a competitive brand are identified as disloyal.

Measures of self-assessed knowledge can indicate self-confidence levels as well as knowledge levels and constitute a better predictor of consumers decision-making strategies (Park and Lessig, 1981). A four items scale measuring the amount of knowledge and experience with the product class was used to capture subjects prior knowledge. This scale developed in an earlier work (Amine, 1993) produced then good reliability and validity properties when tested in two product classes. It measures the amount of information stored in memory and consequently the ability to make a good choice on the basis of internal information search.

176

Cronbach's Alpha reliability scores and percents of variance explained by these three measures were satisfactory and respectively about 0.85 (63.4%) for product importance (one item deleted); 0.80 (61.9%) for prior knowledge and 0.72 (64.2%) for brand loyalty. Factor analyses performed on items measuring each one of these constructs show that they loaded each time together on one principal component showing that the constructs under study are unidimensional. The three measurement scales purged through factor analyses with oblique rotations are presented in the appendix.

4. Results and Discussion

To test our hypotheses, separate regression analyses were conducted first to assess the strength of the relationships between product importance and brand loyalty on the one hand and between prior knowledge and brand loyalty on the other hand. The obtained regression models show that women's perceived importance of tights has a moderate but significant effect on brand loyalty ($t = 4.85$ at $p < 0.000$; Adjusted $R^2 = 0.19$) while their knowledge about tights has a weak effect, even if significant, on her loyalty to a particular brand ($t = 2.95$ at $p < 0.005$; adjusted $R^2 = 0.073$). It appears that perceived importance of tights predicts better consumer brand loyalty (the criterion variable) than knowledge does (the assumed moderator variable).

Our first hypothesis (H1a) assuming that product importance influences significantly and positively the consumer brand loyalty is moderately confirmed even if this relationship is not as strong as supposed (Thompson, 1980). The moderate strength of this relationship could be explained by the fact that importance concerns the product category level where the loyalty is situated on the desaggregate brand level. This finding is consistent with Kapferer and Laurent's (1983) and Amine's (1995) conclusions that some variables such as brand sensitivity would mediate this relationship.

The moderating role of consumer knowledge could be proved if the part of variance of loyalty levels explained by the first regression model with the importance variable only is higher than the percentage explained by the second model using these two variables simultaneously (Baron and Kenny, 1986).

Model 1:   Brand loyalty = f (Product importance) + ε_1

Model 2[1]:   Brand loyalty = f (Product importance, Prior knowledge) + ε_2

When importance and knowledge are included together as independent variables (model 2), regression coefficients estimates of the importance variable decreases significantly from 0.47 (in model 1 where it is used alone) to 0.40. In addition, when comparing the two regression models parameters, we observe that Adjusted Squared R measure of fit varies from 0.19 in model 1 (F-statistic = 23.5; p < 0.000) to 0.17 in model 2 (F-statistic = 11.2; p < 0.001).

The decrease of goodness of fit in model 2 (with importance and knowledge as independent variables) compared to model 1 (only with importance as a predictor variable) shows that the latter better explains loyalty levels than the earlier does. These results confirm the moderating role of consumer knowledge supporting our hypothesis H2 which states that prior knowledge moderates product importance effects on brand loyalty.

Using loyalty as a clustering variable, a classification of the subjects under study was performed. Either hierarchical (average linkage) or non-hierarchical (K-means) clustering procedures were used to compare the stability and robustness of the partitions obtained. A perfect convergence of the results obtained through the two methods is observed for three groups partition providing so the best clustering quality ratio (between-groups to total variance).

The first group (n_1 = 57) encloses the disloyal consumers who frequently switch brands of tights. The second group (n_2 = 19) includes the fairly loyal consumers who could either delay the purchase if their habitual brand of tights is out of stock or switch brands. The third group (n_3 = 27) contains the highly loyal consumers who are emotionally attached to their habitual purchased brand (see Table 1).

As the sizeable group represents disloyal consumers, we can expect the prevalence of tights brand switching. This disloyalty can be explained by the hedonic value associated to tights purchase which improves variety seeking behaviours to maintain a high level of pleasure.

---

[1] In order to avoid multi-collinearity effects between product importance and prior knowledge which correlate significantly, a principal component analysis was conducted on the items measuring these two variables. Then the (independent) factorial axes obtained were introduced in the regression model 2.

178

Our findings show that group mean scores on the loyalty variable (measured on a five-point scale) are significantly different (at 0.001 level) and that variations are quite high between groups and extremely low within groups.

Loyalty Clusters	N	Loyalty mean scores	Average purchase of tights*
Cluster 1: Disloyal Consumers	57	1.75	4.5
Cluster 2: Fairly Loyal Consumers	19	2.95	7
Cluster 3: Highly Loyal Consumers	27	4.25	6.5

* Number of pairs of tights purchased per month

Table 1: Clustering Statistics

The average number of pairs of tights purchased per month for the whole sample is 5.44. When compared with the mean scores obtained in each of the three subgroups, it seems obvious that the group of disloyal consumers purchases significantly less pairs of tights than the two other groups do (fairly and highly loyal). Data in Table 1 shows however that the relation between individual scores of loyalty and the average purchase of tights is not linear especially when loyalty level increases.

A discriminant analysis was conducted to test the fairness of subjects' assignment to the three loyalty groups through product importance and consumer knowledge variables. Importance and knowledge mean scores were calculated for loyalty groups in order to compare them on these discriminant variables.

	The whole sample (N=103)	Disloyal group (n_1=57)	Fairly loyal group (n_2=19)	Highly loyal group (n_3=27)
Importance	2.95	2.62	3.33	3.42
Knowledge	2.79	2.59	3.07	3.05

Table 2: Independent Variables Scores within Clusters

We can observe from Table 2 that there is a significant difference between the „disloyal" group and the two others on the mean scores of product importance and consumer knowledge.

The first group (disloyals) corresponds also to less knowledgeable people about the product class who perceived the latter as less important. This result allows to conclude that low-involved consumers in the product class (tights) are led to low loyalty, but doesn't permit to confirm the alternative hypothesis that high-involvement leads to high loyalty. The mean difference t-tests show that the first group is statistically different from the two others on importance and knowledge scores. Only the first discriminant function was significant at $p < 0.01$.

Independent variables	Disloyal group	Fairly loyal group	Highly loyal group
Importance	2.27	2.56	2.46
Knowledge	1.85	2.50	2.63
Constant*	-5.94	-9.85	-9.56

* After weighting the three groups

Table 3: Discriminant Model Coefficients

The model discriminates between the first group (disloyal consumers) and the two others (fairly and highly loyal consumers) (see Table 3). Especially, 85.7% of the subjects of the earlier group are faithfully assigned when only 58.6% of the overall sample were affected to the right group by the model. This result shows that perceived product importance and consumer knowledge contribute mostly to distinguish between disloyal consumers and more loyal ones. This finding supports clearly our hypothesis (H1b) that low involvement leads to low loyalty.

5. Implications and Further Research

In this paper, an alternative approach for the brand loyalty concept was presented based on a more precise conceptualisation and measurement than previous work has done. Then, the product importance effects on consumer brand loyalty and the moderating role of consumer knowledge were examined. Our results provide mainly reasonable support for our predictions that low brand loyalty is likely to occur when the product class is less important to consumers and that prior knowledge intervenes to moderate product importance effects on brand loyalty. Moreover, if low product importance seems to be a sufficient condition to state that a consumer cannot be committed to a brand in a specific product class, at the opposite high perceived importance appears as a necessary but not sufficient condition to lead to true brand loyalty.

It is reasonable to imagine that consumers could be highly involved in a product category (i.e. wine), without being necessarily loyal to a specific brand, because the product importance is determined by hedonistic or experiential motivations which lead to a variety seeking behaviour. Brand switching will depend in this case on consumption situations such as the sort of meal to be eaten. Consequently, true brand loyalty appears less directly as a result of perceived product importance. The concept of brand sensitivity which is considered in the literature as a mediating variable between product importance and brand loyalty could better explain this relationship (Kapferer and Laurent, 1983). So, one can expect that when a consumer perceives a product class as highly important and if he/she is strongly brand sensitive, it is extremely probable that he/she will be loyal to a particular brand.

Even if it is important for managerial reasons to identify true brand loyalty its occurrence seems to represent only a quarter of the purchase situations met for the product studied. So, due the dominance of low important products in the consumers purchasing behaviour, inertia (or spurious loyalty) is probably so much common that till now researchers and marketing managers were satisfied with using the (restrictive) behavioural approach of brand loyalty. But, the recent research developments on affective and emotional aspects of consumer behaviour allow to expect a more extensive use and a higher relevance of the affective approaches even in brand loyalty area.

Our study doesn't provide much insight on demographic and economic characteristics of the brand-loyal consumer of tights even if our attempt to link brand loyalty to age and occupation did not provide a significant support for these relationships. Moreover, to insure external validity to our results, replication and extension of this study to sizeable consumer samples and to other product categories would provide useful information for marketing practitioners and academic researchers.

References

Alba, J.W. and Hutchinson, J.W. (1987): Dimensions of Consumer Expertise. In: Journal of Consumer Research, Vol. 13, pp. 411-449.

Amine, A. (1993): Measuring the Consumer Information Seeking: Proposition of a Scale. In: Proceedings of the 22nd EMAC Annual Conference, Barcelona, Vol. 1, pp. 91-103.

Amine, A. (1995): Implication du Consommateur et Fidélité à la Marque. In: Actes du Colloque du Laséris, March, Strasbourg, pp. 44-52.

Antil, J.H. (1984): Conceptualization and Operationalization of Involvement. In: Advances in Consumer Research, Vol. 11, pp. 203-209.

Assael, H. (1992): Consumer Behavior and Marketing Action. 4 ed., New York University Press.

Baron, R.M. and Kenny, D.A. (1986): The Moderator-Mediator Variable Distinction in Social Psychological Research: Conceptual, Strategic and Statistical Considerations. In: Journal of Personality and Social Psychology, Vol. 51, No. 6, pp. 1173-1182.

Bloch, P.H. and Richins, M.L. (1983): A Theoretical Model for the Study of Product Importance Perceptions. In: Journal of Marketing Research, Vol. 47, pp. 69-81.

Bloemer, J. and Kasper, H. (1993): Brand Loyalty and Brand Satisfaction: The Case of Buying Audio Cassettes Anew in the Netherlands. In: Proceedings of the 22nd EMAC Annual Conference, Barcelona, Vol. 1, pp. 183-200.

Brucks, M. (1985): The Effects of Product Class Knowledge on Information Search Behavior. In: Journal of Consumer Research, Vol. 12, pp. 1-16.

Celsi, R.L. and Olson, J.C. (1988): The Role of Involvement in Attention and Comprehension Processes. In: Journal of Consumer Research, Vol. 15, pp. 210-224.

Cunningham, S.M. (1967): Perceived Risk and Brand Loyalty, in: D.F. Cox (Ed.), Risk Taking and Information Handling in Consumer Behavior, Boston, Harvard University Press.

Day, G.S. (1969): A Two-Dimensional Concept of Brand Loyalty. In: Journal of Advertising Research, Vol. 9, pp. 29-36.

Houston, M.J. and Rothschild, M.L. (1978): Conceptual and Methodological Perspectives on Involvement. In: Educators' Proceedings of the American Marketing Association, Chicago, pp. 184-187.

Jacoby, J. (1975): Brand Loyalty vs. Repeat Purchasing Behavior. In: Journal of Marketing Research, Vol. 12, November, pp. 484-487.

Jacoby, J. and Kyner, D.B. (1973): A Brand Loyalty Concept: Comments on a Comment. In: Journal of Marketing Research, Vol. 10, February, pp. 1-9.

Kapferer, J-N. and Laurent, G. (1983): La Sensibilité aux Marques: un Nouveau Concept pour la Gestion des Marques, Paris, Fondation Jours de France.

Kass, K.P. (1982): Consumer Habit Forming: Information, Acquisition and Buying Behavior. In: Journal of Business Research, Vol. 10, March, pp. 3-15.

Laurent, G. and Kapferer, J-N. (1985): Measuring Consumer Involvement Profiles. In: Journal of Marketing Research, Vol. 22, pp. 41-53.

Park, C.W. and Lessig, V.P. (1981): Familiarity and its Impacts on Consumer Decision Biases and Heuristics. In: Journal of Consumer Research, Vol. 8, pp. 223-230.

Park, C.W., Mothersbaugh, D.L., and Feick, L. (1994): Consumer Knowledge Assessment. In: Journal of Consumer Research, Vol. 21, pp. 71-82.

Raj, S.P. (1985): Striking a Balance between Brand Popularity and Brand Loyalty. In: Journal of Marketing, Vol. 49, Winter, pp. 53-59.

Robertson, T.S. (1976): Low-Involvement Consumer Behavior. In: Journal of Advertising Research, Vol. 16, pp. 19-24.

Schiffman L.G. and Kanuk L.L. (1987): Consumer Behavior, 3 ed. Prentice-Hall.

Thompson, W. (1980): Brand Loyalty Beats Price in Some Product Categories. In: Marketing News, November 28, pp. 1.

Traylor, M.B. (1981): Product Involvement and Brand Commitment. In: Journal of Advertising Research, Vol. 21, pp. 51-56.

Valette-Florence, P. (1989): Conceptualisation et Mesure de l'Implication. In: Recherche et Applications en Marketing, Vol. 4, pp. 57-78.

Zaichkowsky, J.L. (1985): Measuring the Involvement Construct. In: Journal of Consumer Research, Vol. 12, pp. 341-352.

Appendix

The set of items measuring the three constructs under study are evaluated on a five-point Likert scale ranging from „Strongly Disagree" (1) to „Strongly Agree" (5). In the actual administration of the scales, items were listed in random order.

Brand Loyalty

When I don't find the brand of TIGHTS I usually buy, I prefer delay this purchase.

When I don't find the brand of TIGHTS I usually purchase, I don't mind to visit another store to buy it.

When I don't find the brand of TIGHTS I usually buy, I try another one.[*]

Prior Knowledge

I have a strong prior knowledge about TIGHTS.

I think that I could help those who want to buy TIGHTS.

I can give some advices about TIGHTS purchase if I am asked to.

I have much previous experiences with TIGHTS buying.

I feel that I am not an expert in buying TIGHTS.[*]

Product Importance/Enduring Involvement

TIGHTS is an important product to me.

When buying TIGHTS I feel so pleased.

I can say that TIGHTS is a product that interests me.

For me, TIGHTS means pleasure.

I feel unconcerned with TIGHTS product.[*]

---

[*] Scores obtained on these items were inverted.

Ingo Balderjahn

Empirical Analysis of Price Response Functions

1. The Concept of Price Response Functions
2. The Conjoint Analysis Approach
    2.1. Specification of the Conjoint Model
    2.2. Preference Models
    2.3. Shares-of-Choices
    2.4. Results
3. The Discrete Choice Analysis Approach
    3.1. Specification of the Model
    3.2. The Specification of the Random Utility Model
    3.3. Results
4. Conclusion
References

Empirical Analysis of Price Response Functions

Ingo Balderjahn

Abstract

The price demand function is one of the most popular market response models applied in economics and business. This function is a key element of price management and its knowledge is a prerequisite for optimal pricing. Although the theoretical and managerial relevance of the price demand functions is evident, marketing researchers are not particularly engaged in searching for quantitative methods to appropriately estimate these functions empirically. Conjoint analysis and discrete choice analysis are two quantitative methods to estimate price response functions. The analyses, which both have a link to the consumer behaviour theory, will be described in this article and their application will be demonstrated with to two data sets. Finally, the advantages and disadvantages of both methods will be compared with regard to key criteria for estimating the price response functions empirically.

1. The Concept of Price Response Functions

Price response functions are formal models about the relationship of the price of a product or service as the independent variable and the demand as the price-dependent variable. Other dependent variables such as market share, share-of-choices or individual buying probabilities can also be used. Price response functions are a special class of the general market response models in which the effects of all marketing activities, i.e. product, price, promotion and place, on the buying-decision behaviour are specified (Cooper and Nakanishi, 1990, p. 23).

Knowledge of the price response function is a prerequisite for optimal and rational price decision making (Simon, 1989, p. 13). It appears that price response functions have only limited practical relevance, due to the difficulties in calibrating the function. As a substitute for price response functions, managers often only try to estimate price elasticity. Thus, although the theoretical and practical importance of price response functions is evident, very little is known about empirical methods to estimate that function in an efficient and practical manner.

When conceptualising a price response model we assume from a behavioural point of view that an individual's reaction on price is influenced both by price perception and price

186

evaluation (for other models see e.g. Simon, 1989, pp. 17). If p_{ic} is the price of product i evaluated by consumer c with attributes $\mathbf{s}_c = \{s_{jc}\}$, and x_{ic} stands for the consumer's buying-decision ($x_{ic} = 1$: yes, and $x_{ic} = 0$: no) we derive at the following equation:

$$P_{ic} = P(x_{ic}=1) = f(p_{ic} \mid \mathbf{s}_c, \mathbf{p}), \tag{1}$$

whereas P_{ic} denotes the *choice probability* of individual c, and $\mathbf{p} = \{p_j\}$ contains all competitive product prices.

Traditionally, price response functions are estimated by using regression-based techniques applied on time series data (Börsch-Supan, 1987; Hanssens et al., 1990; Simon, 1989). Due to the high level of aggregation, this type of analysis does not give any indication about individual price preferences. Therefore we want to outline two quantitative methods which utilise findings of the consumer behaviour theory. Both methods use individual preference or choice data. First, we will describe the *conjoint analysis* and provide an example on data concerning students' preferences on several kinds of canteen food collected at the University of Hanover in 1990. Second, we will introduce the *discrete choice analysis,* a multinomial logit approach based on individual choice data, which is an appropriate tool to estimate price response functions. Discrete choice analysis permits to account for individual heterogeneity as well as competitive effects. We will give an example concerning individuals' choices of personal computers to further illustrate its applicability. Finally, the advantages and disadvantages of both methods will be compared with regard to key criteria for estimating the price response functions empirically.

2. The Conjoint Analysis Approach

2.1. Specification of the Conjoint Model

Conjoint analysis is a very popular method in marketing research for estimating individual preferences, market segmentation, and product development (Backhaus et al., 1994; Carroll and Green, 1995; Green and Srinivasan, 1990; Rao and Gautsch, 1982; Wittink et al., 1994). Green and Srinivasan (1978, p. 104) define conjoint analysis as any decompositional method that estimates the structure of an individual's preferences given his/her overall evaluation of a set of alternatives that are pre-specified in terms of levels of different attributes. Recently, some researchers used the term „*choice-based conjoint analysis*" to refer to a procedure which applies quantal choice models (e.g., multinomial logit and probit models) to experimentally collected data (Carrol and Green, 1995, p. 386, Desarbo et al., 1995; Louviere 1988). For the class of decompositional methods which analyse preference data, rather than methods designed to analyse choice data, I prefer to solely use the term „*conjoint analysis*" for two reasons: both approaches differ in their response mode (ratings or rankings instead of choices), and statistical analysis (Chrzan, 1994).

Conjoint analysis is a method that can be used to estimate an individual's price response (Simon, 1989, pp 28). This decompositional approach avoids estimation bias we observe if individuals have to evaluate the price directly. The conjoint analysis procedure to measure the price response function includes two steps. First, the individual's preference structure for a product or service is estimated. Second, the individual's choice or buying behaviour is derived from the estimated preference structure with the help of a choice rule. In applying conjoint analysis, we have to specify products or services as a bundle of attributes with different attribute levels. In the example that follows, canteen food is described by four attributes: starter, main course, dessert, and price. Each attribute is specified using two or three levels, respectively (Figure 1).

<table>
<tr><td><u>starter</u></td><td>salad
soup</td><td><u>dessert</u></td><td>ice-cream
pudding</td></tr>
<tr><td><u>main course</u></td><td>meat
vegetarian</td><td><u>price</u>[1]</td><td>DM 2.60
DM 3.00
DM 3.40</td></tr>
</table>

[1] DM stands for the German currency „Deutsche Mark".

Figure 1: Conjoint analysis specification of canteen food

We use the full-profile approach to collect data. Here, the respondents receive stimulus cards which describe a full menu according to the four attributes. A fractional factorial design (for details see Green and Srinivasan, 1978, p. 109; Louviere, 1988, pp 35) generated by CONJOINT DESIGNER (Bretton Clark, 1990) reduces the number of possible profiles or products from 24 to 8. In our data set these eight menus were rated by a total of 127 students.

2.2. Preference Models

To perform conjoint analysis we can choose one of three appropriate preference models for each attribute (Figure 2). It is „generally assumed that these models are the same for all individuals, but the parameters of the models are permitted to vary across the sample of individuals" (Green and Srinivasan, 1978, p. 104).

$$\bullet \quad \text{part-worth model:} \quad U_i = \sum_{j=1} f_j(z_{ij}) = \sum_{j=1} u_{ij}$$

$$\bullet \quad \text{vector model:} \quad U_i = \beta_1 z_{ij}$$

$$\bullet \quad \text{ideal point model} \quad U_i = \beta_2 z_{ij} + \beta_3 z_{ij}^2$$

z_{ij} denotes the level of the j-th attribute for the i-th profile, and u_{ij}, β_1, β_2, and β_3 denote parameters of the models.

Figure 2: Preference models of conjoint analysis

In our analysis the attributes „starter", „main course", and „dessert" are specified according to the part-worth model, while for the price we applied the vector model as well as the ideal point model. Subsequently, I will only stress the price parameters. In our example, CONJOINT ANALYZER from Bretton Clark (1987) was applied to the data. Utilising conjoint analysis, the means of the individual parameters were: β_1 = -.392, β_2 = .902, and β_3 = -.331. After this *first step*, we know the preference structures of all individuals in our sample.

2.3. Shares-of-Choices

In the *second step* we have to estimate the shares-of-choices, i.e. the number or percentage of students who select the product of interest out of all alternatives in the choice set. For this, we first have to define the relevant *choice set*, i.e. the alternatives that compete with each other, and the product for which we want to estimate the price response functions. In our illustration we assume that the students can choose between a meat and a vegetarian menu, and we want to measure the price response for the meat menu. In the given example, we are primarily interested in the price response concerning the meat menu and, therefore, we fixed the price of the vegetarian menu at DM 2.60. Further, it is assumed that both, meat and vegetarian menu, are combined with salad and pudding, the most preferred combination of the students in our sample.

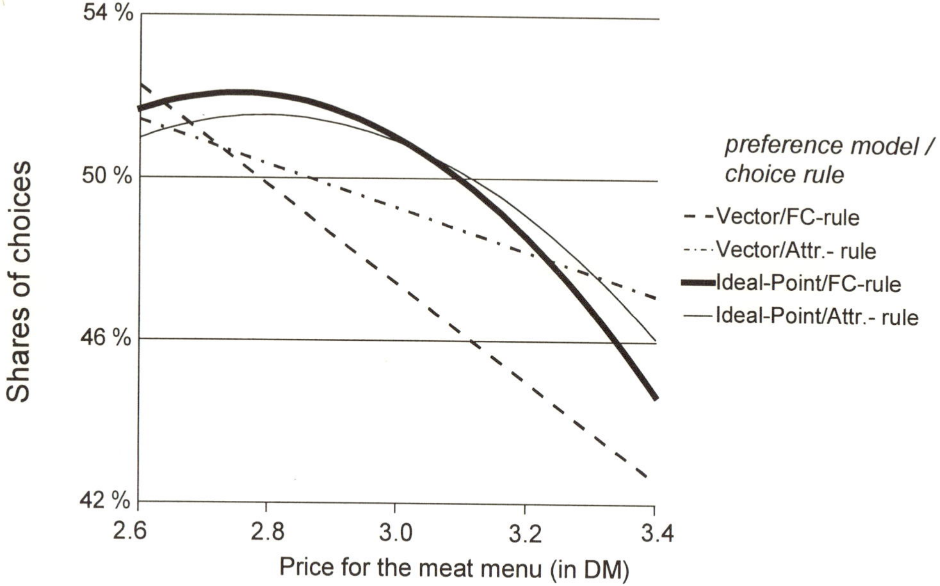

Figure 3: Price response functions for the meat menu applying two different choice rules and two different preference models.

Next, for varying prices of the meat menu we simulate shares of choices, i.e. the number of students who select the meat or vegetarian menu, respectively. To link choices with preferences we have to specify *selection rules* (Green and Srinivasan, 1990, p. 14). According to the *first choice* rule, individuals select that product which accounts for the highest preference or utility value (Louviere, 1988, p. 66). A second rule, the *attraction rule,* is a formula to calculate the individual selection probability. The probability P_{ic} that an individual c selects product i is equal to the ratio of the utility value U_{ic} of product i to the sum of all utility values of the j=1...J-alternatives, i.e. $P_{ic} = U_{ic}/\Sigma\ U_{jc}$. After defining the choice rule, we are able to generate shares of choices for varying prices by aggregating individual reactions. A regression for the shares-of-choices for different preference models (vector model and ideal point model) and different choice rules (first choice rule and attraction rule) on the prices give us the price response function (Balderjahn, 1993, p. 109; Figure 3).

2.4. Results

Figure 3 depicts the estimated price response functions for the meat menu applying two different choice rules and two different preference models. Whereas the ideal point model curves are very similar, the vector model-based curves are obviously different. However, no matter which preference model is applied, the first choice rule always leads to a stronger price effect than the attraction rule. Unfortunately, we are not able to decide with statistical means which of the price response functions outperform the others. The ideal point model curve could be interpreted as an approximation of a *single-kinked price response curve* with a price threshold of DM 3.00 (see Simon 1989, p. 24 for doubly-kinked price response curves). In summary, we have demonstrated how to use the conjoint analysis approach for the empirical estimation of a price response function. Next, we will show that the discrete choice methodology can also be used for that purpose, and which we believe attains even better results than conjoint analysis.

3. The Discrete Choice Analysis Approach

3.1. Specification of the Model

Subsequently, I will shortly outline the basic assumptions and hypotheses that underlie the discrete choice approach (for details see Ben-Akiva and Lerman, 1985). We can distinguish four assumptions and two hypotheses (Figure 4).

<table>
<tr><td>

Assumptions:

    A1: There exist a set of alternatives $\mathbf{A}$ (choice set).

    A2: There exist individual choice sets $\mathbf{A_c} \subseteq \mathbf{A}$ (evoked sets)

    A3: Products are described by a vector $\mathbf{z} = \{z_j\}$ of attributes z_j (j=1...J)

    A4: Individuals are described by a vector $\mathbf{s} = \{s_l\}$ of individual characteristics s_l (l=1...L)

Hypotheses:

    H1: Individuals try to maximise their random utility.

    H2: The buying behaviour is a valid indicator of the underlying preference structure

        (*theory of revealed preferences*)

</td></tr>
</table>

Figure 4: Assumptions and hypotheses of the discrete choice approach

According to the discrete choice model the utility U_{ic} of a product $i \in \mathbf{A}$ is a function of the product attributes z_{ijc} evaluated by consumer c with personal characteristics $\mathbf{s}_c = \{s_{cl}\}$ (Eq. 2).

$$U_{ic} = U_{ic} (\mathbf{z}_{ic}, \mathbf{s}_c, \delta_{ic}) \tag{2}$$

(Balderjahn, 1993, pp 118; Ben-Akiva and Lerman, 1985, pp 55). Further, we assume an *additive utility model* with a deterministic term $v_{ic} = v_{ic} (\mathbf{z}_{ic}, \mathbf{s}_c)$ and disturbances δ_{ic} (Eq.3).

$$U_{ic} = v_{ic} + \delta_{ic} \tag{3}$$

Under the assumptions of the *random utility model,* the selection probability P_{ic} can be specified as

$$P_{ic} = P(i \mid i,j \in \mathbf{A}_c) = P[\delta_{ic} < (v_{ic} - v_{jc})], \text{ and} \tag{4}$$

$$P_{ic} = P(i \mid i,j \in \mathbf{A}_c) = P(U_{ic} \geq U_{jc}; j \in \mathbf{A}_c).$$

P_{ic} is the probability that the utility U_{ic} is greater than U_{jc} for consumer c. The random term δ_{ic} can follow a normal (*probit model*) or an extreme value distribution (*logit model*). Under the assumption that the disturbances are independent and identically extreme-value-distributed, McFadden (1974) has shown that the *multinomial or conditional logit model* is expressed as (Ben-Akiva and Lerman, 1985, p. 103)

$$P_{ic} = \exp (v_{ic}) / \sum \exp (v_{jc}), \text{ and } j \in \mathbf{A}_c. \tag{5}$$

For better illustration of this discrete choice approach, I will subsequently refer to a data set on personal computers (Table 1). A total of 58 respondents had the choice to select one out of the five PCs depicted in Table 1. All respondents were previously informed about performance characteristics of the five computers, and, with one exception, all depicted characteristics were the same for all individuals in our sample. Only the prices for the PCs were selected at random so that they differed completely for each individual. The random sample procedure was based on realistic market prices and price deviations.

BRAND/ Technical Features	COMPAQ DESKPRO 286/40	TANDON PCA 40	COMMO-DORE PC 40/40	HIGH-SCREEN KOMPACT	IBM PS/2 MODEL 50
PROCESSOR	16-BIT 80286	INTEL-80286 8 MHz	80286 10 MHz	286-16 BIT 21 MHz	INTEL 80286 10 MHz
MEMORY (RAM)	640 K	1 MB	512/512 K	1 MB	1 MB
DISC DRIVE	1.2 MB	1.2 MB	1.2 MB	1.2 MB	1.44 MB
FIXED DISC	40 MB	40 MB	40 MB	40 MB	60 MB
GRAPHIC-CARD	HERKULES	HERKULES	AGA(EGA)	EGA	VGA
SCREEN	14"MONO-CHROM	14"MONO-CHROM	14"MONO-CHROM	15"MONO-CHROM	14" COLOUR SCREEN
OPERATING-SYSTEM	MS-DOS 3.3	MS-DOS 3.3	MS-DOS 3.3	MS-DOS 3.3	MS-DOS 3.3/ OS/2
PRICE (exc. tax)	6,000 DM	4,650 DM	5,000 DM	6,200 DM	8,900 DM

Table 1: Eight features of five selected personal computers

3.2. The Specification of the Random Utility Model

We specify the random utility model for this example as follows (eq. 6):

$$U_{ic} = \alpha_i + \beta\, p^*_{ic} + \delta_{ic} \tag{6}$$

where ß is a measure of the marginal disutility of the *price factor* p^*_{ic} with $p^*_{ic} = h(p_{ic})$, and α_i (i=1...5) is the *brand-specific intercept* which contains the effects of all non-pricing factors, (e.g. brand images). For reasons of identification, one α_i is fixed at zero. For our analysis we specify five different utility models by varying the price factor p^*_{ic} (see Table 2 first column). For model A only, we assume a linear relationship between utility and price. For models B to E, the price has a *non-linear effect* on utility, i.e. the higher the price the higher the relative influence of price on utility. As a special case, model E specifies a *piecewise-linear relationship* (Table 2).

We apply LIMDEP for the discrete choice analysis (Greene, 1995). One advantage of discrete choice analysis is that we can test alternative utility models for significance (Balderjahn, 1993, pp 190). Let L(ß) denote the *log-likelihood function* of the underlying discrete choice model. LR(0) and LR(c) are approximately chi-square-distributed *likelihood ratio* *statistics* which test that all coefficients are zero, and that all coefficients, except the alternative-specific constants α, are zero, respectively (Ben-Akiva and Lerman 1985, pp 164). Rho^2 and Rho^{2*} are *goodness-of-fit measures* like the regression rho-square and adjusted rho-squared, respectively. HR means the *hit ratio*, i.e. the true rate of ex-post choices, and PRE is a measure of *reduction in error* if we use the specified model instead of a random model[1]. If we refer to the mentioned statistics above, model D and E show the best results. In our discussion below, we will use the linear model A as the baseline.

Preference Model	L(β)	LR(0)[b]	LR(c)[c]	RHO^2	RHO^{2*}	HR	PRE
A: $v_{ic} = \mu_i + \beta\, p_{ic}$	-77.96	30.7	3.1	.165	.111	37.9	22.4
B: $v_{ic} = \mu_i + \beta\, p_{ic}^2$	-77.43	31.8	4.1	.171	.117	34.5	18.1
C: $v_{ic} = \mu_i + \beta\, p_{ic}^3$	-77.05	32.6	4.9	.175	.121	36.2	20.3
D: $v_{ic} = \mu_i + \beta\, p_{ic}^4$	-76.91	32.9	5.2	.176	.123	37.9	22.4
E: $v_{ic} = \mu_i + \beta_j\, p_{ic}$[a]	-77.19	32.3	4.6	.173	.120	39.7	24.6

a) $\beta_j = \beta_1$ if $p_{ic} \leq$ DM 6,000
    $\beta_j = \beta_2$ if $p_{ic} >$ DM 6,000
b) Model A-D: 5 degrees of freedom; Model E: 6 degrees of freedom
c) Model A-D: 1 degree of freedom; Model E: 2 degrees of freedom

Table 2: Specification of alternative utility models and their statistics

3.3. Results

The study was conducted on a total of 58 students. We will use the TANDON-PC as an example to discuss the results. The estimated utility functions for the TANDON-PC are depicted in Figure 5. The utility measurement units are arbitrary, only differences matter. The curves of the non-linear models D and E are very similar compared to the linear model A. We can conclude that prices up to approximately DM 6,000 are acceptable to customers. Above DM 6,000 the benefit of money increases rapidly.

---

[1] The random model estimates $P_{ik} = 1/I$, an I is the number of alternatives in the choice set.

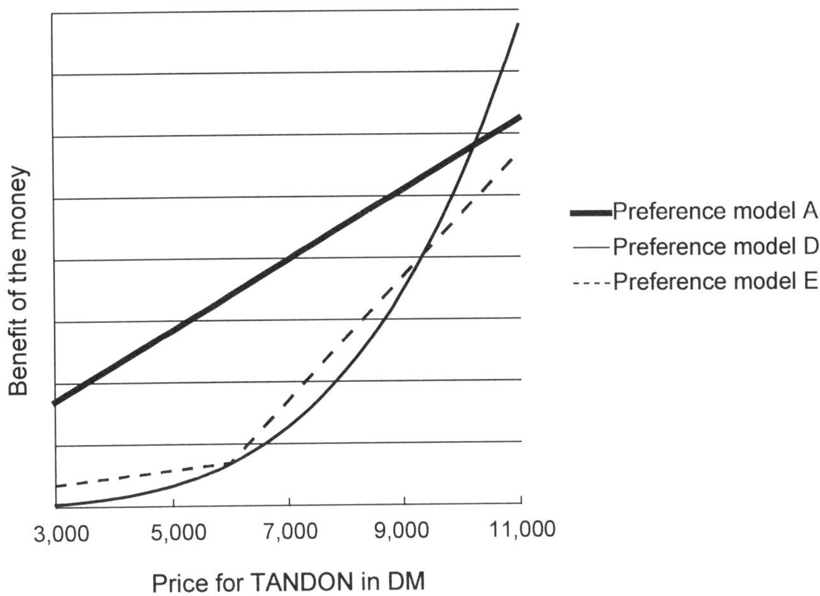

Figure 5: Alternative utility functions

For the underlying preference models, Figure 6 depicts the estimated price response curves. The variable „market share" refers to the part of choices the TANDON-PC held relative to the other four PCs in our choice set (share-of-choices). The prices of all competitive computers are fixed at their mean. Curve E shows a single-kinked price response with a *price threshold* of DM 6,000.

For preference model D, Figure 7 shows the price response curve for the TANDON-PC, assuming different prices for the IBM-PC. Although the price steps of DM 700 are constant, the price response differs, i.e. we have an *asymmetrical price response.* As a consequence of a reduction in the price of the IBM-PC, the TANDON-PC will loose more market share than it will gain if the price for an IBM-PC increases by the same amount.

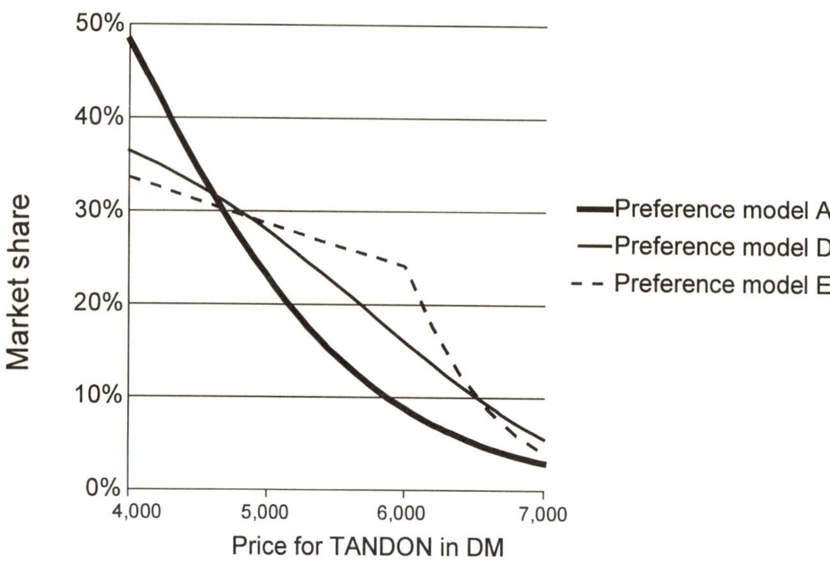

Figure 6: Price response functions for different utility models

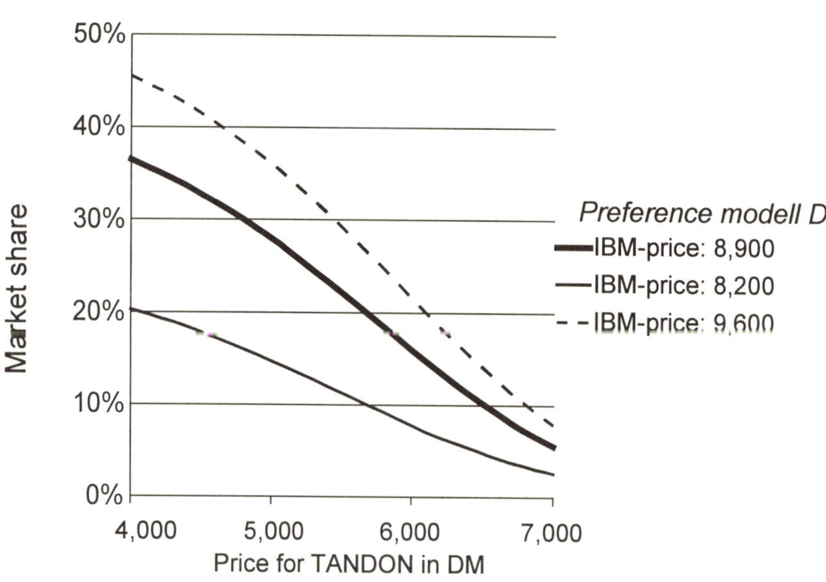

Figure 7: Price response functions for TANDON-PC for alternative prices of the IBM-PC

196

Another advantage of the discrete choice analysis is that it is quite easy to calculate price *elasticities* ε_{mi} for market shares m_i (Ben-Akiva and Lernman, 1985, pp 111). Elasticities are popular measures of the impact of changes in price on demand (Simon, 1989, p. 16). For preference model D, the formula to calculate elasticities is as follows (Ben-Akiva and Lerman, 1985, pp 111; Cooper and Nakanishi 1990, pp 31):

$$\varepsilon_{mi} = 4 \, \beta \, p_{ic}^{4} \, [1 - m_{ic} \, (p_{ic})], \tag{7}$$

where p_{ic} denotes the price for the i-th PC and $i \in A_c$. The price elasticity ε_{mi} for brand i increases if the price increases and the market share decreases. However, the price elasticities are also dependent on prices of competitive brands, too. For example, if IBM increases its price, the price elasticity of TANDON decreases and vice versa (Figure 8). Nevertheless, the reaction is asymmetrical because a lower price for the IBM-PC leads to higher competitiveness of the TANDON-PC.

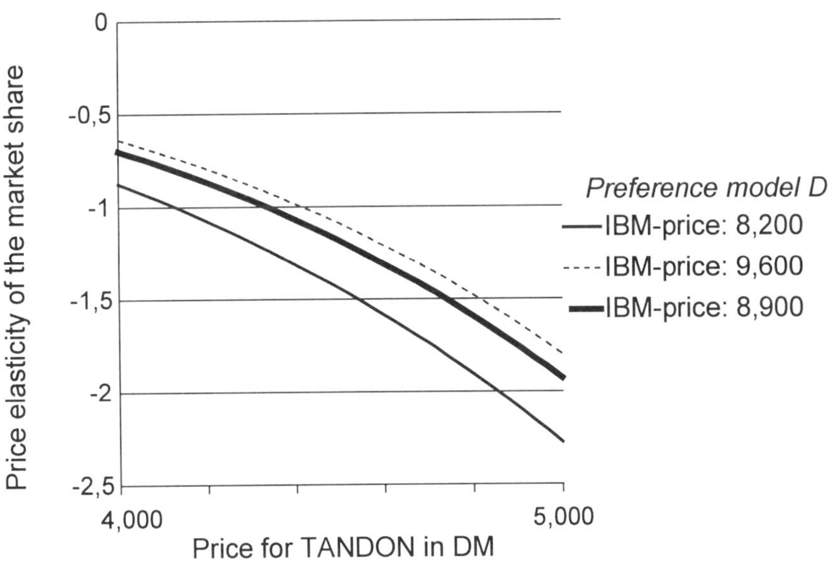

Figure 8: Price elasticity functions for TANDON-PC for alternative prices of the IBM-PC

4. Conclusion

Both approaches, conjoint analysis and discrete choice analysis, are useful tools for the empirical measurement of price response functions. Both consider behavioural aspects and avoid the well-known evaluation bias of traditional direct measurements of price responses (Simon, 1989, p. 27). However, from a conceptual and statistical point of view, the discrete choice approach is superior to the conjoint analysis. Below I will compare both approaches for three important criteria:

- Aggregation problem

  Conjoint analysis is carried out at the individual level. For aggregate price response functions we have the problem on how to aggregate individual preference values. Usually the individual values are averaged. However, this assumes that all part-worths are measured at the same scale, which is an assumption that is not guaranteed (Louviere, 1988, p. 26). Therefore, we propose to aggregate individual price response functions instead of part-worths. Discrete choice analysis is applied on a random sample of an underlying population. Parameters are constant for all individuals, and, thus, no aggregation problems occur.

- Missing link between preference and choice

  Conjoint analysis aims at explaining individual preference structures, not individual choices. Therefore, we have to assume a choice rule which transforms preferences into choices (two-step analysis). Unfortunately, we are not able to test empirically the validity of any choice rule (Green and Krieger, 1988). In discrete choice analysis the theory of revealed preferences connects preferences and choices directly.

- Evoked set problem

  Conjoint analysis assumes that the choice set is the same for all individuals. Discrete choice analysis allows for individually different evoked sets.

In summary, we conclude that conjoint analysis can be used to determine price response functions empirically, but there are several problems, both on the conceptual as well as methodological level that restrict the use of that method. Contrary, discrete choice analysis applies choice data, specifies the utility as a random variable, estimates population parameters, and allows to test the significance of underlying utility models and price response functions. Overall, discrete choice analysis is the more appropriate tool to estimate price response functions.

References

Backhaus, K., Erichson, P., Plinke, W., and Weiber, R. (1994): Multivariate Analysemethoden, 7. ed. Springer: Berlin et al.

Balderjahn, I. (1993): Marktreaktionen von Konsumenten. Duncker & Humblot: Berlin.

Ben-Akiva, M. and Lerman, S.R. (1985): Discrete Choice Analysis: Theory and Application to Travel Demand. MIT Press: Cambridge et al.

Börsch-Supan, A. (1987): Econometric Analysis of Discrete Choice. Berlin.

Bretton Clark (1987): Conjoint Analyzer 2.0. New York.

Bretton Clark (1990): Conjoint Designer 3.0. New York.

Carroll, J.D. and Green, P.E. (1995): Psychometric Methods in Marketing Research: Part I, Conjoint Analysis. In: Journal of Marketing Reserach, Vol. 32, pp. 385-391.

Chrzan, K. (1994): Three Kinds in Order Effects in Choice-Based Conjoint Analysis. In: Marketing Letters, Vol. 5, pp. 165-172.

Cooper, L.G. and Nakanishi, M. (1990): Market-Share Analysis. Kluwer Academic Publishers: Boston et al.

Desarbo, W. S., Ramaswamy, V., and Cohen, S. H. (1995): Market Segmentation with Choice-Based Conjoint Analysis. In: Marketing Letters, Vol. 6, pp. 137-147.

Green, P. E. and Krieger, A. M. (1988): Choice Rules and Sensitivity Analysis in Conjoint Simulators. In: Journal of the Acadamy of Marketing Science, Vol. 16, pp. 114-127.

Green, P.E. and Srinivasan, V. (1978): Conjoint Analysis in Consumer Research: Issues and Outlook. In: Journal of Consumer Reserach, Vol. 5, pp. 103-123.

Green, P.E. and Srinivasan, V. (1990): Conjoint Analyis in Marketing: New developments with Implications for Research and Practice. In: Journal of Marketing, Vol. 54, pp. 3-19.

Greene, W. H. (1995): Limdep 7.0. New York.

Hanssens, D. M., Parsons, L. I., and Schultz, R. L. (1990): Market Resonse Models: Econometric and Time Series Analysis. Boston et al.

Louviere, J.J. (1988): Analyzing Decision Making: Metric Conjoint Analysis. Beverly Hills.

McFadden, D. (1974): Conditional Logit Analysis of Qualitative Choice Behavior. In: Zarembka, P. (Ed.), Frontiers of Econometrics, New York, pp. 105-142.

Rao, V.R.; Gautschi, A. (1982): The Role of Price in Individual Utility Judgements: Development and Empirical Validation of Alternative Models. In: Choice Models for Buyer Behavior in Marketing, Supplement 1, pp. 57-80.

Simon, H. (1989): Price Management. North-Holand: Amsterdam et al.

Wittink, D.R., Vriens, M., and Burhenne, W. (1994): Commercial Use of Conjoint Analysis in Europe: Results and Critical Reflections. In: International Journal of Reserach in Marketing, Vol. 11, pp. 41-52.

Jean-Luc Giannelloni

Optimum Stimulation Level as a Determinant of Exploratory Behaviours: Some Empirical Evidence

1. Introduction
2. Conceptual Framework
    2.1. Optimum Stimulation Level (OSL)
    2.2. Exploratory Consumer Behaviours
    2.3. Theoretical Objectives of the Research
3. Methodology
    3.1. Measuring Optimum Stimulation Level (OSL)
    3.2. Measuring the Dependent Variables
    3.3. Data Collection and Data Analysis Methodology
4. Results
    4.1. Preliminary Analyses
    4.2. Main Results
5. Discussion - Synthesis
    5.1. Theoretical Findings, Limitations, and Perspectives
    5.2. Methodological Findings, Limitations, and Perspectives
    5.3. Empirical Findings, Limitations, and Perspectives
6. Conclusion
References

Optimum Stimulation Level as a Determinant of Exploratory Behaviours: Some Empirical Evidence

Jean-Luc Giannelloni

Abstract

This research aims to bring new evidence of the importance of Optimum Stimulation Level (OSL) in the understanding of consumers' exploratory behaviours. A short-form of the Change Seeker Index is used to test the effect of OSL on information-seeking, variety-seeking and risk-taking behaviours. The psychometric properties of the OSL scale are first assessed, and a structural model is subsequently tested and validated. The scale shows good reliability and validity. In accordance with previous research, OSL has a strong effect on the exploratory behaviours under scrutiny.

1. Introduction

Among the various individual determinants of consumption behaviours, Optimum Stimulation Level (OSL) has probably not received the attention it deserves. The lack of a reliable, valid and easy to use measurement scale is one important reason for this. Steenkamp and Baumgartner (1995) have recently developed and published such a scale. The main objective of this research is to provide further evidence of its reliability and validity. An emphasis will be put on its predictive validity, as we shall test the relationship between OSL and three different exploratory behaviours. But let us start with a brief overview of the literature.

2. Conceptual Framework

2.1. Optimum Stimulation Level (OSL)

OSL can be defined as (Falcy, 1993):

„An ideal level of stimulation to which any individual aspires and that he will try, through his behaviour, to maintain or restore."

Research in consumer behaviour is still mostly relying on the information-processing paradigm, which assumes that any consumption behaviour consists of problem solving, in order to achieve goals (Bettman, 1979). It has nevertheless been recognised that, sometimes, some behaviours are not purposeful, but simply a goal in themselves. These behaviours have been called „exploratory", as they introduce stimuli that can be said to be rewarding in themselves (Maddi, 1961).

These behaviours tend to be motivated by curiosity, which is one of the three classes of basic human motives (Atkinson et al., 1993). The purpose of these curiosity motives is mainly to keep perceptual and intellectual functions work correctly, through regular stimulation (Suedfeld, 1975). Schwartz and Bilsky (1990, p. 889), have included stimulation in their motivational domains of values as it derives from a „*presumed organismic need for variety and stimulation in order to maintain an optimal level of activation*".

This optimal level of activation, or stimulation (referred to as OSL, hereafter) is a key concept affecting the extent to which people engage in exploratory behaviours (Zuckerman, 1979). More precisely, people with high levels of OSL tend to engage more often in exploratory behaviours than people with low levels of OSL (Raju, 1980; Steenkamp and Baumgartner, 1992). Research on OSL is based on very different conceptual approaches (e.g. Fiske and Maddi, 1961). But the three following features are consensus among researchers (Falcy, 1993):

- An individual's OSL is an intermediate situation, between low and high states of stimulation.
- There are stable individual differences in OSL among people, whereas OSL is considered constant for any given individual.
- OSL is related to certain types of behaviours, said to be adaptive, because their only purpose is to increase or lower the level of stimulation at a given time.

At any given moment, an individual will engage in adaptive behaviours, if his level of stimulation at that moment and his OSL are not balanced. If OSL is superior to their current level of stimulation, people will tend to increase their stimulation, and therefore engage in exploratory behaviours; if OSL is inferior to their current level of stimulation, people will tend to decrease their stimulation (Wahlers and Etzel, 1990).

2.2. Exploratory Consumer Behaviours

These behaviours are generally split into four categories: curiosity-motivated, variety-seeking, risk-taking and innovative behaviours (Raju, 1980).

Curiosity-Motivated Behaviours

Curiosity can be defined as a desire for knowledge, with no precise purpose. A distinction is made between a specific and a diversive curiosity-motivated behaviour (Berlyne, 1960). The former consists in exploring a single stimulus in depth, as an answer to that stimulus. On the other hand, diversive curiosity is a tendency to seek stimulation from various sources, as a reaction to a state of boredom; it is not directed towards one single stimulus in particular. Information-seeking belongs to this class of behaviours.

Variety-Seeking

Variety-seeking is a mean of gaining stimulation through purchase behaviours by alternating between familiar objects (e.g. brands, stores). For some product categories, routine decision processes may lead to a situation of boredom and lack of stimulation. By simply changing their usual brand, with no objective reason (e.g. dissatisfaction), consumers complicate their buying process and increase their level of stimulation. Some evidence of a positive relation between OSL and variety-seeking behaviours can be found in the literature (McAlister and Pessemier, 1982; Venkatraman and MacInnis, 1985).

Risk-Taking

Any behaviour includes an element of risk. From a consumer's point of view, the perceived risk linked to a given behaviour can be analysed along two different dimensions. The first one is a dimension of importance: what will happen if I make a wrong choice? The second one is a dimension of uncertainty: what is the (subjective) probability of my making a wrong choice? The more perceived risk in a behaviour, the more this behaviour can be considered as risk-taking (regardless of the „real" risk); risk-taking is arousing, and therefore positively linked to OSL (Wahlers, Dunn, and Etzel, 1986).

Innovative Behaviour

It is the degree to which an individual adopts an innovation (i.e. new products, services, ideas ...) earlier than the others (Midgley and Dowling, 1978). Innovative behaviour is a function of various determinants. (Innate) Innovativeness is one of the most important among these determinants: it is a natural tendency to make innovative decisions independently of the communicated experience of others (Midgley and Dowling, 1978). From a theoretical point of view, OSL should be related to innovativeness, as novelty is arousing and therefore increases stimulation. But the empirical evidence is, at the moment, inconclusive.

2.3. Theoretical Objectives of the Research

The theoretical objective of this research is to show that OSL positively influences information-seeking, variety-seeking and risk-taking. It does not appear theoretically grounded to hypothesise structural relations between these behaviours. This is consistent with previous research in which completely independent experiments have been designed, in order to test the same relations (Steenkamp and Baumgartner, 1992).

The structural relations in the model (i.e. γ_1, γ_2 and γ_3) of Figure 1 are the hypotheses of this research. To state them in a more formal way, we postulate that:

H1: OSL has a positive effect on information-seeking behaviours

H2: OSL has a positive effect on variety-seeking behaviours

H3: OSL has a positive effect on risk-taking behaviours

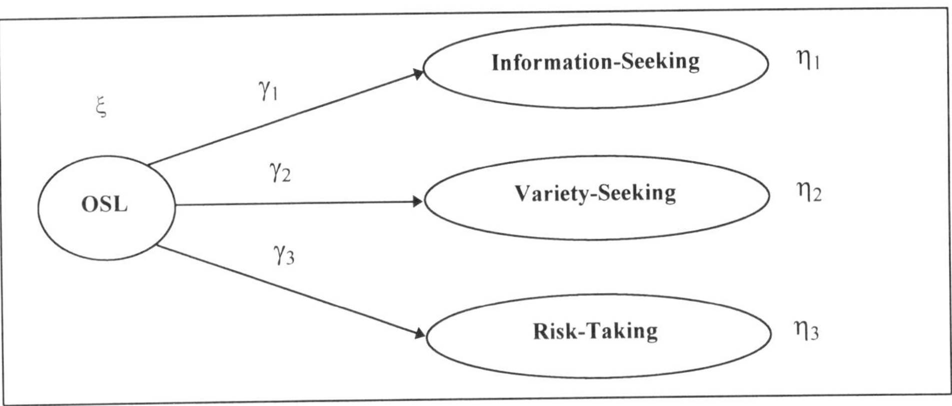

Figure 1: A theoretical model of OSL and three exploratory behaviours

3. Methodology

3.1. Measuring Optimum Stimulation Level (OSL)

A multitude of instruments, based on various conceptual approaches are available. Among others, the Change Seeker Index (CSI) (Garlington and Shimota, 1964), the Arousal

Seeking Tendency (I and II) scales (Mehrabian and Russel ,1973; Mehrabian, 1978), and the Sensation Seeking Scale (SSS) (Zuckerman, 1979) all claim to measure OSL. None of these instruments have proved really satisfactory. For example, Falcy (1993), after having compared Arousal Seeking Tendency I (Mehrabian and Russel, 1973) and Sensation Seeking Scale V (Zuckerman, 1979) recommends building a new scale.

A major weakness of these scales is their length. The shortest one is made of 32 self-report items (Arousal Seeking Tendency II). As a consequence, their factorial structure is often unstable. Recently, Steenkamp and Baumgartner (1995) have developed a very short scale, based on the Change Seeker Index, which „(tries to capture) the need for variation in one's stimulus input in order to maintain optimal functioning" (Garlington and Shimota, 1964). This research was based on previous work in which they concluded that the Change Seeker Index yielded the most consistent results (Steenkamp and Baumgartner, 1992, p. 446).

The Change Seeker Index (CSI) short-form is a seven-item self-report instrument, using 5-point Likert-type scales (Steenkamp and Baumgartner, 1995, p. 98). A confirmatory factor analysis conducted by these authors on the final version of the scale shows a good overall fit: χ^2 (14 df) = 20.34 (p = 0.12), Comparative Fit Index = 0.986; Tucker-Lewis Index = 0.980. Its average reliability is around 0.86. The test of the nomological validity of the CSI short-form yields the same results as those produced by the full CSI. One very interesting result is that the short-form is not, contrary to the full CSI, contaminated with social desirability. Last but not least, the CSI short-form has been cross-culturally validated. It means that it performs equally well with US, Belgian and Dutch samples. In their conclusion, the authors suggest that the scale should be administered to different and more heterogeneous subjects, including samples from other European countries (Steenkamp and Baumgartner, 1995, p. 103).

The methodological objective of this research was to translate, adapt if necessary, and test the psychometric characteristics of the CSI short-form on a French sample.

3.2. Measuring the Dependent Variables

Information-Seeking Tendency

An *ad-hoc* scale has been built. It draws very loosely on the „Echelle de Recherche d'Information" (ERI, Information Seeking Scale) (Amine, 1993). The ERI is made up of 5 dimensions: internal information (experience, acquired knowledge), intensity of information-seeking, external information coming from close personal sources (e.g. parents, friends ...), external information coming from commercial personal sources (e.g. salespeople), external information coming from commercial non-personal sources (e.g. product packaging).

If OSL has any effect on information-seeking behaviours, it is more interesting, in our view, to try to measure it on external information search. Our assumption here is that seeking external information is more stimulating than retrieving one's own knowledge in memory. To be consistent with this assumption, and to shorten the ERI, we have „merged" its four remaining dimensions into one, built upon 5 items. This scale is given in the appendix.

Variety-Seeking Tendency

Several scales exist in the North-American literature (e.g. Raju, 1980; Venkatraman and MacInnis, 1985; Steenkamp and Van Trijp, 1991). We have used a French version of Raju's scale, made of 5 items (6-point Likert scales) (Sirieix et Dubois, 1995; see appendix).

Risk-Taking Tendency

When it comes to measuring, what researchers call risk-taking is actually innovative behaviour (e.g. Raju, 1980; Venkatraman and Price, 1990). But the risk component in the purchase of a new product heavily depends on the product category, and is, in our view, related to situational involvement. If innovative behaviour obviously includes some risk, it is much more than simply risk-taking.

We therefore needed to develop a scale aimed at capturing the idea of risk-taking behaviour. Falcy (1993) has used a scale she called „search for adventure", built upon items linked to (mainly physical) activities objectively including some risk. We drew upon this scale to build our own instrument (4 items, 7-point Likert scales, see appendix).

3.3. Data Collection and Data Analysis Methodology

Data Collection

The data were collected in January 1996. A sample of 360 people was designed, using three crossed quotas, in order to be representative of the population of Chambéry and its suburban area. The empirical context of the research is tourism in a broader sense.

Data Analysis Methodology

We needed to use a methodology that allows the testing of hypotheses at a theoretical level, using empirical data. Therefore, a structural equation modelling approach was used here. First, a series of confirmatory factor analyses was conducted on the four scales, in order to assess their unidimensionality and their reliability. Then, a complete structural model was built and tested by means of an analysis of covariance structure (ACS), using maximum likelihood estimation of the parameters.

4. Results

4.1. Preliminary Analyses

4.1.1. Exploratory Analyses

Three quotas were used to build the sample: gender, age and occupation. Representativity has been achieved on gender and age, but not on occupation. Executives and professionals are slightly over-represented, while blue-collars and non-active people are slightly under-represented ($\chi^2 = 17.9$, df = 8, p = 0.022).

46,81% of the sample are men (53,19% women); 22,93% are aged between 20 and 29, 38,76% between 30 and 49, and 38,31% above 50; 33,49% are clerks and mid-level management people, 19,8% are retired and 14,23% inactive (mainly non-working women).

A first step aimed at eliminating outliers and observations for which data were missing. 347 people, at this stage, remained for subsequent analyses. Most of the items showed means slightly above the average and a reasonable dispersion; in the same way kurtosis and skewness were not extreme. The information-seeking, variety-seeking and OSL scales were therefore considered as „convenient" for analyses based on the normal distribution theory assumption, though none of the items were actually normally distributed. On the contrary, the risk-taking scale showed very low item means, relatively high standard deviations and at least one item with extreme kurtosis and skewness.

The correlation matrices show homogeneous correlation patterns for the OSL, variety-seeking and information-seeking scales. This is exploratory evidence of unidimensional structures. The pattern is more heterogeneous for the risk-taking scale, suggesting that at least one of the items would not correlate on one common factor. Principal components analyses (PCA) have been performed on the four scales, and Table 1 shows a summary of the result.

Scale	Number of items	Average Loading	Average Communality	α	Cumul. % of Var.
Information-Seeking	5	0.724	0.522	0.771	52.4
Variety-Seeking	5	0.808	0.650	0.865	65.1
Risk-Taking	2	0.794	0.630	0.626	72.8
OSL	7	0.756	0.576	0.876	57.6

Table 1: A summary of the exploratory analyses

Due to poor univariate statistics, low item-to-total correlations, and low communalities, two items were removed from the risk-taking scale. The PCA conducted on the two remaining items yields satisfactory results, though no confirmatory analysis can be performed in this situation[1].

4.1.2. Confirmatory Analyses on Measurement Scales

The unidimensional structure of the OSL, information-seeking and variety-seeking scales were confirmed by means of three confirmatory factor analyses, performed with EQS 4 (Bentler, 1993; Bentler and Wu, 1993). As shown in Table 2 below, the three structures are confirmed, showing good overall fits, and high loadings.

Scale	Lowest standardised loading	Average squared loadings	CFI*	χ^2 (df, p)	Average standardised residuals
OSL	0.550	0.507	0.998	13.36 (11. 0.27)	0.0373
Variety-seeking	0.764	0.695	0.996	9.16 (4. 0.06)	0.0127
Information-seeking	0.784	0.662	0.999	5.88 (5. 0.32)	0.0112

* CFI = Comparative Fit Index (Bentler, 1990)

Table 2: Results of confirmatory factor analyses

---

[1] Because the number of parameters to estimate is higher than the number of elements in the data vector (i.e. number of variances and covariances). In that case, the model is said to be under-identified (MacCallum, 1995, p. 29).

The fit statistics are systematically close to 1, with non-significant χ^2 tests. The three scales show average squared loadings higher than 0.5. This means that the latent factors share more than 50% of variance with their indicators, suggesting good convergent validity, according to Fornell and Larcker's terminology (Fornell and Larcker, 1981).

With measurement scales, a „method factor" is often „hidden" in error terms. In other words, a part of the error variance is due to the measurement tool. By allowing the error terms to correlate, or at least part of them, one often achieves a better fit in confirmatory factor analyses. To achieve the results displayed in Table 2, we correlated two error terms of the variety-seeking scale, and 4 error terms of the OSL scale.

4.2. Main Results

The OSL scale has a reliability of 0.876 (α). It is comparable to the result reported by Steenkamp and Baumgartner (1995). Its convergent validity is 0.507 (Table 2). The full model is given in Figure 2. Structural parameters and residual latent errors are reported there. Global fit statistics and other results are given in Table 3. The global fit statistics prove good enough to avoid further steps of model fitting. The χ^2-statistic is highly significant. This is not surprising, as the number of measurement variables is high compared to the number of parameters estimated. A high CFI and low residuals are in themselves fair evidence of a good fit.

Scale	Lowest standardised loading	Average squared loadings	CFI	c^2 (df, p)	Average standardised residuals
OSL	0.551	0.483	0.95	359.57 (143; 0.001)	0.0565
Variety-Seeking	0.790	0.695			
Risk-Taking	0.478	0.583			
Information-Seeking	0.784	0.662			

Table 3: Complete structural model fit statistics and other results

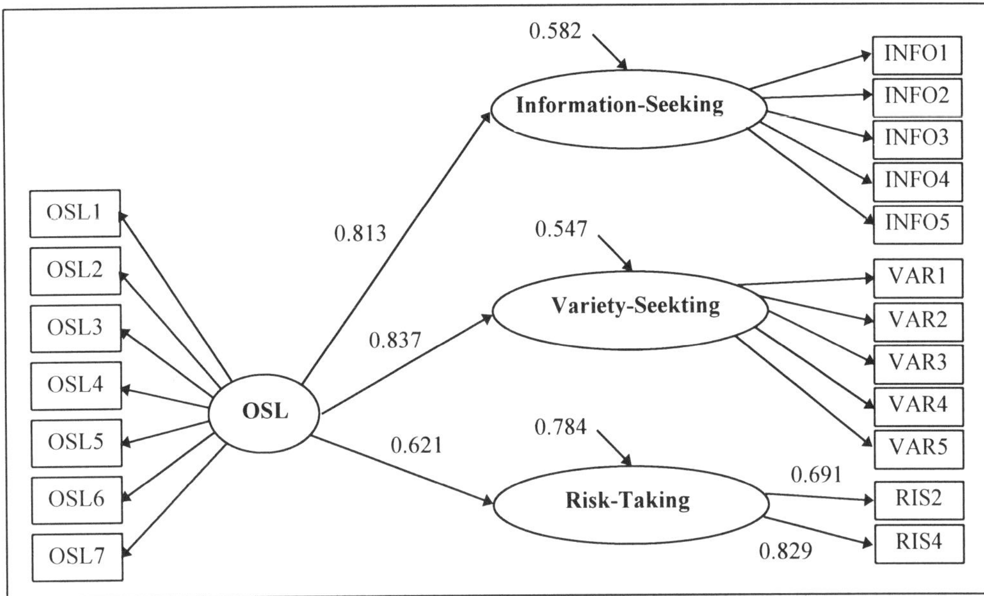

Figure 2: Main results

EQS does not compute correlations between latent factors. The scale's discriminant validity could not, consequently, be directly assessed. We therefore used a more classical estimation approach. We know that Cronbach's alpha is equal to 0.876. In a multitrait-multimethod matrix, discriminant validity is verified when the reliability coefficients (monotrait-monomethod diagonal) are higher than the correlations between constructs (heterotrait-monomethod triangle) (Campbell and Fiske, 1959). As we had assessed our constructs' unidimensionality, we could use aggregate measures for these constructs (total scores) and compute correlation coefficients between them, given in Table 4. All these correlations are lower than OSL's reliability, indicating discriminant validity for this scale.

	OSL	Information-Seeking	Variety-Seeking	Risk-Taking
OSL	1.000			
Information-Seeking	0.258	1.000		
Variety-Seeking	0.667	0.301	1.000	
Risk-Taking	0.554	0.174	0.425	1.000

Table 4: Pearson's correlations between OSL and exploratory behaviours

Nomological validity is relative to the theoretical structure hypothesised in a model. This one must achieve some level of significance and predictive power, otherwise one could question the structural relations postulated between constructs. The nomological validity is given by the average percentage of variance of the endogenous latent constructs accounted for by the exogenous latent constructs (Fornell and Larcker, 1981). In our model, the nomological validity of OSL is given by its predictive power as regards information-seeking, variety-seeking and risk-taking behaviours. Unfortunately, EQS does not yield R^2 for latent constructs. But, as there were only direct effects to take into account, these R^2 coefficients were rather straightforward to compute. We only had to square the three structural coefficients, and compute their mean. The result is 0.583; it means that, on average, OSL explains 58.3% of the variance of the constructs to which it is related.

5. Discussion - Synthesis

5.1. Theoretical Findings, Limitations, and Perspectives

The existence of OSL has been re-assessed. Theory states that OSL is a predictor of exploratory behaviours such as variety-seeking, information-seeking, and risk-taking. This was confirmed here. The effect of OSL on the three behaviours is strong, especially on variety-seeking and information-seeking. This confirms previous research (e.g. Raju, 1980; Venkatraman and MacInnis, 1985; Steenkamp and Baumgartner, 1992). Further research on OSL could focus on its relationship with perceived risk and risk-taking, as risk-taking behaviours are conceptually different from innovative behaviours.

5.2. Methodological Findings, Limitations, and Perspectives

From a methodological point of view, this research brings further evidence of the CSI short-form's reliability and validity. We confirm the scale's unidimensionality, its reliability, and its validity. We would recommend to further examine the scale's construct validity, by means of a structured multitrait-multimethod approach, using structural equation modelling (e.g. Byrne, 1994; Marsh and Grayson, 1995). What Fornell and Larcker (1981) call convergent validity is in fact another form of reliability. It simply indicates that a latent construct shares a significant amount of variance with its indicators. Convergent validity, from a psychometric point of view, is the ability of an instrument to achieve the same results, using two different methods.

Its discriminant validity also remains to be questioned. The OSL and variety-seeking scales are very highly correlated. As the theoretical constructs are different, this suggests that both scales are redundant (i.e. the items are not clearly differentiated by respondents). The correlation found here (r = 0.667) is much higher than that reported by Steenkamp and Baumgartner (1992, r = 0.178) and by Steenkamp and Baumgartner (1995, r = 0.355). In their 1992 paper, these authors used an **actual** variety-seeking behaviour measure; a relatively low correlation is therefore not surprising. In their 1995 paper, though, they used the variety-seeking component of Raju's scale (1980), which is a self-report measure. Our measure is also based, though indirectly, on Raju's work. Two reasons might therefore explain the discrepancy between the two coefficients.

Successive translations and adaptations from English to French have produced variety-seeking items that are very similar, in their meaning, to the OSL items. The only difference is that the former are related to a particular object, whereas the latter are not.

The second reason might be related to the object of measurement used here. When it comes to holidays in a broader sense, OSL and variety-seeking might be very closely associated. A simple cross-tabulation between the two total-score variables gives some evidence of this association (χ^2 = 180.93, df = 9, p = 0.0000; Cramer's v = 0.445). Those who score low on OSL score equally low on variety-seeking in tourism (mainly operationalised as the choice of a vacation site); in the same way, people score average, or high, on both scales. It might therefore be useful to test the OSL scale in several empirical contexts before one can formulate definitive conclusions about its discriminant validity.

5.3. Empirical Findings, Limitations, and Perspectives

The focus of this research was neither empirical, nor managerial. We have paid very little attention to tourism (choice of a vacation site in particular). It is obvious, though, that this object deserves further attention, for a number of reasons. First, because it is one of France's most important economic activities. Hundreds of thousands of jobs depend on the good performance of the French tourist business. From a marketing point of view, it is therefore important to have reliable information on tourists' needs, desires, characteristics, and so on. Second, because research in tourism, at least in France, has not yet achieved, in our view, what one might call a sufficient „state of maturity", most research being due to private businesses and consultants.

6. Conclusion

This research has confirmed the effect of OSL on information-seeking, variety-seeking and risk-taking. As a structural approach has been used, this conclusion is to be considered from a theoretical point of view. This is further evidence of the importance of OSL in consumer behaviour research, as it is related to behaviours that are not, strictly speaking, taken into account by the classical information-processing paradigm. Variety-seeking is particularly interesting, because it most often happens in situations when, according to theory, it should not (low or medium involvement, routine choice ...).

To achieve this theoretical objective, it was necessary to use a reliable and valid tool to measure OSL. Our French version of Steenkamp and Baumgartner's scale (1995) shows here good psychometric properties, at least comparable to their reported results. More empirical evidence is needed, but the scale can already be used with confidence.

Nevertheless, several questions still remain. Should we measure OSL, or an individual's need for stimulation at a given moment in time? It seems that the latter could explain some behaviours much better than OSL. But developing such a measure would surely raise tremendous problems. What is the degree of variability in people's OSL? Is OSL really independent of objects and situations? In other words, is it really constant, for a given individual? These are, among many others, questions that have not been examined in this research and which deserve, further attention.

References

Amine, A. (1993): La recherche d'information par le consommateur: proposition d'une échelle de mesure. In: Recherche et Applications en Marketing, Vol. 8, No. 1, pp. 97-112.

Atkinson, R.L., Atkinson, R.C., Smith, E.E., and Bem, D.J. (1993): Introduction to psychology. 11th ed., Harcourt Brace & Cy International.

Bentler, Peter M. (1990): Comparative Fit Indices in Structural Models. In: Psychological Bulletin, Vol. 107, pp. 238-246.

Bentler, Peter M. (1993): EQS. Structural Equations Program Manual. L.A.: BMDP Statistical Software, Inc.

Bentler, Peter M. and Wu Eric J.C. (1993): EQS/Windows. User's Guide. L.A.: BMDP Statistical Software, Inc.

Berlyne, D.E. (1960): Conflict, Arousal and Curiosity. N.Y.: McGraw-Hill.

Bettman, J.R. (1979): An Information Processing Theory of Consumer Choice: Reading, Mass.: Addison-Wesley.

Byrne, Barbara M. (1994): Structural Equation Modeling with EQS and EQS/Windows. London: Sage Publications.

Campbell, D.T. and Fiske, D.W. (1959): Convergent and Discriminant Validation by Multitrait-Multimethod Matrix. In: Psychological Bulletin, Vol. 56, March, pp. 100-122.

Falcy, S. (1993): Pour une mise en oeuvre du concept de niveau de stimulation optimal dans un contexte français. In: Proceedings of the 9th International Congress dof the Association Française de Marketing, pp. 515-542.

Fiske, D.W. and Maddi, S.R. (1961): Functions of Varied Experience. Homewood, IL: Dorsey.

Fornell, C. and Larcker, D.F. (1981): Evaluating Structural Equation Models with Unobservable Variables and Measurement Error. In: Journal of Marketing Research, Vol. 18, No. 1, pp. 39-50.

Garlington, W.K. and Shimota, H.E. (1964): The Change Seeker Index: A Measure of the Need for Variable Stimulus Input. In: Psychological Reports, Vol. 14, pp. 919-924.

Gerbing, D.W. and Anderson, J.C. (1988): An Updated Paradigm for Scale Development Incorporating Unidimensionality and its Assessment. In: Journal of Marketing Research, Vol. 25, No. 2, pp. 186-192.

Jöreskog, K.G (1971): Statistical Analysis of sets of Congeneric Tests. In: Psychometrika, Vol. 36, No. 2, pp. 109-133.

MacCallum, Robert C. (1995): Model Specification. Procedures, Strategies, and Related Issues. In: R.H. Hoyle (Ed.), Structural Equation Modeling, London: Sage Publications.

Maddi, S.R. (1961): Exploratory Behavior and Variety-Seeking in Man. In: D.W. Fiske and S.R. Maddi (Eds.): Functions of Varied Experience, Homewood, Il: Dorsey, pp. 253-277.

Marsh, Herbert W. and Grayson, David (1995): Latent Variable Models of Multitrait-Multimethod Data. In: R.H. Hoyle (Ed.): Structural Equation Modeling, London: Sage Publications.

McAlister, L. and Pessemier, E. (1982): Variety-seeking behavior: an interdisciplinary review, Journal of Consumer Research, Vol. 9, No. 3, pp. 311-322.

Mehrabian, A. (1978): Characteristic individual reactions to preferred and unpreferred environments. In: Journal of Personality, Vol. 46, December, pp. 717-731.

Mehrabian, A. and Russel, J.A. (1973): A measure of arousal-seeking tendency. In: Environment and Behavior, Vol. 5, September, pp. 315-333.

Midgley, D.F. and Dowling, G.R. (1978): Innovativeness: the concept and its measurement. In: Journal of Consumer Research, Vol. 4, No. 3, pp. 229-242.

Raju, P.S. (1980): Optimum stimulation level: its relationship to personality, demographics and exploratory behavior. In: Journal of Consumer Research, Vol. 7, No. 3, pp. 272-282.

Schwartz, S.H. and Bilsky, W. (1990): Toward a Theory of the Universal Content and Structure of Values: Extensions and Cross-Cultural Replications. In: Journal of Personality and Social Psychology, Vol. 58, No. 5, pp. 878-891.

Sirieix, L. and Dubois, P.L. (1995): Exploration par le lèche vitrine et recherche de variété dans le choix du point de vente: une analyse comparative. In: Recherche et Applications en Marketing, Vol. 10, No. 3, pp. 33-46.

Steenkamp. J.-B. E.M. and Baumgartner. H. (1992): The Role of Optimum Stimulation Level in Exploratory Consumer Behavior. In: Journal of Consumer Research, Vol. 19, No. 3, pp. 434-448.

Steenkamp, J.-B. E.M. and Baumgartner, H. (1995): Development and Cross-Cultural Validation of a Short Form of CSI as a Measure of Optimum Stimulation Level. In: International Journal of Research in Marketing, Vol. 12, No. 2, pp. 97-104.

Steenkamp, J.-B. E.M. and Van Trijp (1991): The Use of LISREL in Validating Marketing Constructs. In: International Journal of Research in Marketing, Vol. 8, No. 3, pp. 283-299.

Suedfeld, P. (1975): The Benefits of Boredom: Sensory Deprivation Considered. In: American Scientist, Vol. 63, pp. 60-69.

Venkatraman, M.P. and MacInnis, D.J. (1985): The Epistemic and Sensory Exploratory Behaviors of Hedonic and Cognitive Consumers. In: Advances in Consumer Research, pp. 102-107.

Venkatraman, M.P. and Price, L.L (1990): Differentiating between Cognitive and Sensory Innovativeness: Concepts, Measurement, and Implications. In: Journal of Business Research, Vol. 20, No. 4, pp. 293-315.

Wahlers, R.G., Dunn, M.G., and Etzel M.J. (1986): The Congruence of Alternative OSL Measures with Consumer Exploratory Behavior Tendencies. In: Advances in Consumer Research, pp. 398-402.

Wahlers, R.G. and Etzel, M.J. (1990): A Structural Examination of Two Optimal Stimulation Level Measurement Models. In: Advances in Consumer Research, pp. 415-425.

Zuckerman, M. (1979): Sensation Seeking: Beyond the Optimal Level of Arousal. Hillsdale, NJ: Lawrence Erlbaum.

Appendix

Information-Seeking: French Wording	Var. Code	Tentative English Translation
Quand je choisis mes vacances, je n'hésite pas à y passer du temps	INFO1	When choosing my holiday, I do not hesitate to spend time on it
Je ne pars pas en vacances sans avoir demandé conseil (agences, offices de tourisme ...)	INFO2	I do not go on holiday without first having asked for advice (travel agencies, tourist offices ...)
Je consulte beaucoup de brochures touristiques avant de partir en vacances	INFO3	I consult many tourist brochures before I go on holiday
Je n'éprouve pas réellement le besoin de m'informer sur mes futures vacances (-)	INFO4	I do not really feel the need to get information about my future vacation (-)
Je suis à l'affût des livres ou des émissions de télé qui concernent ma destination de vacances	INFO5	I am on the watch for books or TV programmes concerning my holiday destination

Variety-Seeking: French Wording	Var. Code	Tentative English Translation
J'aime changer souvent de lieu de vacances	VAR1	I often like to change my place of vacation
Si j'aime un lieu de vacances, je ne vais pas en changer juste pour le plaisir d'essayer autre chose (-)	VAR2	If I like a vacation site, I will not change it simply for the pleasure of trying somewhere else (-)
Je préfère aller sur mon lieu de vacances habituel, plutôt que d'en essayer un dont je ne suis pas sûr (-)	VAR3	I prefer to go to my usual place of vacation, rather than trying one I am not really sure about (-)
Je trouve ennuyeux d'aller en vacances toujours au même endroit	VAR4	I find it boring to always go on holiday at the same place
Quand je me suis habitué à un lieu de vacances, je déteste en changer (-)	VAR5	When I get used to a vacation site, I hate to change (-)

Risk-Taking: French Wording	Var. Code	Tentative English Translation
J'aime aller en vacances dans des pays où il y a du danger (terrorisme, guerre, volcans, climat ...)	RIS1	I like to go on vacation in countries where there is some danger (terrorism, war, volcanoes, weather ...)
En vacances, je cherche à pratiquer des activités telles que le parapente, le saut à l'élastique, le canyoning...	RIS2	When I am on holiday, I try to enjoy activities such as paragliding, benji-jumping, canyoning...
Avant toute chose, en vacances, je cherche à ne pas me blesser (-)	RIS3	First things first: when I am on vacation, I try not to hurt myself (-)
En vacances, je recherche systématiquement l'aventure et l'inattendu	RIS4	When I am on vacation, I systematically look for some adventure and the unexpected

Note: (-) means reversed coding

Björn Walliser and Thomas Froehlicher

The Reaction of German Consumers to French Nuclear Testing

1. Introduction

2. Review of French and German Cultural Differences with Regard to Consumer Behaviour
   2.1. Main Cultural Differences between French and Germans
   2.2. Man-Nature Orientation in France and Germany

3. The German Consumers' Response
   3.1. Quantitative Results of the Content Analysis
   3.2. Qualitative Results of the Content Analysis
   3.3. Results from the Mail Survey

4. Conclusion and Implications

5. Limitations and Future Research

References

The Reaction of German Consumers to French Nuclear Testing

Björn Walliser and Thomas Froehlicher

Abstract

After a review of French-German cultural differences regarding consumer behaviour, the German consumers' response to French nuclear testing is evaluated. A media content analysis indicates that consumer protests are directed against the institution responsible for the tests - the French government - as well as against „innocent" French companies. A mail survey among French subsidiaries in Germany confirms the negative impact of the protests on private firms. Although pressure on these firms comes from different sources and with varying intensity, most of the protests originate at the individual consumer's level. However, most effects seem to be only temporary and do not demand defensive moves with long term consequences from the companies concerned.

1. Introduction

On June 13, 1995, the then newly-elected French President, Jacques Chirac, announced a series of nuclear tests to be effected in the Pacific region. Despite world-wide protests to this plans, a total of six tests were run between September 1995 and January 1996. During this whole period, it was repeatedly suggested that French nuclear policy would have a negative impact on French commercial interests. However, very little efforts was undertaken actually to study the economic consequences of the tests in detail.

This paper aims to describe and analyse the reaction of German consumers to French nuclear policy. The choice of Germany is justified by two factors: Not only is Germany the most important economic partner of France, but also the sensitivity to environmental issues is one of the most prominent cultural differences between both countries. Thus, it seems particularly interesting to examine to what extent, in which way, and for which period of time the German public responded to nuclear tests staged by its neighbour on the opposite side of the globe.

In the first part of this article, the main cultural differences between France and Germany will briefly be summarised. Particular importance will be attached to the man-nature orientation which can be observed in both countries and its implications for marketing, especially consumer behaviour.

Based on a content analysis of French and German media and a mail survey among French subsidiaries in Germany, the second part will then describe the German consumers' response to the tests in detail. Finally, implications for marketing and further research will be drawn.

2. Review of French and German Cultural Differences with Regard to Consumer Behaviour

2.1. Main Cultural Differences between French and Germans

Over the last decades, differences between French and German culture have been studied on many occasions and in different ways. While some authors concentrated mainly on organizational and management aspects of the two (and other) cultures (i.e. Horovitz, 1978; Maurice, Sellier, and Sylvestre, 1993; Bollinger and Hofstede, 1987) others focused on differences in communication (i.e. Hall and Hall, 1984; Albert, Freund, and Koch, 1988; Schröder, 1991; Campbell et al., 1988) or the evolution of values and of the society as a whole (i.e. Stoetzel, 1983; Schnapper and Mendras, 1990; Valette-Florence et al., 1991)[1]. More sectorial contributions come from Schieb (1981), Böcker, Hausruckinger, and Herker (1991), Hetzel and Wissmeier (1991), and Wührer (1991), among others.

Table 1 presents, in a very compressed form, the most important cultural differences found between France and Germany. All of these differences have considerable direct impact on the behaviour of consumers in both countries.

As a result of a higher degree of uncertainty avoidance, German consumers pay more attention to quality norms and product labels when choosing a product. They are more likely to consider their purchase as an investment, thus giving more importance to product attributes such as guarantee and maintenance conditions. At the same time, they are more reluctant to buy products which have not yet proven their reliability.

Lower hierarchical distance in Germany leads to a more homogeneous distribution of income and buying power. The relative difference between the salary of a worker and a com-

---

[1] For a comprehensive review of German and French cultural differences and their implications for marketing before 1991, see Mendel (1991).

pany executive is much less important in Germany than in France (Ardagh, 1987). Besides, hierarchical distance can also be felt in buyer-seller relationships, which in France are more conflict-prone.

Cultural dimensions	France	Germany
uncertainty avoidance	medium to low	medium to high
hierarchical distance	medium	low
individualism / collectivism	individualistic	individualistic
masculinity / femininity	weak feminine orientation	more masculine orientation
family	family extending over two or more generations; low birth rates; women combine family life and professional career; children become autonomous later than in Germany	family mainly limited to household; very low birth rates; women choose between perfect housewife and perfect professional career; children leave home early
religion	mostly Catholic	coexistence of Protestantism (mainly Northern and Eastern regions) and Catholicism (South)
perception of time	polychronic	monochronic
communication	more implicit; indirect; more information embedded in the context	very explicit; direct; more information given, context less important
man-nature orientation	more attempts to dominate and transform nature; less efforts to protect the environment	closer to nature, implying a certain anti-modernism; environmental protection highly valued

Table 1: Main cultural differences between France and Germany, source: adapted from Mendel, 1991

The more feminist orientation of French society can be recognised, among other things, in the types of goods produced and the role of the feminist movement. While many „typically" French products can be seen as feminine products (i.e. cosmetics, „haute couture", luxury products), prominent German products frequently have a masculine orientation (heavy industry, machinery, cars) and image (robustness, reliability).

Even the feminist movement in Germany is more masculine than in France, in the sense that it is more aggressive and strives for example to create separate spaces (bars, cafés, book stores, meeting facilities) for women. The French feminist movement, on the contrary, does not try to exclude men from its activities (Mendel, 1991).

The individualistic orientation of both societies is reflected by the small number of persons typically involved in buying decisions. However, as a result of the broader conception of „family" in France, French people do a lot more of their shopping with their family. Besides, longer opening hours of stores in France allow them to take more time for this activity which has a social function. Producers adapt to this particularity of French society by offering their products in larger containers or family size packages (i.e. mineral water, yoghurt, medicine). Finally, special offers in France more frequently involve quantity rebates than in Germany, where price rebates are more important.

The higher price sensitivity of the German consumer is partly a consequence of his religion. According to Protestant values, the quality-price relationship is fundamental when choosing a product. For consumer goods, this currently translates into priority given to low price; for durable goods, the quality aspect - mainly in the form of durability and solidity - prevails.

Due to their monochronic perception of time, German consumers easily get nervous, if not angry or aggressive, when they have the impression of „loosing time". French consumers are more fatalistic. They accept longer waiting times more easily and are more indulgent, for example, to striking employees.

Compared to France, the diffusion of information is much slower in Germany and depends more strongly on written documents. In general, the German consumer takes his decision only after having informed himself extensively, if possible by consulting „objective" sources. In France, the value of information is more person-dependent, subjective. The reaction of the consumer is more spontaneous and emotional. Being aware of these tendencies, French advertisers try to seduce their audience and make consumers dream.

Being central to this article, the man-nature orientation will be developed in more detail in the following section.

2.2. Man-Nature Orientation in France and Germany

According to Kluckhohn and Strodtbeck (1961), man-nature orientation is one of five basic cultural orientations[2]. It reflects the attitude of the members of a culture towards nature and towards their natural environment. The fundamental question thus being whether mankind strives to dominate nature or to live in harmony with it, important differences between Germany and France can be found.

Germans like nature and respect it. They love to walk and hike, and seek a harmonious relationship with nature. Their efforts to protect the natural environment even implies a certain degree of anti-modernism (Gephardt, 1990). In France, on the contrary, there is a greater tendency to dominate nature. The natural environment is no obstacle to technological progress; it is an inherent problem to modernism. As a result, there is a much larger, and clearly more radical ecological movement in Germany than in France.

The protection of the environment has became a fundamental value in Germany. In a study conducted in fall of 1990 (Millar and Restall, 1991), more than two thirds of all Germans living in the Western part of the country want to „live in harmony with nature" - thus giving this statement the highest priority among a series of values proposed. This has important implications for all economic players in Germany.

Consumers have changed their behaviour. They buy (recyclable) products which harm nature as little as possible. The government contributes to the protection of the environment with fiscal incentives (i.e. catalytic converters, lead-free gasoline) and comparatively severe anti-pollution laws. Companies adapt to the new demands by engineering products which use less energy (i.e. cars), substituting ecologically harmful materials (i.e. in refrigerators), and offering recyclable products. They also demonstrate their ecological responsibility by investing increasing amounts of money in environmental sponsorship.

Several recent events show that the German public's reaction to environmental or health issues is much faster and stronger than in France. When in May 1995 the Royal Dutch/Shell company wanted to sink its off-shore platform „Brent Spar" in the North Sea, German and Dutch consumers were the first to boycott the company's products. Sales of Shell gas stations in several major German cities decreased by more than 50% (Der Spiegel, No. 25, 1995). The French public only became aware of the issue with a time lag of several weeks and reacted in a

---

[2] For a review of the other basic cultural value orientations and their implications for human communication and action, see Usunier and Walliser, 1993, p. 37-46.

224

much less extreme way. The subsequent revelations of major ecological damage due to the oil production of Royal Dutch/Shell in Nigeria were also treated much less extensively in France than in Germany.

„Mad-cow disease" (bovine spongiform encephalopathy, BSE) is another example of different degrees of sensitivity to environmental, and more precisely health issues, in both countries. At the end of the 1980s, the German public began to be aware of the spread of this disease in Great Britain. Although, at that time the possibility of passing the disease on to humans could only be speculated about, consumption of beef declined sharply in Germany. In an effort to counter their losses, German beef producers introduced a product label which guaranteed the German origin of their meat. However, due to the fears of a proportion of the consumers, beef consumption never fully recovered in Germany. In France, the first dramatic decline in beef consumption occurred in the spring of 1996 only, when British government officials agreed that a possible link between the mad-cow disease and the Creutzfeldt-Jakob disease among humans might exist. With a time lag of about six years compared with their German counterparts, French beef producers, in an effort to reassure their clients, introduced a product label („VF" - „Viande Française"[3]) similar to the German one.

Having shown the different levels of sensitivity to environmental issues in both countries, it would be interesting to see how the German public reacted to the resumption of French nuclear testing in the Pacific region.

3. The German Consumers' Response

The central question underlying this research is not so much whether there is a German reaction to French nuclear testing. According to the preceding section, it would be surprising if there wasn't. The main goals of the study are rather:

- to analyse what form this reaction took,
- to estimate when the first reactions took place and how long they lasted,
- and to evaluate the extent to which French companies became a target of the protests.

In a first step, the evaluation of the German consumers' response to the nuclear tests is based on a content analysis of several French and German print media (sections 3.1. and 3.2.).

---

[3] Meaning in English: "French Meat"

The different magazines examined in the period from May 1995 (one month before the announcement of the tests) to March 1996 (two months after the last test) figure in Table 2.

Magazines analysed	France	Germany
„political" magazines	Nouvel Observateur, Le Point, L'Express	Der Spiegel
„economic", „managerial" magazines	L'Expansion MOCI (Moniteur du Commerce Extérieur)	Wirtschaftswoche Manager Magazin
„general interest" magazines	---	Stern

Table 2: Magazines used in the content analysis

Relying on a content analysis of print media assumes that all possible reactions were reported in this media. Since this is not necessarily the case, an additional survey among French subsidiaries in Germany was effected in June 1996, approximately five months after the last test. A four page pre-tested questionnaire including more than fifty mostly dichotomous questions about the type of effect, the duration of the effects, the company reaction and additional company data was mailed to 1280 companies.

A total number of 119 questionnaires were returned of which 117 were usable. This is equivalent to a response rate of 9,1%. Companies of varying size and practically all sectors of activity are represented in the sample. In most cases, questionnaires were answered by top-level company officials. The results of this survey will be presented in a second step (section 3.3).

3.1. Quantitative Results of the Content Analysis

First of all, it should be noted that among the magazines analysed, the German media covered the nuclear tests much more extensively than the French media. Leading French economic magazines such as the „MOCI" or the „L'Expansion" never even mentioned the nuclear tests. While this might be partly comprehensible in the case of the MOCI, which is a publication edited indirectly by the French government itself, it is all the more surprising that „L'Expansion" never took up this issue. Among the German media examined, only the „Manager Magazin" did not report the tests.

The quantitative outcome of the content analysis of the remaining German magazines is presented in Figure 1. Although rather detailed units of measurement can be applied in content analysis (number of words, sentences, lines, size of the text, etc.) the quantitative part of our analysis remained restricted to counting the number of pages (including fractions of pages) of articles dedicated to French nuclear testing as the main subject. For the time period covered (horizontal axis: May to December 1995), the number of pages dedicated to the issue (vertical axis) is presented for each magazine separately and for all magazines combined.

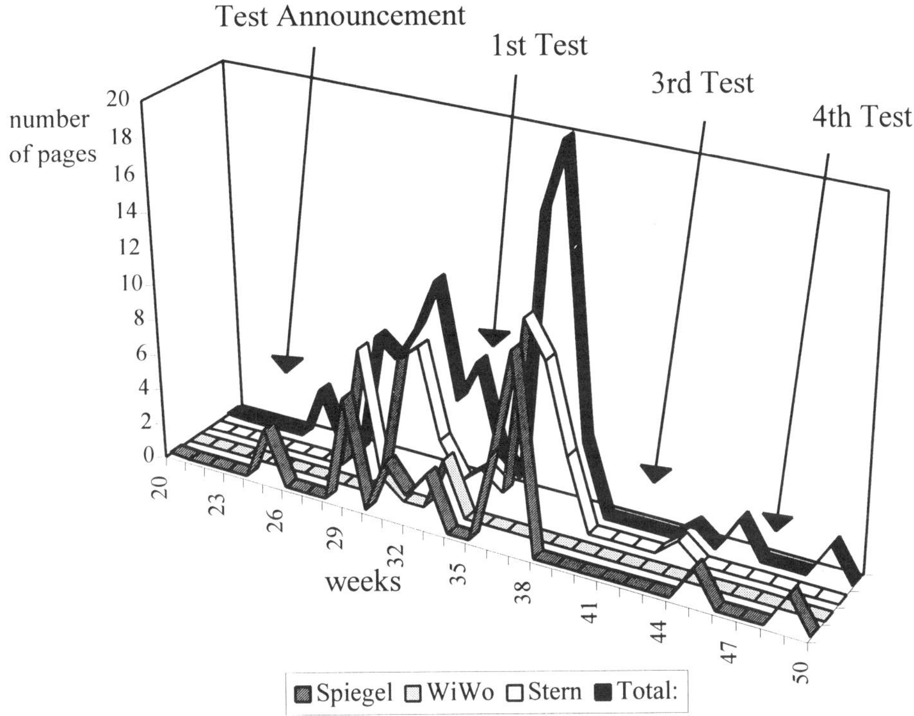

Figure 1: Reports about French nuclear testing in German magazines over time

As can be seen, the issue was first mentioned in „Der Spiegel" shortly after the election of Jacques Chirac as President (end of May, 1995). At that time, however, within an article presenting Jacques Chirac's political programme in general, only 1/8 of a page was dedicated to his plans to resume the tests. Broad coverage started immediately after the announcement of the tests (June 13, 1995). For about eight weeks, the German press reported the new nuclear threat intensively. Then, from mid-August to the beginning of September, the tests draw considerably less media attention. Broad coverage resumed for a short period of time after the first test had actually taken place on September 5 (week 35), and then again, but to a much lesser extent, in October and November after the third and fourth bombs had been detonated. No articles about the French nuclear testing were found after December 1995, although the last test only took place in January 1996.

3.2. Qualitative Results of the Content Analysis

The content analysis of the German media revealed a large number of protests against French nuclear policy. As can be seen in Figure 2, the German public responded to the tests in different ways. On a primary level, actions directly oriented against the French government can be distinguished from deliberate actions against other „innocent" French targets (private companies or individual persons). The resumption of the tests was the consequence of a rather personal decision of President Jacques Chirac - although supported by his right wing political party. The major opposition party as well as a majority of the French public were strongly opposed to this decision. According to a French survey carried out in August 1995, 56% of the French population were against the tests, and 60% wanted Chirac to change his decision (survey made by „Le Parisien", quoted in „Der Spiegel", No. 32, 1995, p. 118). Thus, it seems important to distinguish between protests directed against the person responsible for an action and those against economic, or political actors who had practically no influence on the decision. On a second level, protests initiated by individual consumers or groups of consumers can be distinguished from actions coming from other economic or political actors.

Numberwise, a large majority of the protests against French nuclear policy reported in the German media were directed against French companies and not directly against the French government. Most of these protests were initiated by individual consumers or distributors. However, many actions only had local significance and some were meant to be mostly symbolic. Certain wine dealers in cities such as Munich and Hamburg banned French products from their shops. An estimated 200 restaurants in Hamburg stopped serving French wine. Many of them, however, considered this as a means to stimulate their clients to discuss the issue. Several small islands along the North German coast declared themselves „champagne-free" and „cognac-free" zones (in the same way that other places had declared themselves „nuclear-free zones" during former protests against German or US-American nuclear policies). Not surprisingly, consumer goods with a typical French image seemed to be hit most by the protests (champagne, Bordeaux wine, cognac, cheese, liver paté, French melons, etc.). To a lesser extent, nationalised French companies such as Renault and Air France also became a target.

TARGET OF PROTESTS	INITIATOR OF PROTESTS	
	Individual consumers	Other economic or political actors
French government	- protest letters - e-mail messages	- call for boycott of French State companies (by members of the German Green Party) - collection of signatures (by „Stern" magazine) - organization of protest actions in the Pacific by the media (newspapers, magazines, radio stations)
Other French economic actors	- protests: at Renault subsidiaries in Germany; - call for boycott: champagne, Bordeaux wine, melons, liver paté, calvados, armagnac and other spirits	- call for boycott a) by German wine dealers and restaurants: French fruit, French wine and other spirits; b) by environmental organisations: first boycott French cheese and wine, eventually industrial products; c) politicians: French State companies (i.e. Renault, Air France) - initiation of political protests in France by German wine dealers

Figure 2: Forms of protest against the French nuclear tests

By far the most important action as far as the number of people involved was concerned was initiated by the „Stern" magazine. Between June and September 1995, „Stern" collected a total number of 520 665 signatures against the tests. Among the signatories were several hundred German celebrities (actors, politicians, artists, sportsmen, company executives) depicted week after week in issues of the magazine.

Many consumers from Germany and other parts of the world expressed their discontent via e-mail. The number of messages arriving by this means in the Elysée palace was so significant that the President Chirac's e-mail site had to be closed (Stern, No. 31, 1995, p. 20).

3.3. Results from the Mail Survey

More than 40% of the companies which answered the questionnaire reported that they felt a negative impact from the tests on their business in Germany. For 35% of the companies, consequences were only temporary; another 5,1% indicated ongoing negative effects.

About 15% of the companies interviewed faced a boycott following the nuclear tests. In most cases, this boycott was initiated by consumers or distributors. Besides, the nuclear tests had a considerable negative impact on French companies in Germany in the form of temporary deterioration of the negotiation climate with German business partners (25,6%), temporary or durable image problems (23,1%), loss of time due to the necessity to discuss the issue with business partners (22,2%), protest letters (18,8%), and protest faxes (16,2%). About 17% of the companies reported that their competitors tried to take advantage of the situation by attempting to win additional market shares; 21,4% of the companies indicated a deterioration of their competitive position compared to non-French companies. More than one fifth of the sample suffered from a decrease in sales.

In order to analyse which type of company was typically hit by which type of effects, a correspondance analysis (between test effects and company characteristics) was effected. The results of this analysis can be visualised (Figure 3) on two principal axes with a combined inertia of 43,5% (the third axes only has 13% of inertia, and therefore was not taken into consideration).

The horizontal axis, capturing 24,6% of the total information, permits to classify effects according to their strength. Companies situated on the left-hand side of the graph apparently did not feel affected by the tests (i.e. *K-Way*). Towards the right-hand side, however, the intensity of the effects increases, and the boycott appears as the strongest form of protest. The vertical axis opposes what can be called a „*consumer response*" against a „*company* or *business partner response*". Protest letters are the most frequent form of consumer protest. As some companies indicated, in many cases, protest letters did not come from actual clients but from other consumers. Most of the calls for boycott also originated at the consumer level. With regard to other companies, the deterioritation of the negotiation climate („*bad climate*") was the most common consequence of the tests.

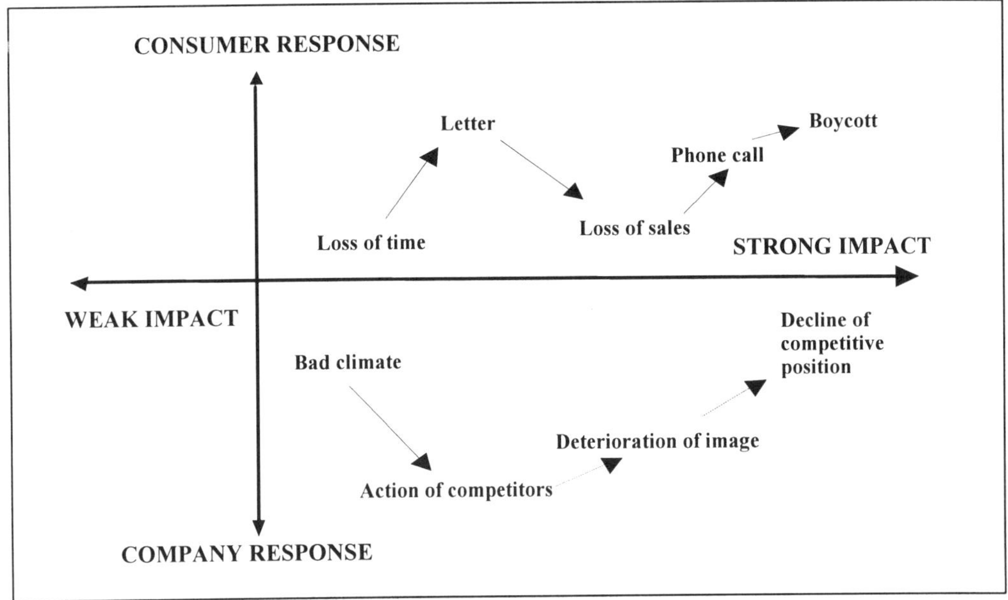

Figure 3: Origin and strength of the test effects

If both axes are taken into consideration simultaneously, two interesting patterns of protest actions and consequences of the tests can be found (as indicated by the arrows in Figure 3). On the consumer side, protest letters are the mildest form of protest. Sending off a letter or a post card is a rather simple act, especially since support was provided in a standardised form by consumer associations, environmental protection groups, and the media. More seriously concerned consumers transmitted their protest via telephone and boycotted French products. For the companies concerned, these actions resulted in a loss of time - and, in the case of stronger protests - a loss of sales (e.g. *Le Bon Pain, Moulinex, Royal Canin*).

Protests from other companies evolved from a deterioration of the negotiation climate to overt competitive moves against French-owned companies (*action of competitors*). This led to image problems and a decline of the competitive position of the companies hit (e.g. *Framatome Connectors*).

Somewhat surprisingly, no significant relationship between the effects and the sector of activity of the companies can be detected. According to the media content analysis, an association between effects and the „food and beverage" category could have been expected. However, effects are clearly associated with the perception of the company as „French", and with the type of clients. The more clients perceived the company products as French, the more frequent were overall effects, deterioration of the negotiation climate, loss of time, sales decrease, and a deterioration of the competitive position. Finally, an evident link between the type of client and the effects appears. Effects can be found much more frequently if the companies' clients are consumers (and not other companies).

4. Conclusion and Implications

This study permits to estimate the economic consequences of French nuclear testing on French companies in Germany. Two major findings with regard to consumer behaviour can be distinguished.

First, it should be noted that German consumers, known to be highly sensitive to environmental issues, took a leading role in a protest movement directed against both the French government and „innocent" private companies. Although pressure on French companies came from different sources and with varying intensity, as is indicated in Figure 4 by the size of the arrows, most of the protests originated at the consumer level. In their mild form, consumer actions typically took the form of protest letters. In more serious cases, consumers called for a boycott of French products, and sometimes induced distributors to take similar measures. Especially in the food and beverage sector, where French products are clearly visible and consumer influence is particularly high, promotion actions for French products were frequently cancelled or postponed.

Environmental protection groups and the media were only marginally involved in direct protest actions against French companies. As the media analysis showed, they also took an important part in the protests but mainly focused their actions on the institution responsible for the tests: the French government. Suppliers were only in one case quoted to be the originators of a boycott.

Inside the French companies, protest actions led to a loss of time, slight tensions among employees, and to several adaptive measures, such as for example employee training to better handle the protests, an intensified search for new clients, and additional communication efforts.

With regard to the companies' business environment, several negative consequences can be observed: image problems, a deterioration of the business climate, minor recruitment problems, and thus ultimately a decline in the competitive position linked to a decrease in sales.

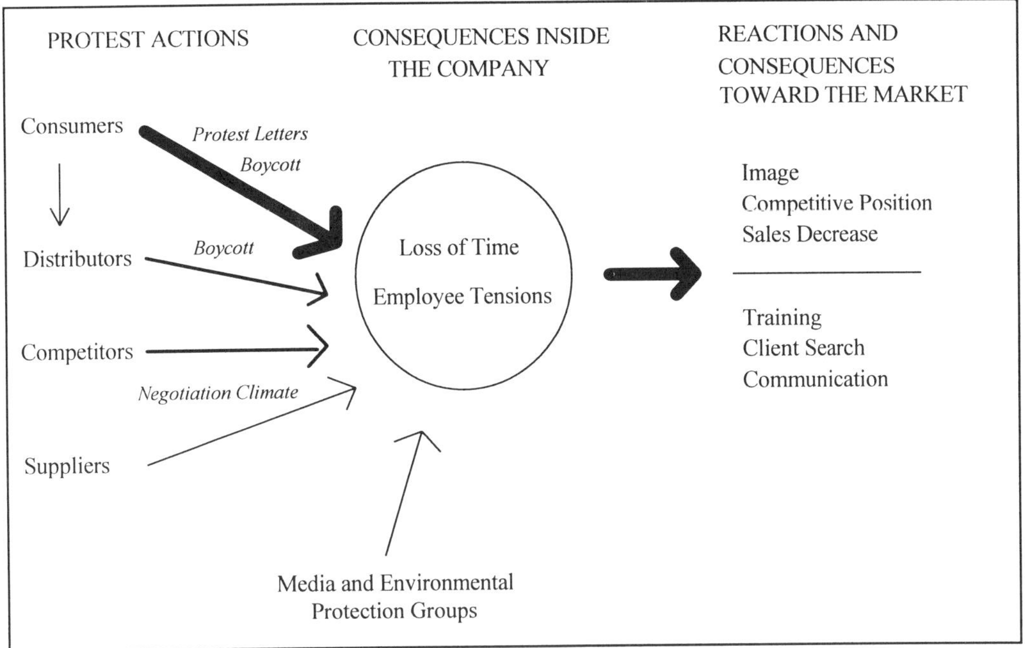

Figure 4: Chain of effects

The second major finding of this research is that the economic effects of the tests seem to be mainly temporary. Calls for boycott and administrative disturbances didn't last much longer than five months. The impact of the protests on sales stopped on average after seven months. No defensive moves with long term consequences, such as a change of the product or company name, significant disinvestments or staff reductions were observed.

This does not mean, however, that there are no long-term consequences at all of the tests. As in any relationship between two friends and neighbours, any dispute leaves behind some traces. Things that happened cannot be made undone. One partner will always remember the other's actions. The French nuclear testing will become part of the German consumers' collective memory. The latter will add the incident to their inventory of reproaches which they will address to their neighbours the next time problems occur. The way the French government decided upon the tests without consulting its major allies and partners did not add to a more trustworthy image of this country in Germany. And in the worst of cases, German consumers will in the future reflect this image on French companies.

According to the results of this research, a foreign-owned company operating in Germany has to be prepared for a series of protest actions if the country with which it is associated takes political decisions which are perceived to be harmful to the environment. The intensity of these reactions depends on the visibility of the foreign character of the company as well as the client structure of the company. The closer companies are to the final consumer, the more likely they are to become a target of protests. Companies selling to other companies seem to be less concerned since business-to-business relations are more governed by long-term (contractual) relations and rational decision making. The individual consumer, on the contrary, is more volatile and emotional in his behaviour.

Although the study doesn't allow to draw conclusions about the effectiveness of alternative defensive measures against the protests, several recommendations can be given. In a first step, companies threatened by consumer actions should train their personnel to handle protests effectively. Telephone calls, fax messages, and letters - even if they are insulting - should be answered in a friendly, patient and consistent way. This training effort needs to be particularly intense for personnel in direct touch with the client, such as for example the sales force.

Unless effects become permanent, companies should not overreact (i.e. should not disinvest) and should not necessarily take up a position for or against the issue. Taking up a position would mean an even deeper involvement with the political debate and risk offending parts of the population either in the home or the foreign country. Instead, efforts have to be made to direct protests to the person or institution responsible for the criticised decision.

5. Limitations and Future Research

Despite the use of different methods to get a realistic idea of the situation (media analysis followed by a mail survey) results should not be generalised. The sample of 117 French subsidiaries in Germany is not representative for all French economic actors operating in Germany. Most importantly pure exporters are not included.

Although no such indications exist, it could be that companies particularly hit by the protests are overrepresented in the sample. These companies could have been more motivated to answer the questionnaire than companies which did not feel concerned by the issue at all.

Similarly, it cannot be excluded that negative effects are exaggerated for personal career reasons. It would have been easy for a subsidiary director to blame the nuclear tests for a sales decrease which was in reality due to poor management.

Future research could focus on sectors where the tests had seemingly above average negative consequences, such as tourism for example. A long-term observation of companies in this sector could reveal the most successful defensive strategies adopted.

Although Germany is the most important economic partner of France, it would also be interesting to compare the consequences of the nuclear testing there with countries such as Australia or New Zealand more directly affected by the issue.

References

Ardagh, J. (1987): Les Allemands. Pierre Belfond: Paris.

Albert, P., Freund, W.S., and Koch, U. (Eds.) (1988): Allemagne-France. Deux paysages médiatiques Peter Lang: Frankfurt a.M., pp. 97-108.

Böcker, F., Hausruckinger, G., and Herker, A. (1991): Pays d'origine et qualités écologiques comme caractéristiques des biens de consommation durables: une analyse comparative du comportement des consommateurs français et allemands. In: Recherche et Applications en Marketing, Vol. 6, No. 3, pp. 5-20.

Bollinger, D. and Hofstede, G. (1987): Les différences culturelles dans le management. Les Editions d'Organisation: Paris.

Campbell, N.G., Graham, J.L., Jolibert, A., and Meissner, H.-G. (1988): Marketing negociations in France, Germany, The United Kingdom and the United States. In: Journal of Marketing, Vol. 52, No. 1, pp. 49-62.

Gephardt, W. (1990): Nature-environnement. In: Leenhardt, J. and Picht, R. (Eds.), Au Jardin des Malentendus, Le commerce franco-allemand des idées, Ed. Hubert Nyssen: Actes du Sud, pp. 353-355.

Hall, E.T. and Hall, M.R. (1984): Les différences cachées. Une étude de la communication internationale. Comment communiquer avec les Allemands. Gruner & Jahr: Hamburg.

Hetzel, P. and Wissmeier, U.K. (1991): L'artiste et l'artisan: une comparaison du marketing des entreprises françaises et allemandes dans les industries de l'habillement. In: Recherche et Applications en Marketing, Vol. 6, No. 3, pp. 5-20.

Horovitz, J. (1978): Allemagne, Grande-Bretagne, France : trois styles de management. In: Revue Française de Gestion, September-October, pp. 8-17.

Kluckhohn, F.R. and Strodtbeck, F.L. (1961): Variations in Value Orientations. Greenwood Press: Westport, CT.

Maurice, M., Sellier, F., and Sylvestre, J.-S. (1983): Politique d'éducation et organisation industrielle en France et en Allemagne. PUF: Paris.

Mendel, D. (1991): Comparaison des cultures allemande et française et implications marketing. In: Recherche et Applications en Marketing, Vol. 6, No. 3, pp. 31-75.

Millar, C. and Restall, C. (1991): The Embryonic Consumer. Markets and Values in Transition in Eastern Europe. In: Conference Proceedings of the 44th E.S.O.M.A.R. Marketing Research Congress, Vol. I, Luxembourg, pp. 593-611.

Schieb, P.-A. (1981): Design industriel: une comparaison France-Allemagne. In: Revue française de gestion, September-October, pp. 80-86.

Schnapper, D. and Mendras, H. (Eds.) (1990): Six manières d'être Européens, Gallimard: Paris.

Schröder, M. (1991): France-Allemagne: la publicité. L'existence de deux logiques de communication. In: Recherche et Applications en Marketing, Vol. 6, No. 3, pp. 97-108.

Der Spiegel (No. 25, 1995): „Versenkt die Shell", May 1995, pp. 22-36.

Der Spiegel (No. 32, 1995): „Teure Tests", July 1995, pp. 118-119.

Stoetzel, J. (1983): Les valeurs du temps présent: une enquête européenne. PUF: Paris.

Usunier, J.-C. and Walliser, B. (1993): Interkulturelles Marketing. Mehr Erfolg im internationalen Geschäft. Gabler: Wiesbaden.

Valette-Florence, P., Grunert, S.C., Grunert, K.G., and Beatty, S. (1991): Une comparaison franco-allemande de l'adhésion aux valeurs personnelles. In: Recherche et Applications en Marketing, Vol. 6, No. 3, pp. 5-20.

Wührer, G.A. (1991): Différences et similarités entre les prestations de service des instituts d'études en France et en RFA. In: Recherche et Applications en Marketing, Vol. 6, No. 3, pp. 5-20.

Frank Wimmer

Environmental Aspects of Consumer Behaviour in Germany

1. Introduction

2. The Difference between Environmentally Friendly and Environmentally Conscious
   Consumer Behaviour

3. The Reasons for Environmentally Friendly Consumer Behaviour
   3.1. Psychological Factors
   3.2. Situational factors

4. The Environmental Consciousness in Germany
   4.1. Theoretical Approaches to the Definition and Measurement of Environmental
        Consciousness
   4.2. Empirical Results on Environmental Consciousness in Germany

5. Environmental Consciousness and Environmental Behaviour

6. Conclusion

References

Environmental Aspects of Consumer Behaviour in Germany

Frank Wimmer

Abstract

In the public discussion in Germany, environmental aspects have recently lost significance. Nevertheless, protection of the environment and ecologically conscious consumer behaviour are of growing importance. The following text deals with methodological problems of empirical studies on environmentally conscious consumer behaviour and provides a report on recent representative survey results.

1. Introduction

„Environmental consciousness and environmental behaviour are miles apart from each other" (Kuhlke, 1993, p. 92). This quote underlines new evidence in empirical social research. According to survey results, Germans appear to be quite environmentally conscious, but most of them are simply paying lip service.

This thesis is the basis of the following discussion: The position of Germans' environmental consciousness and the relationship between *environmental consciousness* and actual *environmental behaviour*. The main questions which need to be addressed are:

1) How can the theoretical construct „environmental consciousness" be defined and empirically measured?

2) What can be learned about the development and the current position of German consumers' environmental consciousness from existing empirical investigations?

3) What is the situation of German consumers' actual environmental behaviour? Which concrete behavioural manners can be viewed as valid indicators for „sustainable consumption" in empirical research?

4) How significant is the relationship between environmental consciousness and selected environmentally relevant consumer behaviour habits? Or vice versa, how large is the behavioural gap between consciousness and behaviour?

5) How can the relationship between environmental consciousness and actual environmental consumer behaviour be explained? Which factors determine this relationship?

2. The Difference between Environmentally Friendly and Environmentally Conscious Consumer Behaviour

Experts have argued a lot about what the best environmental oriented consumer behaviour is. Should automobiles, for example, be driven with the least amount of fuel as possible, should we rely on diesel fuel, or should the use of automobiles be avoided at all? Should drinks, such as milk, be sold in bricks, plastic bags, or in returnable glass bottles or unpackaged? What is „sustainable consumption" actually (see Hansen, Schoenheit, et al., 1994)? In this paper, we choose not to get involved with such arguments among experts.

Let us assume that the purchase of drinks in disposable bottles portrays environmentally friendly behaviour as it contributes to the good of the environment. German consumers are good in this category. In the fruit drinks category, for example, the percentage of reusable bottle purchases has risen in the past 11 years from 13% to ca. 37% (GfK Panel Services, 1995). The remaining percentage portion consists of disposable bottles, cans and cartons. Although this appears to be environmentally friendly, we do not know whether these results are caused by a generally high level of environmental consciousness.

The reason for buying drinks in reusable bottles could simply be that more reusable bottles and less other kinds of packaging are found on store shelves. If the industry and stores were to go back to disposable types of packaging, such as cans (currently seen in the growing percentage of canned beer), consumers' environmental friendliness could be a thing of the past. There is an important difference between *environmentally friendly* and *environmentally conscious* consumer behaviour. The reasons, especially the motives for buying a specific environmentally friendly product are very complex.

3. The Reasons for Environmentally Friendly Consumer Behaviour

There are several reasons for environmentally friendly behaviour of a specific consumer in a specific buying situation (which are also responsible for the use of information before the purchase and the type of product usage and the waste disposal after the purchase): On the one hand there are psychological factors inherent in the consumer besides the environmental consciousness. On the other hand, there are external situational factors at the time of the purchase (Wimmer, 1993, pp. 68; Monhemius, 1993, pp. 90).

3.1. Psychological Factors

At the time of the purchase of an environmentally friendly product many *other values, motives* and *attitudes* may have an influence. The motivation for buying an environmentally friendly product can be in conflict with, for example, the consumer's quality or price expectations or the convenience or social acceptance of the product. Indeed, environmentally friendly products often fall short in terms of quality or they are more expensive and not available in every store. Depending on the *consumer's involvement* with the product and the *perceived risks*, these motives will over-compensate his environmental consciousness.

At the same time, buying an environmentally friendly product normally doesn't give any personal benefits to the consumer, instead it benefits all consumers, the whole society - either today or in the future (social benefits). The more that *social* and *individual benefits* are paired, the more likely the consumer is to buy the environmentally friendly product.

3.2. Situational factors

The correlation between environmental consciousness and environmentally friendly behaviour depends also on specific situational factors at the time and place of purchase (in the store). As we mentioned above, environmentally friendly *products* must first be *available* on the store shelves. Moreover *information* about the environmental advantages of those products must be available to the consumer, for example environmental information or a specific eco-label on the packages or some advice from the store personnel. Without such information, the consumer will not be able to identify environmentally friendly products.

In this paper the complex causes and circumstances of environmentally friendly consumer behaviour can only be briefly mentioned. Whether or not a competition between environmental consciousness and environmentally friendly behaviour can be determined by empirical studies depends additionally on how the consumers are questioned about their environmental consciousness. The problem of how to measure environmental consciousness may involve aspects of personal behaviour or focus on matters not much related to the personal behaviour.

4. The Environmental Consciousness in Germany

4.1. Theoretical Approaches to the Definition and Measurement of Environmental Consciousness

Sociological research, in particular social psychology, sociology and market research, has occupied itself in detail with the construct of environmental consciousness, both in behaviour theory as well as empirical research. But in comparison to the abundance of survey results, only a small amount of theoretical or conceptual contributions exists. There are different definitions for environmental consciousness, and therefore different measurement approaches. As a result, the different empirical data on environmental consciousness of German consumers, respectively citizens, often cannot be compared.

This is not the place, however, to try and come to terms with positions on research in detail. Opposingly, only some central points shall be addressed here.

4.1.1. Different Dimensions of Environmental Consciousness

Environmental consciousness can be seen as a part of the total system of people's values and attitudes, and consequently, will be defined according to different *fundamental dimensions*. It is common knowledge in research that environmental consciousness as *general value* and environmental consciousness as a *basic attitude* should be differentiated (Preisendörfer, 1996, p. 14). In both cases, environmental consciousness can be associated with *different individual dimensions* (Wimmer, 1993, p.51).

- *Environmental consciousness as an ecological value*:

  Values form a very general system for individual orientation. In this context, the following questions can be posed:

  1) Do citizens put high importance on an intact environment as a social problem or goal for Germany?

  2) Do citizens put high importance on the environment, respectively the protection of the environment, within their individual orientations?

- *Environmental consciousness as a fundamental ecological attitude*:

In comparison with general value orientations, (fundamental) attitudes are seen as more object specific and focus more on the overt behaviour of individuals. Here *emotional-affective, cognitive,* as well as *intentional* components can be differentiated corresponding to the common differentiation in social psychology (see Maloney and Ward, 1973, also Kinnear and Taylor, 1973; in German research see Amelang et al., 1977; Kley and Fietkau, 1979; Urban, 1986; Balderjahn, 1986; 1988):

1)   To what extend do people react emotionally to existing environmental problems?

2)   To what extend do people have a great measure of insight into environmental dangers? Do they have a sufficient amount of knowledge about environmental problems?

3)   Does personal commitment to environmentally friendly behaviour exist?

4.1.2. One-dimensional versus Multi-dimensional Operationalisation Concepts

Correspondingly, in empirical studies, environmental consciousness can only be grasped *one-dimensionally* on the basis of isolated indicators or within the framework of more *complex multi-dimensional* operationalisation concepts (Wimmer, 1993, p. 52). In one-dimensional approaches environmental consciousness often is only measured according to the importance of environment as a social problem seen in surveys. On the other hand, in multi-dimensional approaches, respondents are usually given a wide range of statements concerning different aspects of environmental consciousness. Out of the individual responses to each statement, a comprehensive conclusion can be constructed which indicates the level of environmental consciousness. Both the one-dimensional approach as well as the multi-dimensional approach will now be demonstrated by using real survey data.

4.2. Empirical Results on Environmental Consciousness in Germany

In recent years, *representative* data on environmental consciousness in Germany have been collected by several studies. In these studies, one-dimensional approaches as well as multi-dimensional approaches were used. Only a few of these studies were *repeated with the same design,* so that the development of the Germans' environmental consciousness could be analysed:

1) The *Umweltbundesamt* (UBA, Federal Environmental Agency) conducted continual surveys on environmental related attitudes and behavioural manners. These data from 1985 and 1992 can be compared (UBA, 1994, p. 3). In addition, a study was conducted by the UBA in 1996 which is comparable to the results from studies conducted between 1991-1994 by the Institut für Praxis und Sozialforschung (IPOS), Mannheim (see Preisendörfer, 1996).

2) In „*Dialoge*", an empirical work published by *Gruner and Jahr*, repeated studies can be found, which investigate ecological value orientations and intended behaviour over a period of years (Gruner and Jahr, 1995).

3) Similar to the previously mentioned studies, the women's journal *Brigitte* has investigated the development of environmental consciousness in Germany over the years, namely in the context of the so called „*Kommunikationsanalysen*" (Brigitte, 1993).

4) Further surveys on ecological familiarity, attitudes and behaviour of German consumers have been conducted by the *Institute of Marketing at the University of Münster* in 1977, 1985 and 1994 (Bruhn, 1978, 1985; Meffert and Bruhn, 1996).

5) Annual surveys conducted by the German market research institute *GfK Nürnberg*: „People's concerns in Germany" and „Environmental consciousness in Germany" exist since 1985. The results of them will now be presented.

4.2.1. Results on Environmental Consciousness as an Ecological Value

The annual survey „*People's Concerns in Germany*", conducted by GfK since 1985, can be viewed as an example for a strictly *one-dimensional* measurement of environmental consciousness. In this study, a representative population sample is asked to identify what they regard as the most urgent problems facing Germany. Respondents are not bound by previously determined response categories, but are free to state their concerns in open-ended responses.

As *Figure 1* shows, the priority according to environmental protection appears to have fallen consistently since 1988 when environmental protection ranked alongside unemployment as the most urgent problem faced by Germans (Gaspar, 1996, p. 3).

<table>
<tr><td colspan="13">People's Concerns:
Western Germany 1985-1996</td><td></td></tr>
</table>

... percentages of respondents citing stated issues as being urgent tasks to be solved in FRG
(multiple free responses possible)

	1985	1986	1987	1988	1989	1990	1991	1992	1993	1994	1995	1996
1. unemployment	76	65	61	57	39	31	30	31	58	65	58	80
2. asylum-seekers/ foreigner problem	6	27	12	10	9	7	44	73	35	28	23	20
3. pension issues/ -increases	13	14	13	14	8	6	3	3	11	10	11	19
4. *environmental protection*	*41*	*43*	*53*	*57*	*29*	*32*	*26*	*18*	*17*	*17*	*26*	*15*
5. crime	-	-	-	-	-	0,5	2	5	8	16	18	11
6. consolidation of funds	5	2	5	12	3	3	8	8	10	6	7	8
7. securing social benefits	-	-	6	3	-	2	2	2	10	5	7	8
8. housing/rents	1	0	1	2	31	16	19	21	13	15	8	6
9. economic stability/growth	5	5	5	3	-	-	5	5	12	13	6	6
10. inflation	1	1	0	1	2	5	15	10	11	7	8	4
11. health service	-	-	-	-	-	-	2	5	12	5	2	3
12. securing the peace	16	12	22	13	3	6	2	2	2	4	4	2
13. Eastern and German politics	3	2	6	3	47	46	15	13	5	3	3	1
14. right-wing radi-calism	-	-	-	-	-	-	1	4	6	7	2	0,4

Source: GfK Market Research, 1996

Figure 1: People's Concerns: Western Germany 1985-1996

The question is, whether such findings are a *useful measure* of the extent of environmental consciousness in Germany. The only answer to this question is '*no*'. The survey on the 'Nation's Concerns' is not focused primarily upon measuring the environmental consciousness of German citizens. Rather, it gives an indication of the current social concerns in the Federal Republic and in doing so it also strongly reflects the German media's coverage (agenda setting) of the problems (see Wimmer and Wahl, 1995, pp. 31). Furthermore, environmental protection has to compete for its importance in such studies with other problems, so that it is not the absolute significance of environmental protection which is measured, but rather its relative significance when compared with other concerns. If other problems appear to be more pressing, then this does not necessarily mean that the concern of citizens for the environment has actually declined.

In this context, it is also interesting to compare the results of the 'Peoples's Concerns' studies between *East and West Germany*. Such a comparison demonstrates that public opinions in East and West Germany still differ very much from one another and that East Germans have very different concerns than West Germans. Environmental protection continues to have a comparatively low importance in the East, where more pressing economic concerns are evident.

4.2.2. Results on Environmental Consciousness as an Ecological Fundamental Attitude

A methodologically more sophisticated and empirically valid approach is not only to use a single indicator, but to measure environmental consciousness as *a multi-dimensional phenomenon*. Such a theoretical behavioural approach was adopted several years ago by the GfK Nürnberg institute. For a detailed discussion of the methods adopted see Adlwarth and Wimmer, 1986; Wimmer 1988, 1993; Wimmer and Wahl, 1995. In short, the concept underlying the measurement of environmental consciousness encompasses the following list of 11 questions relating to the environment:

1) The preservation of nature is more important to me than further economic growth.

2) Today, people make too much fuss about the environment.

3) The steps currently taken to protect the environment are quite sufficient.

4) I do care much whether the products I use are pollutive or not.

5) The government and industry should begin to protect the environment, not the average citizen.

6) In my household, I cannot do much to protect the environment.

7) I am willing to spend more money on environmentally safe packaging.

8) I am willing to do without a perfectly clean household, if this reduces the strain on the environment.

9) You must impose considerable restrictions on yourself in order to protect the environment.

10) Today, I use considerably less products that are pollutive in my household than in the past.

11) When buying personal hygiene products or detergents, I pay much attention to whether they have any harmful influence on the environment.

The questions refer to different levels and indicators of the phenomenon of environmental consciousness. The first 4 statements focus on *basic attitudes* towards the environment and environmental protection, while statements 5 and 6 are directed towards *personal responsibility* and *perceived consumer effectiveness*. The *willingness to pay higher prices* and *accept functional or personal restrictions* is addressed in questions 7, 8 and 9. Finally, the last statements encompass actual *patterns of behaviour or intended behaviour*.

Since 1985 these statements have been presented annually to the 5,000 West German households participating in a comprehensive consumer panel survey under the responsibility of the GfK Nürnberg institute. In providing the market research institute with continuous information about their purchases, the person who runs the household is simultaneously providing information about their environmental consciousness. Since the households involved in such a consumer panel approximate to a realistic sample of all (West) German households, it is possible to regard these results as representative.

In contrast to other scientific consumer research studies that also aim to be multidimensional, no comprehensive index of environmental consciousness is formed from the responses to the individual statements in this approach. Instead, using *cluster analysis*, different environmental consciousness categories are calculated on the basis of the degree of agreement with the statements. Figure 2 portrays the results of this typology formation for 1995.

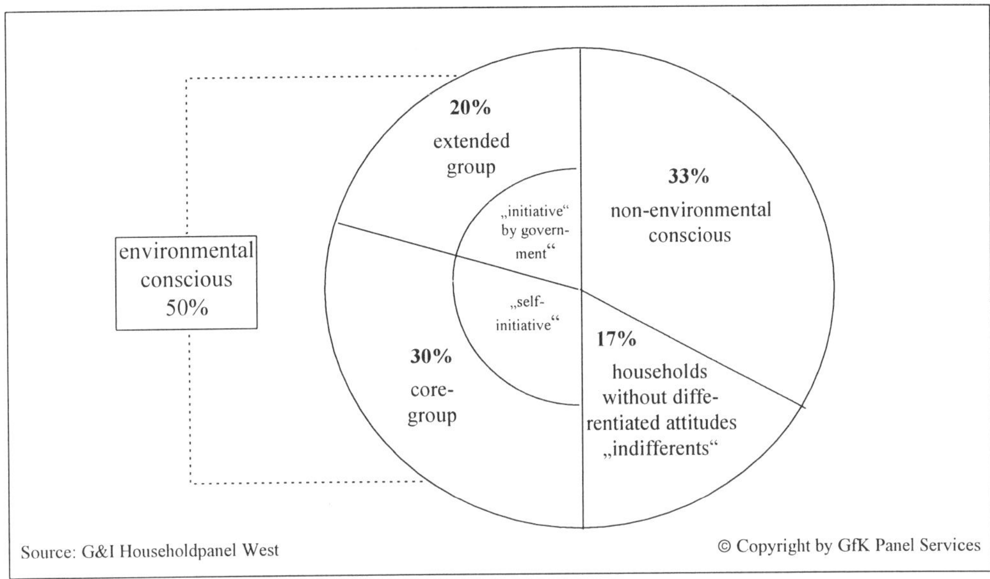

Figure 2: Segments of Environmental Consciousness in West Germany 1995

On the whole, the cluster analysis differentiates between three consumer/household types: the „*environmentally conscious*", the „*not environmentally conscious*" and the „*indifferents*", comprised of those households that fail to fall into either one of the first two categories. People who are „environmentally conscious" and those who are „not environmentally conscious" differ with respect to their agreement or disagreement with the 11 statements. Differences are particularly marked in the extent to which households are prepared to accept significant personal restrictions in order to protect the environment (statement 9). In 1995, 50% of West Germans (more precisely: of people running households in West Germany) belonged to the category defined as being 'environmentally conscious', while 33% had to be classified as being decidedly not environmentally oriented.

The group of '*environmentally conscious*' households can be further subdivided into a *core group* and an *extended group*. Of particular interest here is the core group. This group differs from the others to the extent that its members want to begin protecting the environment themselves and do not assign prime responsibility for doing this to the government or industry (statement 5). The attempt is made to turn *personal involvement*, the individual's *perceived personal responsibility*, into a measure for a more strictly defined environmental consciousness. This core group of West Germans who were particularly environmentally conscious made up 30% of the 1995 sample.

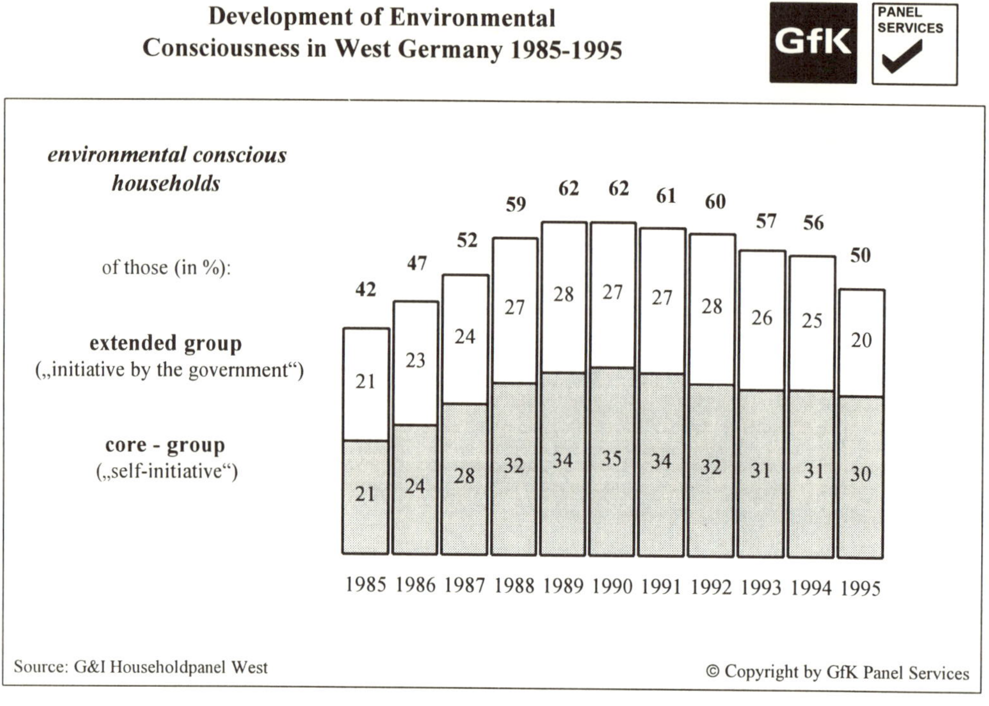

Figure 3: Development of Environmental Consciousness in West Germany 1985-1995

Surveys on the environmental consciousness in Germany using this method have been conducted since 1985 by the GfK Nürnberg institute. This allows an assessment of the *development of environmental consciousness* over time, something which is only rarely possible with empirical behavioural data. *Figure 3* illustrates this development both for the entire group of environmentally conscious people as well as for the core group. There are no other empirical data which could portray a more valid and reliable picture of the state and development of environmental consciousness in Germany. The data show that by 1989 and 1990 the proportion of 'environmentally oriented' people in the West German population had reached its highest level: nearly two-thirds of all households could be classified as environmen-

with over one-third being especially environmentally aware (62% and 35% respectively). Since 1990 there has been a *downward trend*. But this does not significantly affect the overall high level of environmental consciousness in Germany.

5. Environmental Consciousness and Environmental Behaviour

Given the findings outlined above, it is now interesting to assess the manner in which the high level of environmental consciousness in Germany affects the *actual behaviour*. Are we correct to fear that while citizens always give the impression that they are environmentally conscious in surveys, their environmental consciousness and actual environmental behaviour are in fact miles apart? It doesn't help the threatened environment very much if we display high levels of environmental consciousness in surveys, but continue to damage the environment through our actual behaviour.

In contrast to environmental consciousness, the environmental behaviour of citizens (consumers) seems to be a variable which can be measured relatively easily: The purchase or non-purchase of products, the manner and intensity with which products are used and the resulting waste have a considerable effect upon the environment. A wide range of data is available on this topic from commercial market research, particularly with regard to the *purchasing behaviour* of consumers.

Within the context of *consumer panels*, a representative group of consumers and households reports regularly on their purchases. Indeed, these are the same consumers whose environmental consciousness was addressed above using multi-dimensional measurement techniques. As a result of this overlap, it is *uniquely* possible to compare environmental consciousness with the actual behaviour of these consumer households. We don't need to fear that the individual households provide misleading details of their actual behaviour. When we want to analyse what is being purchased, e.g. the quantities of the environmentally friendly or environmentally damaging products, or returnable or disposable packaging materials, all of these topics can be addressed by *examining the regular shopping* reports of the panel households. The information provided on this matter is completely independent of the one-off survey of their environmental consciousness. These panel data form the basis for the selected research findings in *Figure 4*.

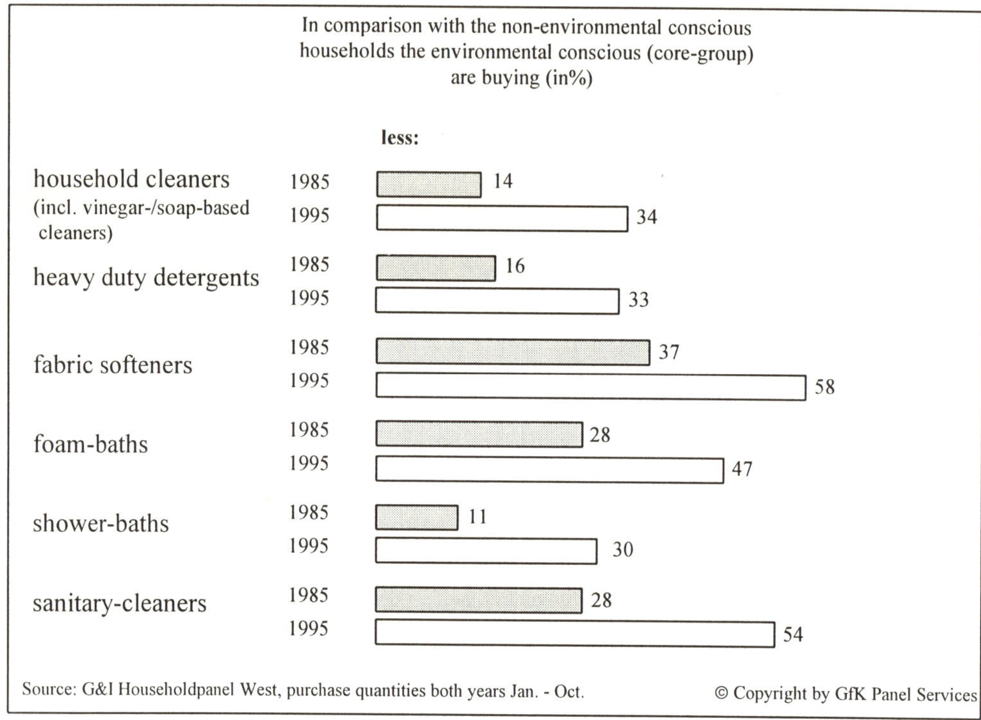

Figure 4: Environmental Consciousness and Purchase Quantities 1985/1995

Overall, the data shows that environmentally conscious consumers and households generally buy fewer *products which damage the environment* than consumers/households that are not environmentally conscious. These data are based on the assumption that heavy duty detergents, toilet cleaning products, fabric softeners etc. are products that damage the environment to a relatively high extend. Furthermore, environmentally conscious consumers do not buy such products less frequently simply because they live in smaller households or because they are older than other consumers. Both, the environmentally conscious and the not environmentally conscious households, are highly comparable in the terms of household size and age. The differences really can be attributed to higher levels of environmental consciousness.

In a final example, attention is paid to consumer behaviour regarding purchases of the more *environmentally friendly returnable bottles* rather than of the less environmentally friendly plastic bags and bricks that are used for fresh milk. In 1995, environmentally conscious households purchased less plastic bags and bricks, but 6% more returnable bottles and 6% more unpackaged milk. This too can be regarded as an indication of the positive connection between environmental consciousness and environmental behaviour - even though a number of other factors also have an important influence.

6. Conclusion

In this paper, it was not possible to discuss the theoretical behavioural factors that govern the relationship between environmental consciousness and environmental behaviour in detail, particularly the question of the circumstances and situations that explain how high levels of environmental consciousness actually determine environmentally friendly behaviour. Nevertheless, the results above allow us to draw the following conclusion: There is a gap between environmental consciousness and overt environmental behaviour, but also a clear*correlation* between both constructs. However, if the consumer has the possibility of behaving in an environmentally friendly manner without having to make significant sacrifices in terms of price, quality, comfort and time, then a close correlation exists between environmental consciousness and environmental behaviour.

References

Adlwarth, W. and Wimmer, F. (1986): Umweltbewußtsein und Kaufverhalten - Ergebnisse einer Verbraucherpanel-Studie. In: Jahrbuch der Absatz- und Verbrauchsforschung, Vol. 32, pp. 166-192.

Amelang, M. et al. (1977): Mitteilung über einige Schritte der Entwicklung einer Skala zum Umweltbewußtsein. In: Diagnostica, Vol. 23, pp. 86-88.

Balderjahn, I. (1986): Das umweltbewußte Konsumentenverhalten - Eine empirische Studie, Berlin.

Balderjahn, I. (1988): Personality Variables and Environmental Attitudes as Predictors of Ecologically Responsible Consumption Patterns. In: Journal of Business Research, Vol. 17, pp. 51-56.

Brigitte (Eds.) (1993): Ach, das bißchen Müll! Umwelt- und Konsumentenverhalten, Hamburg.

Bruhn, M. (1985): Das ökologische Bewußtsein der Konsumenten - Ergebnisse einer Befragung im Zeitvergleich, Workingpaper No. 26 of the Wissenschaftliche Gesellschaft für Marketing und Unternehmensführung, Münster.

Bruhn, M. (1978): Das soziale Bewußtsein von Konsumenten: Erklärungsansätze und Ergebnisse einer empirischen Untersuchung in der Bundesrepublik Deutschland, Vol. 11: Schriftenreihe Unternehmensführung und Marketing, Wiesbaden.

Gaspar, C. (1996): Die Sorgen der Bürger im vereinten Deutschland, Nürnberg.

Gruner & Jahr (Eds.) (1995): Dialoge 4: Berichtsband, Hamburg.

Hansen, U., Schoenheit, I., and Devries, J. (1994): Sustainable Consumption und der Bedarf an unternehmensbezogenen Informationen. In: Forschungsgruppe Konsum und Verhalten (Eds.), Konsumentenforschung, München, pp. 227-244.

Kinnear, T.C. and Taylor, J.R. (1973): The Effect of Ecological Concern on Brand Perceptions. In: Journal of Marketing Research, Vol. 10, pp. 191-197.

Kley, J. and Fietkau, H.J. (1979): Verhaltenswirksame Variablen des Umweltbewußtseins. In: Psychologie und Praxis, Vol. 23. pp. 13-22.

Kuhlke, U. (1993): Sind wir im Umweltschutz nur Maulhelden? In: natur, No. 14, pp. 32-41.

Malony, M.P. and Ward M.P. (1973): Ecology: Let's hear from the People - An Objective Scale for the Measurement of Ecological Attitudes and Knowledges. In: The American Psychologist, Vol. 28, pp. 583-586.

Meffert, H. and Bruhn, M. (1996): Das Umweltbewußtsein von Konsumenten - Ergebnisse einer empirischen Untersuchung in Deutschland im Längsschnittvergleich, Workingpaper No. 99 of the Wissenschaftliche Gesellschaft für Marketing und Unternehmensführung, Münster.

Monhemius, K.C. (1993): Umweltbewußtes Kaufverhalten von Konsumenten - Ein Beitrag zur Operationalisierung, Erklärung und Typologie des Verhaltens in der Kaufsituation, Frankfurt.

Preisendörfer, P. (1996): Umweltbewußtsein in Deutschland 1996, Bonn.

UBA (Umweltbundesamt) (Eds.) (1994): Ermittlung des ökologischen Problembewußtseins der Bevölkerung, Berlin.

Urban, D. (1986): Was ist Umweltbewußtsein? Exploration eines mehrdimensionalen Einstellungskonstruktes. In: Zeitschrift für Soziologie, Vol. 15, pp. 363-377.

Wimmer, F. (1993): Empirische Einsichten in das Umweltbewußtsein und Umweltverhalten der Konsumenten. In: Wagner, G. R. (Eds.), Betriebswirtschaft und Umweltschutz, Stuttgart, pp. 44-78.

Wimmer, F. (1988): Umweltbewußtsein und konsumrelevante Einstellungen und Verhaltensweisen. In: Brandt, A., Hansen, U. et al. (Eds.), Ökologisches Marketing, Frankfurt/New York, pp. 44-85.

Wimmer, F. and Wahl, H. (1995): Value change and environmental awareness in Germany. In: Blühdorn, I., Krause, F., and Scharf, Th. (Eds.), The Green Agenda. Environmental Politics and Policy in Germany, pp. 25-51.

Petra Buchholz

An Investigation of the Handling of Solid Waste in the Consumption Cycle

1. Introduction

2. Waste Behaviour

3. Antecedents of Waste Behaviour

4. Research Design and Models

5. Results and Discussion

6. Conclusion

References

An Investigation of the Handling of Solid Waste in the Consumption Cycle

Petra Buchholz

Abstract

This study investigates the impact of waste-related attitudes on waste behaviour. Waste behaviour is not limited to the separation of waste. In the production-consumption cycle, which covers the buying, using, and separation phase of consumption, a number of buying and using decisions additionally have consequences for the solid waste output (Pieters, 1991). A structural equation model was used to determine which attitudinal and other psychographic variables have an influence on the handling of solid waste. Data for the empirical survey was collected in five large German cities. The total sample size is 1,000 interviews. The results suggest that especially intrinsic and extrinsic motives or the collective value orientation have an influence on waste behaviour. The results presented can provide a foundation for solid waste management strategies of municipalities.

1. Introduction

Despite the fact, that several recycling programs have been established during the last twenty years, the amount of solid waste is still a problem of developed countries. Because consumers' participation in recycling programs has become a pronounced feature in contemporary solid waste management, knowledge is required about the antecedents of participation like attitudes, beliefs, values or intended behaviour (Altenburg et al., 1995). To explain the handling of solid waste, most of the prior research (e.g. Goldenhar, 1991; McCarthy et al., 1994) was focused on the separation of waste. The avoidance and reduction of waste, which both could have an impact on the amount of solid waste too, are subject of this paper additionally. The goal of this paper is to identify attitudinal and other psychographic variables which are useful for explaining why consumers participate in the avoidance, reduction and separation of solid waste.

2. Waste Behaviour

The production-consumption cycle, described by Pieters (1991) and illustrated in Figure 1, shows the material stream of products. It is the starting point of our analysis. Raw materials are the input to the production cycle. Finished goods are distributed and sold to the consumers. The consumption cycle is divided into three phases: the buying, the using and the separation phase. In each of these phases consumers make decisions which are related to waste. Based on this model, we can distinguish between waste-related buying behaviour in the buying phase, waste-related using behaviour in the using phase, and separation behaviour in the separation phase.

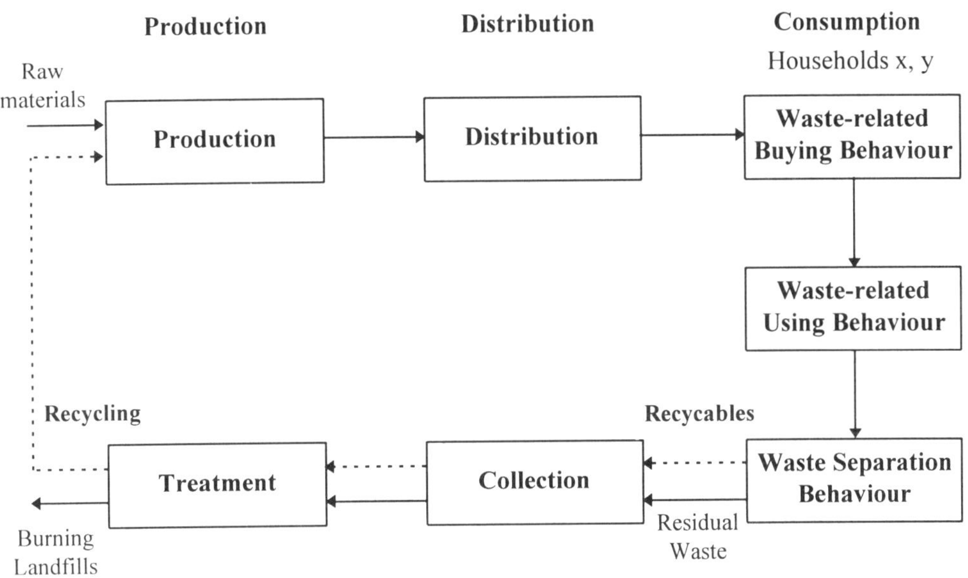

Figure 1: The production-consumption cycle, based on Pieters, 1991, p. 66

To reduce the amount of solid waste consumers have three general options: To avoid waste, to reduce waste, and to separate waste. Waste-related buying behaviour is focused on the avoidance of waste. For example, consumers can avoid buying products with much packaging. Another alternative is to substitute products. Instead of non-returnable bottles private households can choose returnable bottles. This reduces the amount of solid waste. Waste-related using behaviour means that consumers can reduce waste. For instance, they can use products for a long time or may be reuse it. Then they buy products less frequently. This has an impact on the waste output in a fixed period of time. Waste separation behaviour covers all kinds of recycling activities. It depends on the collection system (recycling facilities) how many kinds of recyclables households can separate. Either recyclables are taken to collection containers by consumers or picked up by the garbage collection.

The output from the consumption cycle is solid waste. There are two kinds of waste: Recyclables and residual waste. Most of the recyclables pass a recycling process and are used as secondary raw materials in the production cycle again. Residual waste ends up on landfills or in incinerating plants. In 1990 a so-called Dual System was implemented in Germany. Within this Dual System private companies and municipalities are involved in the collection and treatment of packaging. Due to the introduction of the Dual System a decrease of residual waste is accompanied by an increasing collection of recyclables (Holzapfel, 1996). Despite high participation rates and high recycling rates for most of the recyclables there are two major problems: First, consumers do not correctly sort all recyclables in collection containers or in special bags for recyclables. For instance, green glass is sometimes put into containers for brown glass. The second problem is that recyclables are often put in the garbage can, meant for residual waste only. The impacts of these problems are high recollection costs. The Dual System leads to a tendency of privatisation in waste disposal, especially in the collection and treatment of solid waste. This tasks were covered mainly by the municipalities in the past. Nevertheless, it is a remaining task of municipalities to motivate consumers to participate in the avoidance and separation of solid waste (Balderjahn, 1994). Therefore it is important for municipal solid waste management to know which factors influence waste behaviour.

3. Antecedents of Waste Behaviour

Prior research has stressed the impact of a number of psychographic variables on waste behaviour. The following brief review of literature concentrates on such psychographic variables, which are part of the structural equation model we use for our analysis.

McCarty et al. (1994) have identified values and attitudes as antecedents of recycling behaviour. With a structural modeling framework they found that especially the value orientation „collectivism" has an indirect, but positive effect on recycling. The items that represented collectivism in this study were: „Working hard for the goals of our group", „Being a co-operative participant in group activities", and „Readily helping others in need of help". A study by Vining et al. (1992) shows, that values have a stronger influence on the participation in recycling than general attitudes. This leads to our first hypothesis:

> H_1: A collective value orientation (e.g. the perceived duty as citizen to participate in the avoidance, reduction, and separation of waste) of consumers is expected to be a significant predictor of waste behaviour.

In prior research, constructs like „locus of control" and „perceived consumer effectiveness" were applied in environmental behaviour (Balderjahn, 1986, 1988; Ellen et al., 1991; Goldenhar, 1991). In this context, the constructs deal with the responsibility of consumers, politicians and industry to solve environmental problems. Selected findings are that people, who feel responsible for solving environmental problems, are more likely to engage in recycling (Webster, 1975). On the other hand, Gamba et al. (1994) found that the locus of control variable was not a good discriminator between less and high frequent recyclers. Heterogeneous findings according to these constructs lead to the consideration that the credibility (Kaas, 1994) of politicians and companies in respect to solve environmental problems may be a more important antecedent of waste behaviour. This leads to our second hypothesis:

> H_2: It is expected that, if consumers perceive a low credibility of politicians and industry concerning the solution of environmental problems, they are more likely to engage in the avoidance, reduction, and separation of waste.

Waste-related buying behaviour includes purchasing products which are made out of recycled materials. Research about ecological buying behaviour has shown (Bänsch, 1994; Gierl, 1987) that there could be a lower acceptance of products made out of recycled materials if consumers attribute a lower quality to these products. Therefore, we hypothesise:

> H_3: If consumers attribute a lower quality to products made out of recycled materials, they are less likely to participate in waste-related buying behaviour which includes buying products made out of recycled materials.

Some researchers assume that, the more citizens are informed about environmental or waste issues and the more information they have about this topics, the more they will participate. For instance, Vining et al. (1990) have shown that knowledge about recycling is a better predictor of recycling than environmental attitudes in general. De Young (1988/89) found that a lack of information about recycling leads to a lower participation in waste separation. The relationship between information, knowledge and waste behaviour is covered by the following hypothesis:

H₄: There is a strong relationship between the reported information and knowledge of consumers about environmental issues and the reported engagement in the avoidance, reduction, and separation of waste.

Motivation theories have also been applied to waste behaviour. Two kinds of motivation theories should be mentioned in this context: Intervention studies, which investigate the effectiveness of incentives in an experimental design, and motivational research. A result of intervention studies is for example that monetary incentives like lotteries or monetary rewards have a strong impact on the participation in recycling (Jacobs et al., 1982; Diamond et al., 1991). These extrinsic incentives mostly had short term effects, because the participation decreased when the incentive was withdrawn. Motivational research especially emphasises the importance of intrinsic motives as an antecedent of waste behaviour. Particularly prior research has found, that intrinsic motives like to protect the environment or to save natural resources are related to waste separation behaviour (De Young, 1985/86; Gamba et al., 1994; Oskamp et al., 1991). Based on these findings we assume:

H₅: Intrinsic motives are stronger predictors of waste separation behaviour than extrinsic motives.

This brief review of prior research on antecedents of waste behaviour can only shed a spotlight onto this complex consumer behaviour. In the course of this paper many theoretical constructs are not mentioned. A broader overview of theoretical constructs, which could be related to waste behaviour, gives Matthies (1994).

4. Research Design and Models

In Germany there is a waste rate of about 350 kilograms of residual waste per capita on average a year (Eurostat, 1994). Compared with rural areas, large cities show the highest waste rates. We can observe a small decrease in these figures in 1995 and 1996. That seems to be a result of the introduction of the Dual System. Nevertheless, there is a high potential to avoid and to separate waste in cities. For this reason the empirical survey is focused on cities. We selected 5 of 15 cities in Germany with approximately 500,000 or more inhabitants. These cities are Bremen, Berlin, Leipzig, Düsseldorf and Frankfurt (Main). In May 1995, 200 interviews were conducted in each of these five cities. Respondents (consumers) were selected by quota sampling. The samples are representative with regard to the distribution of the variables sex and age in this cities. In addition to demographic questions, the standardised questionnaire contains questions about attitudes towards waste issues and about waste behaviour.

To analyse the relationships between psychographic variables and waste behaviour we have chosen the structural equation model approach (Long, 1993; Baumgartner et al., 1995). The analysis is performed in two steps: First, observed variables (indicators of the constructs) are linked to unobserved or latent variables (constructs) through a factor analytic model. Second, the causal relationships among these constructs are specified through a structural equation model. Independent variables in this model are the psychographic variables, while statements about waste behaviour have the function of dependent variables.

Waste behaviour covers waste-related buying behaviour ("BUY"), waste-related using behaviour ("USE"), and waste separation behaviour ("DISPOSE"). Each of these measures consists of two items which were taken mainly from prior research (e.g. Altenburg et al., 1993). Waste behaviour was measured by self report on a seven-point-scale from 1="never" to 7= "always". The following Table 1 shows the operationalisation of waste behaviour:

Waste Behaviour	Measures of Waste Behaviour
Waste-related Buying-Behaviour ("BUY")	I buy products with less packaging instead of such with much packaging. (YB1) I buy products out of recycled materials instead of products out of raw materials. (YB2)
Waste-related Using Behaviour ("USE")	I use detergents sparingly. (YU2) I reuse paper. (YU6)
Waste Separation Behaviour ("DISPOSE")	I separate glass bottles. (YD2) I separate newspapers. (YD6)

Table 1: Dependent variables in the structural equation model

These measures of waste behaviour are taken as dependent variables in the structural equation model. Next, the independent variables have to be operationalised. As independent variables we took those psychographic constructs, which were introduced in the short overview of prior research above on the antecedents of waste behaviour (see chapter 3.). Table 2 shows the operationalisation of the psychographic constructs:

Psychographic Constructs	**Indicators of the Constructs**
Collective value orientation ("VALUE")	It is my duty as a citizen to participate in the avoidance and separation of waste. (XV1) We should learn to think more of the community than of ourselves. (XV2)
Credibility ("CREDIT")	Managers in retailing and industry do not really care about solving environmental problems. (XC4) Politicians do not really care about solving environmental problems. (XC5)
Quality perception of products which are made out of recycled materials ("PRODUCT")	Goods made from recycled materials are of poor quality. (XP1) Packaging made from recycled materials carries too many health risks. (XP2)
Attitudes about information/knowledge ("INFO")	I am not confused about what is good and what is bad for the environment. (XI3) I just have the knowledge to evaluate what is good and what is bad for the environment. (XI4)
Intrinsic Motives ("INTRINSIC")	Recycling is an essential part of our society. (XIN2) Recycling conserves natural resources. (XIN4)
Extrinsic Motives ("EXTRINSIC")	Reduced waste fee. (XEX1) Waste fee only for the waste households have produced. (XEX2)

Table 2: Independent variables in the structural equation model

For waste-related attitudes and collective value orientations a seven-point scale from 1 = "strongly disagree" to 7 = "strongly agree" was used. The question for statements about motives was "Please rate which factors might make people, including yourself, more likely to participate in the avoidance and separation of waste". A scale from 1= "unlikely" to 7= "extremely likely" was used.

The expected relationships between the independent and dependent variables were formulated in the hypotheses.

5. Results and Discussion

The hypotheses and variables are combined in a structural equation model. The analysis is performed with the LISREL program (Jöreskog et al., 1994). Because the measures were not normal distributed, we chose a correlation matrix as input matrix for the LISREL procedure (Long, 1993). Estimates of the models' parameters are obtained by unweighted least squares (ULS). Because of missing values the effective number of cases for this model is 686.

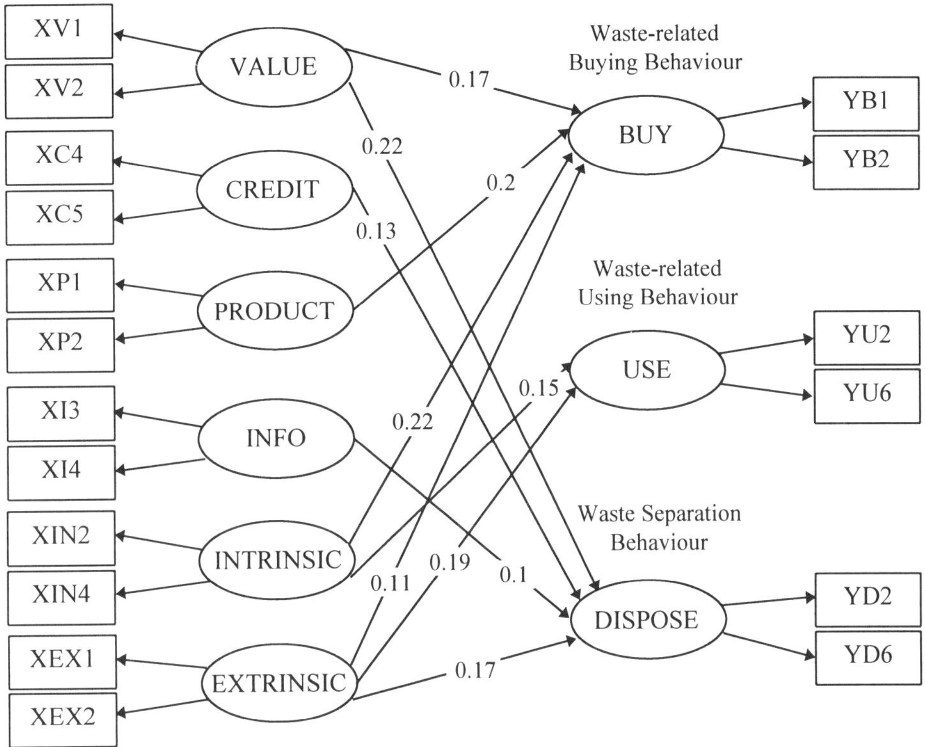

Figure 2: Structural equation model of waste behaviour

To evaluate the model's parameters we used the goodness-of-fit statistics (Long, 1993). This statistic allows a test of the hypothesis that a given model provides an acceptable fit of the observed data. The goodness-of-fit measure (GFI) represents the explained variance of the complete model. In our example, 97% of variance are explained by the complete model. This is an acceptable result in respect to a critical value of 90% explained variance at minimum, which is recommended by literature (for further details see Balderjahn, 1992; Homburg et al., 1995).

The share of unexplained variance is represented by the measure root mean square residual (RMR) and should not exceed 5%. In our example it is 3%. The goodness-of-fit measure adjusted for degrees of freedom (AGFI) should not be lower than 90%. With 94% in our example the AGFI meets this requirement.

The standardised path coefficients illustrate the effects between the independent and the dependent variables. The collective value orientation of consumers has a significant influence (0.17; $p < 0.06$) on waste-related buying and separation behaviour. That partly supports H_1. In this investigation a collective value orientation is not a significant predictor of waste-related using behaviour. If consumers perceive a low credibility of industry and politicians concerning the solution of environmental problems, they are more likely to engage in the separation of waste, as the standardised path coefficient of 0.13 ($p < 0.05$) suggests. The construct „credibility" has no significant relationship with waste-related buying and using behaviour. Therefore credibility seems not to be a good predictor of waste behaviour. This leads to the rejection of H_2. The better consumers attribute the quality of products made out of recycled materials, the more they buy them, as the standardised path coefficient of 0.13 ($p < 0.06$) specifies. This supports H_3. Self reported information and knowledge about environmental issues is not connected with waste behaviour with the exception, that there is a significant relationship (0.1; $p < 0.05$) between the information construct and waste separation behaviour. But this relationship seems too weak to support H_4. The more consumers are in favour of intrinsic motives, the more they participate in waste-related buying and using behaviour, as the standardised path coefficients (0.22 and 0.15; $p < 0.5$) specify. Extrinsic motives have a significant influence ($p < 0.06$) on waste-related buying, using, and separation behaviour. The more people care about the costs of waste, the more they engage in environmentally responsible waste behaviour. The results suggest that waste separation behaviour can be explained better by extrinsic than by intrinsic motives, while waste-related buying behaviour can be explained better by intrinsic than by extrinsic motives. Contrary to our hypothesis H_5, extrinsic motives only show a significant relationship with waste separation behaviour.

6. Conclusion

The analysis has shown, that not all psychographic variables have an influence on waste behaviour in each of the three phases of the consumption cycle. Especially, the strong relationship between extrinsic motives and waste behaviour could have practical implications for solid

264

waste management of municipalities. Obviously, consumers care about the costs of waste. In Germany, waste fees are increasing. This could have demotivating effects on the participation of consumers in the avoidance, reduction, and separation of waste (Frey, 1993). Furthermore, collective value orientation and intrinsic motives could be strengthened by the communication policy of municipalities.

References

Altenburg, U. and Balderjahn, I. (1993): Bestimmungsgründe des Abfallverhaltens privater Haushalte: Ein Vergleich zwischen den Städten Leipzig und Hannover. In: Jahrbuch der Absatz- und Verbrauchsforschung, Vol. 39, No. 1, pp. 61-86.

Altenburg, U., Balderjahn, I., Buchholz, P., and de Vries, W. (1995): Aspekte des Informationsverhaltens von Bürgern bei der Abfallvermeidung und -trennung als Ansatzpunkte für die Informationspolitik von Kommunen. In: Marktforschung und Management, Vol. 39, No. 4, pp. 165-170.

Balderjahn, I. (1986): Das umweltbewußte Konsumentenverhalten. Eine empirische Studie. Berlin.

Balderjahn, I. (1988): Personality Variables and Environmental Attitudes as Predictors of Ecologically Responsible Consumption Patterns. In: Journal of Business Research, Vol. 17, August, pp. 51-56.

Balderjahn, I. (1992): Zur Nutzung ökologischer Konsuminformation. In: Hildebrandt, L., Rudinger, G., and Schmidt, P. (Eds.): Kausalanalysen in der Umweltforschung, Stuttgart, Jena, New York, pp. 155-171.

Balderjahn, I. (1994): Betriebswirtschaftliche Aspekte der Verpackungsverordnung. In: Die Betriebswirtschaft, Vol. 54, No. 4, pp. 481-499.

Bänsch, A. (1994): Die Planung der Lebensdauer von Konsumgütern im Hinblick auf ökonomische und ökologische Ziele. In: Jahrbuch der Absatz- und Verbrauchsforschung, Vol. 40, No. 3, pp. 232-256.

De Young, R. (1985/86): Encouraging environmentally appropriate behavior: The role of intrinsic motivation. In: Journal of Environmental Systems, Vol. 15, pp. 281-292.

De Young, R. (1988/89): Exploring the difference between recyclers and non-recyclers: The role of information. In: Journal of Environmental Systems, Vol. 18, pp. 341-351.

Diamond, W.D. and Loewy, B.Z. (1991): Effects of probabilistic rewards on recycling attitudes and behavior. In: Journal of Applied Social Psychology, Vol. 21, No. 19, pp. 1590-1607.

Ellen, P.S., Wiener, J.L., and Cobb-Walgren (1991): The role of perceived consumer effectiveness in motivating environmentally conscious behaviors. In: Journal of Public Policy & Marketing, Vol. 10, No. 2, pp. 102-117.

Fishbein, M. and Ajzen, I. (1975): Beliefs, attitudes, intention and behavior. Reading, MA: Addison-Wesley.

Frey, B.S. (1993): Motivation as a limit to pricing. In: Journal of Economic Psychology, Vol. 11, pp. 635-644.

Gamba, R.J. and Oskamp, St. (1994): Factors influencing community residents participation in commingled curbside recycling programs. In: Environment and Behavior, Vol. 26, No. 5, pp. 587-612.

Gierl, H. (1987): Ökologische Einstellungen und Kaufverhalten im Widerspruch. In: Markenartikel, Vol. 49, pp. 2-13.

Goldenhar, L.M. (1991): Understanding, predicting and influencing Recycling behavior: The future generation. Michigan: University of Michigan.

Holzapfel, A. (1996): Sinkendes Müllaufkommen - steigende Gebühren. In: Umwelt, Vol. 26, No. 6, pp. 18-19.

Homburg, C. and Baumgartner, H. (1995): Beurteilung von Kausalmodellen. Bestandsaufnahme und Anwendungsempfehlungen. In: Marketing ZFP, Vol. 17, No. 3, pp. 162-176.

Jacobs, H.E. and Bailey, J.S. (1982/83): Evaluating participation in a residential recycling program. In: Journal of Environmental Systems, Vol. 12, pp. 141-152.

Jöreskog, K.G. and Sörbom, D. (1994): New features in LISREL 8. User's Reference Guide 1994, 2nd edition, Chicago: Scientific Software International.

Kaas, K.P. (1994): Ansätze einer institutionenökonomischen Theorie des Konsumentenverhaltens. In: Forschungsgruppe Konsum und Verhalten (Ed.): Konsumentenforschung. Festschrift zum 60. Geburtstag von W. Kroeber-Riel. München, pp. 245-260.

Long, J.S. (1993): Covariance structure models. Sage: California.

Matthies, E. (1994): Umweltproblem „Müll". Eine psychologische Analyse ost- und westdeutscher Sichtweisen. Wiesbaden.

McCarty, J.A. and Shrum, L.J. (1994): The Recycling of Solid Wastes: Personal Values, Value Orientation, and Attitudes about Recycling as Antecedents of Recycling Behavior. In: Journal of Business Research, Vol. 30, May, pp. 53-62.

Oskamp, St., Harrington, M.J., Edwards, T.C., Sherwood, D.L., Okuda, S.M., and Swanson, D.C. (1991): Factors influencing household recycling behavior. In: Environment and Behavior, Vol. 23, No. 4, pp. 494-519.

Pieters, R.G.M. (1991): Changing garbage disposal patterns of consumers: Motivation, ability, and performance. In: Journal of Public Policy & Marketing, Vol. 10, pp. 59-76.

Thøgerson, J. (1994): A model of recycling behaviour, with evidence from Danish source separation programmes. In: International Journal of Research in Marketing, Vol. 11, pp. 145-163.

Vining, J. and Ebreo, A. (1990): What makes a recycler? A comparison of recyclers and nonrecyclers. In: Environment and Behavior, Vol. 22, January, pp. 55-73.

Vining, J. and Ebreo, A. (1992): Predicting Recycling Behavior from Global and Specific Attitudes and changes in Recycling opportunities. In: Journal of Applied Social Psychology, Vol. 22, pp. 1580-1607.

Webster, F.E. (1975): Determining the characteristics of the socially conscious consumer. In: Journal of Consumer Research, Vol. 2, pp. 188-197.

*Rudolf Sinkovics, Thomas Salzberger and Hartmut H. Holz-
müller*

Assessing Measurement Equivalence in Cross-National Consumer Behaviour Research: Principles, Relevance and Application Issues

1. Problem Statement

2. Facets of Equivalence in Cross-National Research

3. Assessment of Cross-National Measurement Equivalence
   3.1. Multiple Group Structural Equation Modeling
   3.2. Latent Trait Theory Based Modeling

4. Measurement Equivalence of the CETSCALE: A Work in Progress Report
   4.1. Culturally Sensitive Transfer of Research Instruments
   4.2. Structural Equation Modeling Based Analysis
   4.3. Latent Trait Theory Based Assessment of Measurement Equivalence

5. Conclusions

References

Assessing Measurement Equivalence in Cross-National Consumer Behaviour Research: Principles, Relevance and Application Issues

Rudolf Sinkovics, Thomas Salzberger and Hartmut H. Holzmüller

Abstract

The increasing globalization of the business environment has pushed cross-national consumer behaviour research to provide useful measures, which capture the domain of the concept in diverse cultural settings and are also powerful in detecting differences. However, current research practice seems not to account for mean-comparability of marketing scales across nations and relies on the „presumed" etic approach for transferability of a scale. On the other hand the transferability of concepts is taken unquestioned and peculiarities of countries and/or their distinct cultures (emic approach) are not integrated into the measurement instrument. This paper will provide a research framework for extending constructs to other countries. Contributions of latent trait theory and structural equation modeling based approaches will be examined as well as other types of replication approaches.

1. Problem Statement

International market research, and thereby *cross-cultural* and *cross-national research*, has become a more and more important issue. On the one hand, managers are faced with rapid internationalisation of business (Levitt, 1983) as markets in many industries become increasingly integrated world-wide (Douglas and Craig, 1992). On the other hand scientists are interested in checking the validity of their theories in the cross-cultural context. Since cross-national research is defined primarily by its method rather than its content, cross-national research, i.e. cross-national comparisons, is always confronted with methodolgical problems (Berry, 1980). Many research endeavours, however, still ignore these problems and, therefore, lack comparability across countries and, consequently, are of questionable quality. Cultural diversities can substantially distract marketing effects and research results (see Assael, 1992; Cateora, 1993; Manrai and Manrai, 1996), which provide no meaningful input for international marketing decisions. Any similarities or differences in the underlying data structures should, in fact, be real and not be artefacts.

The traditional approach to measurement across cultural boundaries and nations can be referred to as „mere" replication research. This approach - which in many cases uses research from the US - implies utilising measurement instruments already established at an earlier time, e.g. a marketing scale that was already applied in a different cultural context is applied in different target-locations. However, the question of cross-national transferability of the scale, i.e. measurement equivalence, is not addressed. Measurement equivalence constitutes the crucial factor for cross-cultural comparisons of research results. „In general, the issue of measurement invariance in cross-national research refers to the question of whether the items in the measurement instrument indicate the latent construct(s) in the same way across countries" (Horn and McArdle, 1992).

2. Facets of Equivalence in Cross-National Research

Basically cross-national research is characterised by the comparative method, which may be regarded as the core of the scientific method (Berry, 1980; Keller, 1982). The comparison of two (or more) cultural groups may be regarded as a quasi-experimental approach (Berry, 1980) with culture as the independent variable. Whenever phenomena might potentially differ in their features across cultures, methodological problems arise. In order to be able to make comparisons in cross-cultural consumer research it is necessary to concentrate on phenomena which share some characteristics. It must be possible to place this core of the phenomena on a single dimension (Berry, 1980). This so-called „dimensional identity" can be attained by using broad concepts, which either share common applicability and utility in diverse cultures („universal concepts") or can be empirically explored out of data sets from two or more cultures („equivalence of data", see Holzmüller, 1995).

When trying to achieve equivalence of data in cross-cultural research, one has to consider several aspects which constitute prerequisites of final data equivalence. Bauer (1989, 1995) provides a framework of these aspects related to different phases of the research process (Figure 1, Bauer, 1989).

Following Bauer's classification, the elements „research topics", „research methods", „research units", „research administration", and „data handling" have to be equivalent. It is important to note that all these facets of equivalence are closely linked and that they cannot be completely separated.

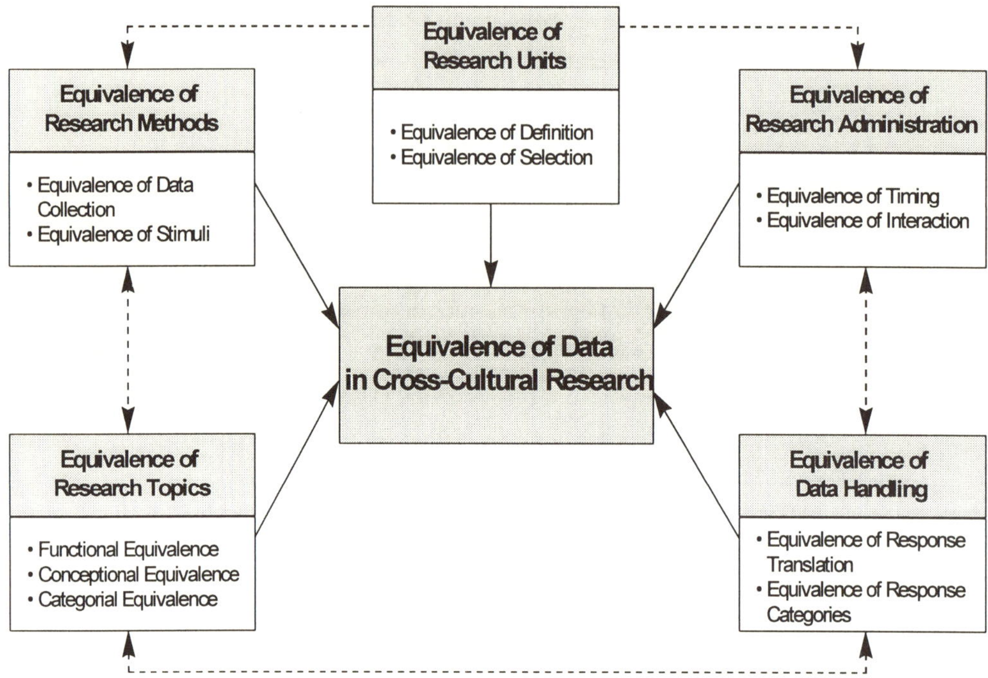

Figure 1: Aspects of equivalence in cross-cultural research (see Bauer, 1989; own translation)

Equivalence of research topics is the basic and, consequently, a very important aspect of data-equivalence in cross-cultural research. Functional equivalence refers to „whether a given concept serves the same function" (Douglas and Craig, 1983) in different cultures. Conceptual equivalence means that the local meaning of concepts and behaviours and the way they are expressed are similar.

Equivalence of research methods requires the selection of data collection techniques that ensure a problem-specific representation of the sample and a comparable internal validity of culture-specific data-collection results (see Kracmar, 1971, pp. 29; Casley and Lury, 1981, pp. 72). Furthermore, *equivalence of research methods* also implies adequate steps to be undertaken to minimise culture-specific response distortions or biases (culture-specific response behaviour).

Equivalence of research units aims at the use of methods which lead to an equivalent representation of several cultural samples, while *equivalence of research administration* can be assumed when time-based factors of influence (e.g., demographic structure, political situation, etc.) are considered adequately as well as interaction-based influences (e.g., interviewer effects)

272

(Bauer, 1989, pp. 178). Finally, *data handling equivalence* has to be taken into account, when concerned with cross-cultural research. This aspect is widely acknowledged and can be operationalized at the level of carefully translated equivalent measures and response categories.

This framework illustrates that rather than attributing the causes of non-equivalent research results solely to the item structure or the translation of the items, there is a variety of further reasons, ranging from data handling to different conceptual operationalisations, which have to be considered as a possible source of non-equivalence. Within this paper we will focus on the overall quality of cross-national research data with respect to its comparability across borders. Since our scope is on the final data and we are not looking at the different stages in the research process, we label the equivalence aspect that is analysed measurement equivalence. This indicates that the assessment of cross-national comparability is based on methods used in measurement theory (Pfanzagl, 1971).

If measurement equivalence cannot be found it is necessary to investigate the earlier steps in the research process in order to identify reasons for the lack of comparability. Possibly erroneous decisions can be eliminated. However, if measurement invariance prevails, we suggest the use of a replication and extension approach. While this leads to a loss of cross-nationally comparable data, it seems to be the only way of applying the (modified) construct in different cultural contexts.

3. Assessment of Cross-National Measurement Equivalence

The cross-cultural measurement equivalence of a scale may empirically be examined by comparing data sets from different cultures. In the following, we will discuss two effective approaches: the multiple group structural equation modeling approach (Mullen, 1995; Steenkamp and Baumgartner, 1996; Singh, 1995) and the Latent Trait Theory (LTT) or Item Response Theory (IRT) approach (Singh, 1996).

3.1. Multiple Group Structural Equation Modeling

The measurement equivalence of cross-cultural data may be examined by the multiple group structural equation modeling (multiple group LISREL) approach (Mullen, 1995; Steenkamp and Baumgartner, 1996). The underlying definition of measurement equivalence involves the following levels of cross-cultural invariance: configural invariance, metric invariance, and scalar invariance (Steenkamp and Baumgartner, 1996; Mullen, 1995). These levels of measurement equivalence represent increasingly stringent forms of invariance, with scalar invariance being the highest and most rigorous type of equivalence (see Figure 2).

Each level of measurement equivalence requires certain criteria to be met. If these criteria are fulfilled, cross-cultural comparisons are possible. The extent to which these comparisons are meaningful, however, depends on the level of invariance shown by the data.

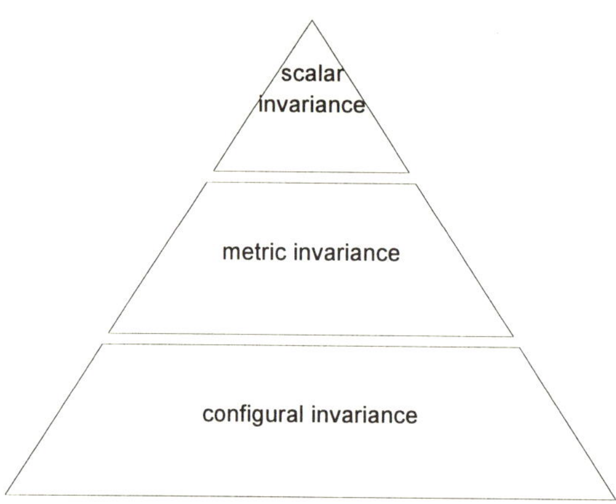

Figure 2: Levels of measurement invariance (Steenkamp and Baumgartner, 1996)

The basic form of invariance, **configural invariance**, refers to the minimal requirement of cross-cultural equivalence. The concept is based on Thurston's simple structure (Horn et al., 1983) developed for the interpretation of exploratory factor analysis. Simple structure means that the loading of a variable is high (preferably near 1) when the item represents an indicator to the factor (salient loadings), and that the loading is low (0 or near 0) when the item does not (non-salient loadings). Given such a structure, each item measures only one dimension. Cross-cultural validity of a marketing scale requires this structure to be the same across cultures. This assumption can be tested by confirmatory factor analysis. Configural invariance holds true, if the items show loadings close to 0 on factors not associated and substantial loadings on factors associated with the item. This has to apply within all samples, irrespectively of the cultural affiliation. Since the factor analysis is a confirmatory analysis, factors are allowed to correlate. Correlations between the factors have to be substantially lower than 1 in order to represent distinct dimensions. When testing for configural invariance, no constraints, whatsoever, are imposed on the magnitude of the salient loadings, i.e. they do not have to be equally high.

Data showing configural invariance qualifies for being tested for **metric invariance**. The model specification, however, has to be altered. Whereas the nonsalient loadings still have to be close to 0, the salient loadings must now correspond across cultures not only in a configural way but also regarding their magnitude. Consequently, the matrices of factor loadings for samples from different cultures have to be the same. Despite the constraints of metric invariance being fulfilled, some form of non-equivalence may still persist. If the data of one sample is exposed to a culture-specific bias as, e.g., expressed by a higher tendency of affirmative answers, a courtesy bias, etc. (Douglas and Craig, 1983), the factor loadings may, however, not be concerned. As a result, metric invariance does not constitute a sufficiently stringent condition for the comparison of absolute scores of measurement as means cannot be compared across cultures.

Mean comparisons are only meaningful, when **scalar invariance** holds. This form of invariance requires equal item intercepts, i.e. the expected values of the observed variables are equal, with all factor scores being equal. Scalar invariance ensures that individuals from different cultures but with the same location on the latent dimension have the same expected value on the observed variables.

In addition to scalar invariance, error variances may be tested for their equivalence, i.e. the reliability of measurement is the same in all samples. Finally, factor variances and covariances (and consequently the factor intercorrelations) may be examined as well.

In empirical marketing research, the question which form of invariance has to be met in order to ensure meaningful comparisons has also to be dealt with. The first research step should consist in considering conceptual aspects. This means that emphasis would stress structural identity, i.e. configural invariance. If configural invariance is achieved without metric and/or scalar invariance at the same time, this may serve as an indicator of the potential transferability of the concept. Nevertheless, since higher levels of invariance do not apply, the operationalisation process (i.e. the scale items) would still need improvement.

With rising demands of replication, higher forms of invariance have to be imposed. Replications in marketing research usually aim at comparing means across cultures. As outlined above, scalar invariance is a prerequisite for such comparisons.

Facing the variety of cultural facets and habits possibly affecting response patterns, it is rather unlikely that full metric or scalar invariance, i.e. the equivalence of all items of a scale, is achieved. The concept of partial invariance accounts for these problems (Steenkamp and Baumgartner, 1996) by limiting the quality constraints to a subset of items.

3.2. Latent Trait Theory Based Modeling

The Latent Trait Theory (LTT) offers a promising alternative to the multiple group LIS-REL approach as a procedure of determining cross-cultural measurement equivalence (Singh, 1996). LTT as a test and measurement theory defines the relationship of observed and latent variables in a different way than Classical Test Theory (CTT), the underlying paradigm of the multiple group structural equation approach. CTT with its well-known basic definition of the observed score expressed as a combination of true score and measurement error refers to continuous variables (Steyer and Eid, 1993). Therefore, the observed score in CTT usually means the score of a scale determined as the sum of several items. In addition, summing up item scores requires interval scale properties to be present on an item level. Opposingly, the relationship between the latent dimension and the observed variable, defined by latent trait models, refers to the response to a single item and is represented by a logistic function. For the answer categories of the observed variables, ordinal scaling is sufficient. Especially in cross-cultural research, the interval scale properties are highly questionable.

A further shortcoming of CTT is the interdependency between personal parameters and item parameters. A personal parameter is, e.g., the respondent's ability in achievement testing or the degree of ethnocentric tendencies in attitude testing. An item parameter may be the item „difficulty" in achievement testing, and the item „affectivity" in attitude testing. In CTT, the item affectivity depends on the sample under scrutiny.

LTT helps to overcome these problems. Many of the different LTT-models feature independence of person and item parameters, i.e. the estimation of item parameters is not affected by the sample structure. Moreover, item parameters and person parameters are measured on the same scale (Hambleton et al., 1991).

3.2.1. Latent Trait Theory-Models

For demonstration purposes, a very simple model will be discussed in the following (Molenaar, 1995). This model - commonly referred to as the Rasch-model - is based on dichotomously scored items measuring the same dimension (assumption of unidimensionality).

For each item one parameter is specified indicating the item's affectivity, hence, the model is called the one-parameter logistic model. Since the LTT model describes the response to an item in accordance with the person parameter (ethnocentrism) and the item parameter (affectivity), the term *Item Response Theory* (IRT) is also used for LTT-models. In the German literature the term „*Probabilistische Testtheorie*" (probabilistic test theory) is used as a synonym for LTT, because the model refers to the probability of agreement.

$$P_i(\theta) = (e^{(\theta - bi)}) / (1 + e^{(\theta - bi)}) \quad ... \; i = 1, 2, ... , n \tag{1}$$

(Hambleton et al., 1991) where

$P_i(\theta)$ is the probability that a randomly chosen respondent with attitude θ agrees to the item i

b_i is the item i affectivity parameter

n is the number of items in the test

e is a transcendental number whose value is 2.718 (correct to three decimals)

The equation of this one-parameter logistic model describes a curve, the so-called item characteristic curve (ICC). This curve defines the probability of agreement in accordance with the location on the underlying latent dimension (θ) and the item affectivity (b_i) as expressed by the function on the curve. For each dichotomous item there is one ICC. The definition of this model implies that all these ICCs are parallel, which means that all items have the same discriminative power.

Regarding the ICC for item 1 in Figure 3 the probability of agreement rises strictly monotonously and asymptotically approaches 1 with increasing attitude. The ICC for an item with higher affectivity has the same shape but is shifted to the right. Given the same location on the latent dimension, the probability of agreement to item 2 is lower than for item 1.

As addressed above, the estimation of item parameters does not depend on the sample structure. In cross-cultural research, item parameters consequently have to be the same, regardless of cultural affiliation, provided the scale is defined in exactly the same manner for all samples. This can be carried out by standardising the expected value of the person parameters to 0. As a result, a scale applicable to all cultures involved is obtained by this process, if large samples are used.

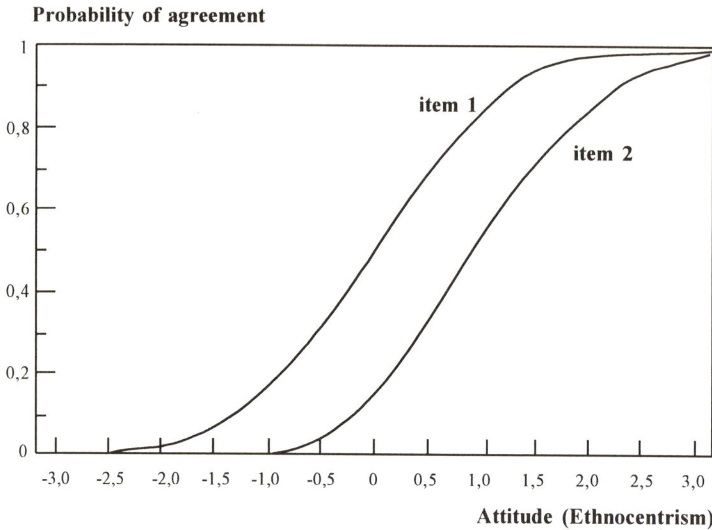

Figure 3: Ideal item characteristic curves (ICCs) for two items

3.2.2. Generalisation of the One-Parameter Logistic Model

The model outlined above may be generalised by introducing further item and/or person parameters (Hambleton et al., 1991; Anderson, 1995; Fischer, 1995; von Davier and Rost 1995; Glas and Verhelst, 1995). The two-parameter logistic model, e.g., defines two item parameters. Besides item affectivity, a further parameter is used to describe the item discrimination. The ICCs may intersect because the constraint of equal discrimination is lifted in this model. Multidimensional models which get along without the premise of unidimensionality generalise person parameters by defining more than one person parameter.

Applied in empirical marketing research, generalisations regarding the item answer categories become even more interesting. Dichotomous scales are not very common, multicategorial or polytomous scales are usually used instead of. This means that the answers to polytomous scales may be dichotomised. Besides the problem of dichotomising odd-numbered categories, dichotomisation always represents a loss of information. Therefore the usage of LTT-models designed for polytomously scored items is more desirable. The ICC of a dichotomous item can be viewed as the threshold between two categories, i.e. agreement and disagreement. In the same manner, the thresholds between each pair of (consecutive) categories of a multicategorial item may be described by an ICC-like curve: the Category Characteristic Curve

278

(CCC). Each item is then characterised by a set of CCCs. There are several models concerning polytomously scored items, which differ in defining constraints on the threshold differences on the latent dimension (e.g., the *rating scale model*, Andrich, 1978; the *equidistance model,* formerly called *dispersion model,* Andrich, 1982; the *dispersion model,* formerly called *successive interval model,* Rost, 1988; the *ordinal* or *partial credit model,* Masters, 1982).

3.2.3. Model Testing and Cross-Cultural Invariance

As outlined above, the estimation of the item parameters is independent of the sample structure. The model test, i.e. the test whether the data fits the LTT model, refers to this. If the item parameters estimated from different samples differ, the model does not hold for that item and has to be considered falsified (Hambleton et al., 1991). When regarding samples from different cultures, as in the case of cross-cultural research, the model test is a test of cross-cultural equivalence at the same time. Therefore, items showing the same item parameters across cultures are appropriate for cross-cultural comparisons. Even comparisons between means may be done, if the same scale is used for different cultures (see scale defining procedures, as mentioned above). If item parameters show culture-specific values (i.e. the estimations of the item parameters differ), the response patterns to this item do not only depend on the latent dimension to be measured but also on cultural factors. Such items are labeled to show „*Differential Item Functioning*" (DIF) and must not be used for cross-cultural comparisons. A statistical method to test differences of item parameters is the chi-square test (Hambleton et al., 1991). Another procedure for detecting DIF may consist in analysing the area between the ICCs for the same items derived from different samples. The smaller this area, the better the equivalence of cross-cultural data.

3.2.4. Culture-Specific and Universal Response Patterns

Culture-specific response patterns can be regarded as deviations from culturally universal patterns taken from an omnicultural, i.e. culturally unbiased, reference sample. When comparing only two cultures, one of both may be arbitrarily chosen as reference culture. Usually, the culture for which the scale was originally developed is taken as the reference culture. Regardless of which culture is seen as the reference group, it is not possible in the case of DIF to draw conclusions about culture-specific and universal response patterns. The identification of universal response patterns requires an omnicultural reference group (Ellis and Kimmel, 1992) which has to be composed of a variety of cultures in order to eliminate any cultural specifics. If culturally homogeneous samples differ from this reference group, culturally specific response patterns prevail.

As opposed to the replication and extension approach, the application of LTT models concentrates on culturally universal items which evoke the same response patterns in all cultures - or at least all those under scrutiny. In terms of etic and emic orientation, this approach would be completely etic-oriented.

3.2.5. Application of Latent Trait Theory-Models

Besides the addressed advantages of LTT, there are quite some practical aspects which limit the application of LTT models. So the initial estimation of item parameters requires large samples. However, the computing procedures involve models and software many researchers might not be familiar with. Furthermore, LTT models are very stringent models and empirical data often falsifies the model even within just one culture (intra-culturally). LTT models require the independence of any pair of items (assumption of local independence, see Hambleton et al., 1991). This requirement may, however, be violated, e.g. when respondents try to answer consistently.

4. Measurement Equivalence of the CETSCALE: A Work in Progress Report

The CETSCALE (Consumer ethnocentristic tendencies scale), an instrument that allows to measure consumer ethnocentrism, was initially developed by Shimp and Sharma (1987) in the United States. Consumer Ethnocentrism (Shimp and Sharma, 1987) serves as an alternative attempt explaining some aspects of consumer behaviour, suggesting that domestic consumers evaluate their own country's products as more desirable than those originating from foreign manufacturers. Because of the sound methodology used to develop the instrument and the relevance for international marketing, it stimulated research on that topic in other countries (Netemeyer et al., 1991; Herche, 1992; Good and Huddleston, 1995). The replication studies that have been published until now, focused primarily on nomological validation and application issues. However, none of the earlier studies tested measurement equivalence. So far only

Steenkamp and Baumgartner (1996) used measurement theory based methods to assess the equivalence of CETSCALE data collected in different countries.

The research project in Austria was designed to overcome some of the shortcomings in the CETSCALE related international research by using a stepwise and more comprehensive framework to rate and assess the measurement equivalence of the instrument. Figure 4 depicts a general framework for research in the cross-national context, exemplified by consumer ethnocentrism studies.

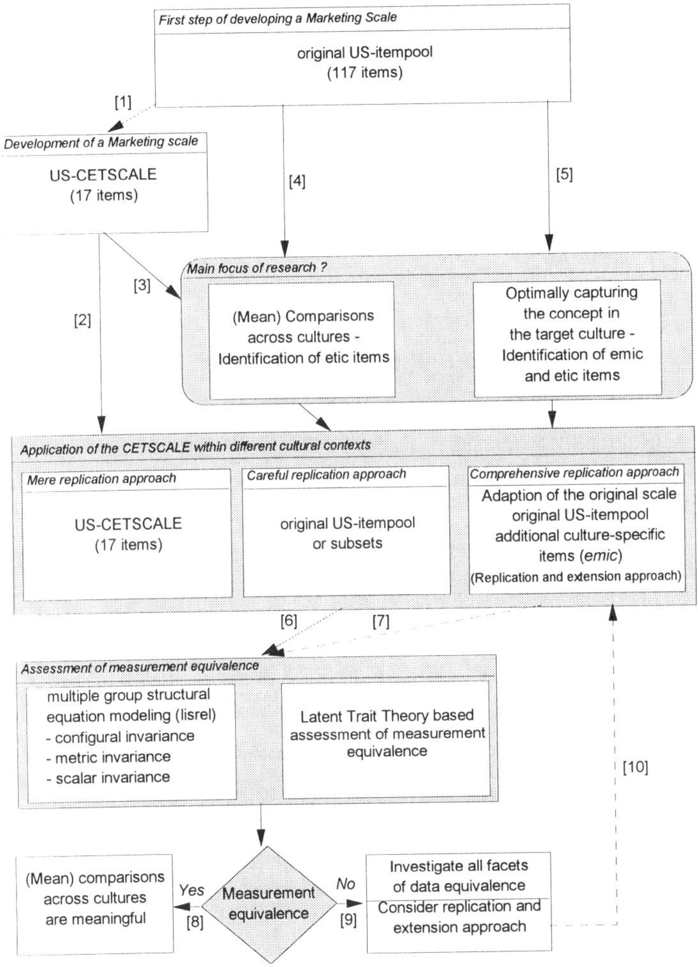

Figure 4: Approaches for extending constructs to other countries - CETSCALE application

Generally, the development of a marketing scale starts with the generation of a comprehensive item pool which captures the domain of the construct (Churchill, 1979). This item pool is subsequently to be reduced to a smaller number of items by item selection and reduction techniques (Anderson and Gerbing, 1988). When developing the US-CETSCALE Shimp and Sharma (1987) ended up with a pool of 117 items after qualitative item generation procedures. This set of items was truncated to the number of 17 items, capturing consumer ethnocentric tendencies (US-CETSCALE, see Figure 4[1]). The application of the CETSCALE in different cultural contexts may either aim at identifying cross-culturally valid, i.e. etic items in order to make meaningful mean comparisons, or it may aim at optimally capturing the concept within one specific culture. These two main orientations determine which approach to choose.

The mere replication approach (Figure 4[2]) is confined to translating the items, collecting data, and comparing results. Possible problems of data and measurement equivalence, however, are not investigated. Measurement equivalence is assumed rather than tested.

In sharp contrast, the more careful replication approach refers to either the original item pool (Figure 4[4], 117 consumer ethnocentrism items) or to subsets (Figure 4[3]). After data collection the measurement equivalence has to be investigated (Figure 4[6]). As outlined earlier, we suggest two effective approaches: the multiple group structural equation modeling approach and the Latent Trait Theory based approach.

If the replication focuses on optimally capturing the concept within one specific culture, a comprehensive replication has to be done by applying the replication and extension approach. The approach starts with the original item pool. Moreover, additional items are generated reflecting specific facets of the target culture. If these additional items turn out to be valid, the new scale contains emic items. Those items which are used by the new scale and the original US-scale are the common denominator and can be regarded as „derived etic" items (Holzmüller, 1995). For the items in common the measurement equivalence may be investigated using the same approaches as mentioned above (Figure 4[7]).

If measurement equivalence is shown by the data (Figure 4[8]), mean comparisons are meaningful. If the hypothesis of measurement equivalence has to be rejected (Figure 4[9]), all facets of data equivalence (depicted in Figure 1) have to be (re-)investigated. Alternatively, a more comprehensive pool of items may be used, in order to re-assess measurement equivalence. Moreover, a replication and extension approach has to be considered, if measurement equivalence cannot be achieved (Figure 4[10]).

The Austrian research project started with the replication and extension approach in Austria in order to include not only the culturally universal core of the concept (etic aspects) but also Austrian specifics (emic aspects). Future steps will refer to the assessment of the measurement equivalence by both, structural equation modeling and the Latent Trait Theory based approach.

From a methodological point of view, it seems to be appropriate to go for a universal scale first, and to broaden the concept in a second run, only if necessary. However, it seems to be reasonable to keep the possible failure to construct a measurement-equivalent scale in mind and be prepared for answers why this could happen. Therefore, in order to enhance „research economy" while data collection, it may be advisable to include some additional open statements to the problem or concept during the first questionnaire administration.

4.1. Culturally Sensitive Transfer of Research Instruments

As outlined at the beginning of this paper, we promote the idea that replications - if they are to increase common knowledge in the scientific marketing area (Rosenthal and Rosnow, 1984; Collins, 1985) - have to be carefully designed. Whenever the rigid framework of assessing configural, metric or even scalar invariance does not seem applicable, a carefully designed replication and extension approach („comprehensive replication") should be used.

The Austrian study tried to cope with this problem by broadening the research approach. Careful scale construction as well as selective replication and extension procedures helped to include Austrian culture standards in the scale. The procedures involved the re-establishment of the original US-item pool in Austria and a refinement of diverse facets of the ethnocentrism phenomenon. Qualitative interview statements, data categorisation and correspondence analysis as well as common data reduction techniques, such as exploratory and confirmatory factor analyses and item-to-total-correlations were used.

While Shimp and Sharma's US-CETSCALE comprises only 17 items, the AT-CETSCALE comprises a total of 21 items. Both scales have 11 items in common, the AT-CETSCALE contains 4 more items out of the re-established item pool and 1 item which does not have a cultural counterpart in the US. The common denominator, i.e. the 11 items shared, can be regarded as „derived ethics" items (Holzmüller, 1995, S. 153).

4.2. Structural Equation Modeling Based Analysis

Steenkamp and Baumgartner (1996) analysed three data sets of a 10-item version of the CETSCALE. Data was collected in Belgium, Great Britain and Greece. Whereas configural invariance held for the three samples, full metric invariance did not. This means some of the item loadings differed significantly across cultures. Therefore four factor loadings were set free, partial metric invariance was tested and finally supported.

When testing for scalar invariance, three intercepts were set free in addition to the intercepts of those items where metric invariance did not hold. Partial scalar invariance for all three samples under scrutiny was supported for 4 items. Building on the procedure to assess measurement equivalence, as proposed by Steenkamp and Baumgartner (1996) we plan to extend this research by including Austrian and Korean data. Especially Korean data looks promising in this specific research area, because of the sound diversities in social and economic life compared to European data.

4.3. Latent Trait Theory Based Assessment of Measurement Equivalence

Considering the fundamental differences of LTT vs. CTT (see chapter 3.1.1) it seems reasonable to further investigate LTT/IRT models. The empirical analysis of the cross-cultural equivalence of the CETSCALE by means of LTT/IRT will be demonstrated by using several samples collected in Austria. These samples will be compared with a Korean sample. The model specification will first focus on multicategorial models. Alternatively dichotomised data will be analysed by means of simpler LTT/IRT models (Ellis and Kimmel, 1992; Singh, 1996).

Any model of this sort will, however, be based on the original pool of 117 items. So the IRT-approach starts with the same item base as the replication and extension approach. This is mainly due to the simple fact that the larger the item pool, the more likely a reasonable number of cross-culturally invariant items may be found. As opposed to the replication and extension approach, IRT explicitly wants to avoid emic items but identify etic items instead. If the number of such items with culturally universal response patterns is too small to represent a scale, the LTT approach will be confined to several inner-Austrian samples. In this way the determination of subcultural equivalence of the CETSCALE could serve as a fall-back position (e.g. analysis of different Austrian regions in terms of their CETSCALE score).

The application of the LTT approach represents a valuable theoretical contribution to cross-cultural research, regardless of the actual results of the measurement equivalence assessment of the CETSCALE. If data shows measurement equivalence, LTT serves as a theoretically satisfying basis of mean comparability. If, however, measurement equivalence does not hold, LTT indicates that cross-cultural comparability cannot be achieved. In this case, LTT gives an argument for the use of the replication and extension approach.

5. Conclusions

This paper provides a research framework for useful replication research. The „mere replication approach" (translate items, collect data, compare results) usually relies on the cross-cultural transferability of a scale („presumed" etic approach). As suggested, whenever comparisons of means are intended, the „presumed" etic approach is not sufficient. For mean comparisons of cross-cultural research data, equivalence issues have to be carefully examined. Both the multiple group LISREL and the latent trait theory approach offer opportunities to test cross-cultural invariance. Whenever methodological restrictions do not allow meaningful metric equivalence, the authors suggest using the „comprehensive replication" approach. A comprehensive replication can be seen as a careful adaptation and extension of a concept to a target country, insofar it is an emic approach (Douglas and Craig, 1983). This „emic" orientation aims at integrating peculiarities of countries and/or their distinct cultures into the measurement instrument.

By confining to culturally universal, i.e. etic, items, culture-specific facets are, however, neglected. It is up to the researcher and his/her research objective whether a broadening replication and extension („comprehensive replication") approach is used or whether one wants to focus on the culturally invariant core of a marketing concept. Future findings and additional data sets from different cultures will show whether latent trait theory is applicable in the field of consumer ethnocentric tendencies.

References

Anderson, E.B. (1995): Polytomous Rasch models and their estimation, In: Fischer, G.H. and Molenaar, I.W. (Eds.): Rasch models, foundations, recent developments, and applications, Springer, New York, pp. 271-292.

Anderson, J.C. and Gerbing, D.W. (1988): Structural equation modeling in practice: A review and recommended two-step approach. In: Psychological Bulletin, Vol. 103, pp. 411-423.

Andrich, D. (1978): A rating formulation for ordered response categories. In: Psychometrika, Vol. 43, pp. 561-573.

Andrich, D. (1982): An extension of the Rasch model for ratings providing both location and dispersion parameters. In: Psychometrika, Vol. 47, pp. 105-113.

Bauer, E. (1989): Übersetzungsprobleme und Übersetzungsmethoden bei einer multinationalen Marketingforschung. In: Jahrbuch der Absatz- und Verbrauchsforschung, No. 2, pp. 174-205.

Berry, J.W. (1980): Introduction to methodology, In: Triandis, H.C. and Berry, J.W. (Eds.): Handbook of Cross-Cultural Psychology, Vol.2: Methodology, Boston.

Casley, D.J. and Lury, D.A. (1981): Data collection in developing countries. Oxford, N.Y.

Churchill, G.A. (1979): A paradigm for developing better measures of Marketing constructs. In: Journal of Marketing Research, Vol. 16, February, pp. 64-73

Collins, H.M. (1985): Changing order: replication and induction in scientific practice. Sage: Beverly Hills, CA.

Douglas, S.P. and Craig, C.S. (1992): Advances in international marketing. In: International Journal of Research in Marketing, Vol. 9, pp. 291-318.

Douglas, S.P. and Craig, C.S. (1983): International marketing research. Prentice-Hall: Englewood Cliffs.

Ellis, B.B. and Kimmel, H.D. (1992): Identification of unique cultural response patterns by means of Item response theory. In: Journal of Applied Psychology, Vol. 77, No. 2, pp. 177-184.

Fischer, G.H. (1995): The derivation of polytomous Rasch models. In: Fischer, G.H. and Molenaar, I.W. (Eds.): Rasch models, foundations, recent developments, and applications. Springer, New York, pp. 293-306.

Glas, C.A.W. and Verhelst, N.D. (1995): Tests of fit for polytomous Rasch models. In: Fischer, G.H. and Molenaar, I.W. (Eds.): Rasch models, foundations, recent developments, and applications. Springer, New York, pp. 325-352.

286

Good, L.K. and Huddleston, P. (1995): Ethnocentrism of Polish and Russian consumers: are feelings and intentions related? In: International Marketing Review, Vol.12, No. 5, pp. 35-48.

Hambleton, R.K. and Swaminathan, H. (1996): Item response theory - principles and applications, 8 ed. Kluwer Nijhoff Publishing: Boston.

Hambleton, R.K., Swaminathan, H., and Rogers, H.J. (1991): Fundamentals of item response theory. SAGE: Newbury Park.

Herche, J. (1992): A note on the predictive validity of the CETSCALE. In: Journal of the Academy of Marketing Science, Vol. 20, No. 3, pp. 261-264.

Holzmüller, H.H. (1995): Konzeptionelle und methodische Probleme in der interkulturellen Management- und Marketingforschung. Schäffer-Poeschel: Stuttgart.

Horn, J.L., McArdle, J., and Mason, R. (1983): When is invariance not invariant: A practical scientist's look at the ethereal concept of factor invariance. In: The Southern Psychologist, Vol. 1, No. 4, pp. 179-188.

Horn, J.L. and McArdle, J.J. (1992): A Practical and Theoretical Guide to Measurement Invariance in Aging Research. In: Experimental Aging Research, Vol. 18, No. 3, pp. 117-144.

Kracmar, J.Z. (1971): Marketing research in developing countries. New York, NY.

Levitt, T. (1983): The globalization of markets. In: Harvard Business Review, Vol. 61, May-June, pp. 92-102.

Manrai, L.A. and Manrai, A.K. (1996): Current issues in the cross-cultural and cross-national consumer research. In: Journal of International Consumer Marketing, Vol.8, No.3/4, pp. 9-22.

Masters, G.N. (1982): A Rasch model for partial credit scoring. In: Psychometrika, Vol. 47, pp. 149-174.

Molenaar, I.W. (1995): Some background for the item response theory and the Rasch model. In: Fischer, G.H. and Molenaar, I.W. (Eds.): Rasch models, foundations, recent developments, and applications. Springer, New York, pp. 3-14.

Mullen, M.R. (1995): Diagnosing measurement equivalence in cross-national research, In: Journal of International Business Studies, Third Quarter, pp. 573-596.

Netemeyer, R.G., Durvasula, S., and Lichtenstein, D.R. (1991): A cross-national assessment of the reliability and validity of the CETSCALE. In: Journal of Marketing Research, Vol. 28, pp. 320-327.

Pfanzagl, J. (1971): Theory of measurement. Physica: Würzburg.

Rost, J. (1988): Measuring attitudes with a threshold model drawing on a traditional scaling concept. In: Applied Psychological Measurement, Vol. 12, pp. 397-409.

Shimp, T.A. and Sharma, S. (1987): Consumer ethnocentrism: construction and validation of the CETSCALE. In: Journal of Marketing Research, Vol. 14, pp. 280-289.

Singh, J. (1995): Measurement issues in cross-national research. In: Journal of International Business Studies, Third Quarter, pp. 597-617.

Singh, J. (1996): A latent trait theory approach to measurement issures in marketing research: principles, relevance and application, In: Proceedings of the EMAC Annual Conference, Budapest.

Steenkamp, J.B. and Baumgartner, H. (1996): Assessing invariance of measurement instruments in cross-national consumer research, Work in progress paper, Leuven.

Steyer, R. and Eid, M. (1993): Messen und Testen. Springer: Berlin.

von Davier, M. and Rost, J. (1995): Polytomous mixed Rasch models. In: Fischer, G.H. and Molenaar, I.W. (Eds): Rasch models, foundations, recent developments, and applications, Springer, New York, pp. 371-382.

François d'Hauteville and Ronald E. Goldsmith

Measuring Cross Cultural Acceptance of an Innovation: The Case of Low-Alcohol Wine

1. Introduction

2. Theoretical Background and Hypotheses

3. Method
   3.1. Samples
   3.2. Questionnaire and Variables

4. Analyses and Results
   4.1. Dimensionality and Internal Consistency of Theoretical Construct Scales
   4.2. Associations with Wine Consumption and Theoretical Constructs
   4.3. Low-Alcohol Wine and Consumer Demographics
   4.4. Correlations among Variables

5. Discussion

6. Conclusions

References

Measuring Cross Cultural Acceptance of an Innovation: The Case of Low-Alcohol Wine

François d'Hauteville and Ronald E. Goldsmith[1]

Abstract

This paper describes a study based on data from 409 consumers in three countries: the US (n = 121), Germany (n = 113), and France (n = 175). The study participants completed a questionnaire asking them to describe their wine related attitudes and behaviours. The focus of the study was on the effects of consumer demographics (sex, age, and country) and of consumer characteristics (frequency of wine use, wine involvement, wine innovativeness, wine knowledge, and opinion seeking about wine) on the probability of future purchase of a new beverage, a low-alcohol wine. The results suggest there was more interest in trying the new low-alcohol wine in Germany than in France or the US; and women expressed slightly more interest in the new product than men in all three countries. Although wine involvement, wine innovativeness, and opinion seeking about wine are not significantly related to the intention of purchasing low-alcohol wine, they appear to be reliable constructs that may be used for international comparisons.

1. Introduction

Studies from sociologists and anthropologists (Padilla, 1992) show that cultural background is a determinant factor of consumer preferences for food and beverages. For strategic planners and marketing managers in the food and beverages industries, it is important to assess these national differences, as well as the tendencies concerning globalization of markets (d'Hauteville, 1996). It may be quite easy to compare what products people actually buy, eat or drink. It is more difficult however to explain or predict these differences, particularly when it comes to launching new products on international markets.

In this paper, we compare attitudes towards a new product, low-alcohol wine, in three countries: US, Germany, and France. We hypothesise that latent attitude constructs such as

---

[1] This research was supported by a Summer Research Grant from the College of Business, Florida State University, Tallahassee to the second author.

involvement, innovativeness, expertise and opinion seeking may be adequate indicators of cultural differences.

First, we analyse for each national sample the validity of the constructs used in the survey. Then we look at the existing relationships between the intention of purchasing low-alcohol wine and these latent variables, but also with typical demographic variables such as sex or country of origin. Finally, we discuss these relations and the quality of the variables as cross-cultural measures.

2. Theoretical Background and Hypotheses

Many characteristics of consumer personality and lifestyle influence the buyer behaviour. One of the most important constructs yet identified by consumer researchers is „enduring involvement" or the feelings of interest, enthusiasm, and excitement that many consumers feel toward specific product categories (Bloch, 1986). When consumers are aroused and interested in a product field, they exhibit a variety of related attitudes and behaviours that are important in understanding patterns of consumer behaviour. Involvement with a product field has been identified as an important precursor of knowledge, innovativeness, and opinion leadership in the particular product field (Flynn and Goldsmith, 1993a; 1993b; Goldsmith and Flynn, 1992).

In light of the research on cultural differences among consumers, we can propose as first hypothesis to be tested in this study that we expect consumers to differ in their levels of involvement, product knowledge, innovativeness, and opinion leadership across the three countries under study.

Lacking detailed information about wine consumption among consumers in these three countries, however, we can not draw exact hypotheses about which country's consumers will score higher or lower on these variables. Nevertheless, a general knowledge of cross-cultural wine consumption suggests that the two European countries should demonstrate higher levels of the wine-related variables than the US consumers (see Academic American Encyclopaedia, 1994; Aigrain et al., 1990; Lelong, 1990). In contrast, the pattern of relationships among the constructs involvement, knowledge, innovativeness, and opinion leadership should be positive regardless of the studied country because these constructs represent more universal consumer attitudes and behaviours. Thus, the second hypothesis is that all four variables will be positively correlated with each other in the samples from all three countries. These four constructs should also be positively correlated with wine consumption, as they have been characterised to be important indicators of usage rate in other studies (Flynn and Goldsmith, 1993a; 1993b; Goldsmith and Flynn, 1992, d'Hauteville, 1994). Consequently, our third hypothesis is that the four constructs will be positively correlated with self-reported wine usage. Our fourth hypothesis is that higher levels of wine involvement, knowledge, innovativeness, and opinion leadership should be positively correlated with willingness to try the new low-alcohol wine product as they reflect greater interest and concern with wine and an eagerness to try new products in this product field.

3. Method

3.1. Samples

Convenience samples were deemed appropriate because the purpose of the study was not to provide point and interval estimates of the variables, but to test the relationships among them, and thus are adequate for this purpose (Calder et al., 1981).

The US data was collected with questionnaires distributed to undergraduate students in marketing classes at a large US south-eastern university. The sample (n = 121) consisted of 69 men and 51 women with one missing value for sex. The average age was 22.1 years (SD = 2.2)[2]. The German data was gathered from business students at the University of Berlin. The sample (n = 113) consisted of 39 men and 70 women, with 4 missing values for sex. The average age was 27.6 years (SD = 5.9). The French data was collected from business students at the Ecole Nationale Superieure d'Agronomie in Montpellier. The sample (n = 175) consisted of 75 men and 100 women. The mean age was 21.3 years (SD = 3.2). Analysis of variance (see Table 1) indicated that the average age of German students was higher than that of US and French students (p < .05). The relatively „youth" of the samples is also appropriate as wine consumption is prevalent among young people (Simmons Market Research Bureau, 1990; Aigrain et al., 1990; Lelong, 1990).

Table 1 depicts some variables used in the questionnaire, and Table 2 shows the results of two-tailed t-tests comparing mean scores between men and women within each country for all the variables. Only in France was a significant difference in the average age between men (mean = 22.2 years) and women (mean = 20.7 years).

---

[2] SD: Standard Deviation of the mean.

Variable		Values	Mean	SD	Cronbach's Alpha
Age	USA	18-33	22.1 [a]	2.2	
	Germany	22-55	27.6 [b]	5.9	
	France	19-52	21.3 [a]	3.2	
Times	USA	0-7	0..56 [a]	0.98	
per Week*	Germany	0-10	1.44 [b]	1.62	
	France	0-12	1.48 [b]	1.88	
How	USA	1-5	2.70 [a]	1.23	
Often?*	Germany	1-5	3.16 [b]	1.22	
	France	1-5	2.89 [a]	0.99	
Usage	USA	4-29	9.8 [a]	5.6	.93
	France	4-29	11.6 [b]	5.4	.88
Involvement	USA	3-15	7.4 [a]	3.1	.94
	Germany	3-14	8.2 [a]	3.0	.88
	France	3-15	9.3 [b]	3.6	.93
Innovativeness	USA	6-30	14.6 [a]	5.6	.90
	Germany	6-23	14.6 [a]	4.2	.75
	France	6-28	14.4 [a]	5.5	.84
Perceived	USA	6-42	19.3 [b]	8.5	.90
Knowledge	Germany	6-39	17.5 [a]	8.3	.87
	France	9-42	20.1 [b]	8.2	.85
Real	USA	0-10	4.96 [a]	1.9	
Knowledge	France	0-12	8.24 [b]	2.1	
Opinion	USA	6-42	29.1 [b]	8.2 ·	.91
Seeking	Germany	6-41	22.6 [a]	9.6	.88
	France	6-48	33.2 [c]	8.2	.89
Likely	USA	1-9	3.11 [a]	2.30	
to Try*	Germany	1-9	4.55 [b]	3.01	
	France	1-9	3.39 [a]	2.44	
Purchase	USA	3-21	8.39 [a]	4.6	.91
Intention	France	3-21	8.73 [a]	5.1	.95

*Single Item Measure

a, b, c Items with the same superscript letter are not statistically different ($p < .05$) by one-way ANOVA.

Table 1: Descriptive statistics

Variable		Men			Women			t-value	2-tail sig.
		Cases	Mean	SD	Cases	Mean	SD		
Age	USA	69	22.1	1.7	50	22.1	2.7	0.11	.912
	Germany	38	27.1	5.8	70	27.8	6.1	-0.60	.551
	France	75	22.2	4.6	100	20.7	1.1	2.78*	.007
Times per Week	USA	69	.42	1.0	51	0.74	0.9	-1.74	.084
	Germany	39	1.5	1.9	69	1.25	1.1	0.91	.366
	France	74	2.4	2.5	100	0.84	0.8	5.06*	.000
How Often?	USA	69	2.5	1.2	51	3.0	1.3	-2.17	.032
	Germany	39	3.1	1.3	70	3.2	1.2	-0.12	.906
	France	75	3.2	1.0	100	2.7	0.9	3.69	.000
Usage	USA	69	8.8	5.5	51	11.2	5.4	-2.30	.023
	France	73	13.8	6.2	100	10.1	4.0	4.53	.000
Involvement	USA	69	6.9	3.2	51	8.1	2.9	-2.13	.036
	Germany	39	8.2	3.1	70	8.2	2.9	0.01	.989
	France	75	10.3	3.6	100	8.6	3.4	3.09	.002
Innovativeness	USA	69	14.4	6.0	51	14.8	5.0	-0.46	.644
	Germany	38	14.6	4.2	70	14.5	4.2	0.14	.888
	France	75	15.4	5.7	100	13.6	5.2	2.15	.033
Perceived Knowledge	USA	69	20.2	8.9	51	18.1	7.9	1.33	.188
	Germany	39	18.5	7.3	69	16.6	8.3	1.20	.233
	France	75	22.4	8.5	100	18.4	7.6	3.25	.001
Real Knowledge	USA	69	5.0	1.8	51	5.0	1.9	-0.14	.886
	France	75	8.5	2.1	100	8.0	2.1	1.68	.095
Opinion Seeking	USA	68	28.2	8.0	51	30.2	8.5	-1.29	.201
	Germany	39	22.0	8.9	68	23.3	10.2	-0.68	.501
	France	75	31.0	8.8	100	34.8	7.4	-3.07	.002
Likely to Try	USA	68	2.8	2.3	51	3.5	2.3	-1.75	.083
	Germany	39	3.9	2.7	69	4.9	3.1	-1.81	.074
	France	74	3.3	2.4	99	3.5	2.5	-0.48	.631
Purchase Intention	USA	61	7.7	4.8	47	9.3	4.3	-1.81	.072
	France	62	8.2	5.3	80	9.2	5.1	-1.16	.249

*Separate Variance Estimates

Table 2: T-tests for mean differences between men and women

3.2. Questionnaire and Variables

In addition to demographic questions, the questionnaire contained scales to measure the wine consumption and the latent constructs. The English questionnaire was translated into French and German by native speakers and then back-translated into English to ensure equivalent meaning (Brislin et al., 1973). The German questionnaire was somewhat shorter than the US and French questionnaires because it did not contain the RAND usage, real wine knowledge, or purchase intention scales, all described below.

Wine Consumption

Three measures were used to describe how frequently respondents purchased and consumed wine. The first question was: „How many times per week on average would you say you drink wine, either socially or with meals?" This variable was labelled „*Times (per Week)*". The second question asked was „How often do you buy wine, either by the bottle or by the glass?" We used a five-point rating scale (5 = frequently, 4 = sometimes, 3 = rarely, 2 = almost never, and 1 = never). This variable was labelled „*(How) Often*". The third measure consisted of four questions asking how often the respondent currently drank wine, how much was drunk in a day, how often it was purchased, and how much was spent each month. These items were taken from the RAND Health Insurance Experiment Habit Batteries (Manning 1991, pp. 147-156). Statements were scored using six-point and nine-point basis respectively. These four items were factor analysed and a single factor was extracted. They were subsequently summed to form a multi-item index labelled „*Usage*". Descriptive statistics for the three criterion variables appear in Table 1. Comparisons across the three countries showed that the German and French students reported consuming more wine than the US students, as might be expected given national wine consumption statistics showing that more wine is consumed per capita in both France and Germany than in the US (Academic American Encyclopaedia, 1994; Biddle and Gordon, 1996; Hall, 1986).

Table 2 shows that in the US women reported consuming more wine than men, consistent with published data (Flaste, 1994; Simmons Market Research Bureau, 1990); in Germany wine consumption appeared to be about equal between men and women; and in France, men reported consuming more wine than women.

Theoretical Constructs

Four theoretical constructs were measured and hypothesised to be possible predictors of the survey participants' likelihood to purchase the new low-alcohol wine product. These were involvement with wine, wine innovativeness, knowledge of wine, and opinion seeking for wine.

Involvement was operationalized with a three-item Likert scale developed by Mittal and Lee (1989) which showed to be both reliable and valid by Goldsmith and Emmert (1991).

Wine innovativeness was measured by a six-item Likert scale, the Domain Specific Innovativeness Scale (DSI), developed by Goldsmith and Hofacker (1991) and validated repeatedly (Flynn and Goldsmith, 1993a; 1993b; Goldsmith and Flynn, 1992).

Knowledge of wine was measured in two ways. First, a six-item Likert scale measured subjective or self-perceived knowledge of what consumers think they know about a product category (labelled as „*(Self-)Perceived Knowledge*"). Second, a measure of actual wine knowledge was composed for this study and included in the US and French questionnaire (labelled as „*Real Knowledge*"). This multiple choice test contained twelve questions about wine with four possible answers for each question. The consumer's score was the total number of right answers. The correlations between the „perceived knowledge" scale and the „real knowledge" test were .28 for the US students and .51 for the French students. Table 1 shows that on average US and French students reported that they thought they know more about wine than German students, and the French students scored much higher on real wine knowledge than the US ones.

Opinion seeking for wine was conceptualised as the extent to which a consumer would take advice from others before wine purchasing and consumption decisions. The construct was measured by a six-item Likert scale shown to be valid and reliable by Flynn, Goldsmith, and Eastman (1996).

Purchase Intention

We asked the respondents whether they would probably buy the new low-alcohol wine using two separate measures. The first consisted of a single statement, „If a non- or low-alcoholic wine were to appear on the market, how likely would you try it?" followed by a nine-point rating scale anchored by „not so likely" and „very likely", respectively. This question appeared on all three questionnaires and is labelled „*Likely to Try*".

A second scale was only included in the US and French questionnaire. This was a three-item, seven-point, bi-polar adjective scale described by Yi (1990). The item asked was: „If a non- or low-alcoholic wine were to appear in the market, how likely would you buy a bottle to try it?" and the response formats contained the adjectives „likely-unlikely," „possible-impossible," and „probable-improbable". After the appropriate responses were reverse-scored, the three items were summed up to form a total score labelled „*Purchase Intention*".

Descriptive statistics for these two measures are shown in Table 1. They appeared to possess convergent validity as they were highly correlated both in the US sample (r = .74) and in the French sample (r = .85).

4. Analyses and Results

4.1. Dimensionality and Internal Consistency of Theoretical Construct Scales

Each multi-item scale was separately factor analysed (principal component factor analysis) to evaluate its dimensionality. For each country all scales have shown to be unidimensional. Internal consistency was measured by computing Cronbach's alpha coefficient for each multi-item scale measuring involvement, innovativeness, perceived knowledge, opinion seeking, and intention to try (likely to try). These value are shown in Table 1. They were uniformly above the recommended level of .80 (Nunnally, 1978) with the exception of the DSI (scale to measure innovativeness) for the German sample (.75). A comparison with reported alpha coefficients in consumer behaviour research (Peterson 1994) revealed relatively good results.

4.2. Associations with Wine Consumption and Theoretical Constructs

The three measures of wine usage, „Times", „Often", and „Usage", were all highly correlated, as one might expect, with r's ranging from .50 to .81 across the three countries. They were uncorrelated, however, with either „Likely to Try" or „Purchase Intention" (see Table 3). The hypothetical constructs, „Wine Involvement", „Wine Innovativeness", „Perceived" and „Real Knowledge of Wine", and „Wine Opinion Seeking", were correlated with the two measures of the „Likelihood to Try" the new low-alcohol wine. These correlation coefficients are shown in Table 3. However, none of the correlations were significant, suggesting that interest in trying the new low-alcohol wine product was not related to any aspect of current wine consumption, interest, or knowledge, as we expected with our fourth hypothesis.

Variable Names	Likely To Try	Purchase Intention
US Sample (n = 121)		
Age	.03	-.01
Times	.07	.07
Often	-.02	.02
Usage	-.04	.06
Involvement	-.03	.16
Innovativeness	-.02	.08
Self-Perceived Knowledge	-.05	.04
Real Knowledge	.01	.06
Opinion Seeking	-.03	-.00
German Sample (n = 113)		
Age	.04	
Times	-.09	
Often	-.13	
Usage	xxx	
Involvement	-.02	
Innovativeness	.04	
Self-Perceived Knowledge	-.06	
Real Knowledge	xxx	
Opinion Seeking	.12	
French Sample (n = 175)		
Age	.14	.14
Times	-.03	-.02
Often	-.03	.05
Usage	-.10	.03
Involvement	-.04	.11
Innovativeness	-.03	.16
Self-Perceived Knowledge	-.02	.09
Real Knowledge	-.12	-.11
Opinion Seeking	.14	.06

Table 3: Correlations of purchase intention of a new low-alcohol wine with other variables

4.3. Low-Alcohol Wine and Consumer Demographics

To determine whether an interest in trying the new low-alcohol wine product was associated with the consumer characteristics of age, sex, and country, correlation analysis and analysis of variance were used. Table 3 shows that age was uncorrelated in the three samples with either „ Likely to Try" or „Purchase Intention". An analysis of variance (ANOVA) was performed, with „Likely to Try" as dependent variable, and with sex and country (US, Germany, France) as independent variables. The analysis shows no statistically significant interaction effect (p > .05), but both main effects are significant. Across the three countries, women indicate that they will more likely try low-alcohol wine (mean = 3.95) than men (mean = 3.24); with F = 4.82; p = .029.

Examination of the country-by-country comparisons shown in Table 2 above reveal that women in each country show a higher acceptance of low-alcohol wine than men, but the differences are not statistically significant before the data was aggregated for all three countries, indicating a consistent but weak effect for sex. The main effect for country is significant (F = 8.83; p < .001). The German students report a higher likelihood of trying the low-alcohol wine (mean = 4.56) than either the US or French students (means of 3.13 and 3.39, respectively).

When the „Purchase Intention" scale was used in ANOVA as dependent variable, the results were similar. The interaction between sex and country is not significant, but the main effect for sex is significant (F = 4.1; p = .044), with women reporting a greater purchase intention (mean = 9.24) than men (mean = 7.94). The main effect for country is not significant, showing that the US and French means are not statistically different for „Purchase Intention" (8.43 and 8.73), which confirms previous results on likelihood of purchase for these two groups.

4.4. Correlations among Variables

Table 4 shows that, for all samples, there is a statistically significant correlation (p < .01) between frequency of use („Times per Week" and „Usage") and each of the constructs: „Innovativeness", „Involvement", and „Perceived Knowledge". It also shows these three variables are correlated with each other in all three samples (p < .01). „Opinion Seeking" is negatively correlated with „Times per Week" for the French and American samples (p < .01). The negative relation measured on the German sample is not significant. „Opinion Seeking" is also negatively correlated to „Innovativeness" and „Involvement", although the significance level is only obtained at the p < .05 level for the French sample. The negative correlation between

„Opinion Seeking" and „Perceived Knowledge" shows a higher level of significance (p < .01 for the German and French sample, p < .05 for the US sample).

Variables	1	2	3	4	5	6	7	8	9
US Sample (n = 121)									
1. Age	--								
2. Times per Week	.16	--							
3. How Often?	.29**	.58**	--						
4. Innovativeness	.18	.55**	.67**	--					
5. Involvement	.19*	.60**	.73**	.73**	--				
6. Perceived Knowledge	.19*	.51**	.63**	.74**	.66**	--			
7. Real Knowledge	.18	.08	.34**	.24**	.28**	.28**	--		
8. Opinion Seeking	.04	-.33**	-.14	-.14	-.14	-.19*	.01	--	
9. Usage	.31**	.81**	.77**	.74**	.80**	.66**	27**	-.21**	--
German Sample (n = 113)									
1. Age	--								
2. Times per Week	.17	--							
3. How Often?	.07	.61**	--						
4. Innovativeness	-.01	.34**	.49**	--					
5. Involvement	-.01	.55**	.67**	.57**	--				
6. Perceived Knowledge	.02	.40**	.52**	.52**	.66**	--			
7. Real Knowledge							--		
8. Opinion Seeking	-.29**	-.14	-.17	.01	-.09	-.26**		--	
French Sample (n = 175)									
1. Age	--								
2. Times per Week	.34**	--							
3. How Often?	.23**	.50**	--						
4. Innovativeness	.16*	.36**	.54**	--					
5. Involvement	.17*	.42**	.63**	.69**	--				
6. Perceived Knowledge	.22**	.46**	.58**	.61**	.78**	--			
7. Real Knowledge	.18*	.28**	.28**	.37**	.46**	.51**	--		
8. Opinion seeking	-.29**	-.25**	-.18*	-.15*	-.14*	-.27**	.21**	--	
9. Usage	.33**	.68**	.72**	.61**	.71**	.67**	.42**	-.26**	--

* p < .05 ** p < .01

Table 4: Correlations among variables

5. Discussion

The main limitations of this study are that the convenience sample restricts our ability to draw generalisations about the populations of the three countries; both because the samples were not random and the respondents are selected from the relatively homogeneous groups of students consumers. Because many of the findings (e.g., French and German students reported consuming more wine than the Americans) do correspond to reported results in other studies, however, we can express some confidence concerning the direction, but not in regard to the strength of the relationships under scrutiny. However, the multi-item scales demonstrated high internal consistency, and multiple measures used for usage and purchase intention demonstrated high convergent validity.

Comparing latent constructs measures between the three groups proved to be interesting. Our results show that there are significant differences in wine involvement between American and European students, as expected in our first hypothesis. These results confirm d'Hauteville's findings (1994) concerning German, British and French groups of consumers, suggesting that involvement in wine may be considered as a measure of cultural differences. In contrast, DSI measures showed no difference in the three groups, because it is a specific construct, which is more closely related to individual personality.

As expected in hypothesis 2, we have found that involvement, DSI, and perceived knowledge are correlated with each other in all three samples. We have also shown that these variables are related to either frequency of wine consumption or usage for each of the three samples, which is quite consistent with expectations (our third hypothesis). Opinion seeking is negatively related to perceived knowledge for all samples, which is in line with Flynn et al. (1996) conceptualisation of this measurement scale.

From the theoretical perspective, it is generally expected that product involvement in a product category should be positively related to new product adoption in this category (Valette-Florence and Roehrich, 1993). Our findings reveal however that one cannot simply assume that involvement in a product category such as wine will necessarily lead consumers to try a new product that „sounds" like it belongs to that category. The analyses show that wine enthusiasts have little interest in the new low-alcohol wine. It is probably that consumers perceive the new product as being too far from a typical wine because it lacks alcohol and therefore reject it as an element of the product class in which they are interested. These results confirm d'Hauteville's findings (1994) concerning British, German and French consumers interest in low-alcohol wine in relation to involvement in wine. In this study, it worked out that frequent consumers of light products showed a higher level of purchase intention than wine drinkers, suggesting that low-alcohol wine might be perceived as more fitting within the light products category than within wine.

We also found that neither DSI, perceived knowledge, real knowledge, nor opinion seeking were significantly related to intention to try or the purchase intention, as we would have normally expected (Gatignon and Robertson, 1992). We may apply the same reasoning as we used about involvement: if we assume that low-alcohol wine is not associated with the target category of product, then we may also assume that the information processing about this new product does not benefit of a particular respondents' attention. In this case, domain innovativeness, perceived knowledge and opinion seeking, do not function as appropriate descriptors of the individual-product relationship. The amount of perceived difference between a new product and the target product category may also play a mediating role in the expected relation between the variables influencing the person-object relation and new product adoption.

From the managerial perspective, it appears that marketers of low-alcohol wines should concentrate on marketing to women as the most likely target market and that cross-culturally, Germany seems to represent the most promising market for the product at this time. This is very consistent with previous findings: d'Hauteville (1994) shows that German consumers are much more involved with light products than French consumers, and that they express a significantly greater acceptance of the low-alcohol wine concept. Moreover, the results suggest that marketers of a new low-alcohol wine will meet difficulties in positioning the new product as a type of wine, because wine enthusiasts seem to reject it as part of their choice set. In fact, the marketers should develop another positioning strategy to market this product. This may be what some marketers have already attempted. Hannon (1996) describes the newly developing interest in the US for low-alcohol wines and shows that a „healthy product" positioning seems to be the chosen strategy for these brands. It is too early with regard to the actual stage in the product life cycle to determine whether this is successful or not.

6. Conclusions

The purpose of this study was to assess whether the likelihood of purchasing a new low-alcohol wine product could be predicted by either consumer characteristics (wine usage, age, sex, country) or by theoretical constructs (wine involvement, wine innovativeness, wine knowledge, or opinion seeking for wine). Data from three samples of student consumers from the US, Germany, and France were analysed. We expected the three sample to differ on levels of involvement, DSI, and perceived knowledge in relation to wine.

The German consumers expressed a greater likelihood of trying the new product and women in all three countries expressed a somewhat greater likelihood of trying it.

The results showed that neither wine usage nor the theoretical constructs were systematically associated with acceptance of the low-alcohol wine. The explanation may be a different position in the consumer's mind for the low-alcohol wine and the target wine category based on a comparison of the attributes of both. These insights should be studied in other product categories for confirmation or disconfirmation and suggests that consumer researchers might measure the perceptions of consumers regarding a new product's membership in a given product category as part of their study of consumer reaction to new products.

The findings show that standardised instruments developed to measure the hypothetical constructs, involvement, innovativeness, perceived knowledge, opinion seeking, and purchase intention, appear to be valid and reliable in cross-cultural research. Both French and German researchers can use these scales in studies of their populations and expect psychometrically valid results.

References

Academic American Encyclopaedia (1994): Per Capita Wine Consumption Ranked by Country in 1991. Grolier Electronic Publishing, Inc.

Aigrain, P., D. Boulet, J.P. Laporte, and J.L. Lambert (1990): La Consommation de Vin des Français. In: Coll. Notes et Documents, INRA/ESR: Montpellier.

Biddle, Nina A. and Jeanne Gordon (1996): To Your Health? In: Newsweek, January 22, 1996, pp. 52-54.

Bloch, Peter H. (1986): The Product Enthusiast: Implications for Marketing Strategy. In: Journal of Consumer Marketing, Vol. 3, No. 3, pp. 51-62.

Brislin, R. W., W. J. Loner, and R. M. Thorndike (1973): Cross-Cultural Research Methods. Wiley.

Calder, B.J., L.W. Phillips, and A.M. Tybout (1981): Designing Research for Application. In: Journal of Consumer Research, Vol. 8, September, pp.197-207.

D'Hauteville, Francois (1994): Un Modèle d'Acceptation du Nouveau Produit par le Consommateur: Cas du Vin allégé en Alcool. Doctorate thesis, University of Montpellier 2.

D'Hauteville, Francois (1996): Marketing Global et Mondialisation des Marchés Agro-Alimentaires, le Rôle Perturbateur du Consommateur et du Distributeur. In: Economie Rurale, July, pp. 22-27.

Flaste, Richard (1994): Grape Nuts. In: Allure, November, pp. 98-99.

Flynn, L.R. and R.E. Goldsmith (1993a): A Validation of the Goldsmith and Hofacker Innovativeness Scale. In: Educational and Psychological Measurement, Vol. 53, No 4, pp. 1005-1116.

Flynn, L.R. and R.E. Goldsmith (1993b): Identifying Innovators in Consumer Service Markets. In: Service Industries Journal, Vol. 13, No. 3, pp. 97-109.

Flynn, L.R., R.E. Goldsmith, and J. Eastman (1996): Opinion Leaders and Opinion Seekers: Two New Measurement Scales. In: Journal of the Academy of Marketing Science, Vol. 24, No. 2, pp. 137-147.

Gatignon, H. and T.S. Robertson, (1992).: Innovative Decision Process. In: Robertson T.S. and H.H. Kassarjian (Eds.), Handbook of Consumer Behavior, Prentice Hall: Englewood Cliffs, pp.316-348.

Goldsmith, R.E. and J. Emmert (1991): Measuring Product Category Involvement: A Multitrait-Multimethod Study. In: Journal of Business Research, Vol. 23, No. 4, pp. 363-371.

Goldsmith, R.E. and L.R. Flynn (1992): Identifying Innovators in Consumer Product Markets. In: European Journal of Marketing, Vol. 26, No. 12, pp. 42-55.

Goldsmith, R.E. and C.H. Hofacker (1991): Measuring Consumer Innovativeness. In: Journal of the Academy of Marketing Science, Vol. 19, No. 3, pp. 209-221.

Hall, Trish (1986): Tough Times: Wine Industry Finds It May Be Its Own Worst Enemy. In: Wall Street Journal, May 3.

Hannon, Kerry (1996): No alcohol - and good for the heart? In: U.S. News & World Report, May 20, 1996, p. 70.

Lelong, P. (1990): Le Marché des Nouveaux Produits Allégés et Aromatisés à Base de Vins en Europe. Centre Français du Commerce Exterieur: Paris.

Manning, Willard G. (1991): The Costs of Poor Health Habits. Harvard University Press: Cambridge, MA.

Mittal, B. and M. Lee (1989): A Causal Model of Consumer Involvement. In: Journal of Economic Psychology, Vol. 10, pp. 363-389.

Nunnally, Jum C. (1978): Psychometric Theory. McGraw Hill: New York.

Padilla, Martine (1992): Le Concept de Modèle de Consommation Alimentaire et la Théorie de la Consommation. In: Economies et Sociétés, AG 21, p. 6.

Peterson, Robert A. (1994): A Meta-analysis of Cronbach's Coefficient Alpha. In: Journal of Consumer Research, Vol. 21, September, pp. 381- 391.

Simmons Market Research Bureau (1990): Study of Media and Markets. Vol. P-17, 0064.

Valette-Florence, P. and Roehrich, G. (1993): Une Approche Causale du Comportement d'Achat Innovateur. In: Economie et Sociétés, Sciences de Gestion, No. 19, October, pp. 75-106.

Yi, Youjae (1990): Cognitive and Affective Priming Effects of the Context for Print Advertisements. In: Journal of Advertising, Vol. 12, No. 2, pp. 40-48.

Tina M. Lowrey, Cele Otnes and L.J. Shrum

Consumer Ambivalence: Perspectives Gained from Shopping with Consumers

1. Introduction

2. Wedding as Case Study

3. Research Design

4. Analysis and Writing of Text

5. Findings

6. Advantages of our Research Method

7. Disadvantages of our Research Method

8. Conclusion

References

Consumer Ambivalence:
Perspectives Gained from Shopping with Consumers

Tina M. Lowrey, Cele Otnes and L.J. Shrum

Abstract

Researchers have investigated the role of emotions in a variety of consumption contexts. However, the construct of mixed emotions, or ambivalence, has not been fully explored. In our study of wedding planning, the concept of ambivalence emerged from the naturalistic text generated by interviewing and shopping with consumers. In this chapter, we describe the research method we used, as well as how we arrived at our final interpretation and explication of „consumer ambivalence". Finally, we discuss the advantages and disadvantages of our method.

1. Introduction

Research on emotion has had a long tradition in the study of consumer behaviour. Until recently, it has been treated primarily as an unidimensional construct, with positive and negative emotions representing bipolar anchors on a single emotion continuum. However, recent theorizing on the nature of emotions has pointed out that positive and negative emotions may in fact be independent of each other such that a person may hold both positive and negative emotions simultaneously (Diener and Emmons, 1984; Hajda, 1968; Kris, 1984).

Our goals for this chapter are two-fold. First, we intend to articulate the concept of *consumer ambivalence* by pinpointing the antecedents of consumers' mixed emotions and exploring the coping strategies consumers use to deal with their ambivalence. We do this within the context of a case study of wedding planning. Second, we explicate the particular research methodology we used (shopping with consumers) and offer insights into how our employment of various qualitative data collection methods (e.g., depth interviews, participant observation) within one study provide rich data that are useful in understanding complex and dynamic consumer thoughts and behaviours.

2. Wedding as Case Study

One of the initial purposes of our research was to explore whether Rook's (1985) framework for consumption rituals was applicable in the context of wedding planning. That is, we sought to identify the scripts, artifacts, roles and audiences inherent during the wedding planning process. We soon realized, however, that both brides and grooms expressed strong emotions during this process. Initially, we categorized these emotional experiences as either positive or negative. However, we found that this dichotomous approach to emotions failed to capture the many instances of ambivalence that appeared in our text. Indeed, the majority of emotional experiences reported by our informants were mixed, rather than purely positive or negative. In many of these instances, the informants were aware of their mixed emotions. But at other times, informants seemed to be unaware of the ambivalent nature of their emotions. For example, when the interviewer asked: „Did you experience any positive emotions when shopping for wedding-related items?", one bride, Lynn, replied:

> *Probably the biggest joy that I got was my dress ... I was ... up in Chicago ... [It was] the second dress I tried on ... and the people there were just very, very rude, so I didn't get the dress up there ... so the girl ordered it for me here ... so when we got the dress, it was like the generic version [of] the original dress I tried on. What happened was ... it was during [the Persian Gulf] war ... [and] people were pushing their weddings up so far, and so fast. So instead of the actual hand-sewn dresses, they were mass-producing them ... so, I sat in the showroom, and just cried and cried because I mean, I didn't need the dress right away, you know. And they ended up giving my money back, and I went up and bought the sample in Chicago. It was a frustrating time, but it all worked out.*

What is so remarkable about this example is that Lynn was relating an incident that led to the experience of positive emotions. As her story begins, she claims that her biggest joy was her dress, yet proceeds to relate other emotions she experienced during the process as well: anger, disappointment, and regret. Her story, and the stories of all of our informants, led us to believe that the appropriate focus of our paper should be on the consumer ambivalence that arose while brides planned their weddings, rather than on an oversimplistic positive-negative dichotomy. Thus, we offer the following definition of *consumer ambivalence*:

Consumer ambivalence is the simultaneous or sequential experience of multiple emotional states, as a result of the interaction between internal factors and external interactions with objects, people, institutions, and/or cultural phenomena in market-oriented contexts, that can have direct and/or indirect ramifications for prepurchase, purchase, or postpurchase attitudes and behaviour.

For a thorough discussion of the concept of consumer ambivalence, see Otnes et al. (in press).

3. Research Design

Our project featured several stages of data collection. Stage 1 consisted of same-sex focus groups conducted with brides and grooms in June and July of 1991. In Stage 2, nine of the brides that had participated in the earlier focus groups were recruited for in-depth interviews. Stage 3 consisted of shopping trips conducted with these brides. In Stages 4 and 5, the same brides were again interviewed and accompanied on wedding-related shopping trips. Finally, for Stage 6, four additional brides were recruited in June of 1995 for a follow-up study. In describing how we conducted our research, we follow a template for interpretive researchers offered by Altheide and Johnson (1994), which is useful for understanding the particular context of our study.

Contexts (History, Physical Setting, Environment)

All stages of the research were conducted in a Midwestern city in the US (population approximately 100,000), where a major state university is located (approximately 30,000 students). In the earliest stages of our research, the US had been involved in the Persian Gulf war and was recovering from an economic downturn. These events often affected wedding planning for our informants.

The initial focus groups were conducted in a seminar room at the university. Interviews were held with informants in their homes or other locations of their choice. Shopping trips included accompanying brides to bridal shops, caterers, florists, fabric stores, and other speciality shops.

Number of Participants, Key Individuals

Two focus groups were conducted with 19 brides and two focus groups were conducted with 15 grooms. Group sizes ranged from six to ten, as recommended in the literature (Kreuger, 1988). Participants were paid $25.00 each. The 13 key informants (the nine brides in Stages 2-5 and the four brides in Stage 6) were paid an additional $40.00 each. In Stages 2-5, a researcher/informant ratio of 1:3 was maintained; in Stage 6, this ratio was 1:4. With one exception, all informants were White, all were between the ages of 18 and 35, and either enrolled at the university or working full-time.

Activities

Focus groups explored wedding artifacts, scripts, performance roles, and the role of the audience (Rook, 1985), and also helped us generate questions for the in-depth phases. Groups were videotaped and the text transcribed. Personal interviews lasted from 45 to 60 minutes, were audiotaped and the text transcribed. Although interviews were structured (McCracken, 1988), informants were also encouraged to discuss any topic related to wedding planning that arose. During shopping trips, researchers observed brides selecting gowns, flowers, catering menus, and other items. Shopping trips lasted 45 to 90 minutes. Rather than audiotaping these interactions, researchers created detailed field notes immediately after each trip. In all, over 600 pages of text were generated. To ensure the trustworthiness of our interpretation, we employed multiple researchers who had multiple encounters with informants, triangulated interpretations across researchers and authors, and the first author (who had not participated in data collection) served as external auditor of the text.

Schedules, Temporal Order

Focus groups were held in June and July of 1991, and lasted 60 to 90 minutes. In Stages 2-5, each key informant was interviewed, accompanied on a shopping trip, interviewed again, and accompanied on a final shopping trip (for a thorough description of our methodology, see Otnes et al., 1995).

Division of Labour, Hierarchies

Six individuals were involved in data collection: the second author (female), the third author (male), and four female undergraduates. The second author devised the research design and questions, and moderated all but one grooms' focus group (conducted by the third author). The undergraduates were enrolled in a minority research program at the university. The students recruited informants by placing flyers in bridal salons in the community, and also screened responses to ads placed in the campus paper. They observed all focus groups, and were trained in interviewing and shopping with consumers via role-playing exercises. The second author met with the students for 2 to 4 hours each week for the duration of the project and offered suggestions and comments to improve interactions during the interviews. Students completed all fieldwork. The first and second authors read over all field notes and interviews and interpreted text. The first author (female) was not involved in data collection and thus brought a fresh perspective to the interpretation of the text, and to the write-up of the paper. The third author assisted in the interpretation and final write-up of the paper.

Routines and Variations

We scheduled our interactions with key informants so we could observe wedding planning as a process. Thus, whenever possible, interviews and shopping trips were spaced one week to ten days apart. This allowed us to develop questions for the second interview based on observations made during the first shopping trip.

Significant Events: Origins and Consequences

In addition to the Persian Gulf war, the most significant events observed were the budgetary constraints that led some brides to exclude desired items from their weddings. We discuss how this situation was often accompanied by consumer ambivalence.

Team Members' Perspectives and Meanings

For two reasons, the student researchers' stance in the field could be considered „naive". First, none had ever planned a wedding, and only one had ever been in a wedding party. Thus, they were often unfamiliar with aspects of wedding planning. We believe this perspective was beneficial, because as brides carefully explained their activities, they often revealed (intentionally or unintentionally) their own attitudes and opinions toward them.

Moreover, the researchers were all African-American females, whereas our informants were White. Students were thus trained to carefully note when their own values differed from those of informants. Although racial differences could conceivably have caused conflicts, all informants were advised of the research program, and all willingly participated in the study.

We held these assumptions at the onset of this study: 1) all brides, regardless of age, would regard their weddings as key events in their lives (supported); 2) older brides would be more financially responsible for their weddings, and would thus exhibit more control over decisions (only somewhat supported); and 3) wedding planning would be accompanied by intense emotions (supported).

Social Rules and Basic Patterns of Order

Our brides revealed that the customs surrounding Midwestern weddings dictated a „sit-down dinner" at the reception. The inability to provide this dinner often led to dramatic emotional experiences by the bride. Another custom that disturbed brides, and often led to ambivalence, was the bridal registry. Finally, even though some brides planned relatively modest weddings, and not all were held in a church, all selected formal wedding gowns.

4. Analysis and Writing of Text

Within single interactions with informants, and across the wedding planning process, consumer ambivalence was both recognized and unrecognized by our informants. Thus, our interpretation is both emic and etic. The interpretive process went through several iterations (Huberman and Miles, 1994), involving negotiation in order to arrive at an agreed-upon meaning of the text. We then created a „quasi-public text", shared with several colleagues (Denzin, 1994), all of whom influenced the final paper. Our paper thus adheres to a „mainstream realist" style (Denzin, 1994).

5. Findings

We discovered that there were four major categories of ambivalence, with antecedents and coping strategies that were, for the most part, unique. For a more thorough discussion of our findings, see Otnes et al. (in press).

Expectation vs. Reality

The first major category resulted from a difference between the brides' expectations and the reality of a given consumption situation. These conflicts arose either due to product-specific expectations (as the quote from Lynn earlier in the paper implies, regarding her wedding gown) or retailer-specific expectations (such as one bride's positive predisposition - later negated - towards a florist). Not surprisingly, coping strategies that brides employed in these instances included merchandise return, change of purchasing venue, „toughing it out" with a given retailer, or assertiveness on the part of the bride with a particular retailer.

Overload

The second major category arose from overload, either task overload or product overabundance. With task overload, brides (and grooms) were overwhelmed with the variety of tasks involved in planning a wedding. With product overabundance, brides were overwhelmed by the number of choices available for completing a single task. As might be expected, coping strategies for this type of ambivalence included simplification of the wedding in order to reduce the number of tasks to be performed, seeking assistance from others (such as mothers, friends, etc.), and, ironically, extensive information search. Although extensive information search might help brides feel that they were being thorough, we feel that this, in turn, added to their sense of being overwhelmed!

Role Conflict with Purchase Influencers

Another major category of ambivalence stemmed from role conflict with various purchase influencers (primarily family members, or future in-laws). It is not uncommon for a ritual as significant as a wedding to be fraught with differences of opinion between the bride and groom, or between the couple and their respective families (particularly when the parents are paying for the ceremony). There were several incidents of such role conflict with our informants. Perhaps unfortunately, the only two coping strategies evident in our text were resignation and compromise. With resignation, brides simply gave in to whatever was expected of them. With compromise, brides attempted to have some say in the final outcome. Both of these strategies resulted in increased, rather than reduced, ambivalence.

314

Custom and Value Conflict

The final major category of ambivalence resulted from a conflict between the customs surrounding the typical wedding ceremony and the personal values of the brides. In some instances, brides were resistant to a particular custom, such as the bridal registry, which some perceived as too materialistic. In other instances, brides wanted to adhere to specific customs, but were unable to do so. This was particularly true with the custom of a sit-down dinner after the ceremony, which can be quite expensive, and several of our brides simply could not afford this. Finally, we had brides that wanted to personalize their weddings in ways that were objectionable to others. For instance, one of our brides wished to have her dog participate in the ceremony. One coping strategy was to resign themselves to the situation at hand (such as in the case of being unable to provide a sit-down dinner). Another strategy was to modify their weddings in order to allow for personalization, while at the same time providing mandated items that were expected by others. A final strategy was defiant non-purchase of sanctioned items, or a refusal to „give in" to the expectations of others. Regardless of the strategy used, the bride's happiness was often tinged with anxiety and regret.

6. Advantages of our Research Method

There are both advantages and disadvantages of the particular method we used in this study. Below we have briefly outlined the major advantages of shopping with consumers (for a more detailed explanation of these, see Otnes et al., 1995).

Type of Data Generated

We believe that shopping with consumers enables researchers to record informant-driven experiences in the retail setting more accurately and thoroughly than other methods. Unlike in-store observation, where the informant is typically unaware of the researcher's presence, actually shopping with consumers allows researchers to both observe and interact with the informant. Interviewing, of course, only provides recollections of consumption activities, but is an important data collection technique. We combined interviewing with the more active, timely method of shopping with consumers in order to take advantage of the strengths of each.

Proximity to Consumers

Shopping with consumers allows researchers to actively participate in and question specific behaviours on the part of the informants. Researchers can observe the behaviour of informants in checkout lines, customer service departments, and even dressing room waiting areas. Additionally, several instances occur where the researcher accompanies the informants in transit to and from the retail setting. This allows for additional reflection on the part of the informant, and adds to the time that researchers can interact with informants.

Access to Shopping Agendas

Because of the nature of the method, informants are often eager to share with researchers their agendas for the day's shopping. In addition, informants often point out their own particular behaviours that they perceive to be noteworthy, or attempt to explain the reasons for their behaviour. In contrast, even the most informant-driven, phenomenological interviews about shopping (Thompson et al., 1989) generally yield information that consumers perceive to be important at the time of the interview, rather than what may have been important in the retail setting. Likewise, researchers who passively observe consumers have little or no access to the agendas of the shoppers they are observing.

Potential to Enhance Future Interactions

Because researchers are able to record informant-driven experiences, future interactions with informants tend to be more relevant and enlightening. And, when combined with interviews, researchers can verify interpretations from the shopping trips with the informants. This lends a longitudinal aspect to such a research project, as researchers interact with the informants over time. In addition, the combination of shopping trips and interviews allows informants to reflect on their behaviour, and helps them define their own activities and rationales. Thus, the informants become active observers of their own consumer behaviour, as well as that of others.

Potential to Enhance Trust

Our experience reveals that shopping with consumers expedites the process of building trusting relationships with informants. Building such relationships leads to a „cooperation paradigm" (Wallendorf and Belk, 1989), wherein the two parties engage in shared activities and experiences. In our experience, shopping with consumers led to such relationships, much more so than interviews would have done alone.

7. Disadvantages of our Research Method

As mentioned previously, the method of shopping with consumers has weaknesses as well. These are outlined briefly below.

Effectiveness as Stand-Alone Method

The sole use of shopping with consumers may not be sufficient for researchers to gain a thorough understanding of their informants. Rather, we recommend combining this active method with the more reflective method of interviews. This allows both for experiential learning, as well as in-depth conversations with informants. While shopping, conversations tend to be fragmented. Thus, by combining shopping with consumers with personal interviews, researchers are able to probe more thoroughly and question their observations without interruption.

Costs

Shopping with consumers requires intense levels of participation on the part of informants. Thus, monetary incentives paid to informants are typically higher than those for interviews or other methods. In addition, the time required by the researcher to accompany informants on trips, prepare detailed field notes immediately upon completion of such trips, and to prepare semi-structured interviews for other phases of the project is immense (not to mention the vast effort required to transcribe and analyze text at later stages). Therefore, researchers should seriously question whether they have the time, energy, and temperament to utilize shopping with consumers as a method.

Potential for Informant Reactance

Although we feel that shopping with consumers allows for trusting relationships to develop, it must be understood that certain unattractive behaviours may be hidden (or desirable behaviours highlighted) by informants. Particularly in early stages of the interaction, an informant may wish to „put her best face forward“ by acting in an unnatural manner. However, in our experience, we felt that such performance anxiety quickly dissipated as researchers got to know their informants.

Need for Researcher/Informant Similarity

In most instances, informants will naturally feel more comfortable with researchers who are similar to them. This desire for similarity may manifest itself in terms of gender or race, but may be most important in terms of personalities and/or attitudes and opinions. Thus, researchers may find themselves in the position of being less than forthcoming about their own values and attitudes. Of course, this is true of virtually all research methods. However, it can become uncomfortable in situations where trusting relationships are presumably being built.

8. Conclusion

In summary, we have found that shopping with consumers is a valuable method, particularly when combined with personal interviews. We have used this method in a study of Christmas shopping as well, with positive results (Otnes et al., 1993). In addition, we have continued to employ shopping with consumers in an ongoing, longitudinal study of Christmas shopping (Lowrey and Otnes, 1996). In these two studies, we have found that shopping with consumers has yielded far greater insights than we could have imagined, or could have achieved with other methods.

In addition to the interesting findings in our Christmas research, we found that employing this method in our study of wedding planning also allowed us to uncover the interesting, and underexplored, phenomenon of consumer ambivalence. As mentioned previously, our informants had intense emotional experiences during the planning of their weddings, as we had suspected. However, we had not realized beforehand how „mixed“ these emotional experiences would be for our informants. It was only through interacting with them over time, in a variety of settings, that their ambivalence emerged.

In addition to the ritualistic contexts which we have studied, consumer ambivalence should be examined in other ritualistic contexts. We believe too, however, that consumer ambivalence may be evident in more „everyday" contexts. That is, we feel that mixed emotions may emerge in non-ritualistic consumption situations as well. We hope that other researchers will be encouraged to continue to investigate consumer ambivalence in an attempt to more fully understand this complex phenomenon.

References

Altheide, D.L. and Johnson, J.M. (1994): Criteria for Assessing Interpretive Validity in Qualitative Research. In: Denzin, N.K. and Lincoln, Y.S. (Eds.), Handbook of Qualitative Research, Sage: Thousand Oaks, pp. 485-499.

Denzin, N.K. (1994): The Art and Politics of Interpretation. In: Denzin, N.K. and Lincoln, Y.S. (Eds.), Handbook of Qualitative Research, Sage: Thousand Oaks, pp. 500-515.

Diener, E. and Emmons, R.A. (1984): The Independence of Positive and Negative Affect. In: Journal of Personality and Social Psychology, Vol., 47, pp. 1105-1117.

Hajda, J. (1968): Ambivalence and Social Relations. In: Sociological Focus, Vol. 2, pp. 21-28.

Huberman, A.M. and Miles, M.B. (1994): Data Management and Analysis Methods. In: Denzin, N.K. and Lincoln, Y.S. (Eds.), Handbook of Qualitative Research, Sage: Thousand Oaks, pp. 428-444.

Kris, A.O. (1984): The Conflicts of Ambivalence. In: Psychoanalytic Study of the Child, Vol. 39, pp. 213-233.

Krueger, R.A. (1988): Focus Groups: A Practical Guide for Applied Research, Sage: Newbury Park.

Lowrey, T.M. and Otnes, C. (1996): A Longitudinal Study of Christmas Gift-Giving, unpublished manuscript.

McCracken, G. (1988): The Long Interview, Sage: Newbury Park.

Otnes, C., Lowrey, T.M., and Kim, Y. (1993): Gift Selection for Easy and Difficult Recipients: A Social Roles Interpretation. In: Journal of Consumer Research, Vol. 20, pp. 229-244.

Otnes, C., Lowrey, T.M., and Shrum, L.J. (in press): Toward an Understanding of Consumer Ambivalence. In: Journal of Consumer Research.

Otnes, C., McGrath, M.A., and Lowrey, T.M. (1995): Shopping with Consumers: Usage as Past, Present, and Future Research Technique. In: Journal of Retailing and Consumer Services, Vol. 2, pp. 97-110.

Rook, D.W. (1985): The Ritual Dimension of Consumer Behavior. In: Journal of Consumer Research, Vol. 12, pp. 252-264.

Thompson, C.J., Locander, W.B., and Pollio, H.R. (1989): Putting Consumer Experience Back Into Consumer Research: The Philosophy and Method of Existential-Phenomenology. In: Journal of Consumer Research, Vol. 16, pp. 133-146.

Wallendorf, M. and Belk, R. W. (1989): Assessing Trustworthiness in Naturalistic Consumer Research. In: Hirschman, E.C. (Ed.), Interpretive Consumer Research, Association for Consumer Research: Provo, pp. 69-84.

Günther Botschen and Eva Thelen

Hard versus Soft Laddering: Implications for Appropriate Use

1. Introduction

2. Factors Affecting the Predictive Validity of Soft- and Hard Laddering

3. Method
   3.1. Sample and Procedure
   3.2. Questionnaire

4. Results

5. Conclusions

6. Limitations of the Study and Suggestions for Future Research

References

Hard versus Soft Laddering: Implications for Appropriate Use

Günther Botschen and Eva Thelen

Abstract

Means-end chain theory and laddering as the corresponding interviewing technique find increased acceptance in marketing research. According to Olson (1995) means-end chains are hierarchical cognitive structures that model the basis for personal relevance by relating consumers' product or service knowledge to their self-knowledge. Two techniques have been used in empirical studies to collect laddering data: „soft laddering", an in-depth, one-on-one interviewing technique, and „hard laddering", a paper-and-pencil version using a structured questionnaire. Up to now research comparing the results of soft and hard laddering isstill missing. The objective of this study is to compare the two techniques based on validity criteria recently developed by Grunert and Grunert (1995). The authors show that soft and hard laddering produce comparable results.

1. Introduction

Laddering and means-end chains are one of the most promising developments in consumer research within the last decade. It is an approach which takes consumers' individuality seriously and at the same time comes up with quantitative results. It is rooted in a cognitive approach, and allows for emotional and unconscious factors or, at least, semi-conscious factors (Grunert, Grunert, and Sorenson, 1995).

According to Olson (1995) means-end chains are hierarchical cognitive structures that model the basis for personal relevance by relating consumers' product or service knowledge to their self-knowledge. The lower levels of a means-end hierarchy contain concrete and abstract knowledge about product/service attributes/preferences and their linkages to the functional and abstract consequences/benefits of product/service use. Some means-end chains may connect these psycho-social consequences to abstract self knowledge about the consumer's life goals and values. Consumers see products/services as self-relevant to the extent that their product/service knowledge or expectations about attributes and functional consequences is connected, via means-end structures, to their self-knowledge about desirable psychological consequences and values (Walker and Olson, 1991; Olson, 1989). Figure 1 gives an example of a consumer's cognitive structure according to means-end theory.

Levels of Means-End Chains	Concrete Attributes →	Abstract Attributes →	Functional Consequences →	Psycho-Social Consequences →	Instrumental Values →	Terminal Values
Example	Price →	Good quality →	Can easily handle it →	Others see me as special →	Being center of attention →	Self-esteem
Motor-Cycle Triumph Speed Triple 900	98 H.P. →	Powerful engine →	Can perfectly accelerate →	Feel very strong ↗		

Figure 1: Excerpt of a consumer's cognitive structure according to „means-end theory"

In means-end theory a basic hierarchical model is assumed, in which cognitive categories of different levels of abstraction are interlinked in chains and networks. Further it is assumed that behavioural motivation is derived by linking cognitive categories corresponding to concrete objects, e.g. products, services, stores or behaviour, with cognitive categories at a high degree of abstraction, like values. Based on these considerations it should be possible to explain/predict actual behaviour with regard to these concrete objects by specifying how, in a given situation, parts of the cognitive structure are retrieved and used to guide behaviour (Grunert and Grunert, 1995). Increased acceptance and use of a new approach inevitably leads to the identification of unresolved issues and problems. Many of these unresolved problems are related to the collection and analysis of laddering data.

Originally laddering referred to an in-depth, one-on-one interviewing technique used to develop an understanding of how consumers translate the attributes of products/services into meaningful associations with respect to self, following means-end theory (Olson and Reynolds, 1983; Gutman, 1982). This type of laddering involved a tailored interviewing technique format using primarily a series of directed probes, typified by the „Why is that important to you?" question, with the expressed goal of determining sets of linkages between the key perceptual elements across the range of attributes, consequences and values (Reynolds and Gutman, 1988). Most of the published means-end chains studies use this type of interview, where the respondent's natural flow of speech is restricted as little as possible which later on was called „soft" laddering (Grunert and Grunert, 1995).

Walker and Olson (1991) developed a paper-and-pencil version of the laddering technique. Here laddering is accomplished through a structured questionnaire in which subjects first state their reasons for wanting to do something or preferring a certain product, service, store or behaviour, and then indicate, why the given reason is important to them. Data collection methods that do not involve personal interviews at all, like self-administered questionnaires and computerised data collection devices are designated as „hard" laddering (Grunert and Grunert, 1995).

Both techniques have been used in different empirical studies (Baker and Knox 1995; Botschen et al., 1995; Bagozzi and Dabholkar 1994, Pieters, Baumgartner, and Stad, 1994; Klenosky, Gengler, and Mulvey, 1988; Young and Feigin, 1975) and came up with promising results. What is still missing is research comparing the results of soft and hard laddering (Grunert and Grunert, 1995). Should a test of convergent validity show that both techniques lead to similar results, one could conclude that hard laddering is the preferable technique, since it is easier to administer and less costly. Different results would request an investigation of predictive validity in a larger context.

Following the suggestions of Pieters (1992) and Grunert and Grunert (1995) the objective of this study is to compare the data collection, coding and results of hard and soft laddering to provide researchers with recommendations concerning the appropriate use of hard and soft laddering. The comparison of the two techniques is based on the validity criteria recently developed by Grunert and Grunert (1995). The better the technique fulfils these criteria, the higher will be the predictive validity. In the empirical study the two types of laddering techniques will be applied for measuring the cognitive structures underlying women's choicebehaviour for fashion shops and clothing.

2. Factors Affecting the Predictive Validity of Soft- and Hard Laddering

Grunert and Grunert (1995) developed four criteria that laddering procedures should meet in order to increase predictive validity of the laddering procedure.

1) Raw data should be a result more of the respondent's cognitive structures and processes than of the researcher's cognitive structures and processes.

This criterion calls for open methods, in which each respondent can formulate her/his own cognitive categories. Any type of closed questioning violates this criterion as long as the cognitive categories used by respondent and researcher do not equal. In respect to the start of a laddering interview free elicitation tasks seem more promising than triadic sorting as long as one can expect that respondents are familiar with the product, service, behaviour or store under investigation. In this case respondents should be capable to associate the determinant concrete attributes. The generation of concrete attributes is typically restricted to three or four salient choice criteria, which increases the likelihood of their relevance for buyingbehaviour. Considering these prerequisites the free elicitation task seems to be appropriate for the soft and hard laddering approach. Given that the free elicitation task is limited to three or four determinant attributes we agree with Grunert and Grunert (1995) that soft and hard laddering meets the first criterion, because the respondents are free to use their own cognitive categories. We assume that both techniques generate the same amount and content of attributes although there might be some interviewer bias using the soft laddering approach. Due to the face-to-face contact between respondent and interviewer, attributes with a high degree of social desirability may be favoured and attributes with low social acceptability may be avoided.

Hard laddering forces the respondent to produce linear ladders one by one. Thiscan be misleading in the case of multifinality; the same attribute may lead to different consequences and in the case of equifinality, a single consequence may be based on multiple attributes (Pieters, 1993), which often occur in complex cognitive structures. For instance, a salesperson's friendliness may lead to uncertainty reduction for the customer with respect to the product s/he is looking for, and it may also directly lead to a more pleasant shopping experience for the customer (multifinality). Or both being helpful and keeping distance may provide the customer the opportunity to gain an overview of the available merchandise in the store and to make a good choice (equifinality) (Pieters, Botschen and Thelen, 1996). Hard laddering in the way it is used until now cannot reveal these complex cognitive structures. Modifications of the technique would be necessary to allow respondents to give more than one reason why something is important for him or to give only one reason for the importance of multiple attributes or consequences. Although the development of a suitable instruction seems theoretically possible, the answering task for the respondents would become too complex and biased.

As a consequence of this restriction we assume that soft laddering generates more consequences and the overall picture of the cognitive structure of respondents shown in the hierarchical value map will yield a bigger amount of linkages between attributes consequences and values.

2) The data collection should not involve strategic processes atypical for the target situation.

Two types of cognitive processes can usually be distinguished. Automatic cognitive processes are unconscious, not subject to limitations, and quite invariant to different task requirements. Perceiving familiar external stimuli, linking them to stored cognitive categories, and retrieving information from memory based on retrieval cues are examples for automatic cognitive processing. Strategic cognitive processes are conscious, subject to capacity limitations, and easily adapted to task requirements.

Criterion 2 refers to the problem that predictive ability is embedded when the respondent uses different strategic processes in the data collection and in the target situation. Grunert and Grunert (1995) basically propose two ways of solving this problem:

- to make sure that the strategic processes in the data collection situation are very similar to those one expects in the target situation, or

- to find a data collection situation with minimal strategic processing.

Retrieval processes in the laddering situation can conveniently be explained by spreading activation theory (Grunert and Grunert, 1995; Anderson, 1983; Anderson and Pirolli, 1984; Collins and Loftus, 1975). The spreading activation is assumed to be a fast, parallel automatic process. The question „Why is that important to you?" activates the cognitive category which the respondent has named last. Activation spreads from this category throughout the network, causing retrieval of additional categories, if the associations between the categories are strong enough. Grunert and Grunert (1995) pointed out that deviations from this „ideal" laddering process can occur when the cognitive structure with regard to the product in question is especially weak or especially sophisticated. The interviewer has considerable influence on the amount of strategic processing in the laddering interview by his decision on when to stop probing. If the respondent has little or medium knowledge about the object under investigation s/he may construct new associations to meet the interviewers demands.

Respondents with comprehensive knowledge about the researched object may find it difficult to follow the hierarchical format of hard and soft laddering although a interviewer can detect the process and steer the interview accordingly again supporting more strategic processes atypical for the target situation.

The „soft" approach is potentially better in handling the types of problems on the respondent's side caused by weak or elaborate cognitive structures. On the other hand, it obviously increases the extent of cognitive processing on the interviewer side, which may introduce new biases. The interviewer must try to make sense of the answers and relate them to the means-end model. „Hard" laddering is an attempt to avoid the interviewer's influence on the results. On the other hand the given amount of boxes in the questionnaire can lead the respondents to fill out all the boxes. Instructions should draw attention to the fact that it is not necessary to fill out all the boxes.

3) *Coding should preferably be based on cognitive categories widely shared among customers, researchers, and users of research results, and not on the researcher's idiosyncratic cognitive categories.*

Coding means grouping different answers together which, for the purpose of the following analysis, will be regarded as equal. Hereby the meaning the researcher attaches to the material and the meaning the respondent originally attached to the material should not be too divergent. Grouping of answers is based on the researcher's estimate of the semantic distance between the various answers, and hence on her/his cognitive structure. One could expect that the more context information a data collection device supplies, the easier will be the process of assigning meaning. Due to the fact that soft-laddering generates more redundant and contextual information than hard laddering does, we expect the reconstruction of meanings in the coding phase easier and interjudge reliability of coders to be higher for soft laddering data.

Grunert and Grunert's (1995) fourth criteria that the algorithm used for data reduction (aggregation) should be based on theory about cognitive structure and processes has no impact whether data is collected and coded by soft or hard laddering and therefore will not be considered furthermore.

3. Method

3.1. Sample and Procedure

A total of 40 female customers of an exclusive clothing shop in Innsbruck, a town in the western part of Austria, were interviewed for the study. Subjects were asked to participate in the interview after having shopped any clothing items. They had to go through a soft and hard laddering procedure for two different laddering tasks. Half of the respondents had to start with the soft laddering task and continue with the hard laddering. The other half began the interview with the hard laddering and afterwards was laddered by interviewers. One laddering task focused on the important attributes and underlying motivations for an ideal fashion store; the other laddering task on the important attributes and underlying motivations for ideal women's clothing items.

The verbal laddering interviews were conducted by two Ph. D. students who are well trained and have already participated in other laddering studies. Some additional demographic data was collected at the end of the interview. The whole interview took 30 minutes on average.

Due to the fact that all interviews took place in the same clothing store after having bought any clothing items we could make sure that the strategic processes in the data collection situation is very similar to those one expects in the target situation.

3.2. Questionnaire

First respondents were asked to fill out a paper and-pencil laddering interview that had been applied in previous research (Olson and Walker 1991; Pieters and Baumgartner, 1992; Pieters, Baumgartner, and Allen 1995; Pieters, Botschen, and Thelen, 1996). The hard laddering was accomplished through a structured questionnaire in which subjects were asked:

> „Please think about the attributes or characteristics of your ideal women's fashion store (women's clothing items) that would have maximised your satisfaction with the store (clothing item)".

On the next page three sequences of boxes appear. Each sequence contains five boxes. The text above the first box in each sequence reads „I would like that my ideal fashion (clothing item) store is ... or has ...". Respondents were asked to write in the first box of the first sequence the desired characteristic or attribute of their ideal fashion store which first comes up to their mind being as specific and exact as possible.

After that they were asked to think about another characteristic or attribute that they would have liked that their ideal fashion store has or displays and to write this in the first box of the second sequence and then think about a third attribute or characteristic and write it in the first box of the third sequence.

The instructions to complete the rows were the following:

> *„Once you have done this, proceed to the second box of the first sequence. The text above reads „... that is important to me because ...". Indicate in this box why the characteristic or attribute of your ideal fashion store (clothing item) is important to you. After you have indicated that, proceed to the third box of the first sequence. The text reads*

*„... that is important to me because then ...“. Indicate in the third box why what you in-
dicated in the second box is important for you. Proceed in the same way with the fourth
and fifth box of the first sequence. If you really don't know why something that you indicated in a previous box is important to you, you can leave the following box open. When
you have completed the first sequence, proceed to the second and third sequence. "*

Figure 2 shows the paper and pencil laddering version of the ideal fashion store which is
identical with the paper and pencil version of the ideal clothing item.

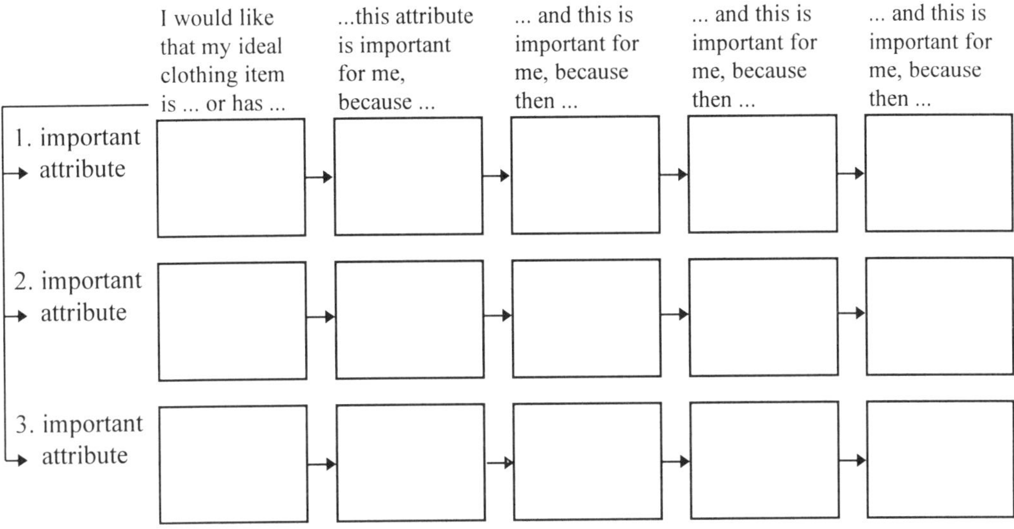

Figure 2: Paper and pencil version of women's clothing hard laddering

The soft laddering procedure started with the same entrance sentence and continued
with the question. „ What are the three most important attributes or characteristics which come
up to your mind?“ After having written down the three attributes the interviewer continued the
soft laddering procedure by going back to the first mentioned attribute asking„Why is ..... for
your ideal fashion store important ?“. Then the interviewer followed the standard soft laddering
procedure.

4. Results

Because responses obtained in laddering interviews are typically rather idiosyncratic, it
is necessary to perform a content analysis and classify the raw data into a limited number of
response categories (Reynolds and Gutman, 1988). In the present case the 40 responses to the

laddering interviews were content analysed using standard procedures by two independent judges and grouped into 33 meaning categories for the laddering of fashion stores and 26 meanings for the laddering of women's clothing. Two corrections to the data were made. If a person gave two consecutive responses that belonged to the same meaning category, only the first response was coded. Also, if a person returned to the same meaning category after one intermediate response to another category, the last response was not coded. In both cases, the sequence of responses express circularity (Pieters, Baumgartner, and Stad, 1994).

The coding was done by three researchers independently. Interjudge agreement is shown in Table 1. Disagreements were resolved through discussion so that all responses were classified.

Percentage of agreement Proportional Reduction in Loss (Rust and Cooil, 1994)	Soft Laddering	Hard Laddering
Fashion store	70 % .90	86% .98
Women's clothing	75% .93	87% .98

Table 1: Interjudge agreement in coding

Interjudge agreement was found to be higher in hard laddering than in soft laddering. In the present case additional context information in soft laddering did not lead to higher interjudge agreement as we expected.

In a first step of analysis the results obtained from the two laddering techniques were compared using the frequencies of the meanings (Table 2).

The results show that soft and hard laddering do only marginally differ in respect to the identified meanings. In the case of the ideal fashion store two more meanings („rebuying, buying" and „ good looking") out of 33 meanings could be identified at the consequence level using the hard laddering technique. In the case of the ideal women's clothing the meaning „no annoyance" was mentioned applying soft laddering and „love everything beautiful" was added in hard laddering. This strong overlap between identified meanings supports our assumption, that the content of attributes will not differ between the two techniques. The marginal differences on the consequence level and the conformity of meanings at the value level let us conclude that both techniques are equally suited for the identification of meanings.

Attributes	Soft	Hard	Consequences	Soft	Hard
Store design	13	7	Obliging	3	2
Assortment	17	14	Comfortable	11	4
Competent personnel	17	13	Good Shopping experience	2	1
Friendly personnel	5	8	Find what I am looking for	4	1
Presentation of merchandise	10	5	Free Decision	17	9
Price-Value	1	8	Store Profile	3	7
Quality	9	6	Good looking	0	5
Service	3	4	Individuality	12	5
Distant personnel	10	2	Buying, Rebuying	0	7
			No annoyance	3	3
Values			Durability	10	5
Joy	2	4	Latest fashion	6	4
Self-esteem	6	4	Practical	10	2
Impress others	4	5	Product information	5	2
Feeling good	13	16	Reduces uncertainty	18	14
			Right clothing	4	6
			Nice to look at	7	1
			Saves Money	2	11
			No Search	5	1
			Saves time	8	5

Table 2: Frequencies of meanings for fashion stores

A comparison of the frequencies of the meanings within and between the two research subjects shows that soft laddering tends to produce higher frequencies within the meanings. The strongest differences occur on the attribute level for the fashion store 85 versus 67 naming and on the level of consequences, 130 versus 95 mentioned consequences in the fashion store example and 108 versus 98 in the women's clothing example. These differences may be caused by two reasons. First, the used version of hard laddering does not allow forked answers, one attribute or consequence cannot lead at the same time to more than one following consequence. Second, in the soft laddering approach higher frequencies of consequences may be caused by interviewer influences. Only well trained interviewers will prevent respondents from developing artificial cognitive structures, by asking additional „why is that important for you?" questions without too strongly initiating strategic processing at the respondents side. In this study we could not found strong differences of frequencies of meanings at the attribute level in the women's clothing example (55 vs. 56) and at the value level (25 vs. 29, fashion store and 23 vs. 23, women's clothing).

A comparison of the frequencies of specific meanings between hard and soft laddering in the two subjects of investigation shows that in 36% (12 out of 33) of the cases frequencies of hard laddering meanings succeed frequencies of soft laddering for the fashion store example and in 46 % (12 out of 26) of the cases frequencies of hard laddering meanings succeed or equaled frequencies of soft laddering for the women's clothing example. Taking into account that the used version of hard laddering did not permit forked answers, that potential biases through interviewers in the soft laddering can be hardly excluded and that the respondents cognitive structure can be considered as medium comprehensive, hard laddering can be evaluated as equally suited as soft laddering to determine relevant attributes and underlying motivations at this stage of comparative analysis.

Following Reynolds and Gutman (1988), in a next step two asymmetric dominance matrices were constructed, in which the attributes, benefits/consequences, and values act as the row and column elements, and in which the cells contain the frequency in which a particular column element is mentioned after a particular row element, aggregated across subjects and ladders. Only direct linkages between meanings are entered, and the diagonal is empty, as a particular row element cannot be mentioned after itself.

The means-end structure was constructed by depicting all connections between meanings that form active cells at a selected cut-off level of 2 (Pieters, Baumgartner, and Stad, 1994).

Figure 3 show the aggregate hierarchical value maps (HVM) of fashion store and allows a comparison of the determined linkages in the cognitive structures produced by hard and soft laddering.

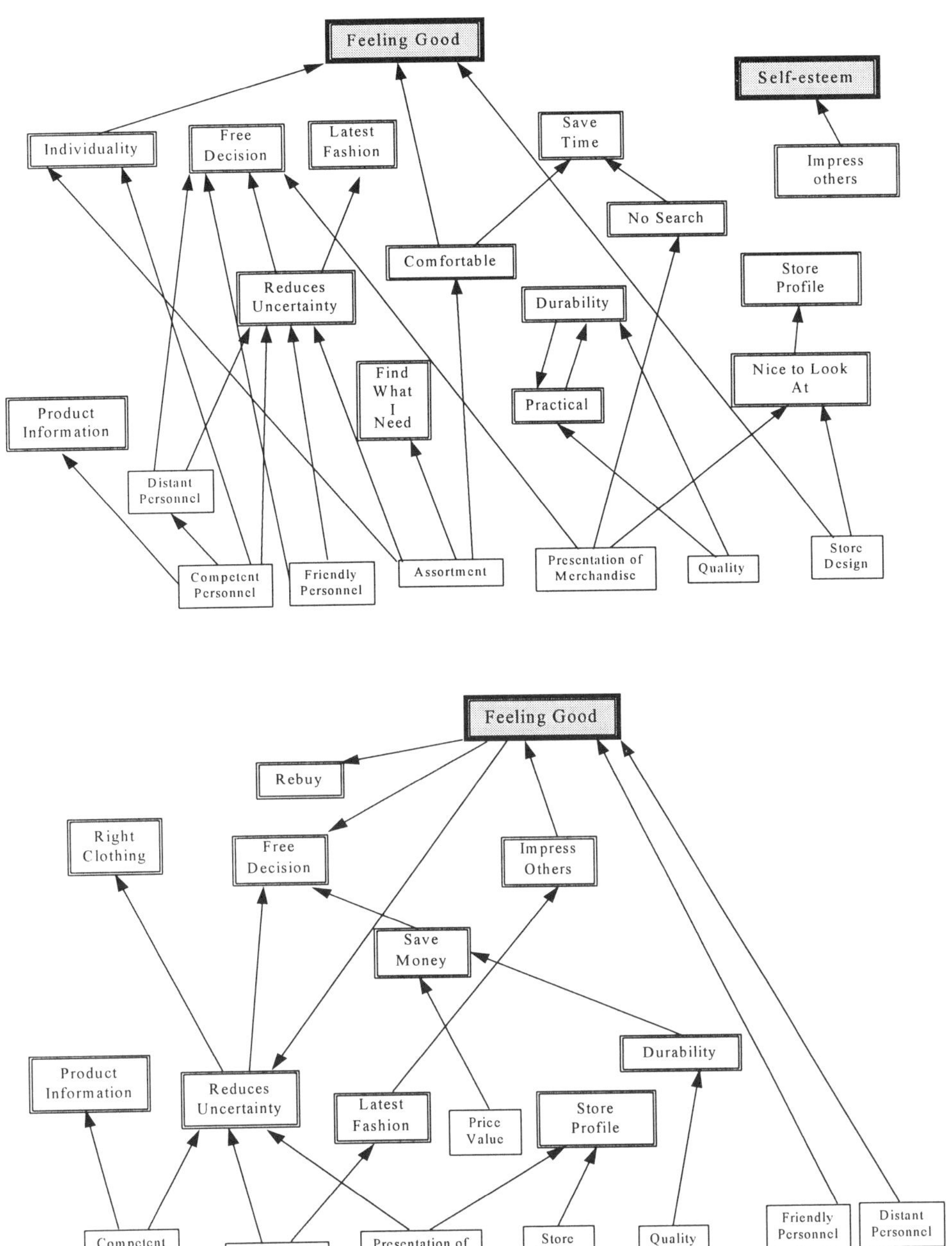

Figure 3: Hierarchical value maps of fashion store using soft laddering (at top) and hard laddering (at bottom) at a cut-off level of 2

At the chosen cut-off level of 2 the amount of meanings included in the HVM do not differ in respect to the applied laddering technique. In the case of the fashion store soft laddering revealed a less complex structure at the attribute level and a more complex structure on the consequence and value level. In the case of the women's clothing example hard laddering comes up with a more complex structure on the attribute level and on the consequence level. Central consequences and values e.g. „reduces uncertainty", „durability", and „feeling good" in the fashion store example and „easy to care", „durability", „cosy to wear", and „feeling good" are equally considered in the corresponding HVM of hard and soft laddering. From the analysis of the aggregated HVM both techniques seem to be equally suitable to measure medium comprehensive cognitive structures.

To get a better inside into the structures the local diagnostics centrality and abstractness were calculated following the suggestions of Pieters et al. (1995). Abstractness is hereby defined as the extent to which meanings are predominantly means or ends in the perception of customers. Centrality is defined as the extent to which a meaning is connected to all meanings in the implication matrix. Figure 4 shows the algorithms for calculating these measures.

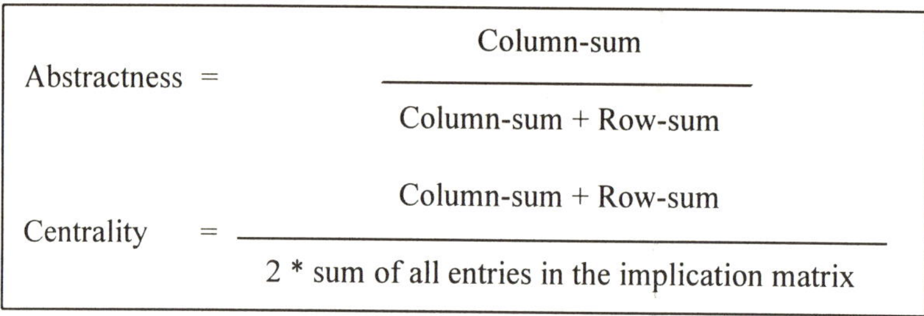

$$\text{Abstractness} = \frac{\text{Column-sum}}{\text{Column-sum} + \text{Row-sum}}$$

$$\text{Centrality} = \frac{\text{Column-sum} + \text{Row-sum}}{2 * \text{sum of all entries in the implication matrix}}$$

Figure 4: Calculation of local diagnostics

As expected the abstractness on the attribute level is low, ranging from .00 to .36 for fashion stores and .00 to .17 for women's clothing. On the consequence level it ranges from .44 to 1.00 for fashion stores and .38 to 1.00 for women's clothing.

In soft laddering more meanings are ends of means-end chains compared to hard laddering. On the value level abstractness goes from .5 to 1.00 for fashion stores and from .67 to 1.00 for women's clothing. The comparison of the local diagnostics abstractness of meanings between soft and hard laddering shows similar results on the attribute and value level for both subjects under investigation. On the consequence level the abstractness of some meanings differs. For fashion stores abstractness is slightly lower in hard laddering than in soft laddering. This overall tendency could not be found in the results for women's clothing.

334

Next the local diagnostic centrality was used for a comparison between hard and soft laddering. Centrality ranges from .01 to .16 for the fashion store and from .01 to .06 for women's clothing. In many cases centrality of meanings in soft laddering equals centrality of meanings in hard laddering. For some meanings on the attribute, consequences, and value level differences can be observed but no general tendency can be perceived according to soft or hard laddering.

In the next step results were compared using the average length and width of means-end chains (MEC). The average length was calculated as the average amount of meanings in the ladders. Width was calculated as the average amount of ladders one respondent had for a specific attribute. Table 3 shows that soft and hard laddering do not differ in respect to the length of MEC, but that significant differences occur in respect to the width of MEC. Hard laddering does not allow forked answers, therefore the differences in width are not surprising. Looking at the results in detail, the significant differences in average widths can be traced to only a few attributes, „competent personnel" in the laddering of fashion stores and„quality" in the laddering of women's clothing. Obviously these attributes have very complex meaning structures. Due to the restrictions in the design of the written questioning technique hard laddering is less capable of measuring these complex structures. In some cases respondents tried to overcome these restrictions on their own by writing more than one consequence into one box.

	Soft laddering	Hard laddering	Significance
Length of MEC Fashion	3.5	3.2	
Length of MEC Store	3.4	3.6	
Width of MEC Fashion	1.3	1.1	.03
Width of MEC Store	1.4	1.1	.00

Table 3: Comparison of length and width of MEC

For a final comparison convergent validity of hard and soft laddering was examined. To test convergent validity of soft and hard laddering five measures were used in correlation analyses: frequency of meanings, links going into a single meaning, links going out of a single meaning, abstractness and centrality. Table 4 shows the results.

	Fashion Stores		Women's Clothing	
	Correlation Coefficient	Significance	Correlation coefficient	Significance
Frequency of meanings	.53	.00	.72	.00
Links going in	.48	.01	.88	.00
Links going out	.74	.00	.54	.00
Abstractness	.82	.00	.75	.00
Centrality	.47	.01	.62	.00

Table 4: Convergent validity of hard and soft laddering

All correlation coefficients are significant and range from .47 for centrality (fashion stores) to .88 for links going in (women's clothing). Soft and hard laddering results show sufficient convergent validity.

5. Conclusions

The preceeding steps of comparative analysis between soft and hard laddering demonstrate that both techniques are suited to identify relevant characteristics or attributes of desired products, services, and behaviour and their corresponding underlying motivations. Convergent validity indicates that hard and soft laddering produce comparable results. Some observed differences slightly indicate that soft laddering is more capable of identifying complex underlying motivations mainly on the level of functional and socio-psychological consequences. Due to the fact that this may be caused by the interviewer during the verbal questioning and the rather limited design of the hard laddering which does not provide forked answers, we conclude that hard laddering seems to be equally appropriate as long as the cognitive structure can be considered as medium comprehensive. In the case of very weak or highly sophisticated cognitive structures of respondents we assume that application of soft laddering may be more advantageous. A trained interviewer can more easily detect the process and steer the interview although at the same time strategic processing at the respondents side may be initiated.

Considering important additional criteria like ease to administer, amount of costs, and appropriateness to analyse representative samples, hard laddering seems to be superior to soft laddering to measure medium comprehensive cognitive structures. Hard laddering is easier to administer and less costly and therefore appropriate to analyse representative samples. Hard laddering shows less interviewer bias in respect to social desirability, and additional context information did not improve reliability of coding in this study.

6. Limitations of the Study and Suggestions for Future Research

This study was designed to analyse medium comprehensive cognitive structures although no explicit measurement of the level of comprehensiveness of cognitive structures was used. Future research should be extended to weak and sophisticated cognitive structures. Therefore a better comprehensiveness measurement should be developed. Constructs like involvement and expertise should be considered. Comparisons of the different methods should integrate technique evaluations by interviewers and respondents. Finally research should focus on modifications of hard laddering to improve measurement of more comprehensive structures, e.g. allowing forked answers.

References

Anderson, J. R. (1983): A spreading activation theory of memory. In: Journal of Verbal Learning and Verbal Behaviour, Vol. 22, pp. 261-295.

Bagozzi, R. P. and P. A. Dabholkar (1994): Consumer Recycling Goals and Their Effect on Decisions to Recycle: A Means-End Chain Analysis. In: Psychology & Marketing, Vol. 11, No. 4, pp. 313-340.

Baker, S. and S. Knox (1995): Mapping Consumer Cognitions in Europe. In: M. Bergadaa (Ed.), Marketing Today and for the 21st Century, Proceedings of the 24th EMAC conference, pp. 81-100.

Botschen, G., L. Bstieler, A. Hemetsberger, and M. Schieferer (1995): Diagnosing Means-End Structures to Determine the Degree of Potential Marketing-Program Standardization. In: Smith S. (Ed.), Proceedings of the Fifth Symposium on Cross-Cultural Consumer and Business Studies, Hongkong, pp. 169-176.

Botschen, G., E. Thelen, and R. Pieters (1996): Using Means-End Structures for Benefit Segmentation in a Service Industry. In: Mühlbacher H. et al. (Eds.), Focus Dienstleistungsmarketing, Gabler Verlag, Wiesbaden (forthcoming).

Collins, A. M. and E. F. Loftus (1975): A spreading activation theory of semantic processing. In: Psychological Review, Vol. 82, pp. 407-428.

Grunert, K. G. and S. C. Grunert (1995): Measuring subjective meaning structures by the laddering method. Theoretical considerations and methodological problems. In: International Journal of Research in Marketing. Special Issue: Means-end chains, Jerry Olson (Guest Editor), Vol. 12, pp. 209-227.

Grunert, K.G., S.C. Grunert, and E. Sorenson (1995): Means-End Chains and Laddering: An Inventory of Problems and an Agenda for Research. Working paper No. 34, November, Centre for Market Surveillance, Research and Strategy for the Food Sector, Aarhus, Denmark.

Gutman, J. (1982): A means-end model based on consumer categorization processes. In: Journal of Marketing, Vol. 46, pp. 60-72.

Jolly, J. P., T. J. Reynolds, and J. W. Slocum Jr. (1988): Application of Means-End Theory for Understanding the Cognitive Bases of Performance Appraisal. In: Organizational Behaviour and Human Decision Processes, Vol. 41, No. 2, pp. 153-179.

Klenosky, D. B., Ch. E. Gengler, and M. S. Mulvey (1993): Understanding the Factors Influencing Ski Destination Choice: A Means-End Analytic Approach. In: Journal of Leisure Research, Vol. 25, No. 4, pp. 362-379.

Olson, J. C. (1995): Introduction. In: International Journal of Research in Marketing. Special Issue: Means-end chains, Jerry Olson (Guest Editor), Vol. 12, pp. 189-191.

Olson, P. (1989): Theoretical Foundations of Means-End Chains. In: Werbeforschung & Praxis, No 5, pp. 174-178.

Olson, J. C. and T. J. Reynolds (1983): Understanding consumers' cognitive structures: Implications for advertising strategy. In: Percy, L. and A. Woodside (Eds.), Advertising and Consumer Psychology. Lexington, MA: Lexington Books.

Pieters, R. (1993): A Control view on the behaviour of Consumers: Turning the Triangle. In: Van Raaij, W.F. and G. J. Bamossy (Eds.), European Advances in Consumer Research, Vol. 1, pp. 507-512.

Pieters, R. and H. Baumgartner (1992): A Means-End Approach to Consumer Goal Structure. Working paper, Erasmus University.

Pieters, R., H. Baumgartner, and D. Allen (1995): A means-end chain approach to consumer goal structures. In: International Journal of Research in Marketing. Special Issue: Means-end chains, Jerry Olson (Guest Editor), Vol. 12, pp. 227-244.

Pieters, R., H. Baumgartner, and H. Stad (1994): Diagnosing Means-End Structures: The Perception of Word-processing Software and the Adaptive-Innovative Personality of Managers. In: Bloemer, J., Lemmink, J., and H. Kaspar (Eds.), Proceedings of the 23rd EMAC conference, Maastricht, pp. 749-763.

Pieters, R., G. Botschen, and E. Thelen (1996): A Hierarchical Model of Customer Expectations about Salespeople Behaviour. In: Proceedings of 5th Annual Frontiers in Services Conference, Vanderbilt University, Nashville.

Reynolds, T. J. and J. Gutman (1988): Laddering theory, method, analysis, and interpretation. In: Journal of Advertising Research, Vol. 28, pp. 11-31.

Rust, T. R. and B. Cooil (1994): Reliability Measures for Qualitative Data. Theory and Implications. In: Journal of Marketing Research, Vol. 31, February, pp. 1-14.

Walker, B. A. and J. C. Olson (1991): Means-end chains: connecting products with self. In: Journal of Business Research, Vol. 22, pp. 111-118.

Young, S. and B. Feigin (1975): Using the Benefit Chain for Improved Strategy Formulation. In: Journal of Marketing, Vol. 39, July, pp. 72-74.

About the Contributors

Dr. Abdelmajid Amine, Associate Professor of Marketing at the IRG Research Center, Marketing Department of E.S.A. (Ecole Supérieure des Affaires), University of Paris Val de Marne, Créteil, France

Prof. Dr. Ingo Balderjahn, Professor of Business Administration and Marketing and Head of the Department of Marketing, School of Business Administration and Economics, University of Potsdam, Potsdam, Germany

Dr. Gary Baumgartner, Associate Professor at the Faculty of Applied Economics (DGES), Center for Business Research (CERAG), University Pierre Mendès France, Grenoble, France

Dr. Günther Botschen, Associate Professor at the Department of Marketing and Retailing, University of Innsbruck, Innsbruck, Austria

M.Sc. Lone Bredahl, Research Assistant at the MAPP: Centre for Market Surveillance, Research and Strategy for the Food Sector, Aarhus School of Business, Aarhus, Denmark

M.Sc. Karen Brunsø, Ph. D. student at the MAPP: Centre for Market Surveillance, Research and Strategy for the Food Sector, Aarhus School of Business, Aarhus, Denmark

Dipl.-Ök. Petra Buchholz, Research Assistant at the Department of Business Adminstration and Marketing, Faculty of Economics, University of Leipzig, Leipzig, Germany

Prof. Dr. Franz-Rudolf Esch, Professor of Business Administration and Marketing and Head of the Department of Marketing - Business Administration I, Justus-Liebig University Gießen, Gießen, Germany

Dr. Thomas Froehlicher, Assistant Professor of Strategy at the Graduate School of Management (IECS), Robert Schuman University, Strasbourg, France

Dr. Marie-Laure Gavard-Perret, Associate Professor of Marketing at the Institute of Research in Business Management (IREGE$_{Marketing}$), University of Savoie, Chambéry, France

Dr. Jean-Luc Giannelloni, Associate Professor of Marketing at the Institute of Research in Business Management (IREGE$_{Marketing}$), University of Savoie, Chambéry, France

Dr. Ronald E. Goldsmith, Professor of Marketing at the Marketing Department, College of Business, Florida State University, Tallahassee, FL, USA

Dr. Thomas C. O'Guinn, Professor at the Department of Advertising, College of Communications, University of Illinois, Urbana-Champaign, USA

Prof. Dr. Klaus G. Grunert, Professor of Marketing at the Aarhus School of Business and Director of the MAPP: Centre for Market Surveillance, Research and Strategy for the Food Sector, Aarhus School of Business, Aarhus, Denmark

Dr. François d'Hauteville, Lecturer at the Department of Economics and Business Management, National School of Agronomic Engineering, Montpellier, France

Dr. Patrick Hetzel, Associate Professor at the Research Center I.R.I.S., Institute of Business Administration, University Jean Moulin Lyon 3, Lyon, France

Dr. Hartmut H. Holzmüller, Associate Professor of Marketing at the Department of Marketing, Vienna University of Economics and Business Administration, Vienna, Austria

Prof. Ph.D. Alain Jolibert, Professor at the Business School (ESA), Center for Business Research (CERAG), University Pierre Mendès France, Grenoble, France

Dr. Sigrid Joseph, Associate Lecturer at Dauphine University, Centre of Research Dauphine Marketing Strategy Prospective, Paris, France

Dr. Tina M. Lowrey, Associate Professor of Marketing at the Department of Marketing, College of Business, Rider University, Lawrenceville, NJ, USA

Prof. Dr. Jean Moscarola, Professor of Marketing and Information Systems at the Institute Universitaire Professionnalisé d'Annecy and Member of the Institue of Research in Business Management (IREGE*Marketing*), University of Savoie, Annecy/Chambéry, France

Yorick Odin, Ph. D. student in Management Science at the Ecole Supérieure des Affaires de Grenoble, University Pierre Mendès France - Grenoble II, Grenoble, France

Dr. Cele Otnes, Associate Professor of Advertising at the Department of Advertising, College of Communications, University of Illinois, Urbana-Champaign, USA

Mag. Thomas Salzberger, Assistant Professor at the Department of Marketing, Vienna University of Economics and Business Administration, Vienna, Austria

Dr. L.J. Shrum, Assistant Professor at the Department of Marketing, Faculty of Management, Rutgers University, New Brunswick, NJ, USA

Mag. Rudolf Sinkovics, Assistant Professor at the Department of Marketing, Vienna University of Economics and Business Administration, Vienna, Austria

Dr. Eva Thelen, Associate Professor at the Department of Marketing and Retailing, University Innsbruck, Innsbruck, Austria

Prof. Dr. Pierre Valette-Florence, Professor of Marketing and Quantitative Methods at the Ecole Supérieure des Affaires de Grenoble, University Pierre Mendès France - Grenoble II, Grenoble, France

Prof. Dr. Eric Vernette, Professor of Marketing at the University of Savoie and Head of the Marketing Group of the Institute of Research in Business Management (IREGE$_{Marke\text{-}ting}$), University of Savoie, Chambéry, France

Jean-Yves Vinais, Ph. D. student in Management Science at the Ecole Supérieure des Affaires de Grenoble, University Pierre Mendès France - Grenoble II, Grenoble, France

Dr. Björn Walliser, Associate Professor of Marketing at the Graduate School of Management (IECS), Robert Schuman University Strasbourg, Strasbourg, France

Prof. Dr. Frank Wimmer, Professor of Business Administration and Marketing and Head of the Department of Business Administration and Marketing, Otto-Friedrich University Bamberg, Bamberg, Germany

Ihre **Meinung** zählt!

Um unsere Fachliteratur an Ihren Wünschen auszurichten und weiter
zu verbessern, sind wir an Ihrer Meinung interessiert.
Deshalb bitten wir Sie freundlichst um Ihre Mitarbeit. Vielen Dank!

Aus welchem Buch stammt dieser Fragebogen?___________________
____

Welche Erwartungen hatten Sie an das Buch?___________________
____
____

Wurden Ihre Erwartungen erfüllt?   ❏ ja   ❏ nein   ❏ teilweise

Wie beurteilen Sie den Inhalt?_______________________________
____
____

Wie bewerten Sie die typografische Gestaltung? (Textanordnung, Schrift-
größe, Lesbarkeit, Abbildungen)______________________________
____
____

Wie beurteilen Sie den Preis? ❏ sehr preisgünstig ❏ angemessen ❏ zu teuer

Was könnte man besser machen?______________________________
____
____

Sonstiges____
____
____

Und so erreichen Sie uns:
Fax 07 11/21 94-119 • Telefon 07 11/21 94-112
Schäffer-Poeschel Verlag • Joachim Bader • PF 103241 • 70028 Stuttgart
e-mail: bader@schaeffer-poeschel.de • Internet: http://www.schaeffer-poeschel.de